Knowledge Graphs

Synthesis Lectures on Data, Semantics, and Knowledge

Editor
Ying Ding, *University of Texas at Austin*
Paul Groth, *University of Amsterdam*

Founding Editor Emeritus
James Hendler, *Rensselaer Polytechnic Institute*

Synthesis Lectures on Data, Semantics, and Knowledge is edited by Ying Ding of the University of Texas at Austin and Paul Groth of the University of Amsterdam. The series focuses on the pivotal role that data on the web and the emergent technologies that surround it play both in the evolution of the World Wide Web as well as applications in domains requiring data integration and semantic analysis. The large-scale availability of both structured and unstructured data on the Web has enabled radically new technologies to develop. It has impacted developments in a variety of areas including machine learning, deep learning, semantic search, and natural language processing. Knowledge and semantics are a critical foundation for the sharing, utilization, and organization of this data. The series aims both to provide pathways into the field of research and an understanding of the principles underlying these technologies for an audience of scientists, engineers, and practitioners.

Topics to be included:

- Knowledge graphs, both public and private

- Linked Data

- Knowledge graph and automated knowledge base construction

- Knowledge engineering for large-scale data

- Machine reading

- Uses of Semantic Web technologies

- Information and knowledge integration, data fusion

- Various forms of semantics on the web (e.g., ontologies, language models, and distributional semantics)

- Terminology, Thesaurus, & Ontology Management

- Query languages

Knowledge Graphs

Aidan Hogan, Eva Blomqvist, Michael Cochez, Claudia d'Amato, Gerard de Melo, Claudio Gutierrez, Sabrina Kirrane, José Emilio Labra Gayo, Roberto Navigli, Sebastian Neumaier, Axel-Cyrille Ngonga Ngomo, Axel Polleres, Sabbir M. Rashid, Anisa Rula, Lukas Schmelzeisen, Juan Sequeda, Steffen Staab, and Antoine Zimmermann

ISBN: 978-3-031-00790-3   paperback
ISBN: 978-3-031-01918-0   PDF
ISBN: 978-3-031-00113-0   hardcover

DOI 10.1007/978-3-031-01918-0

A Publication in the Springer series
SYNTHESIS LECTURES ON DATA, SEMANTICS, AND KNOWLEDGE

Lecture #22
Series Editors: Ying Ding, *University of Texas at Austin*
               Paul Groth, *University of Amsterdam*
Founding Editor Emeritus: James Hendler, *Rensselaer Polytechnic Institute*
Series ISSN
Print 2691-2023   Electronic 2691-2031

Knowledge Graphs

Aidan Hogan
DCC, Universidad de Chile; IMFD

Eva Blomqvist
Linköping University

Michael Cochez
Vrije Universiteit Amsterdam and Discovery Lab,
Elsevier

Claudia d'Amato
University of Bari

Gerard de Melo
HPI, University of Potsdam and Rutgers University

Claudio Gutierrez
DCC, Universidad de Chile; IMFD

Sabrina Kirrane
WU Vienna

José Emilio Labra Gayo
Universidad de Oviedo

Roberto Navigli
Sapienza University of Rome

Sebastian Neumaier
St. Pölten University of Applied Sciences

Axel-Cyrille Ngonga Ngomo
DICE, Universität Paderborn

Axel Polleres
WU Vienna

Sabbir M. Rashid
Tetherless World Constellation, Rensselaer
Polytechnic Institute

Anisa Rula
University of Brescia

Lukas Schmelzeisen
Universität Stuttgart

Juan Sequeda
data.world

Steffen Staab
Universität Stuttgart and University of Southampton

Antoine Zimmermann
École des mines de Saint-Étienne

SYNTHESIS LECTURES ON DATA, SEMANTICS, AND KNOWLEDGE #22

ABSTRACT

This book provides a comprehensive and accessible introduction to knowledge graphs, which have recently garnered notable attention from both industry and academia. Knowledge graphs are founded on the principle of applying a graph-based abstraction to data, and are now broadly deployed in scenarios that require integrating and extracting value from multiple, diverse sources of data at large scale.

The book defines knowledge graphs and provides a high-level overview of how they are used. It presents and contrasts popular graph models that are commonly used to represent data as graphs, and the languages by which they can be queried before describing how the resulting data graph can be enhanced with notions of schema, identity, and context. The book discusses how ontologies and rules can be used to encode knowledge as well as how inductive techniques—based on statistics, graph analytics, machine learning, etc.—can be used to encode and extract knowledge. It covers techniques for the creation, enrichment, assessment, and refinement of knowledge graphs and surveys recent open and enterprise knowledge graphs and the industries or applications within which they have been most widely adopted. The book closes by discussing the current limitations and future directions along which knowledge graphs are likely to evolve.

This book is aimed at students, researchers, and practitioners who wish to learn more about knowledge graphs and how they facilitate extracting value from diverse data at large scale. To make the book accessible for newcomers, running examples and graphical notation are used throughout. Formal definitions and extensive references are also provided for those who opt to delve more deeply into specific topics.

KEYWORDS

knowledge graphs, graph databases, knowledge graph embeddings, graph neural networks, ontologies, knowledge graph refinement, knowledge graph quality, knowledge bases, artificial intelligence, semantic web, machine learning

Contents

Preface

The origins of this book can be traced back to a Dagstuhl Seminar, held in 2018, on the topic of Knowledge Graphs. At the time of the seminar, the topic was quickly becoming mainstream in academia and industry, but there were conflicting messages as to what a "knowledge graph" was. Much of the discussion of the seminar centered on this question, and there were divergent opinions as to how knowledge graphs could (or should) be defined; how they relate to previous concepts such as graph databases, knowledge bases, ontologies, RDF graphs, property graphs, semantic networks, etc.; and how the emerging area of Knowledge Graphs should be positioned with respect to the established areas of Artificial Intelligence, Big Data, Databases, Graph Theory, Logic, Machine Learning, Knowledge Representation, Natural Language Processing, Networks (in their various forms), and the Semantic Web. As the discussion continued, a consensus began to emerge: Knowledge Graphs, as a topic, involves a novel confluence of techniques stemming from previously disparate scientific communities, with the unifying goal of developing novel graph-based techniques for better integrating and extracting value from diverse knowledge sources at large scale.

As a follow-up to the seminar, the attendees agreed that in order to foster this unifying view of Knowledge Graphs, there was a need for a manuscript that would serve as a general introduction to the area. This manuscript would:

- motivate knowledge graphs and the value of abstracting data as graphs;

- survey the historical context of knowledge graphs and the key initiatives leading to their popularization;

- draw together disparate views of knowledge graphs into a unifying definition;

- provide an introduction to the key techniques that knowledge graphs enable, relating to querying, validation, reasoning, learning, refinement, enrichment, quality assessment, and more besides;

- describe how knowledge graphs are used in practice, surveying the companies using knowledge graphs, the applications they are used for, the open knowledge graphs that have been published, etc.; and

- delineate future research directions for knowledge graphs.

The manuscript would then serve as an introductory text for students, practitioners and researchers new to the area, helping to form a consensus in terms of what is a knowledge graph, laying the foundations for future developments.

The goal of preparing this manuscript was an ambitious one, and involved drawing together and distilling down a vast amount of literature on a diverse range of topics into a set of key concepts described in an accessible way. For this reason, the manuscript has been prepared by many authors, who have lent their knowledge and expertise to the preparation of specific sections. A short version of the manuscript was first published as a tutorial paper [Hogan et al., 2021], consisting of an abridged version of the first five chapters of this book, along with a summary of how knowledge graphs are used in practice, and conclusions. However, there was not enough space to describe all of the important developments in the area. This led us to publish this book, which further includes topics relating to the creation, enrichment, quality assessment, refinement and publication of knowledge graphs, as well as formal definitions, a historical perspective, and extended discussion throughout.

The book is divided into ten chapters. Chapter 1 provides a general introduction to the area, defines the concept of a "knowledge graph", and provides a high-level overview of how knowledge graphs are currently being used. Chapter 2 presents and contrasts popular graph models that are commonly used to represent data as graphs, and the languages by which they can be queried. Chapter 3 describes how the resulting data graph can be enhanced with notions of schema, identity, and context. Chapter 4 discusses how ontologies and rules can be used to encode knowledge, and how they enable deductive forms of reasoning. Chapter 5 delves into how inductive techniques—based on statistics, graph analytics, machine learning, etc.—can be used to encode and extract knowledge. Chapter 6 is dedicated to techniques for the creation and enrichment of knowledge graphs from legacy sources of data. Chapter 7 enumerates a variety of quality measures that can be used to assess a knowledge graph in terms of its fitness for use in a variety of applications. Chapter 8 presents key methods for the refinement of knowledge graphs, with the goal of improving their completeness and correctness. Chapter 9 provides a survey of the open and enterprise knowledge graphs that have emerged in recent years, along with the industries within which, and the applications for which, they have been most widely adopted. Chapter 10 wraps up the book with discussion of the current limitations and future directions along which knowledge graphs are likely to evolve. An Appendix further covers knowledge graphs from an historical perspective, establishing their significance in the broader context of the academic study of data and knowledge, as well as surveying prior definitions of "knowledge graphs" from the literature.

A key aim of this book is to be accessible to a broader audience. While background knowledge of related topics such as Databases, Logic, Machine Learning, Semantic Web, etc., will help to understand some of the particular topics mentioned, such a background is not necessary to follow the general concepts described within. The book aims to motivate and illustrate the various concepts it introduces from a practical perspective, and in order to be as accessible as possible, relies heavily on an example-driven presentation using a graphical notation. For the reader wishing to dig more into the technical minutiae, we complement this discussion with formal definitions throughout; however, the reader more interested in understanding the general concepts and their rationale will find the discussion to be self-contained if they choose to skip the definitions presented in visually distinctive boxes.

The book serves as an entry point for those new to the topic, and may thus serve as a useful textbook for university courses, for researchers who are venturing into the topic for the first time, and for practitioners who wish to understand more about how knowledge graphs might be of use within their company or organization, or indeed, how to maximize the value of the knowledge graphs that they are currently developing. Readers who are already active within specific sub-areas of Knowledge Graphs may further appreciate the technical definitions included, the references to other literature provided, and the broader perspective that this book offers in terms of the other related sub-areas and how they complement each other.

By drawing together diverse techniques from disparate areas, Knowledge Graphs has become an exciting topic in terms of both research and applications. We expect to see growing interest on this topic as the years advance, and indeed hope that this book will help to more firmly establish the foundations of this topic, and to foster future developments upon these foundations, potentially by its readers.

Aidan Hogan, Eva Blomqvist, Michael Cochez, Claudia d'Amato, Gerard de Melo, Claudio Gutierrez, Sabrina Kirrane, José Emilio Labra Gayo, Roberto Navigli, Sebastian Neumaier, Axel-Cyrille Ngonga Ngomo, Axel Polleres, Sabbir M. Rashid, Anisa Rula, Lukas Schmelzeisen, Juan Sequeda, Steffen Staab, and Antoine Zimmermann
September 2021

Acknowledgments

We thank the organizers and attendees of the Dagstuhl Seminar on "Knowledge Graphs." We also thank those who provided feedback on this content.

Hogan was funded by Fondecyt Grant No. 1181896. Hogan & Gutierrez were funded by ANID Millennium Science Initiative Program, Code ICN17_002. Cochez did part of the work while employed at Fraunhofer FIT, Germany and was later partially funded by Elsevier's Discovery Lab. Kirrane, Ngonga Ngomo, Polleres & Staab received funding through the project "Know-Graphs" from the European Union's Horizon program under the Marie Skłodowska-Curie grant agreement No. 860801. Kirrane & Polleres were supported by the European Union's Horizon 2020 research and innovation programme under grant 731601. Labra was supported by the Spanish Ministry of Economy and Competitiveness (Society challenges: TIN2017-88877-R). Navigli was supported by the MOUSSE ERC Grant No. 726487 under the European Union's Horizon 2020 research and innovation programme. Rashid was supported by IBM Research AI through the AI Horizons Network. Schmelzeisen was supported by the German Research Foundation (DFG) grant STA 572/18-1.

Aidan Hogan, Eva Blomqvist, Michael Cochez, Claudia d'Amato, Gerard de Melo, Claudio Gutierrez, Sabrina Kirrane, José Emilio Labra Gayo, Roberto Navigli, Sebastian Neumaier, Axel-Cyrille Ngonga Ngomo, Axel Polleres, Sabbir M. Rashid, Anisa Rula, Lukas Schmelzeisen, Juan Sequeda, Steffen Staab, and Antoine Zimmermann
September 2021

CHAPTER 1

Introduction

Though the phrase "knowledge graph" has been used in the literature since at least 1972 [Schneider, 1973], the modern incarnation of the phrase stems from the 2012 announcement of the Google Knowledge Graph [Singhal, 2012], followed by further announcements of the development of knowledge graphs by Airbnb [Chang, 2018], Amazon [Krishnan, 2018], eBay [Pittman et al., 2017], Facebook [Noy et al., 2019], IBM [Devarajan, 2017], LinkedIn [He et al., 2016], Microsoft [Shrivastava, 2017], Uber [Hamad et al., 2018], and more besides. The growing industrial uptake of the concept proved difficult for academia to ignore: more and more scientific literature is being published on knowledge graphs, which includes books (e.g., Fensel et al. [2020], Kejriwal et al. [2021], Pan et al. [2017], Qi et al. [2020]), as well as papers outlining definitions (e.g., Ehrlinger and Wöß [2016]), novel techniques (e.g., Lin et al. [2015], Pujara et al. [2013], Wang et al. [2014]), and surveys of specific aspects of knowledge graphs (e.g., Paulheim [2017], Wang et al. [2017]).

Underlying all such developments is the core idea of using graphs to represent data, often enhanced with some way to explicitly represent knowledge [Noy et al., 2019]. The result is most often used in application scenarios that involve integrating, managing, and extracting value from diverse sources of data at large scale [Noy et al., 2019]. Employing a graph-based abstraction of knowledge has numerous benefits in such settings when compared with, for example, a relational model or NoSQL alternatives. Graphs provide a concise and intuitive abstraction for a variety of domains, where edges capture the (potentially cyclical) relations between the entities inherent in social data, biological interactions, bibliographical citations and co-authorships, transport networks, and so forth [Angles and Gutiérrez, 2008]. Graphs allow maintainers to postpone the definition of a schema, allowing the data—and its scope—to evolve in a more flexible manner than typically possible in a relational setting, particularly for capturing incomplete knowledge [Abiteboul, 1997]. Unlike (other) NoSQL models, specialized graph query languages support not only standard relational operators (joins, unions, projections, etc.), but also navigational operators for recursively finding entities connected through arbitrary-length paths [Angles et al., 2017]. Standard knowledge representation formalisms—such as ontologies [Brickley and Guha, 2014, Hitzler et al., 2012, Mungall et al., 2012] and rules [Horrocks et al., 2004, Kifer and Boley, 2013]—can be employed to define and reason about the semantics of the terms used to label and describe the nodes and edges in the graph. Scalable frameworks for graph analytics [Malewicz et al., 2010, Stutz et al., 2016, Xin et al., 2013a] can be leveraged for computing centrality, clustering, summarization, etc., in order to gain insights about the domain being described. Various representations have also been developed that support applying machine learning techniques both directly and indirectly over graphs [Wang et al., 2017, Wu et al., 2019].

In summary, the decision to build and use a knowledge graph opens up a range of techniques that can be brought to bear for integrating and extracting value from diverse sources of data at large scale. The goal of this book is to motivate and give a comprehensive introduction to knowledge graphs: to describe their foundational data models and how they can be queried; to discuss representations relating to schema, identity, and context; to discuss deductive and inductive ways to make knowledge explicit; to present a variety of techniques that can be used for the creation and enrichment of graph-structured data; to describe how the quality of knowledge graphs can be discerned and how they can be refined; to discuss standards and best practices by which knowledge graphs can be published; and to provide an overview of existing knowledge graphs found in practice. Our intended audience includes researchers and practitioners who are new to knowledge graphs. As such, we do not assume that readers have specific expertise on knowledge graphs.

Knowledge graph   The definition of a "*knowledge graph*" remains contentious [Bergman, 2019, Bonatti et al., 2018, Ehrlinger and Wöß, 2016], where a number of (sometimes conflicting) definitions have emerged, varying from specific technical proposals to more inclusive general proposals; we address these prior definitions in Appendix A. Herein we adopt an inclusive definition, where we view a knowledge graph as *a graph of data intended to accumulate and convey knowledge of the real world, whose nodes represent entities of interest and whose edges represent relations between these entities.* The graph of data (aka *data graph*) conforms to a graph-based data model, which may be a *directed edge-labeled graph*, a *property graph*, etc. (we discuss concrete alternatives in Chapter 2). By *knowledge*, we refer to something that is *known*. Such knowledge may be accumulated from external sources, or extracted from the knowledge graph itself. Knowledge may be composed of simple statements, such as "*Santiago is the capital of Chile*," or quantified statements, such as "*all capitals are cities.*" Simple statements can be accumulated as edges in the data graph. If the knowledge graph intends to accumulate quantified statements, a more expressive way to represent knowledge—such as *ontologies* or *rules*—is required. *Deductive methods* can then be used to entail and accumulate further knowledge (e.g., "*Santiago is a city*"). Additional knowledge—based on simple or quantified statements—can also be extracted from and accumulated by the knowledge graph using *inductive methods*.

Knowledge graphs are often assembled from numerous sources, and as a result, can be highly diverse in terms of structure and granularity. To address this diversity, representations of *schema*, *identity*, and *context* often play a key role, where a *schema* defines a high-level structure for the knowledge graph, *identity* denotes which nodes in the graph (or in external sources) refer to the same real-world entity, while *context* may indicate a specific setting in which some unit of knowledge is held true. As aforementioned, effective methods for *extraction*, *enrichment*, *quality assessment*, and *refinement* are required for a knowledge graph to grow and improve over time.

In practice   Knowledge graphs aim to serve as an ever-evolving shared substrate of knowledge within an organization or community [Noy et al., 2019]. We distinguish two types of knowledge graphs in practice: *open knowledge graphs* and *enterprise knowledge graphs*. Open knowledge graphs are published online, making their content accessible for the public good. The most prominent examples—DBpedia [Lehmann et al., 2015], Freebase [Bollacker et al., 2007b], Wikidata [Vrandečić and Krötzsch, 2014], YAGO [Hoffart et al., 2011], etc.—cover many domains and are either extracted from Wikipedia [Hoffart et al., 2011, Lehmann et al., 2015], or built by communities of volunteers [Bollacker et al., 2007b, Vrandečić and Krötzsch, 2014]. Open knowledge graphs have also been published within specific domains, such as media [Raimond et al., 2014], government [Hendler et al., 2012, Shadbolt and O'Hara, 2013], geography [Stadler et al., 2012], tourism [Alonso Maturana et al., 2018, Kärle et al., 2018, Lu et al., 2016, Zhang et al., 2019], life sciences [Callahan et al., 2013], and more besides. Enterprise knowledge graphs are typically internal to a company and applied for commercial use-cases [Noy et al., 2019]. Prominent industries using enterprise knowledge graphs include Web search (e.g., Bing [Shrivastava, 2017], Google [Singhal, 2012]), commerce (e.g., Airbnb [Chang, 2018], Amazon [Dong, 2019, Krishnan, 2018], eBay [Pittman et al., 2017], Uber [Hamad et al., 2018]), social networks (e.g., Facebook [Noy et al., 2019], LinkedIn [He et al., 2016]), finance (e.g., Accenture [Okorafor and Ray, 2019], Banca d'Italia [Bellomarini et al., 2019], Bloomberg [Meij, 2019], Capital One [Branum and Sehon, 2019], Wells Fargo [Newman, 2019]), among others. Applications include search [Shrivastava, 2017, Singhal, 2012], recommendations [Chang, 2018, Hamad et al., 2018, He et al., 2016, Noy et al., 2019], personal agents [Pittman et al., 2017], advertising [He et al., 2016], business analytics [He et al., 2016], risk assessment [Dalgliesh, 2016, Tobin, 2017], automation [Henson et al., 2019], and more besides. We will provide more details on the use of knowledge graphs in practice in Chapter 10.

Running example   To keep the discussion accessible, throughout the book we present concrete examples in the context of a hypothetical knowledge graph relating to tourism in Chile (loosely inspired by related use-cases [Kärle et al., 2018, Lu et al., 2016]). The knowledge graph is managed by a tourism board that aims to increase tourism in the country and promote new attractions in strategic areas. The knowledge graph itself will eventually describe tourist attractions, cultural events, services, businesses, travel routes, etc. Some applications the organization envisages are to:

- create a tourism portal that allows visitors to search for attractions, upcoming events, and other related services (in multiple languages);

- gain insights into tourism demographics in terms of season, nationalities, etc.;

- analyze sentiment about tourist attractions, including positive reviews, summaries of complaints about events and services, crime reports, etc.;

- understand tourism trajectories: the sequence of attractions, events, etc., that tourists often visit;

- cross-reference these tourism trajectories with currently available flights, buses, etc., to suggest new strategic routes for public transport;

- offer personalized recommendations of places to visit;

- and so forth.

Outline   The remainder of the book is structured as follows.

Chapter 2 outlines graph data models and the languages used to query them.

Chapter 3 describes representations of schema, identity, and context for graphs.

Chapter 4 presents deductive formalisms for representing and entailing knowledge.

Chapter 5 describes inductive techniques for learning from graphs.

Chapter 6 discusses the creation and enrichment of knowledge graphs.

Chapter 7 enumerates dimensions for assessing knowledge graph quality.

Chapter 8 discusses various techniques for knowledge graph refinement.

Chapter 9 introduces principles and protocols for publishing knowledge graphs.

Chapter 10 surveys some prominent knowledge graphs and their applications.

Chapter 11 concludes with future directions for knowledge graphs.

Appendix A outlines the historical background for knowledge graphs.

CHAPTER 2

Data Graphs

At the foundation of any knowledge graph is the principle of first applying a graph abstraction to data, resulting in an initial data graph. We now discuss a selection of graph-structured data models that are commonly used in practice to represent data graphs. We then discuss the primitives that form the basis of graph query languages used to interrogate such data graphs.

2.1 MODELS

Leaving aside graphs, let us assume that the tourism board from our running example has not yet decided how to model relevant data about attractions, events, services, etc. The board first considers using a tabular structure—in particular, relational databases—to represent the required data, and though they do not know precisely what data they will need to capture, they begin to design an initial relational schema. They begin with an Event table with five columns:

Event(<u>name</u>, venue, type, <u>start</u>, end)

where <u>name</u> and <u>start</u> together form the primary key of the table in order to uniquely identify recurring events. But as they start to populate the data, they encounter various issues: events may have multiple names (e.g., in different languages), events may have multiple venues, they may not yet know the start and end date-times for future events, events may have multiple types, and so forth. Incrementally addressing these modeling issues as the data become more diverse, they generate internal identifiers for events and adapt their relational schema until they have:

$$\text{EventName}(\underline{id}, \underline{name}), \text{EventStart}(\underline{id}, start), \text{EventEnd}(\underline{id}, end), \qquad (2.1)$$
$$\text{EventVenue}(\underline{id}, \underline{venue}), \text{EventType}(\underline{id}, \underline{type})$$

With the above schema, the organization can now model events with 0–n names, venues, and types, and 0–1 start dates and end dates (without needing nulls).

Along the way, the board has to incrementally change the schema several times in order to support new sources of data. Each such change requires a costly remodeling, reloading, and reindexing of data; here we only considered one table. The tourism board struggles with the relational model because they do not know, *a priori*, what data will need to be modeled or what sources they will use. But once they reach the latter relational schema, the board finds that they can integrate further sources without more changes: with minimal assumptions on *multiplicities* (1–1, 1–n, etc.) this schema offers a lot of flexibility for integrating incomplete and diverse data.

In fact, the refined, flexible schema that the board ends up with—as shown in (2.1)—is modeling a set of binary relations between entities, which indeed can be viewed as modeling a graph. By instead adopting a graph data model from the outset, the board could forgo the need for an upfront schema, and could define any (binary) relation between any pair of entities at any time.

We now introduce graph data models popular in practice [Angles et al., 2017].

2.1.1   DIRECTED EDGE-LABELED GRAPHS

A directed edge-labeled graph (sometimes known as a *multi-relational graph* [Balazevic et al., 2019a, Bordes et al., 2013, Nickel and Tresp, 2013]) is defined as a set of nodes—like (Santiago), (Arica), (EID16), (2018-03-22 12:00)—and a set of directed labeled edges between those nodes, like (Santa Lucía)—city→(Santiago). In the case of knowledge graphs, nodes are used to represent entities and edges are used to represent (binary) relations between those entities. Figure 2.1 provides an example of how the tourism board could model event data as a directed edge-labeled graph. The graph includes data about the names, types, start and end date-times, and venues for events.[1] Adding information to such a graph typically involves adding new nodes and edges (with some exceptions discussed later). Representing incomplete information requires simply omitting a particular edge; for example, the graph does not yet define a start/end date-time for the Food Truck festival.

Modeling data as a graph in this way offers more flexibility for integrating new sources of data, compared to the standard relational model, where a schema must be defined upfront and followed at each step. While other structured data models such as trees (XML, JSON, etc.) would offer similar flexibility, graphs do not require organizing the data hierarchically (should venue be a parent, child, or sibling of type for example?). They also allow cycles to be represented and queried (e.g., note the directed cycle in the routes between Santiago, Arica, and Viña del Mar).

A standardized data model based on directed edge-labeled graphs is the Resource Description Framework (RDF) [Cyganiak et al., 2014], which has been recommended by the W3C. The RDF model defines different types of nodes, including *Internationalized Resource Identifiers* (IRIs) [Dürst and Suignard, 2005] which allow for global identification of entities on the Web; *literals*, which allow for representing strings (with or without language tags) and other datatype values (integers, dates, etc.); and *blank nodes*, which are anonymous nodes that are not assigned an identifier (for example, rather than create internal identifiers like EID15, EID16, in RDF, we have the option to use blank nodes). We will discuss these different types of nodes further in Section 3.2 when we speak about issues relating to identity.

---

[1]We draw bidirectional edges as (Viña del Mar)←bus→(Arica), which more concisely depicts two directed edges: (Viña del Mar)—bus→(Arica) and (Viña del Mar)←bus—(Arica). Also while some naming conventions recommend more complete edge labels that include a verb, such as has venue or is valid from, in this book, for presentation purposes, we will omit the "has" and "is" verbs from such labels, using simply venue or valid from.

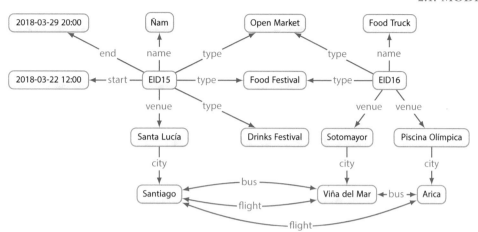

Figure 2.1: Directed edge-labeled graph describing events and their venues.

We now formally define a directed edge-labeled graph, where we denote by **Con** a countably infinite set of constants.

Definition 2.1 Directed edge-labeled graph.   A *directed edge-labeled graph* is a tuple $G = (V, E, L)$, where $V \subseteq$ **Con** is a set of nodes, $L \subseteq$ **Con** is a set of edge labels, and $E \subseteq V \times L \times V$ is a set of edges.

Example 2.2   In reference to Figure 2.1, the set of nodes V has 15 elements, including `Arica`, `EID16`, etc. The set of edges E has 23 triples, including (`Arica`,`flight`,`Santiago`). Bidirectional edges are represented with two edges. The set of edge labels L has 8 elements, including `start`, `flight`, etc.

Definition 2.1 does not state that V and L are disjoint: though not present in the example, a node can also serve as an edge-label. The definition also permits that nodes and edge labels can be present without any associated edge. Either restriction could be explicitly stated—if necessary—in a particular application while still conforming to a directed edge-labeled graph.

For ease of presentation, we may treat a set of (directed labeled) edges $E \subseteq V \times L \times V$ as a directed edge-labeled graph (V, E, L), in which case we refer to the graph induced by E assuming that V and L contain all and only those nodes and edge labels, respectively, used in E. We may similarly apply set operators on directed edge-labeled graphs, which should be interpreted as applying to their sets of edges; for example, given $G_1 = (V_1, E_1, L_1)$ and

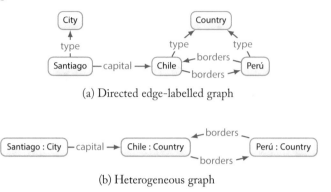

(a) Directed edge-labelled graph

(b) Heterogeneous graph

Figure 2.2: Comparing directed edge-labeled graphs and heterogeneous graphs.

$G_2 = (V_2, E_2, L_2)$, by $G_1 \cup G_2$ we refer to the directed edge-labeled graph induced by $E_1 \cup E_2$.

2.1.2   HETEROGENEOUS GRAPHS

A heterogeneous graph [Hussein et al., 2018, Wang et al., 2019, Yang et al., 2020] (or *heterogeneous information network* [Sun and Han, 2012, Sun et al., 2011]) is a directed graph where each node and edge is assigned one type. Heterogeneous graphs are thus akin to directed edge-labeled graphs—with edge labels corresponding to edge types—but where the type of node forms part of the graph model itself, rather than being expressed with a relation (as seen in Figure 2.2). An edge is called *homogeneous* if it is between two nodes of the same type (e.g., borders in Figure 2.2); otherwise it is called *heterogeneous* (e.g., capital in Figure 2.2). Heterogeneous graphs allow for partitioning nodes according to their type, for example, for the purposes of machine learning tasks [Hussein et al., 2018, Wang et al., 2019, Yang et al., 2020]. Conversely, such graphs typically only support a one-to-one relation between nodes and types, which is not the case for directed edge-labeled graphs (see, for example, the node Santiago with zero types and EID15 with multiple types in Figure 2.1).

We next define the notion of a heterogeneous graph.

Definition 2.3   Heterogeneous graph.   A *heterogeneous graph* is a tuple $G = (V, E, L, l)$, where $V \subseteq \mathbf{Con}$ is a set of nodes, $L \subseteq \mathbf{Con}$ is a set of edge/node labels, $E \subseteq V \times L \times V$ is a set of edges, and $l : V \to L$ maps each node to a label.

Example 2.4   In reference to Figure 2.2b, the set of nodes V has three elements: `Santiago`, `Chile`, and `Perú`. The set of edges E has three triples, including (`Santiago`,`capital`,`Chile`). The set of edge labels L has four elements: `capital`, `borders`, `City`, `Country`. Finally, with respect to the node labels, l(`Santiago`) = `City`, l(`Chile`) = `Country`, and l(`Perú`) = `Country`.

In heterogeneous graphs, edge and node labels are often called *types*. By defining edges with labels as per directed edge-labeled graphs—rather than separately labeling edges with l—two nodes can be related by n edges with n different labels; for example, we can represent both (`Santiago`, `capital`, `Chile`) and (`Santiago`, `country`, `Chile`) as edges in the heterogeneous graph.

2.1.3   PROPERTY GRAPHS

Property graphs constitute an alternative graph model that offers additional flexibility when modeling more complex relations. Consider integrating incoming data that provide further details on which companies offer fares on which flights, allowing the board to better understand available routes between cities (for example, on national airlines). In the case of directed edge-labeled graphs, we cannot directly annotate an edge like (Santiago)—flight→(Arica) with the company (or companies) offering that route. But we could add a new node denoting a flight, connect it with the source, destination, companies, and mode, as shown in Figure 2.3a. Applying this modeling to all routes in Figure 2.1 would, however, involve significant changes.

The property graph model was thus proposed to offer additional flexibility when modeling data as a graph [Angles et al., 2017, Miller, 2013]. A property graph allows a set of *property-value* pairs and a *label* to be associated with both nodes and edges. Figure 2.3b depicts an example of a property graph with data analogous to Figure 2.3a. We use property-value pairs on edges to model the companies. The type of relation is captured by the label `flight`. We further use node labels to indicate the types of the two nodes, and property-value pairs for their latitude and longitude.

Property graphs are prominently used in graph databases, such as Neo4j [Angles et al., 2017, Miller, 2013]. Property graphs can be converted to/from directed edge-labeled graphs [Angles et al., 2019, Hernández et al., 2015] (per, e.g., Figure 2.3b). In summary, directed edge-labeled graphs offer a more minimal model, while property graphs offer a more flexible one. Often the choice of model will be secondary to other practical factors, such as the implementations available for different models, etc.

We formally define a property graph.

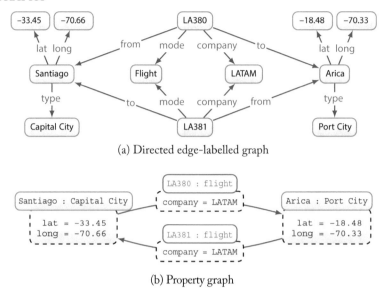

(a) Directed edge-labelled graph

(b) Property graph

Figure 2.3: Comparing directed edge-labeled graphs and property graphs.

Definition 2.5 Property graph. A *property graph* is a tuple $G = (V, E, L, P, U, e, l, p)$, where $V \subseteq \mathbf{Con}$ is a set of node ids, $E \subseteq \mathbf{Con}$ is a set of edge ids, $L \subseteq \mathbf{Con}$ is a set of labels, $P \subseteq \mathbf{Con}$ is a set of properties, $U \subseteq \mathbf{Con}$ is a set of values, $e : E \to V \times V$ maps an edge id to a pair of node ids, $l : V \cup E \to 2^L$ maps a node or edge id to a set of labels, and $p : V \cup E \to 2^{P \times U}$ maps a node or edge id to a set of property-value pairs.

Example 2.6 Returning to Figure 2.3b:

- the set V contains `Santiago` and `Arica`;

- the set E contains `LA380` and `LA381`;

- the set L contains `Capital City`, `Port City`, and `flight`;

- the set P contains `lat`, `long`, and `company`;

- the set U contains -33.45, -70.66, `LATAM`, -18.48, and -70.33;

- the mapping e gives, for example, $e(\text{LA380}) = (\text{Santiago}, \text{Arica})$;

- the mapping l gives, for example, $l(\text{Santiago}) = \{\text{Capital City}\}$ and $l(\text{LA380}) = \{\text{flight}\}$; and

- the mapping p gives, for example, $p(\text{LA380}) = \{(\text{company}, \text{LATAM})\}$ and $p(\text{Santiago}) = \{(\text{lat}, -33.45), (\text{long}, -70.66)\}$.

Unlike previous definitions [Angles et al., 2017], we allow a node or edge to have several values for a given property. In practice, systems like Neo4j [Miller, 2013] may rather support this by allowing a single array (i.e., list) of values.

2.1.4 GRAPH DATASET

Although graphs can be merged by taking their union, it is often desirable to manage several graphs rather than one monolithic graph; for example, it may be beneficial to manage multiple graphs from different sources, making it possible to update or refine data from one source, to distinguish untrustworthy sources from more trustworthy ones, and so forth. A graph dataset then consists of a set of *named graphs* and a *default graph*. Each named graph is a pair of a graph ID and a graph. The default graph is a graph without an ID, and is referenced "by default" if a graph ID is not specified. Figure 2.4 provides an example where events and routes are stored in two named graphs, and the default graph manages metadata about the named graphs. Graph names can also be used as nodes in a graph. Furthermore, nodes and edges can be repeated across graphs, where the same node in different graphs will typically refer to the same entity, allowing data on that entity to be integrated when merging graphs. Though the example depicts a dataset of directed edge-labeled graphs, the concept generalizes straightforwardly to datasets of other types of graphs.

An RDF dataset is a graph dataset model standardized by the W3C [Cyganiak et al., 2014] where each graph is an RDF graph, and graph names can be blank nodes or IRIs. A prominent use-case for RDF datasets is to manage and query *Linked Data* composed of inter-linked documents of RDF graphs spanning the Web. When dealing with Web data, tracking the source of data becomes of key importance [Bonatti et al., 2011, Dividino et al., 2009, Zimmermann et al., 2012]. We will discuss Linked Data later in Section 3.2 and further discuss provenance in Section 3.3.

We formally define a graph dataset. We assume that all data graphs featured in a given graph dataset follow the same model (directed edge-labeled graph, heterogeneous graph, property graph, etc.).

Definition 2.7 Graph dataset. A *named graph* is a pair (n, G) where G is a data graph, and $n \in \mathbf{Con}$ is a graph name. A *graph dataset* is a pair $D = (G_D, N)$ where G_D is a data graph called the *default graph* and N is either the empty set, or a set of named graphs

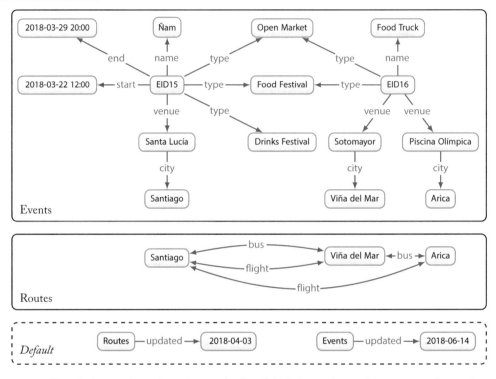

Figure 2.4: Graph dataset based on directed edge-labeled graphs with two named graphs and a default graph describing events and routes.

$\{(n_1, G_1), \ldots (n_k, G_k)\}$ ($k > 0$) such that if $i \neq j$ then $n_i \neq n_j$ (for all $1 \leq i \leq k, 1 \leq j \leq k$).

Example 2.8 Figure 2.4 provides an example of a directed edge-labeled graph dataset D consisting of two named graphs and a default graph. The default graph does not have a name associated with it. The two graph names are Events and Routes; these are also used as nodes in the default graph.

2.1.5 OTHER GRAPH DATA MODELS

The previous models are popular examples of graph representations. Other graph data models exist with *complex nodes* that may contain individual edges [Angles and Gutiérrez, 2008, Hartig and Thompson, 2014] or nested graphs [Angles and Gutiérrez, 2008, Berners-Lee and Connolly, 2011] (sometimes called *hypernodes* [Levene and Poulovassilis, 1989]). Likewise, the mathematical notion of a *hypergraph* defines *complex edges* that connect sets rather than pairs of nodes. In our view, a knowledge graph can adopt any such graph data model based on nodes and edges: often data can be converted from one model to another (see Figure 2.3a vs. Figure 2.3b). In the rest of the paper, we prefer discussing directed edge-labeled graphs given their relative succinctness, but most discussion extends naturally to other models.

2.1.6   GRAPH STORES

A variety of techniques have been proposed for storing and indexing graphs, facilitating the efficient evaluation of queries (as discussed next). Directed edge-labeled graphs can be stored in relational databases either as a single relation of arity three (*triple table*), as a binary relation for each property (*vertical partitioning*), or as *n*-ary relations for entities of a given type (*property tables*) [Wylot et al., 2018]. Custom (so-called *native*) storage techniques have also been developed for a variety of graph models, providing efficient access for finding nodes, edges, and their adjacent elements [Angles and Gutiérrez, 2008, Miller, 2013, Wylot et al., 2018]. A number of systems further allow for distributing graphs over multiple machines based on popular NoSQL stores or custom partitioning schemes [Janke and Staab, 2018, Wylot et al., 2018]. For further details we refer to the book chapter by Janke and Staab [2018] and the survey by Wylot et al. [2018] dedicated to this topic.

2.2   QUERYING

A number of languages have been proposed for querying graphs [Angles et al., 2017], including the SPARQL query language for RDF graphs [Harris et al., 2013]; and Cypher [Francis et al., 2018], Gremlin [Rodriguez, 2015], and G-CORE [Angles et al., 2018] for querying property graphs. We refer to Seifer et al. [2019] for an investigation of the popularity of these languages. Underlying these query languages are some common primitives, including (basic) graph patterns, relational operators, path expressions, and more besides [Angles et al., 2017]. We now describe these core features for querying graphs in turn, starting with basic graph patterns.

2.2.1   BASIC GRAPH PATTERNS

At the core of every structured query language for graphs lie *basic graph patterns* [Angles et al., 2017, Consens and Mendelzon, 1990], which follow the same model as the data graph being queried (see Section 2.1), additionally allowing variables as terms.[2] Terms in basic graph patterns are thus divided into constants, such as (Arica) or venue, and variables, which we prefix with question marks, such as (?event) or ?rel. A basic graph pattern is then evaluated against the data graph by generating mappings from the variables of the graph pattern to constants in the data graph such

---

[2]The terms of a directed edge-labeled graph are its nodes and edge-labels. The terms of a property graph are its ids, labels, properties, and values (as used on either edges or nodes).

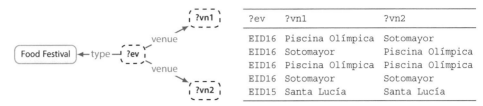

?ev	?vn1	?vn2
EID16	Piscina Olímpica	Sotomayor
EID16	Sotomayor	Piscina Olímpica
EID16	Piscina Olímpica	Piscina Olímpica
EID16	Sotomayor	Sotomayor
EID15	Santa Lucía	Santa Lucía

Figure 2.5: Basic directed edge-labeled graph pattern (left) with mappings generated over the directed edge-labeled graph of Figure 2.1 (right).

that the image of the graph pattern under the mapping (replacing variables with the assigned constants) is contained within the data graph.

Figure 2.5 provides an example of a basic graph pattern looking for the venues of Food Festivals, along with the possible mappings generated by the graph pattern against the data graph of Figure 2.1. In some of the presented mappings (the last two listed), multiple variables are mapped to the same term, which may or may not be desirable depending on the application. Hence a number of semantics have been proposed for evaluating basic graph patterns [Angles et al., 2017], among which the most important are: *homomorphism-based semantics*, which allows multiple variables to be mapped to the same term such that all mappings shown in Figure 2.5 would be considered results; and *isomorphism-based semantics*, which requires variables on nodes and/or edges to be mapped to unique terms, thus excluding the latter three mappings of Figure 2.5 from the results. Different languages may adopt different semantics for evaluating basic graph patterns; for example, SPARQL adopts a homomorphism-based semantics, while Cypher adopts an isomorphism-based semantics specifically on edges (while allowing multiple variables to map to one node).

As we will see in later examples (particularly Figure 2.7), basic graph patterns may also form cycles (be they directed or undirected), and may replace edge labels with variables. Basic graph patterns in the context of other models can be defined analogously by allowing variables to replace constants in any position of the model.

We formalize basic graph patterns first for directed edge-labeled graphs, and subsequently for property graphs [Angles et al., 2017]. For these definitions, we introduce a countably infinite set of *variables* **Var** ranging over (but disjoint from: **Con** ∩ **Var** = ∅) the set of constants. We refer generically to constants and variables as *terms*, denoted and defined as **Term** = **Con** ∪ **Var**. We define a basic graph pattern for a model by simply replacing constants with terms (that may be variables). Though we focus on directed edge-labeled graphs and property graphs, basic graph patterns for other graph models can be defined analogously.

Definition 2.9   Basic directed edge-labeled graph pattern.   We define a *basic directed edge-labeled graph pattern* as a tuple $Q = (V, E, L)$, where $V \subseteq$ **Term** is a set of node terms, $L \subseteq$ **Term** is a set of edge terms, and $E \subseteq V \times L \times V$ is a set of edges (triple patterns).

Example 2.10   Returning to the example of Figure 2.5:

- the set V contains the constant Food Festival and variables ?event, ?ven1, and ?ven2;

- the set E contains four edges, including (?event, type, Food Festival); and

- the set L contains the constants type and venue.

A basic property graph pattern is also defined by introducing variables.

Definition 2.11   Basic property graph pattern.   We define a *basic property graph pattern* as a tuple $Q = (V, E, L, P, U, e, l, p)$, where $V \subseteq$ **Term** is a set of node id terms, $E \subseteq$ **Term** is a set of edge id terms, $L \subseteq$ **Term** is a set of label terms, $P \subseteq$ **Term** is a set of property terms, $U \subseteq$ **Term** is a set of value terms, $e : E \rightarrow V \times V$ maps an edge id term to a pair of node id terms, $l : V \cup E \rightarrow 2^L$ maps a node or edge id term to a set of label terms, and $p : V \cup E \rightarrow 2^{P \times U}$ maps a node or edge id term to a set of pairs of property-value terms.

Toward defining the results of evaluating a basic graph pattern over a data graph (following the same model), we first define a partial mapping $\mu : $ **Var** $\rightarrow$ **Con** from variables to constants, whose *domain* (the set of variables for which it is defined) is denoted by $\mathrm{dom}(\mu)$. Given a basic graph pattern Q, let **Var**(Q) denote the set of all variables appearing in (some recursively nested element of) Q. We further denote by $\mu(Q)$ the image of Q under μ, meaning that any variable $v \in$ **Var**$(Q) \cap \mathrm{dom}(\mu)$ is replaced in Q by $\mu(v)$. Observe that when **Var**$(Q) \subseteq \mathrm{dom}(\mu)$, then $\mu(Q)$ is a data graph (in the corresponding model of Q).

Next, we define the notion of containment between data graphs. For two directed edge-labeled graphs $G_1 = (V_1, E_1, L_1)$ and $G_2 = (V_2, E_2, L_2)$, we say that G_1 is a *sub-graph* of G_2, denoted $G_1 \subseteq G_2$, if and only if $V_1 \subseteq V_2$, $E_1 \subseteq E_2$, and $L_1 \subseteq L_2$.[a] Conversely, in property graphs, nodes can often be defined without edges. For two property graphs $G_1 = (V_1, E_1, L_1, P_1, U_1, e_1, l_1, p_1)$ and $G_2 = (V_2, E_2, L_2, P_2, U_2, e_2, l_2, p_2)$, we say that G_1 is a *sub-graph* of G_2, denoted $G_1 \subseteq G_2$, if and only if $V_1 \subseteq V_2$, $E_1 \subseteq E_2$, $L_1 \subseteq L_2$, $P_1 \subseteq P_2$, $U_1 \subseteq U_2$, for all $x \in E_1$ it holds that $e_1(x) = e_2(x)$, and for all $y \in E_1 \cup V_1$ it holds that $l_1(y) \subseteq l_2(y)$ and $p_1(y) \subseteq p_2(y)$.

We are now ready to define the evaluation of a basic graph pattern.

Definition 2.12   Evaluation of a basic graph pattern.   Let Q be a basic graph pattern and let G be a data graph (in the same model). We then define the *evaluation of the basic graph pattern Q over the data graph G*, denoted $Q(G)$, to be the set of mappings $Q(G) = \{\mu \mid \mu(Q) \subseteq G \text{ and } \mathrm{dom}(\mu) = \mathbf{Var}(Q)\}$.

Example 2.13   Figure 2.5 enumerates all of the mappings given by the evaluation of the depicted basic graph pattern over the data graph of Figure 2.1. Each non-header row indicates a mapping μ.

The final results of evaluating a basic graph pattern may vary depending on the choice of semantics: the results under *homomorphism-based semantics* are defined as $Q(G)$. Conversely, under *isomorphism-based* semantics, mappings that send two edge variables to the same constant and/or mappings that send two node variables to the same constant may be excluded from the results. Henceforth, we assume the more general *homomorphism-based semantics*.

---

[a]Given, for example, $G_1 = (\{a\}, \{(a, b, a)\}, \{b, c\})$ and $G_2 = (\{a, c\}, \{(a, b, a)\}, \{b\})$, we remark that $G_1 \not\subseteq G_2$ and $G_2 \not\subseteq G_1$: the former has a label not used on an edge while the latter has a node without an incident edge. In concrete data models like RDF where such cases of nodes or labels without edges cannot occur, the sub-graph relation $G_1 \subseteq G_2$ holds if and only if $E_1 \subseteq E_2$ holds.

2.2.2   COMPLEX GRAPH PATTERNS

A (basic) graph pattern transforms an input graph into a table of results (as shown in Figure 2.5). We may then consider using the relational algebra to combine and/or transform such tables, thus forming more complex queries from one or more graph patterns. Recall that the relational algebra consists of unary operators that accept one input table, and binary operators that accept two input tables. Unary operators include projection (π) to output a subset of columns, selection (σ) to output a subset of rows matching a given condition, and renaming of columns (ρ). Binary operators include union ($\cup$) to merge the rows of two tables into one table, difference ($-$) to remove the rows from the first table present in the second table, and joins ($\bowtie$) to extend the rows of one table with rows from the other table that satisfy a join condition. Selection and join conditions typically include equalities ($=$), inequalities ($\leq$), negation ($\neg$), disjunction ($\vee$), etc. From these operators, we can further define other (syntactic) operators, such as intersection ($\cap$) to output rows in both tables, anti-join ($\triangleright$, aka *minus*) to output rows from the first table for which there are no join-compatible rows in the second table, left-join ($\bowtie$, aka *optional*) to perform a join but keeping rows from the first table without a compatible row in the second table, etc.

Basic graph patterns can then be expressed in a subset of relational algebra (namely π, σ, ρ, $\bowtie$). Assuming, for example, a single ternary relation $G(s, p, o)$ representing a graph—i.e., a table G with three columns s, p, o—the query of Figure 2.5 can be expressed in relational

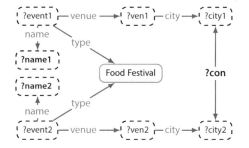

?name1	?con	?name2
Food Truck	bus	Food Truck
Food Truck	bus	Food Truck
Food Truck	bus	Ñam
Food Truck	flight	Ñam
Food Truck	flight	Ñam
Ñam	bus	Food Truck
Ñam	flight	Food Truck
Ñam	flight	Food Truck

Figure 2.6: Complex graph pattern (left) with mappings generated over the graph of Figure 2.1 (right).

algebra as:

$$\pi_{ev,vn1,vn2}$$
$$(\sigma_{p=\text{type}\wedge o=\text{Food Festival}\wedge p_1=p_2=\text{venue}}(\rho_{s/ev}(G \bowtie \rho_{p/p_1,o/vn1}(G) \bowtie \rho_{p/p_2,o/vn2}(G)))),$$

where $\bowtie$ denotes a *natural join*, meaning that equality is checked across pairs of columns with the same name in both tables (here, the join is thus performed on the subject column s). The result of this query is a table with a column for each variable: $ev, vn1, vn2$. However, not all queries using π, σ, ρ and $\bowtie$ on G can be expressed as basic graph patterns; for example, we cannot choose which variables to project in a basic graph pattern, but rather must project all variables not fixed to a constant.

Graph query languages such as SPARQL [Harris et al., 2013] and Cypher [Francis et al., 2018] allow the full use of relational operators over the results of graph patterns, giving rise to *complex graph patterns* [Angles et al., 2017]. Figure 2.6 presents an example of a complex graph pattern with projected variables in bold, choosing particular variables to appear in the final results. In Figure 2.7, we give another example of a complex graph pattern looking for food festivals or drinks festivals not held in Santiago, optionally returning their start date and name (where available).

Complex graph patterns can give rise to duplicate results; for example, the first result in Figure 2.6 appears twice since ?city1 matches Arica and ?city2 matches Viña del Mar in one result, and vice-versa in the other. Query languages then offer two semantics: *bag semantics* preserves duplicates according to the multiplicity of the underlying mappings, while *set semantics* (typically invoked with a DISTINCT keyword) removes duplicates from the results.

We now formally define complex graph patterns.

Definition 2.14 Complex graph pattern. *Complex graph patterns* are defined recursively, as follows.

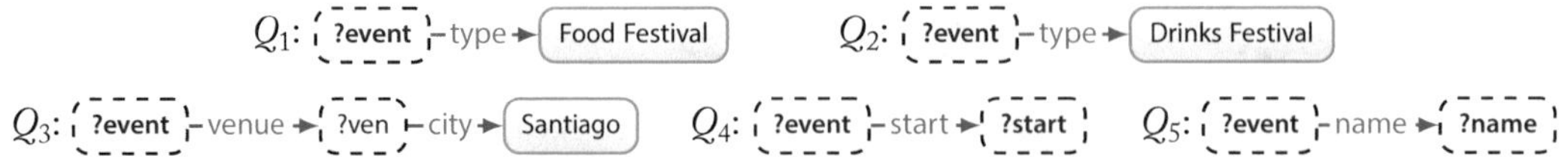

Q_1: [?event]–type→ [Food Festival] Q_2: [?event]–type→ [Drinks Festival]

Q_3: [?event]–venue→ [?ven]–city→ [Santiago] Q_4: [?event]–start→ [?start] Q_5: [?event]–name→ [?name]

$$Q := ((((Q_1 \cup Q_2) \triangleright Q_3) \bowtie Q_4) \bowtie Q_5), \quad Q(G) =$$

?event	?start	?name
EID16		Food Truck

Figure 2.7: Complex graph pattern (Q) with mappings generated ($Q(G)$) over the graph of Figure 2.1 (G).

- If Q is a basic graph pattern, then Q is a *complex graph pattern*.

- If Q is a complex graph pattern, and $V \subseteq \mathbf{Var}(Q)$, then $\pi_V(Q)$ is a *complex graph pattern*.

- If Q is a complex graph pattern, and R is a selection condition with Boolean and equality connectives $(\wedge, \vee, \neg, =)$, then $\sigma_R(Q)$ is a *complex graph pattern*.

- If both Q_1 and Q_2 are complex graph patterns, then $Q_1 \bowtie Q_2$, $Q_1 \cup Q_2$, $Q_1 - Q_2$ and $Q_1 \triangleright Q_2$ are also *complex graph patterns*.

We now define the evaluation of complex graph patterns. Given a mapping μ, for a set of variables $V \subseteq \mathbf{Var}$ let $\mu[V]$ denote the mapping μ' such that $\mathrm{dom}(\mu') = \mathrm{dom}(\mu) \cap V$ and $\mu'(v) = \mu(v)$ for all $v \in \mathrm{dom}(\mu')$ (in other words, $\mu[V]$ projects the variables V from μ). Letting R denote a Boolean selection condition and μ a mapping, we denote by $\mu \models R$ that μ satisfies the Boolean condition. Finally, we define two mappings μ_1 and μ_2 to be *compatible*, denoted $\mu_1 \sim \mu_2$, if and only if $\mu_1(v) = \mu_2(v)$ for all $v \in \mathrm{dom}(\mu_1) \cap \mathrm{dom}(\mu_2)$ (i.e., they map common variables to the same constant). We are now ready to provide the definition.

Definition 2.15 Complex graph pattern evaluation.   Given a complex graph pattern Q, if Q is a basic graph pattern, then $Q(G)$ is defined per Definition 2.12. Otherwise, $Q(G)$ is defined as follows:

$$\pi_V(Q)(G) = \{\mu[V] \mid \mu \in Q(G)\}$$
$$\sigma_R(Q)(G) = \{\mu \mid \mu \in Q(G) \text{ and } \mu \models R\}$$
$$Q_1 \bowtie Q_2(G) = \{\mu_1 \cup \mu_2 \mid \mu_1 \in Q_2(G), \mu_2 \in Q_1(G) \text{ and } \mu_1 \sim \mu_2\}$$
$$Q_1 \cup Q_2(G) = \{\mu \mid \mu \in Q_1(G) \text{ or } \mu \in Q_2(G)\}$$
$$Q_1 - Q_2(G) = \{\mu \mid \mu \in Q_1(G) \text{ and } \mu \notin Q_2(G)\}$$
$$Q_1 \triangleright Q_2(G) = \{\mu \mid \mu \in Q_1(G) \text{ and } \nexists \mu_2 \in Q_2(G) \text{ such that } \mu \sim \mu_2\}$$

Based on these operators, we can define some additional syntactic operators, such as the *left-join* (⋈, aka *optional*):

$$Q_1 ⋈ Q_2(G) = (Q_1(G) ⋈ Q_2(G)) \cup (Q_1(G) \triangleright Q_2(G)).$$

We call such operators *syntactic* as they do not add expressivity.

Example 2.16   Figure 2.7 illustrates a complex graph pattern and its evaluation.

2.2.3   NAVIGATIONAL GRAPH PATTERNS

A key feature that distinguishes graph query languages is the ability to include *path expressions* in queries. A path expression r is a regular expression that allows for matching arbitrary-length paths between two nodes using a *regular path query* (x, r, y), where x and y can be variables or constants (or even the same term). The base path expression is where r is a constant (an edge label). Furthermore, if r is a path expression, then r^* (*Kleene star*: zero-or-more) is also a path expression. Finally, if r_1 and r_2 are path expressions, then $r_1 \mid r_2$ (*disjunction*) and $r_1 \cdot r_2$ (*concatenation*) are also path expressions. A related notion is that of *2-way regular path queries*, which also allow for querying inverse paths; specifically, if r is path expression, then it is a *2-way path expression*, and if r is a *2-way path expression*, then r^- (*inverse*) is a *2-way path expression*. Henceforth we will refer generically to both the 1-way and 2-way variants as path expressions and regular path queries.

Regular path queries can be evaluated under different semantics. For example, (Arica, bus*, ?city) evaluated against the graph of Figure 2.1 may match the paths shown in Figure 2.8. In fact, since a cycle is present, an infinite number of paths are potentially matched. For this reason, restricted semantics are often applied, returning only the shortest paths, or paths without repeated nodes or edges (as in the case of Cypher).[3] Rather than returning paths, another option is to instead return the (finite) set of pairs of nodes connected by a matching path (as in the case of SPARQL 1.1).

Regular path queries can then be used in basic graph patterns to express *navigational graph patterns* [Angles et al., 2017], as shown in Figure 2.9, which illustrates a query searching for food festivals in cities reachable (recursively) from Arica by bus or flight. Furthermore, when regular path queries and graph patterns are combined with operators such as projection, selection, union, difference, and optional, the result is known as *complex navigational graph patterns* [Angles et al., 2017].

---

[3]Mapping variables to paths requires special treatment [Angles et al., 2017]. Cypher [Francis et al., 2018] returns a string that encodes a path, upon which certain functions such as length(·) can be applied. G-CORE [Angles et al., 2018], on the other hand, allows for returning paths, and supports additional operators on them, including projecting them as graphs, applying cost functions, and more besides.

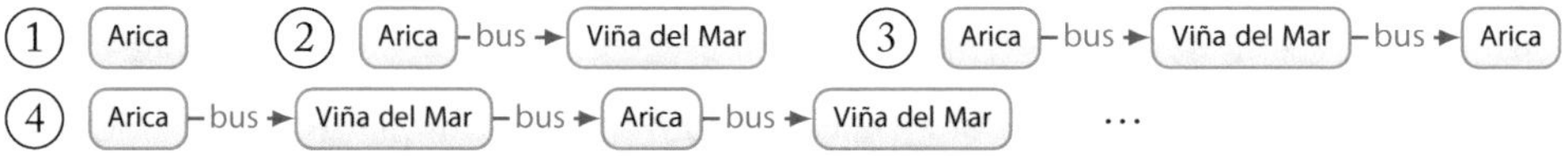

Figure 2.8: Example paths matching (`Arica, bus*, ?city`) over the graph of Figure 2.1.

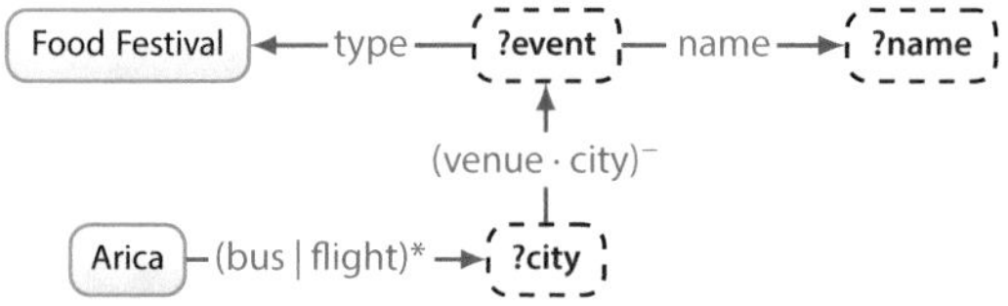

?event	?name	?city
EID15	Ñam	Santiago
EID16	Food Truck	Arica
EID16	Food Truck	Viña del Mar

Figure 2.9: Navigational graph pattern (left) with mappings generated over the graph of Figure 2.1 (right).

We first define path expressions and regular path queries.

Definition 2.17 Path expression. A constant (edge label) c is a *path expression*. Furthermore, if r, r_1, and r_2 are path expressions, then:

- r^- (*inverse*) and r^* (*Kleene star*) are *path expressions* and

- $r_1 \cdot r_2$ (*concatenation*) and $r_1 \mid r_2$ (*disjunction*) are *path expressions*.

We now define the evaluation of a path expression on a directed-edge labeled graph under the SPARQL 1.1-style semantics whereby the endpoints (pairs of start and end nodes) of the path are returned [Harris et al., 2013].

Definition 2.18 Path evaluation (directed edge-labeled graph). Given a directed edge-labeled graph $G = (V, E, L)$ and a path expression r, we define the *evaluation of r over G*, denoted $r[G]$, as follows:

$$\begin{aligned}
r[G] &= \{(u, v) \mid (u, r, v) \in E\} \text{ (for } r \in \mathbf{Con)} \\
r^-[G] &= \{(u, v) \mid (v, u) \in r[G]\} \\
r_1 \mid r_2[G] &= r_1[G] \cup r_2[G] \\
r_1 \cdot r_2[G] &= \{(u, v) \mid \exists w \in V : (u, w) \in r_1[G] \text{ and } (w, v) \in r_2[G]\} \\
r^*[G] &= V \cup \bigcup_{n \in \mathbb{N}^+} r^n[G]
\end{aligned}$$

where by r^n we denote the nth-concatenation of r (e.g., $r^3 = r \cdot r \cdot r$).

The evaluation of a path expression on a property graph $G = (V, E, L, P, U, e, l, p)$ can be defined analogously by adapting the first definition (in the case that $r \in$ **Con**) as follows:

$$r[G] = \{(u, v) \mid \exists x \in E : e(x) = (u, v) \text{ and } l(e) = r\}.$$

The rest of the definitions then remain unchanged.

Query languages may support additional operators, some of which are syntactic (e.g., r^+ is sometimes used for one-or-more, but can be rewritten as $r \cdot r^*$), while others may add expressivity such as the case of SPARQL [Harris et al., 2013], which allows a limited form of negation in expressions (e.g., $!r$, with r being a constant or the inverse of a constant, matching any path not labeled r).

Next, we define a regular path query and its evaluation.

Definition 2.19   Regular path query.   A *regular path query* is a triple (x, r, y) where $x, y \in$ **Con** $\cup$ **Var** and r is a path expression.

Definition 2.20   Regular path query evaluation.   Let G denote a directed edge-labeled graph, c, c_1, $c_2 \in$ **Con** denote constants and z, z_1, $z_2 \in$ **Var** denote variables. Then the *evaluation of a regular path query* is defined as follows:

$$
\begin{aligned}
(c_1, r, c_2)(G) &= \{\mu_\emptyset \mid (c_1, c_2) \in r[G]\} \\
(c, r, z)(G) &= \{\mu \mid \mathrm{dom}(\mu) = \{z\} \text{ and } (c, \mu(z)) \in r[G]\} \\
(z, r, c)(G) &= \{\mu \mid \mathrm{dom}(\mu) = \{z\} \text{ and } (\mu(z), c) \in r[G]\} \\
(z_1, r, z_2)(G) &= \{\mu \mid \mathrm{dom}(\mu) = \{z_1, z_2\} \text{ and } (\mu(z_1), \mu(z_2)) \in r[G]\},
\end{aligned}
$$

where $\mu_\emptyset$ denotes the empty mapping such that $\mathrm{dom}(\mu) = \emptyset$ (the join identity).

Definition 2.21   Navigational graph pattern.   If Q is a basic graph pattern, then Q is a *navigational graph pattern*. If Q is a navigational graph pattern and (x, r, y) is a regular path query, then $Q \bowtie (x, r, y)$ is a *navigational graph pattern*.

The definition of the evaluation of a navigational graph pattern then follows from the previous definition of a join and the definition of the evaluation of a regular path query (for a directed edge-labeled graph or a property graph, respectively). Likewise, *complex navigational graph patterns*—and their evaluation—are defined by extending this definition in the natural way with the same operators from Definition 2.14 following the same semantics seen in Definition 2.15.

2.2.4   OTHER FEATURES

Thus far, we have discussed features that form the practical and theoretical foundation of any query language for graphs [Angles et al., 2017]. However, specific query languages for graphs may support other features, such as aggregation (GROUP BY, COUNT, etc.), more complex filters and datatype operators (e.g., range queries on years extracted from a date), federation for querying remotely hosted graphs over the Web, languages for updating graphs, support for entailment, etc. For more information, we refer to the documentation of the respective query languages (e.g., Angles et al. [2018], Harris et al. [2013]) and to the survey by Angles et al. [2017].

2.2.5   QUERY INTERFACES

Knowledge graphs are often queried by non-expert users who may not be able to express their information needs in terms of a particular graph query language. Different types of interfaces have thus been proposed in order to assist users in querying data graphs. Such interfaces may support, for example, the following.

Faceted browsing: Users start by specifying a simple search, such as a keyword search, a type of node like Food Festival, or possibly other kinds of search. They are then presented with a set of matching results, and a set of facets, which are typically attributes (e.g., venue) and values (e.g., Santa Lucía) present in the current results set. Selecting a value for a facet restricts the current results set to include only results with the indicated value; this selection process can be applied iteratively to restrict results per multiple facets. Often the faceted criteria are translated into and evaluated as graph queries. Though relatively intuitive for users, such systems typically support acyclic queries that generate lists of results (analogous to graph queries that project a single variable), and rarely support more expressive queries. Examples of faceted browsing systems for graphs include VisiNav [Harth, 2010], Broccoli [Bast and Buchhold, 2013], SemFacet [Arenas et al., 2016], GraFa [Moreno-Vega and Hogan, 2018], etc.

Query building: Users are provided with a form or graphical interface that can be used to specify a graph query without needing to understand the syntax of a specific query language. Such query builders allow for incrementally adding nodes or edges to the query, assisted by features such as auto-completion, previewing intermediate results, and graph navigation. Query builders typically allow for expressing queries equivalent to (cyclic) basic graph patterns, but may not support more expressive features of query languages as described herein. Graph query builder systems include Smeagol [Clemmer and Davies, 2011], QueryVOWL [Haag et al., 2015], VIIQ [Jayaram et al., 2015a], Sparklis [Ferré, 2017], RDF Explorer [Vargas et al., 2019], and more besides.

Query-by-example: Users provide examples of positive and sometimes negative answers to their queries. For example, they may provide as positive examples the nodes (Arica), (Santiago), and (Viña del Mar), and as negative examples the nodes (Chile) and (Lima), where the system will then "reverse engineer" a query that returns positive examples but not negative examples (in this case, the query proposed may return nodes of type City whose country is Chile). Query-by-example systems typically support basic graph patterns, and may not support more expressive querying features. They are useful in cases where users have examples of what they are looking for, but are not necessarily sure of the query they need to retrieve similar examples. Query-by-example systems for graphs include GQBE [Jayaram et al., 2015b] and SPARQLByE [Diaz et al., 2016].

Question answering: Users express their queries as questions in natural language; for example, they might ask "*What food festivals will be held in Arica?*" The question answering system will then generate answers from the graph based on its best interpretation of the question. We identify three types of question answering system. *Navigation-based systems* identify entities/nodes from the graph that are mentioned in the query, and then attempt to navigate edges from those nodes whose labels best match the question; for example, they may match the nodes (Food Festival) and (Arica) in the graph based on the question, and from there, try to navigate edges in the graph whose labels match the question in order to find answers. *Template-based systems* rather pre-suppose a fixed list of question templates expressed in the query language, with placeholder variables that will be replaced with entities/nodes detected in the question; a template matched for the previous example may be of the form "*What X will be held in Y?*" *Translation-based systems* attempt to translate the question into a query in the structured query language, using (typically neural) machine translation techniques. The latter two types of question answering systems can additionally return a graph query that explains the answers generated. Question answering systems are often very intuitive to use, but may not always return correct results, particularly when considering complex questions/queries. Examples of question answering systems for knowledge graphs include Treo [Freitas et al., 2011], NFF [Hu et al., 2018], TemplateQA [Zheng et al., 2018], WDAqua-core1 [Diefenbach et al., 2020], and more besides.

Such query interfaces enable non-expert users to formulate queries over graphs, which in turn broadens the potential impact of knowledge graphs.

C H A P T E R   3

Schema, Identity, and Context

In this chapter we describe extensions of the data graph—relating to schema, identity, and context—that provide additional structures for accumulating knowledge. Henceforth, we refer to a *data graph* as a collection of data represented as nodes and edges using one of the models discussed in Chapter 2. We refer to a *knowledge graph* as a data graph potentially enhanced with representations of schema, identity, context, ontologies, and/or rules. These additional representations may be embedded in the data graph, or layered above. Representations for schema, identity and context are discussed now, while ontologies and rules will be discussed in Chapter 4.

3.1 SCHEMA

One of the benefits of modeling data as graphs—versus, for example, the relational model—is the option to forgo or postpone the definition of a schema. However, when modeling data as graphs, schemata *can* be used to prescribe a high-level structure and/or semantics that the graph follows or should follow. We discuss three types of graph schemata: *semantic*, *validating*, and *emergent*.

3.1.1 SEMANTIC SCHEMA

A semantic schema allows for defining the meaning of high-level terms (aka *vocabulary* or *terminology*) used in the graph, which facilitates reasoning over graphs using those terms. Looking at Figure 2.1, for example, we may notice some natural groupings of nodes based on the types of entities to which they refer. We may thus decide to define *classes*, such as `Event`, `City`, etc., to denote these groupings. In fact, Figure 2.1 already illustrates three low-level classes—`Open Market`, `Food Market`, `Drinks Festival`—grouping similar entities with an edge labeled type. We may subsequently wish to capture some relations between these classes. In Figure 3.1, we present a class hierarchy for events where children are defined to be *sub-classes* of their parents such that if we find an edge `EID15`—type→`Food Festival` in our graph, we may also *infer* that `EID15`—type→`Festival` and `EID15`—type→`Event` hold in the graph.

Aside from classes, we may also wish to define the semantics of edge labels, aka *properties*. Returning to Figure 2.1, we may consider that the properties city and venue are *sub-properties* of a more general property location, such that given an edge `Santa Lucía`—city→`Santiago`, for example, we may also infer that `Santa Lucía`—location→`Santiago` must hold as an edge in the graph. We may also consider, for example, that bus and flight are both sub-properties of a more general property connects to. Along these lines, properties may also form a hierarchy similar to what we saw for classes. We

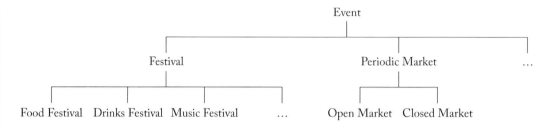

Figure 3.1: Example class hierarchy for `Event`.

Table 3.1: Definitions for sub-class, sub-property, domain, and range

Feature	Definition	Condition	Example
Subclass	c –subc. of→ d	x –type→ c implies x –type→ d	City –subc. of→ Place
Subproperty	p –subp. of→ q	x –p→ y implies x –q→ y	venue –subp. of→ location
Domain	p –domain→ c	x –p→ y implies x –type→ c	venue –domain→ Event
Range	p –range→ c	x –p→ y implies y –type→ c	venue –range→ Venue

may further define the *domain* of properties, indicating the class(es) of entities for nodes from which edges with that property extend; for example, we may define that the domain of connects to is a class `Place`, such that given the previous sub-property relations, we infer Arica —type→ Place. Conversely, we may define the *range* of properties, indicating the class(es) of entities for nodes to which edges with that property extend; for example, we may define that the range of city is a class `City`, inferring Arica —type→ City.

A prominent standard for defining a semantic schema for (RDF) graphs is the *RDF Schema (RDFS)* standard [Brickley and Guha, 2014], which allows for defining sub-classes, sub-properties, domains, and ranges among the classes and properties used in an RDF graph, where such definitions can be serialized as a graph. We illustrate the semantics of these features in Table 3.1 and provide a concrete example of definitions in Figure 3.2 for a sample of terms used in the running example. These definitions can then be embedded into a data graph. More generally, the semantics of terms used in a graph can be defined in much more depth than seen here, as is supported by the *Web Ontology Language (OWL)* standard [Hitzler et al., 2012] for RDF graphs. We will return to such semantics later in Chapter 4.

Semantic schemata are typically defined for incomplete graph data, where the absence of an edge between two nodes, such as Viña del Mar —flight→ Arica, does not mean that the relation does not hold in the real world. Therefore, from the graph of Figure 2.1, we cannot assume that there is no flight between Viña del Mar and Arica. In contrast, if the *Closed World Assumption (CWA)* were adopted—as is the case in many classical database systems—it would be assumed that the

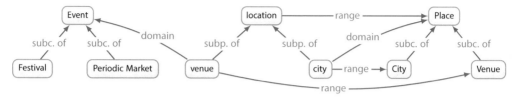

Figure 3.2: Example schema with sub-classes, sub-properties, domains, and ranges.

data graph is a complete description of the world, thus allowing to assert with certainty that no flight exists between the two cities. Systems that do not adopt the CWA are said to adopt the *Open World Assumption* (*OWA*). Considering our running example, it would be unreasonable to assume that the tourism organization has complete knowledge of everything describable in its knowledge graph, and hence adopting the OWA appears more appropriate. However, it can be inconvenient if a system is unable to definitely answer "*yes*" or "*no*" to questions such as "*is there a flight between Arica and Viña del Mar?*," especially when the organization is certain that it has complete knowledge of the flights. A compromise between OWA and CWA is the *Local Closed World Assumption* (*LCWA*), where portions of the data graph are assumed to be complete.

3.1.2   VALIDATING SCHEMA

When graphs are used to represent diverse, incomplete data at large scale, the OWA is the most appropriate choice for a *default* semantics. But in some scenarios, we may wish to guarantee that our data graph—or specific parts thereof—are in some sense "complete." Returning to Figure 2.1, for example, we may wish to ensure that all events have at least a name, a venue, a start date, and an end date, such that applications using the data—e.g., one that sends event notifications to users—can ensure that they have the minimal information required. Furthermore, we may wish to ensure that the city of an event is *stated to be* a city (rather than *inferring* that it is a city). We can define such constraints in a validating schema and validate the data graph with respect to the resulting schema, listing constraint violations (if any). Thus, while semantic schemata allow for inferring new graph data, validating schemata allow for validating a given data graph with respect to some constraints.

A standard way to define a validating schema for graphs is using *shapes* [Knublauch and Kontokostas, 2017, Labra Gayo et al., 2017, Prud'hommeaux et al., 2014]. A shape *targets* a set of nodes in a data graph and specifies *constraints* on those nodes. The shape's target can be defined in many ways, such as targeting all instances of a class, the domain or range of a property, the result of a query, nodes connected to the target of another shape by a given property, etc. Constraints can then be defined on the targeted nodes, such as to restrict the number or types of values taken on a given property, the shapes that such values must satisfy, etc.

A *shapes graph* is formed from a set of interrelated shapes. Shapes graphs can be depicted as UML-like class diagrams, where Figure 3.3 illustrates an example of a shapes graph based on

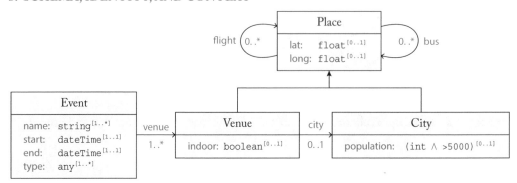

Figure 3.3: Example shapes graph depicted as a UML-like diagram.

Figure 2.1, defining constraints on four interrelated shapes. Each shape—denoted with a box like $\boxed{\text{Place}}$, $\boxed{\text{Event}}$, etc.—is associated with a set of constraints. Nodes conform to a shape if and only if they satisfy all constraints defined on the shape. Inside each shape box are placed constraints on the number (e.g., [1..*] denotes one-to-many, [1..1] denotes precisely one, etc.) and types (e.g., string, dateTime, etc.) of nodes that conforming nodes can relate to with a property (e.g., name, start, etc.). Another option is to place constraints on the number of nodes conforming to a particular shape that the conforming node can relate to with a property (thus generating edges between shapes); for example, $\boxed{\text{Event}} \xrightarrow[1..*]{\text{venue}} \boxed{\text{Venue}}$ denotes that conforming nodes for $\boxed{\text{Event}}$ must relate to at least one node with the property venue that conforms to the $\boxed{\text{Venue}}$ shape. Shapes can inherit the constraints of parent shapes—with inheritance denoted with an △ connector—as in the case of $\boxed{\text{City}}$ and $\boxed{\text{Venue}}$, whose conforming nodes must also conform to the $\boxed{\text{Place}}$ shape.

Given a shape and a targeted node, it is possible to check if the node conforms to that shape or not, which may require checking conformance of other nodes; for example, the node $\boxed{\text{EID15}}$ conforms to the $\boxed{\text{Event}}$ shape not only based on its local properties, but also based on conformance of $\boxed{\text{Santa Lucía}}$ to $\boxed{\text{Venue}}$ and $\boxed{\text{Santiago}}$ to $\boxed{\text{City}}$. Conformance dependencies may also be recursive, where the conformance of $\boxed{\text{Santiago}}$ to $\boxed{\text{City}}$ requires that it conforms to $\boxed{\text{Place}}$, which requires that $\boxed{\text{Viña del Mar}}$ and $\boxed{\text{Arica}}$ conform to $\boxed{\text{Place}}$, and so on. Conversely, $\boxed{\text{EID16}}$ does not conform to $\boxed{\text{Event}}$, as it does not have the start and end properties required by the example shapes graph.

When declaring shapes, the data modeler may not know in advance the entire set of properties that some nodes can have (now or in the future). An *open shape* allows the node to have additional properties not specified by the shape, while a *closed shape* does not. For example, if we add the edge $\boxed{\text{Santiago}} \text{—founder→} \boxed{\text{Pedro de Valdivia}}$ to the graph represented in Figure 2.1, then $\boxed{\text{Santiago}}$ only conforms to the $\boxed{\text{City}}$ shape if the shape is defined as open (since the shape does not mention founder).

Practical languages for shapes often support additional Boolean features, such as conjunction (AND), disjunction (OR), and negation (NOT) of shapes; for example, we may say that all the values of venue should conform to the shape $\boxed{\text{Venue } and \text{ (} not \text{ City)}}$, making explicit that venues in the data graph should not be directly given as cities. However, shapes languages that freely combine recursion and negation may lead to semantic problems, depending on how their semantics are defined. To illustrate, consider the following case inspired by the barber paradox [Labra Gayo et al., 2017], involving a shape BARBER whose conforming nodes shave at least one node conforming to PERSON *and* (*not* BARBER). Now, given (only) Bob —shave→ Bob with Bob conforming to PERSON, does Bob conform to BARBER? If *yes*—if Bob conforms to BARBER—then Bob violates the constraint by not shaving at least one node conforming to PERSON *and* (*not* BARBER). If *no*—if Bob does not conform to BARBER—then Bob satisfies the BARBER constraint by shaving such a node. Semantics to avoid such paradoxical situations have been proposed based on stratification [Boneva et al., 2017], partial assignments [Corman et al., 2018], and stable models [Gelfond and Lifschitz, 1988].

Although validating schemata and semantic schemata serve different purposes, they can complement each other. In particular, a validating schema can take into consideration a semantic schema, such that, for example, validation is applied on the data graph including inferences. Taking the class hierarchy of Figure 3.1 and the shapes graph of Figure 3.3, for example, we may define the target of the EVENT shape as the nodes that are of type Event (the class). If we first apply inferencing with respect to the class hierarchy of the semantic schema, the EVENT shape would now target EID15 and EID16. The presence of a semantic schema may, however, require adapting the validating schema. Taking into account, for example, the aforementioned class hierarchy would require defining a relaxed cardinality on the type property. Open shapes may also be preferred in such cases rather than enumerating constraints on all possible properties that may be inferred on a node.

Two shapes languages have recently emerged for RDF graphs: *Shape Expressions* (*ShEx*), published as a W3C Community Group Report [Prud'hommeaux et al., 2014]; and *SHACL* (*Shapes Constraint Language*), published as a W3C Recommendation [Knublauch and Kontokostas, 2017]. These languages support the discussed features (and more) and have been adopted for validating graphs in a number of domains relating to health care [Thornton et al., 2019], scientific literature [Hammond et al., 2017], spatial data [Car et al., 2019], among others. More details about ShEx and SHACL can be found in the book by Labra Gayo et al. [2017]. A recently proposed language that can be used as a common basis for both ShEx and SHACL reveals their similarities and differences [Labra Gayo et al., 2019]. A similar notion of schema has been proposed by Angles [2018] for property graphs.

We formally define shapes following the conventions of Labra Gayo et al. [2019].

Definition 3.1 Shape.   A *shape* ϕ is defined as:

$$
\begin{array}{lll}
\phi & ::= & \top & \text{true} \\
& | & \Delta_N & \text{node belongs to the set of nodes } N \\
& | & \Psi_{\text{cond}} & \text{node satisfies the Boolean condition cond} \\
& | & \phi_1 \wedge \phi_2 & \text{conjunction of shape } \phi_1 \text{ and shape } \phi_2 \\
& | & \neg\phi & \text{negation of shape } \phi \\
& | & @s & \text{reference to shape with label } s \\
& | & \widehat{p}\phi\{\min, \max\} & \text{between min and max outward edges (inclusive)} \\
& & & \text{with label } p \text{ to nodes satisfying shape } \phi
\end{array}
$$

where $\min \in \mathbb{N}_{(0)}$, $\max \in \mathbb{N}_{(0)} \cup \{*\}$, with "$*$" indicating unbounded.

Definition 3.2 Shapes schema.   A *shapes schema* is defined as a tuple $\Sigma = (\Phi, S, \lambda)$ where Φ is a set of shapes, S is a set of shape labels, and $\lambda : S \to \Phi$ is a total function from labels to shapes.

Example 3.3   The shapes schema from Figure 3.3 can be expressed as:

$$
\begin{array}{lll}
\boxed{\text{Event}} & \mapsto & \widehat{\text{name}}\Delta_{\texttt{string}}\{1, *\} \wedge \widehat{\text{start}}\Delta_{\texttt{dateTime}}\{1, 1\} \wedge \widehat{\text{end}}\Delta_{\texttt{dateTime}}\{1, 1\} \\
& & \wedge\widehat{\text{type}}\top\{1, *\} \wedge \widehat{\text{venue}}@\boxed{\text{Venue}}\{1, *\} \\
\boxed{\text{Venue}} & \mapsto & @\boxed{\text{Place}} \wedge \widehat{\text{indoor}}\Delta_{\texttt{boolean}}\{0, 1\} \wedge \widehat{\text{city}}@\boxed{\text{City}}\{0, 1\} \\
\boxed{\text{City}} & \mapsto & @\boxed{\text{Place}} \wedge \widehat{\text{population}}(\Delta_{\texttt{int}} \wedge \Psi_{>5000})\{0, 1\} \\
\boxed{\text{Place}} & \mapsto & \widehat{\text{lat}}\Delta_{\texttt{float}}\{0, 1\} \wedge \widehat{\text{long}}\Delta_{\texttt{float}}\{0, 1\} \\
& & \wedge\widehat{\text{flight}}@\boxed{\text{Place}}\{0, *\} \wedge \widehat{\text{bus}}@\boxed{\text{Place}}\{0, *\}
\end{array}
$$

For example, $\boxed{\text{Event}}$ is a shape label (an element of S) that maps to a shape (an element of ϕ). This mapping is defined by λ.

In a shapes schema, shapes may refer to other shapes, giving rise to a graph that is sometimes known as the *shapes graph* [Knublauch and Kontokostas, 2017]. Figure 3.3 illustrates a shapes graph of this form.

The semantics of a shape is defined in terms of the evaluation of that shape over each node of a given data graph. The semantics of a shapes schema, in turn, is the result of evaluating each shape of the schema over each node of a given data graph; the result of this evaluation is a *shapes map*.

Definition 3.4 Shapes map.   Given a directed edge-labeled graph $G = (V, E, L)$ and a shapes schema $\Sigma = (\Phi, S, \lambda)$, a *shapes map* is a (partial) mapping $\sigma : V \times S \to \{0, 1\}$.

The shapes map σ is a way of labeling the nodes of G with the labels of shapes from S. If $\sigma(v, s) = 1$, then node v is labeled s (possibly among other labels); otherwise if $\sigma(v, s) = $

0, then node v is not labeled s. The precise semantics depends on whether or not σ is a total or partial mapping: whether or not it is defined for every pair in $V \times S$. Herein we present the semantics for the more straightforward case wherein σ is assumed to be a total shapes map.

Definition 3.5   Shape evaluation.   Given a shapes schema $\Sigma = (\Phi, S, \lambda)$, a directed edge-labeled graph $G = (V, E, L)$, a node $v \in V$ and a total shapes map σ, the *shape evaluation function* $[\phi]^{G,v,\sigma} \in \{0, 1\}$ is defined as follows:

$$
\begin{aligned}
[\top]^{G,v,\sigma} &= 1 \\
[\Delta_N]^{G,v,\sigma} &= 1 \text{ iff } v \in N \\
[\Psi_{\text{cond}}]^{G,v,\sigma} &= 1 \text{ iff } \text{cond}(v) \text{ is true} \\
[\phi_1 \wedge \phi_2]^{G,v,\sigma} &= \min\{[\phi_1]^{G,v,\sigma}, [\phi_2]^{G,v,\sigma}\} \\
[\neg\phi]^{G,v,\sigma} &= 1 - [\phi]^{G,v,\sigma} \\
[@s]^{G,v,\sigma} &= 1 \text{ iff } \sigma(v, s) = 1 \\
[\hat{p}\phi\{\min, \max\}]^{G,v,\sigma} &= 1 \text{ iff } \min \le |\{(v, p, u) \in E \mid [\phi]^{G,u,\sigma} = 1\}| \le \max
\end{aligned}
$$

If $[\phi]^{G,v,\sigma} = 1$, then v is said to *satisfy* ϕ in G under σ.

Typically for the purposes of validating a graph with respect to a shapes schema, a *target* is defined that requires certain nodes to satisfy certain shapes.

Definition 3.6   Shapes target.   Given a directed edge-labeled graph $G = (V, E, L)$ and a shapes schema $\Sigma = (\Phi, S, \lambda)$, a *shapes target* $T \subseteq V \times S$ is a set of pairs of nodes and shape labels from G and Σ, respectively.

The nodes that a shape targets can be selected based on a manual selection, based on the type(s) of the nodes, based on the results of a graph query, etc. [Corman et al., 2018, Labra Gayo et al., 2019].

Last, we define the notion of a valid graph under a given shapes schema and target based on the existence of a shapes map satisfying certain conditions.

Definition 3.7   Valid graph.   Given a shapes schema $\Sigma = (\Phi, S, \lambda)$, a directed edge-labeled graph $G = (V, E, L)$, and a shapes target T, we say that G *is valid under* Σ *and* T if and only if there exists a shapes map σ such that, for all $s \in S$ and $v \in V$ it holds that $\sigma(v, s) = [\lambda(s)]^{G,v,\sigma}$, and $(v, s) \in T$ implies $\sigma(v, s) = 1$.

Example 3.8   Taking the graph G from Figure 2.1 and the shapes schema Σ from Figure 3.3, first assume an empty shapes target $T = \{\}$. If we consider a shapes map where, e.g., $\sigma(\boxed{\text{EID15}}, \boxed{\text{EVENT}}) = 1$, $\sigma(\boxed{\text{Santa Lucía}}, \boxed{\text{VENUE}}) = 1$, $\sigma(\boxed{\text{Santa Lucía}}, \boxed{\text{PLACE}}) = 1$, etc., but where $\sigma(\boxed{\text{EID16}}, \boxed{\text{EVENT}}) = 0$ (as it does not have the required values for start and end), etc., then

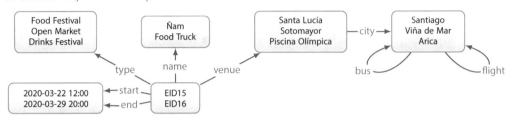

Figure 3.4: Example quotient graph simulating the data graph in Figure 2.1.

we see that G is valid under Σ and T. However, if we were to define a shapes target T to ensure that the Event shape targets EID15 and EID16—i.e., to define T such that $\{(\text{EID15}, \text{Event}), (\text{EID16}, \text{Event})\} \subseteq T$—then the graph would no longer be valid under Σ and T since EID16 does not satisfy Event.

The semantics we present here assumes that each node in the graph either satisfies or does not satisfy each shape labeled by the schema. More complex semantics—for example, based on Kleene's three-valued logic [Corman et al., 2018, Labra Gayo et al., 2019]—have been proposed that support partial shapes maps, where the satisfaction of some nodes for some shapes can be left as undefined. Shapes languages in practice may support other more advanced forms of constraints, such as counting on paths [Knublauch and Kontokostas, 2017]. In terms of implementing validation with respect to shapes, work has been done on translating constraints into sets of graph queries, whose results are input to a SAT solver for recursive cases [Corman et al., 2019].

3.1.3 EMERGENT SCHEMA

Both semantic and validating schemata require a domain expert to explicitly specify definitions and constraints. However, a data graph will often exhibit latent structures that can be automatically extracted as an *emergent schema* [Pham et al., 2015] (aka *graph summary* [Čebirić et al., 2019, Liu et al., 2018, Spahiu et al., 2016]).

A framework often used for defining emergent schema is that of *quotient graphs*, which partition groups of nodes in the data graph according to some equivalence relation while preserving some structural properties of the graph. Taking Figure 2.1, we can intuitively distinguish different *types* of nodes based on their context, such as event nodes, which link to venue nodes, which in turn link to city nodes, and so forth. In order to describe the structure of the graph, we could consider six partitions of nodes: *event, name, venue, class, date-time, city*. In practice, these partitions may be computed based on the class or shape of the node. Merging the nodes of each partition into one node while preserving edges leads to the quotient graph shown in Figure 3.4: the nodes of this quotient graph are the partitions of nodes from the data graph and an edge

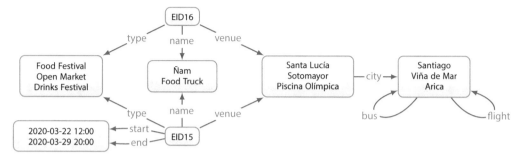

Figure 3.5: Example quotient graph bisimilar with the data graph in Figure 2.1.

$(X)\text{-}y\text{-}(Z)$ is included the quotient graph if and only if there exists $x \in X$ and $z \in Z$ such that $(x)\text{-}y\text{-}(z)$ is in the original data graph.

There are many ways in which quotient graphs may be defined, depending not only on how nodes are partitioned, but also how the edges are defined. Different quotient graphs may provide different guarantees with respect to the structure they preserve. Formally, we can say that every quotient graph *simulates* its input graph (based on the *simulation relation* of set membership between data nodes and quotient nodes), meaning that for all $x \in X$ with x an input node and X a quotient node, if $(x)\text{-}y\text{-}(z)$ is an edge in the data graph, then there must exist an edge $(X)\text{-}y\text{-}(Z)$ in the quotient graph such that $z \in Z$; for example, the quotient graph of Figure 3.4 simulates the data graph of Figure 2.1. However, this quotient graph seems to suggest (for instance) that (EID16) would have a start and end date in the data graph when this is not the case. A stronger notion of structural preservation is given by *bisimilarity*, which in this case would further require that if $(X)\text{-}y\text{-}(Z)$ is an edge in the quotient graph, then for all $x \in X$, there must exist a $z \in Z$ such that $(x)\text{-}y\text{-}(z)$ is in the data graph; this is not satisfied by (EID16) in the quotient graph of Figure 3.4, which does not have an outgoing edge labeled start or end in the original data graph. Figure 3.5 illustrates a bisimilar version of the quotient graph, splitting the *event* partition into two nodes reflecting their different outgoing edges. An interesting property of bisimilarity is that it preserves forward-directed paths: given a path expression r without inverses and two bisimilar graphs, r will match a path in one graph if and only if it matches a corresponding path in the other bisimilar graph. One can verify, for example, that a path matches $(x)\text{---}_{\text{city}\cdot(\text{flight}|\text{bus})^*}\text{---}(z)$ in Figure 2.1 if and only if there is a path matching $(X)\text{---}_{\text{city}\cdot(\text{flight}|\text{bus})^*}\text{---}(Z)$ in Figure 3.5 such that $x \in X$ and $z \in Z$.

There are many ways in which quotient graphs may be defined, depending on the equivalence relation that partitions nodes. Furthermore, there are many ways in which other similar or bisimilar graphs can be defined, depending on the (bi)simulation relation that preserves the data graph's structure [Čebirić et al., 2019]. Such techniques aim to *summarize* the data graph into a higher-level topology. In order to reduce the memory overhead of the quotient graph, in practice, nodes may rather be labeled with the cardinality of the partition and/or a high-level label (e.g., *event, city*) for the partition rather than storing the labels of all nodes in the partition.

Various other forms of emergent schema not directly based on a quotient graph framework have also been proposed; examples include emergent schemata based on relational tables [Pham et al., 2015], and based on formal concept analysis [González and Hogan, 2018]. Emergent schemata may be used to provide a human-understandable overview of the data graph, to aid with the definition of a semantic or validating schema, to optimize the indexing and querying of the graph, to guide the integration of data graphs, and so forth. We refer to the survey by Čebirić et al. [2019] dedicated to this topic for further details.

Emergent schemata are often based on the notion of a quotient graph.

Definition 3.9   Quotient graph.   Given a directed edge-labeled graph $G = (V, E, L)$, a graph $\mathcal{G} = (\mathcal{V}, \mathcal{E}, L)$ is a *quotient graph* of G if and only if:

- $\mathcal{V}$ is a partition of V without the empty set, i.e., $\mathcal{V} \subseteq (2^V - \emptyset)$, $V = \bigcup_{U \in \mathcal{V}} U$, and for all $U \in \mathcal{V}$, $W \in \mathcal{V}$, it holds that $U = W$ or $U \cap W = \emptyset$; and

- $\mathcal{E} = \{(U, l, W) \mid U \in \mathcal{V}, W \in \mathcal{V} \text{ and } \exists u \in U, \exists w \in W : (u, l, w) \in E\}$.

A quotient graph can "merge" multiple nodes into one node, keeping the edges of its constituent nodes. For an input graph $G = (V, E, L)$, there is an exponential number of possible quotient graphs based on partitions of the input nodes. On one extreme, the input graph is a quotient graph of itself (turning nodes like ⓤ into singleton nodes like ⟨{u}⟩). On the other extreme, a single node ⟨V⟩, with all input nodes, and loops (V, l, V) for each edge-label l used in the set of input edges E, is also a quotient graph. Quotient graphs typically fall somewhere in between, where the partition $\mathcal{V}$ of V is often defined in terms of an *equivalence relation* $\sim$ on the set V such that $\mathcal{V} = \sim / V$; i.e., $\mathcal{V}$ is defined as the *quotient set* of V with respect to $\sim$; for example, we might define an equivalence relation on nodes such that $u \sim v$ if and only if they have the same set of defined types, where $\sim / V$ is then a partition whose parts contain all nodes with the same types. Another way to induce a quotient graph is to define the partition in a way that preserves some of the topology (i.e., connectivity) of the input graph. One way to formally define this idea is through *simulation* and *bisimulation*.

Definition 3.10   Simulation.   Given two directed edge-labeled graphs $G = (V, E, L)$ and $G' = (V', E', L')$, let $R \subseteq V \times V'$ be a relation between the nodes of G and G', respectively. We call R a *simulation* on G and G' if, for all $(v, v') \in R$, the following holds:

- if $(v, p, w) \in E$ then there exists w' such that $(v', p, w') \in E'$ and $(w, w') \in R$.

If a simulation exists on G and G', we say that G' *simulates* G, denoted $G \leadsto G'$.

Definition 3.11 Bisimulation. If R is a simulation on G and G', we call it a *bisimulation* if, for all $(v, v') \in R$, the following condition holds:

- if $(v' p, w') \in E'$ then there exists w such that $(v, p, w) \in E$ and $(w, w') \in R$.

If a bisimulation exists on G and G', we call them *bisimilar*, denoted $G \approx G'$.

Bisimulation ($\approx$) is then an equivalence relation on graphs. By defining the (bi)simulation relation R in terms of set membership $\in$, every quotient graph simulates its input graph, but does not necessarily bisimulate its input graph. This gives rise to the notion of *bisimilar quotient graphs*.

Example 3.12 Figures 3.4 and 3.5 exemplify quotient graphs for the graph of Figure 2.1. Figure 3.4 simulates but is not bisimilar to the data graph. Figure 3.5 is bisimilar to the data graph. Often the goal will be to compute the most concise quotient graph that satisfies a given condition; for example, the nodes without outgoing edges in Figure 3.5 could be merged while preserving bisimilarity.

3.2 IDENTITY

Figure 2.1 uses nodes like (Santiago), but to which Santiago does this node refer? Do we refer to Santiago de Chile, Santiago de Cuba, Santiago de Compostela, or do we perhaps refer to the indie rock band Santiago? Based on edges such as (Santa Lucía)—city→(Santiago), we may deduce that it is one of the three cities mentioned (not the rock band), and based on the fact that the graph describes tourist attractions in Chile, we may further deduce that it refers to Santiago de Chile. Without further details, however, *disambiguating* nodes of this form may rely on heuristics prone to error in more difficult cases. To help avoid such ambiguity, first we may use globally-unique identifiers to avoid naming clashes when the knowledge graph is extended with external data, and second we may add external identity links to disambiguate a node with respect to an external source.

3.2.1 PERSISTENT IDENTIFIERS

Assume we wished to compare tourism in Chile and Cuba, and we have acquired an appropriate knowledge graph for Cuba similar to the one we have for Chile. We can merge two graphs by taking their union. However, as shown in Figure 3.6, using an ambiguous node like (Santiago) may yield a *naming clash*: the node is referring to two different real-world cities in both graphs, where the merged graph indicates that Santiago is a city in both Chile and Cuba (rather than

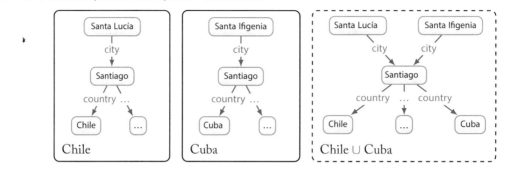

Figure 3.6: Result of merging two graphs with ambiguous local identifiers.

two distinct cities).[1] To avoid such clashes, long-lasting *persistent identifiers* (*PIDs*) [Hakala, 2010] can be created in order to uniquely identify an entity; examples of PID schemes include *Digital Object Identifiers* (*DOIs*) for papers, *ORCID iDs* for authors, *International Standard Book Numbers* (*ISBNs*) for books, *Alpha-2 codes* for counties, and more besides.

In the context of the Semantic Web, the RDF data model goes one step further and recommends that global Web identifiers be used for nodes and edge labels. However, rather than adopt the *Uniform Resource Locators (URLs)* used to identify the location of *information resources* such as webpages, RDF 1.1 proposes to use *Internationalized Resource Identifiers (IRIs)* to identify *non-information resources* such as cities or events.[2] Hence, for example, in the RDF representation of Wikidata [Vrandečić and Krötzsch, 2014]—a knowledge graph proposed to complement Wikipedia, discussed in more detail in Chapter 10—while the URL https://www.wikidata.org/wiki/Q2887 refers to a webpage that can be loaded in a browser providing human-readable metadata about Santiago, the IRI http://www.wikidata.org/entity/Q2887 refers to the city itself. Distinguishing the identifiers for the webpage and the city itself avoids naming clashes; for example, if we use the URL to identify both the webpage and the city, we may end up with an edge in our graph, such as (with readable labels below the edge):

Such an edge leaves ambiguity: was Pedro de Valdivia the founder of the webpage, or the city? Using IRIs for entities distinct from the URLs for the webpages that describe them avoids such ambiguous cases, where Wikidata thus rather defines the previous edge using less ambiguous identifiers, as follows:

---

[1]Such a naming clash is not unique to graphs, but could also occur if merging tables, trees, etc.

[2]Uniform Resource Identifiers (URIs) can be Uniform Resource Locators (URLs), used to locate information resources, and Uniform Resource Names (URNs), used to name resources. Internationalized Resource Identifiers (IRIs) are URIs that allow Unicode (e.g., `http://example.com/Ñam`).

[http://www.wikidata.org/entity/Q2887]——http://www.wikidata.org/prop/direct/P112——▶[http://www.wikidata.org/entity/Q203534]

[Santiago (IRI)]   [founded by (IRI)]   [Pedro de Valdivia (IRI)]

using IRIs for the city, person, and founder of, distinct from the webpages describing them. These Wikidata identifiers use the prefix http://www.wikidata.org/entity/ for entities and the prefix http://www.wikidata.org/prop/direct/ for relations. Such prefixes are known as *namespaces*, and are often abbreviated with prefix strings, such as `wd:` or `wdt:`, where the latter edge can then be written more concisely using such abbreviations as the edge (wd:Q2887)—wdt:P112—▶(wd:Q203534).

If HTTP IRIs are used to identify the graph's entities, when the IRI is looked up (via HTTP), the web-server can return (or redirect to) a description of that entity in formats such as RDF. This further enables RDF graphs to link to related entities described in external RDF graphs over the Web, giving rise to *Linked Data* [Berners-Lee, 2006, Heath and Bizer, 2011] (discussed in Chapter 9). Though HTTP IRIs offer a flexible and powerful mechanism for issuing global identifiers on the Web, they are not necessarily persistent: websites may go offline, the resources described at a given location may change, etc. In order to enhance the persistence of such identifiers, *Persistent URL (PURL)* services offer redirects from a central server to a particular location, where the PURL can be redirected to a new location if necessary, changing the address of a document without changing its identifier. The persistence of HTTP IRIs can then be improved by using namespaces defined through PURL services.

3.2.2 EXTERNAL IDENTITY LINKS

Assume that the tourist board opts to define the `chile:` namespace with an IRI such as `http://turismo.cl/entity/` on a web-server that they control, allowing nodes such as (chile:Santiago)—a shortcut for the IRI (http://turismo.cl/entity/Santiago)—to be looked up over the Web. While using such a naming scheme helps to avoid naming clashes, the use of IRIs does not necessarily help ground the identity of a resource. For example, an external geographic knowledge graph may assign the same city the IRI (geo:SantiagoDeChile) in their own namespace, where we have no direct way of knowing that the two identifiers refer to the same city. If we merge the two knowledge graphs, we will end up with two distinct nodes for the same city, and thus not integrate their data.

There are a number of ways to ground the identity of an entity. The first is to associate the entity with uniquely-identifying information in the graph, such as its geo-coordinates, its postal code, the year it was founded, etc. Each additional piece of information removes ambiguity regarding which city is being referred to, providing (for example) more options for matching the city with its analogue in external sources. A second option is to use *identity links* to state that a local entity has the same identity as another *coreferent* entity found in an external source; an instantiation of this concept can be found in the OWL standard, which defines the `owl:sameAs` property relating coreferent entities. Using this property, we could state the edge (chile:Santiago)—owl:sameAs—▶(geo:SantiagoDeChile) in our RDF graph, thus establishing an identity link between the corresponding nodes in both graphs. Rather than specifying pairwise identity links between all knowledge graphs, it suffices if two knowledge graphs provide corresponding identity links to the same external knowledge graph, such as DBpedia or Wikidata; for example, if the local knowledge graph provides an identity link to Wikidata indicating (chile:Santiago)—owl:sameAs→(wd:Q2887), while the remote knowledge graph has the identity link (geo:SantiagoDeChile)—owl:sameAs→(wd:Q2887), then we can infer (chile:Santiago)—owl:sameAs→(geo:SantiagoDeChile). The semantics of `owl:sameAs` defined by the OWL standard then allows us to combine the data for both nodes. Such semantics will be discussed later in Chapter 4. Ways in which identity links can be computed will also be discussed later in Chapter 8.

3.2.3   DATATYPES

Consider the two date-times on the left of Figure 2.1: how should we assign these nodes persistent/global identifiers? Intuitively it would not make much sense, for example, to assign IRIs to these nodes since their syntactic form directly tells us what they refer to: specific dates and times in March 2020. This syntactic form is further recognizable by machine, meaning that with appropriate software, we could order such values in ascending or descending order, extract the year, etc.

Most practical data models for graphs allow for defining nodes that are datatype values. RDF uses *XML Schema Datatypes* (*XSD*) [Peterson et al., 2012], among others, where a datatype node is given as a pair (l, d) where l is a lexical string, such as "2020-03-29T20:00:00," and d is an IRI denoting the datatype, such as `xsd:dateTime`. The node is then denoted ("2020-03-29T20:00:00"^^xsd:dateTime). Datatype nodes in RDF are called *literals* and are not allowed to have outgoing edges. Other datatypes commonly used in RDF data include `xsd:string`, `xsd:integer`, `xsd:decimal`, `xsd:boolean`, etc. If the datatype is omitted, the value is assumed to be of type `xsd:string`. Applications built on top of RDF can then recognize these datatypes, parse them into datatype objects, and apply equality checks, normalization, ordering, transformations, etc., according to their standard definition. In the context of property graphs, Neo4j [Miller, 2013] also defines a set of internal datatypes on property values that includes numbers, strings, Booleans, spatial points, and temporal values.

3.2.4   LEXICALIZATION

Global identifiers for entities will sometimes have a human-interpretable form, such as (chile:Santiago), but the identifier strings themselves do not carry any formal semantic significance. In other cases, the identifiers used may not be human-interpretable by design. In Wikidata, for instance, Santiago de Chile is identified as (wd:Q2887), where such a scheme has the advantage of providing better persistence and of not being biased to a particular human language. As a real-world example, the Wikidata identifier for Eswatini ((wd:Q1050)) was not affected when the country changed its name from Swaziland, and does not necessitate choosing between languages for creating (more readable) IRIs such as (wd:Eswatini) (English), (wd:eSwatini) (Swazi), (wd:Esuatini) (Spanish), etc.

Since identifiers can be arbitrary, it is common to add edges that provide a human-interpretable label for nodes, such as (wd:Q2887)—rdfs:label→("Santiago"), indicating how people may refer to the subject node linguistically. Linguistic information of this form plays an important role in grounding knowledge such that users can more clearly identify which real-world entity a particular node in a knowledge graph actually references [de Melo, 2015]; it further permits cross-referencing entity labels with text corpora to find, for example, documents that potentially speak of a given entity [Martínez-Rodríguez et al., 2020]. Labels can be complemented with aliases (e.g., (wd:Q2887)—skos:altLabel→("Santiago de Chile")) or comments (e.g., (wd:Q2887)—rdfs:comment→("Santiago is the capital of Chile")) to further help ground the node's identity.

Nodes such as ("Santiago") denote string literals, rather than an identifier. Depending on the specific graph model, such literal nodes may also be defined as a pair (s, l), where s denotes the string and l a language code; in RDF, for example we may state (chile:City)—rdfs:label→("City"@en), (chile:City)—rdfs:label→("Ciudad"@es), etc., indicating labels for the node in different languages. In other models, the pertinent language can rather be specified, e.g., via metadata on the edge. Knowledge graphs with human-interpretable labels, aliases, comments, etc. (in various languages) are sometimes called (*multilingual*) *lexicalized knowledge graphs* [Bonatti et al., 2018].

3.2.5   EXISTENTIAL NODES

When modeling incomplete information, we may in some cases know that there must exist a particular node in the graph with particular relationships to other nodes, but without being able to identify the node in question. For example, we may have two co-located events (chile:EID42) and (chile:EID43) whose venue has yet to be announced. One option is to simply omit the venue edges, in which case we lose the information that these events have a venue and that both events have the same venue. Another option might be to create a fresh IRI representing the venue, but semantically this becomes indistinguishable from there being a known venue. Hence some graph models permit the use of existential nodes, represented here as a blank circle:

These edges denote that there exists a common venue for (chile:EID42) and (chile:EID42) without identifying it. Existential nodes are supported in RDF as blank nodes [Cyganiak et al., 2014], which are also commonly used to support modeling complex elements in graphs, such as *RDF lists* [Cyganiak et al., 2014, Hogan et al., 2014]. Figure 3.7 exemplifies an RDF list, which uses blank nodes in a linked-list structure to encode order. Though existential nodes can be convenient, their presence can complicate operations on graphs, such as deciding if two data graphs have the same structure modulo existential nodes [Cyganiak et al., 2014, Hogan, 2017]. Hence methods for *skolemizing* existential nodes in graphs—replacing them with canonical labels—have been proposed [Hogan, 2017, Longley and Sporny, 2019]. Other authors rather call to minimize the use of such nodes in graph data [Heath and Bizer, 2011].

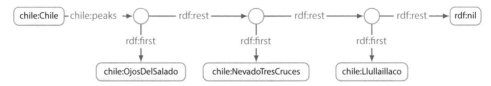

Figure 3.7: RDF list representing the three largest peaks of Chile, in order.

3.3 CONTEXT

Many (arguably *all*) facts presented in the data graph of Figure 2.1 can be considered true with respect to a certain *context*. With respect to *temporal context*, ⬭Santiago⬭ has existed as a city since 1541, flights from ⬭Arica⬭ to ⬭Santiago⬭ began in 1956, etc. With respect to *geographic context*, the graph describes events in Chile. With respect to *provenance*, data relating to ⬭EID15⬭ were taken from—and are thus said to be true with respect to—the Ñam webpage on January 4, 2020. Other forms of context may also be used. We may further combine contexts, such as to indicate that ⬭Arica⬭ is a Chilean city (*geographic*) since 1883 (*temporal*) per the Treaty of Ancón (*provenance*).

By context we herein refer to the *scope of truth*, i.e., the context in which some data are held to be true [Guha et al., 2004, McCarthy, 1993]. The graph of Figure 2.1 leaves much of its context implicit. However, making context explicit can allow for interpreting the data from different perspectives, such as to understand what held true in 2016, what holds true excluding webpages later found to have spurious data, etc. As seen previously, context for graph data may be considered at different levels: on individual nodes, individual edges, or sets of edges (sub-graphs). We now discuss various representations by which context can be made explicit at different levels.

3.3.1 DIRECT REPRESENTATION

The first way to represent context is to consider it as data no different from other data. For example, the dates for the event ⬭EID15⬭ in Figure 2.1 can be seen as representing a form of temporal context, indicating the temporal scope within which edges such as ⬭EID15⬭—venue→⬭Santa Lucía⬭ are held true. Another option is to change a relation represented as an edge, such as ⬭Santiago⬭—flight→⬭Arica⬭, into a node, such as seen in Figure 2.3a, allowing us to assign additional context to the relation. While in these examples context is represented in an ad hoc manner, a number of specifications have been proposed to represent context as data in a more standard way. One example is the *Time Ontology* [Cox et al., 2017], which specifies how temporal entities, intervals, time instants, etc.—and relations between them such as *before*, *overlaps*, etc.—can be described in RDF graphs in an interoperable manner. Another example is the *PROV Data Model* [Gil et al., 2013], which specifies how provenance can be described in RDF graphs, where entities (e.g., graphs, nodes, physical document) are derived from other entities, are generated and/or used by activities (e.g., extraction, authorship), and are attributed to agents (e.g., people, software, organizations).

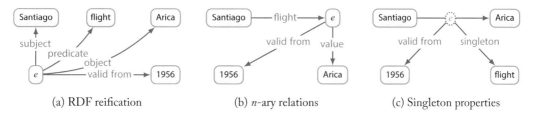

(a) RDF reification   (b) *n*-ary relations   (c) Singleton properties

Figure 3.8: Three representations of temporal context on a directed labeled edge.

3.3.2 REIFICATION

Often we may wish to directly define the context of edges themselves; for example, we may wish to state that the edge (Santiago)—flight→(Arica) is valid from 1956. While we could use the pattern of turning the edge into a node—as illustrated in Figure 2.3a—to directly represent such context, another option is to use *reification*, which allows for making statements about statements in a generic manner (or in the case of a graph, for defining edges about edges). In Figure 3.8 we present three forms of reification that can be used for modeling temporal context on the aforementioned edge within a directed edge-labeled graph [Hernández et al., 2015]. We use *e* to denote an arbitrary identifier representing the edge itself to which the context can be associated. Unlike in a direct representation, *e* represents an edge, not a flight. RDF reification [Cyganiak et al., 2014] (Figure 3.8a) defines a new node ⓔ to represent the edge and connects it to the source node (via subject), target node (via object), and edge label (via predicate) of the edge. In contrast, *n*-ary relations [Cyganiak et al., 2014] (Figure 3.8b) connect the source node of the edge directly to the edge node ⓔ with the label of the edge; the target node of the edge is then connected to ⓔ (via value). Finally, singleton properties [Nguyen et al., 2014] (Figure 3.8c) rather use *e* as an edge label, connecting it to a node indicating the original edge label (via singleton). Other forms of reification have been proposed in the literature, including, for example, NdFluents [Giménez-García et al., 2017]. In general, a reified edge does not assert the edge it reifies; for example, we may reify an edge to state that it is no longer valid. We refer to Hernández et al. [2015] for further comparison of reification alternatives.

3.3.3 HIGHER-ARITY REPRESENTATION

As an alternative to reification, we can use higher-arity representations for modeling context. Taking again the edge (Santiago)—flight→(Arica), Figure 3.9 illustrates three higher-arity representations of temporal context. First, we can use a named graph (Figure 3.9a) to contain the edge and then define the temporal context on the graph name. Second, we can use a property graph (Figure 3.9b) where the temporal context is defined as a property on the edge. Third, we can use *RDF** [Hartig, 2017] (Figure 3.9c): an extension of RDF that allows edges to be defined as nodes. Among these options, the most flexible is the named graph representation, where we can assign context to multiple edges at once by placing them in one named graph; for example, we

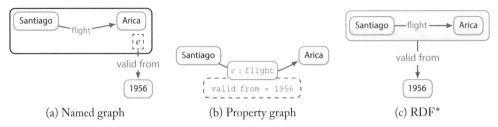

(a) Named graph   (b) Property graph   (c) RDF*

Figure 3.9: Three higher-arity representations of temporal context on an edge.

can add more edges to the named graph of Figure 3.9a that are also valid from 1956. The least flexible option is RDF*, which, in the absence of an edge id, does not permit different groups of contextual values to be assigned to an edge; for example, if we add four contextual values to the edge (Chile)—president→(M. Bachelet) to state that it was valid from 2006 until 2010 and valid from 2014 until 2018, we cannot pair the values, but may rather have to create a node to represent different presidencies (in the other models, we could have used two named graphs or edge ids).

3.3.4   ANNOTATIONS

Thus far, we have discussed representing context in a graph, but we have not spoken about automated mechanisms for reasoning about context; for example, if there are only seasonal summer flights from (Santiago) to (Arica), we may wish to find other routes from Santiago for winter events taking place in (Arica). While the dates for buses, flights, etc., can be represented directly in the graph, or using reification, writing a query to manually intersect the corresponding temporal contexts will be difficult. An alternative is to consider *annotations* that provide mathematical definitions of a contextual domain and key operations over that domain that can be applied automatically.

Some annotations model a particular contextual domain; for example, *Temporal RDF* [Gutiérrez et al., 2007] allows for annotating edges with time intervals, such as (Chile)—$\overset{president}{[2006, 2010]}$→(M. Bachelet), while *Fuzzy RDF* [Straccia, 2009] allows for annotating edges with a degree of truth such as (Santiago)—$\overset{climate}{0.8}$→(Semi-Arid), indicating that it is more-or-less true—with a degree of 0.8—that Santiago has a semi-arid climate.

Other forms of annotation are domain-independent; for example, *Annotated RDF* [Dividino et al., 2009, Udrea et al., 2010, Zimmermann et al., 2012] allows for representing context modeled as *semi-rings*: algebraic structures consisting of domain values (e.g., temporal intervals, fuzzy values, etc.) and two operators to combine domain values: *meet* and *join*.[3] We provide an example in Figure 3.10, where G is annotated with values from a temporal domain using sets of integers (1–365) to represent days of the year. For brevity we use intervals, where, e.g., $\{[150, 152]\}$ denotes the set $\{150, 151, 152\}$. Query Q then asks for flights from Santiago to cities

---

[3]The *join* operator for annotations is different from the join operator for relational algebra.

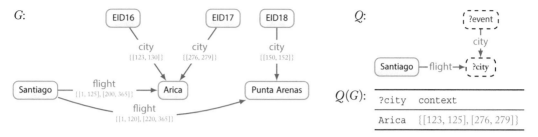

Figure 3.10: Example query on a temporally annotated graph.

with events; this query will check and return an annotation reflecting the temporal validity of each answer. To derive these answers, we require a conjunction of annotations on compatible flight and city edges, using the *meet operator* to compute the annotation for which both edges hold. The natural way to define meet here is as the intersection of sets of days, where, for example, applying meet on the event annotation $\{[150, 152]\}$ and the flight annotation $\{[1, 120], [220, 365]\}$ for (Punta Arenas) leads to the empty time interval $\{\}$, which may thus lead to the city being filtered from the results (depending on the query evaluation semantics). However, for (Arica), we find two different non-empty intersections: $\{[123, 125]\}$ for (EID16) and $\{[276, 279]\}$ for (EID17). Given that we are interested in just the city (a projected variable), we can combine the two annotations for (Arica) using the *join operator*, returning the annotation in which either result holds true. The natural way to define join here is as set union, giving $\{[123, 125], [276, 279]\}$.

We define an annotation domain per Zimmermann et al. [2012].

Definition 3.13 Annotation domain.   Let A be a set of *annotation values*. An *annotation domain* is an idempotent, commutative semi-ring $D = \langle A, \oplus, \otimes, \bot, \top \rangle$.

This definition can then instantiate specific domains of context. Letting D be a semiring imposes that, for any values a, a_1, a_2, a_3 in A, the following hold:

- $(a_1 \oplus a_2) \oplus a_3 = a_1 \oplus (a_2 \oplus a_3)$

- $(\bot \oplus a) = (a \oplus \bot) = a$

- $(a_1 \oplus a_2) = (a_2 \oplus a_1)$

- $(a_1 \oplus a_2) = (a_2 \oplus a_1)$

- $(a_1 \otimes a_2) \otimes a_3 = a_1 \otimes (a_2 \otimes a_3)$

- $(\top \otimes a) = (a \otimes \top) = a$

- $a_1 \otimes (a_2 \oplus a_3) = (a_1 \otimes a_2) \oplus (a_1 \otimes a_3)$

- $(a_1 \oplus a_2) \otimes a_3 = (a_1 \otimes a_3) \oplus (a_2 \otimes a_3)$

- $(\bot \otimes a) = (a \otimes \bot) = \bot$

The requirement that it be idempotent further imposes the following:

- $(a \oplus a) = a$

Finally, the requirement that it be commutative imposes the following:

- $(a_1 \otimes a_2) = (a_2 \otimes a_1)$

Idempotence induces a partial order: $a_1 \leq a_2$ if and only if $a_1 \oplus a_2 = a_2$. Imposing these conditions on the annotation domain allow for reasoning and querying to be conducted over the annotation domain in a well-defined manner. Annotated graphs can then be defined in the natural way.

Definition 3.14   Annotated directed edge-labeled graph.   Letting $D = \langle A, \oplus, \otimes, \bot, \top \rangle$ denote an idempotent, commutative semi-ring, we define an *annotated directed edge-labeled graph* (or *annotated directed edge-labeled graph*) as $G = (V, E_A, L)$ where $V \subseteq \mathbf{Con}$ is a set of nodes, $L \subseteq \mathbf{Con}$ is a set of edge labels, and $E_A \subseteq V \times L \times V \times A$ is a set of edges annotated with values from A.

Example 3.15   Figure 3.10 exemplifies query answering on a graph annotated with days of the year. Formally this domain can be defined as follows: $A = 2^{\mathbb{N}_{[1,365]}}$, $\oplus = \cup$, $\otimes = \cap$, $\top = \mathbb{N}_{[1,365]}$, $\bot = \emptyset$, where one may verify that $D = \langle 2^{\mathbb{N}_{[1,365]}}, \cup, \cap, \mathbb{N}_{[1,365]}, \emptyset \rangle$ is indeed an idempotent, commutative semi-ring.

3.3.5   OTHER CONTEXTUAL FRAMEWORKS

Other frameworks have been proposed for modeling and reasoning about context in graphs. A notable example is that of *contextual knowledge repositories* [Homola and Serafini, 2012], which allow for assigning individual (sub-)graphs to their own context. Unlike in the case of named graphs, context is explicitly modeled along one or more dimensions, where each (sub-)graph takes a value for each dimension. Each dimension is associated with a partial order over its values—e.g., 2020-03-22 $\preceq$ 2020-03 $\preceq$ 2020—enabling the selection and combination of sub-graphs that are valid within contexts at different granularities. Schuetz et al. [2020] similarly propose a form of contextual OnLine Analytic Processing (OLAP), based on a data cube formed by dimensions where each cell contains a knowledge graph. Operations such as "*slice-and-dice*" (selecting knowledge according to given dimensions), as well as "*roll-up*" (aggregating knowledge at a higher level) are supported. We refer the reader to the respective papers for more details [Homola and Serafini, 2012, Schuetz et al., 2020].

.

C H A P T E R   4

Deductive Knowledge

As humans, we can *deduce* more from the data graph of Figure 2.1 than what the edges explicitly indicate. We may deduce, for example, that the Ñam festival (EID15) will be located in Santiago, even though the graph does not contain an edge EID15 —location→ Santiago. We may further deduce that the cities connected by flights must have some airport nearby, even though the graph does not contain nodes referring to these airports. In these cases, given the data as premises, and some general rules about the world that we may know *a priori*, we can use a deductive process to derive new data, allowing us to know more than what is explicitly given by the data. These types of general premises and rules, when shared by many people, form part of "*commonsense knowledge*" [McCarthy, 1990]; conversely, when rather shared by a few experts in an area, they form part of "*domain knowledge*," where, for example, an expert in biology may know that *hemocyanin* is a protein containing copper that carries oxygen in the blood of some species of *Mollusca* and *Arthropoda*.

Machines, in contrast, do not have *a priori* access to such deductive faculties; rather they need to be given formal instructions, in terms of premises and *entailment regimes*, facilitating similar deductions to what a human can make. In this way, we will be making more of the meaning (i.e., *semantics*) of the graph explicit in a machine-readable format. These entailment regimes formalize the conclusions that logically follow as a consequence of a given set of premises. Once instructed in this manner, machines can (often) apply deductions with a precision, efficiency, and scale beyond human performance. These deductions may serve a range of applications, such as improving query answering, (deductive) classification, finding inconsistencies, etc. As a concrete example involving query answering, assume we are interested in knowing *the festivals located in Santiago*; we may straightforwardly express such a query as per the graph pattern shown in Figure 4.1. This query returns no results for the graph in Figure 2.1: there is no node named Festival, and nothing has (directly) the location Santiago. However, an answer (Ñam) could be automatically entailed were we to state that x being a Food Festival *entails* that x is a Festival, or that x having venue y in city z *entails* that x has location z. How, then, should such entailments be captured? In Section 3.1.1 we already discussed how the former entailment can be captured with sub-class relations in a semantic schema; the second entailment, however, requires a more expressive entailment regime than seen thus far.

In this chapter, we discuss ways in which more complex entailments can be expressed and automated. Though we could leverage a number of logical frameworks for these purposes—such as First-Order Logic, Datalog, Prolog, Answer Set Programming, etc.—we focus on *ontologies*,

$Q:$?name ⟵ name ⟶ ?festival —type→ Festival / —location→ Santiago

Figure 4.1: Graph pattern querying for names of festivals in Santiago.

which constitute a formal representation of knowledge that, importantly for us, can be represented as a graph. We then discuss how these ontologies can be formally defined, how they relate to existing logical frameworks, and how reasoning can be conducted with respect to such ontologies.

4.1   ONTOLOGIES

To enable entailment, we must be precise about what the terms we use mean. Returning to Figure 2.1, for example, and examining the node (EID16) more closely, we may begin to question how it is modeled, particularly in comparison with (EID15). Both nodes—according to the class hierarchy of Figure 3.1—are considered to be events. But what if, for example, we wish to define two pairs of start and end dates for (EID16) corresponding to the different venues? Should we rather consider what takes place in each venue as a different event? What then if an event has various start and end dates in a single venue: would these also be considered as one (recurring) event, or many events? These questions are facets of a more general question: *what precisely do we mean by an "event"*? Does it happen in one contiguous time interval or can it happen many times? Does it happen in one place or can it happen in multiple? There are no "correct" answers to such questions—we may understand the term "event" in a variety of ways, and thus the answers are a matter of *convention*.

In the context of computing, an *ontology*[1] is then a concrete, formal representation of what terms mean within the scope in which they are used (e.g., a given domain). For example, one event ontology may formally define that if an entity is an "event," then it has precisely one venue and precisely one time instant in which it begins. Conversely, a different event ontology may define that an "event" can have multiple venues and multiple start times, etc. Each such ontology formally captures a particular perspective—a particular *convention*. Under the first ontology, for example, we could not call the Olympics an "event," while under the second ontology we could. Likewise ontologies can guide how graph data are modeled. Under the first ontology we may split (EID16) into two events. Under the second, we may elect to keep (EID16) as one event with two venues. Ultimately, given that ontologies are formal representations, they can be used to automate entailment.

Like all conventions, the usefulness of an ontology depends on the level of agreement on what that ontology defines, how detailed it is, and how broadly and consistently it is adopted.

[1]The term stems from the philosophical study of *ontology*, concerning the kinds of entities that exist, the nature of their existence, what kinds of properties they have, and how they may be identified and categorized.

Adoption of an ontology by the parties involved in one knowledge graph may lead to a consistent use of terms and consistent modeling in that knowledge graph. Agreement over multiple knowledge graphs will, in turn, enhance the interoperability of those knowledge graphs.

Among the most popular ontology languages used in practice are the *Web Ontology Language* (*OWL*) [Hitzler et al., 2012],[2] recommended by the W3C and compatible with RDF graphs; and the *Open Biomedical Ontologies Format* (*OBOF*) [Mungall et al., 2012], used mostly in the biomedical domain. Since OWL is the more widely adopted, we focus on its features, though many similar features are found in both [Mungall et al., 2012]. Before introducing such features, however, we must discuss how graphs are to be *interpreted*.

4.1.1   INTERPRETATIONS AND MODELS

We as humans may *interpret* the node (Santiago) in the data graph of Figure 2.1 as referring to the real-world city that is the capital of Chile. We may further *interpret* an edge (Arica)—flight→(Santiago) as stating that there are flights from the city of Arica to this city. We thus interpret the data graph as another graph—what we here call the *domain graph*—composed of real-world entities connected by real-world relations. The process of interpretation, here, involves *mapping* the nodes and edges in the data graph to nodes and edges of the domain graph.

Along these lines, we can abstractly define an *interpretation* of a data graph as being composed of two elements: a domain graph, and a mapping from the *terms* (nodes and edge-labels) of the data graph to those of the domain graph. The domain graph follows the same model as the data graph; for example, if the data graph is a directed edge-labeled graph, then so too will be the domain graph. For simplicity, we will speak of directed edge-labeled graphs and refer to the nodes of the domain graph as *entities*, and to its edges as *relations*. Given a data graph and an interpretation, while we denote nodes in the data graph by (Santiago), we will denote the entity it refers to in the domain graph by ⦂Santiago⦂ (per the mapping of the given interpretation). Likewise, while we denote an edge by (Arica)—flight→(Santiago), we will denote the relation by ⦂Arica⦂⸺flight⟹⦂Santiago⦂ (again, per the mapping of the given interpretation). In this abstract notion of an interpretation, we do not require that ⦂Santiago⦂ or ⦂Arica⦂ be the real-world cities, nor even that the domain graph contain real-world entities and relations: an interpretation can have any domain graph and mapping.

Why is such an abstract notion of interpretation useful? The distinction between nodes/edges and entities/relations becomes important when we define the meaning of ontology features and entailment. To illustrate this distinction, if we ask whether there is an edge labeled flight between (Arica) and (Viña del Mar) for the data graph in Figure 2.1, the answer is *no*. However, if we ask if the entities ⦂Arica⦂ and ⦂Viña del Mar⦂ are connected by the relation flight, then the answer depends on what assumptions we make when interpreting the graph. Under the Closed World Assumption (CWA), if we do not have additional knowledge, then the answer is a definite *no*—since what is not known is assumed to be false. Conversely, under the Open World

---

[2]We could include RDF Schema (RDFS) in this list, but it is largely subsumed by OWL, which extends its core.

Assumption (OWA), we cannot be certain that this relation does not exist as this could be part of some knowledge not (yet) described by the graph. Likewise under the Unique Name Assumption (UNA), the data graph describes *at least two* flights to `Santiago` (since `Viña del Mar` and `Arica` are assumed to be different entities and, therefore, `Arica`—flight→`Santiago` and `Viña del Mar`—flight→`Santiago` must be different edges). Conversely, under No Unique Name Assumption (NUNA), we can only say that there is *at least one* such flight since `Viña del Mar` and `Arica` may be the same entity with two "names."

These assumptions (or lack thereof) define which interpretations are valid, and which interpretations *satisfy* which data graphs. We call an interpretation that satisfies a data graph a *model* of that data graph. The UNA forbids interpretations that map two data terms to the same domain term. The NUNA allows such interpretations. Under the CWA, an interpretation that contains an edge `x`-p►`y` in its domain graph can only satisfy a data graph from which we can entail `x`-p►`y`. Under the OWA, an interpretation containing the edge `x`-p►`y` can satisfy a data graph not entailing `x`-p►`y` so long it does not explicitly contradict that edge. OWL adopts the NUNA and OWA, which is the most general case: multiple nodes/edge-labels in the graph may refer to the same entity/relation-type (per the NUNA), and anything not entailed by the data graph is *not* assumed to be false as a consequence (per the OWA).

A graph interpretation—or simply interpretation—captures the assumptions under which the semantics of a graph can be defined. We define interpretations for directed edge-labeled graphs, though the notion extends naturally to other graph models (assuming the data and domain graphs follow the same model).

Definition 4.1 Graph interpretation. A *(graph) interpretation* I is defined as a pair $I = (\Gamma, \cdot^I)$ where $\Gamma = (V_\Gamma, E_\Gamma, L_\Gamma)$ is a (directed edge-labeled) graph called the *domain graph* and $\cdot^I : \mathbf{Con} \to V_\Gamma \cup L_\Gamma$ is a partial mapping from constants to terms in the domain graph.

We denote the domain of the mapping $\cdot^I$ by $\mathrm{dom}(\cdot^I)$. For interpretations under the UNA, the mapping $\cdot^I$ is required to be injective, while with no UNA (NUNA), no such requirement is necessary.

Interpretations that *satisfy* a graph are then said to be *models* of that graph.

Definition 4.2 Graph model. Let $G = (V, E, L)$ be a directed edge-labeled graph. An interpretation $I = (\Gamma, \cdot^I)$ *satisfies* G if and only if the following hold:

- $V \cup L \subseteq \mathrm{dom}(\cdot^I)$;

- for all $v \in V$, it holds that $v^I \in V_\Gamma$;

- for all $l \in L$, it holds that $l^I \in L_\Gamma$; and

- for all $(u, l, v) \in E$, it holds that $(u^I, l^I, v^I) \in E_\Gamma$.

If I *satisfies* G we call I a *(graph) model* of G.

4.1.2 ONTOLOGY FEATURES

Beyond our base assumptions, we can associate certain patterns in the data graph with *semantic conditions* that define which interpretations satisfy it; for example, we can add a semantic condition to enforce that if our data graph contains the edge (p)–subp. of→(q), then any edge x–p→y in the domain graph of the interpretation must also have a corresponding edge x–q→y to satisfy the data graph. These semantic conditions then form the features of an ontology language. In what follows, to aid readability, we will introduce the features of OWL using an abstract graphical notation with abbreviated terms. For details of concrete syntaxes, we rather refer to the OWL and OBOF standards [Hitzler et al., 2012, Mungall et al., 2012]. Likewise, we present semantic conditions over interpretations for each feature in the same graphical format;[3] further details of these conditions will be described later in Section 4.1.3.

Individuals

In Table 4.1, we list the main features supported by OWL for describing *individuals* (e.g., Santiago, EID16), sometimes distinguished from classes and properties. First, we can *assert* (binary) relations between individuals using edges such as (Santa Lucía)–city→(Santiago). In the condition column, when we write x–y→z, for example, we refer to the condition that the relation is given in the domain graph of the interpretation; if so, the interpretation satisfies the axiom. OWL further allows for defining relations to explicitly state that two terms refer to the *same* entity, where, e.g., (Región V)–same as→(Región de Valparaíso) states that both refer to the same region (per Section 3.2); or that two terms refer to *different* entities, where, e.g., (Valparaíso)–diff. from→(Región de Valparaíso) distinguishes the city from the region of the same name. We may also state that a relation does not hold using *negation*, which can be serialized as a graph using a form of reification (see Figure 3.8a).

Properties

In Section 3.1.1, we already discussed how *sub-properties*, *domains*, and *ranges* may be defined for properties. OWL allows such definitions, and further includes other features, as listed in Table 4.2. We may define a pair of properties to be *equivalent*, *inverses*, or *disjoint*. We can further define a particular property to denote a *transitive*, *symmetric*, *asymmetric*, *reflexive*, or *irreflexive* relation. We can also define the multiplicity of the relation denoted by properties, based on being *functional* (many-to-one) or *inverse-functional* (one-to-many). We may further define a *key* for a class, denoting the set of properties whose values uniquely identify the entities

---

[3]We abbreviate "if and only if" as "iff" whereby "ϕ iff ψ" can be read as "if ϕ then ψ" and "if ψ then ϕ."

Table 4.1: Ontology features for individuals

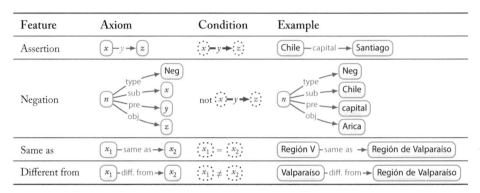

of that class. Without adopting a Unique Name Assumption (UNA), from these latter three features we may conclude that two or more terms refer to the same entity. Finally, we can relate a property to a *chain* (a path expression only allowing concatenation of properties) such that pairs of entities related by the chain are also related by the given property. Note that for the latter two features in Table 4.2 we require representing a list, denoted with a vertical notation; while such a list may be serialized as a graph in a number of concrete ways, OWL uses RDF lists (see Figure 3.7).

Classes

In Section 3.1.1, we discussed how class hierarchies can be modeled using a *sub-class* relation. OWL supports sub-classes, and many additional features, for defining and making claims about classes; these additional features are summarized in Table 4.3. Given a pair of classes, OWL allows for defining that they are *equivalent*, or *disjoint*. Thereafter, OWL provides a variety of features for defining novel classes by applying set operators on other classes, or based on conditions that the properties of its instances satisfy. First, using set operators, one can define a novel class as the *complement* of another class, the *union* or *intersection* of a list (of arbitrary length) of other classes, or as an *enumeration* of all of its instances. Second, by placing restrictions on a particular property p, one can define classes whose instances are all of the entities that have: *some value* from a given class on p; *all values* from a given class on p;[4] have a specific individual as a value on p (*has value*); have themselves as a reflexive value on p (*has self*); have at least, at most or exactly some number of values on p (*cardinality*); and have at least, at most or exactly some number of values on p from a given class (*qualified cardinality*). For the latter two cases, in

---

[4]While something like (flight)◄─prop─(DomesticAirport)─all─►(NationalFlight) might appear to be a more natural example for ALL VALUES, this would be problematic as the corresponding *for all* condition is satisfied when no such node exists, so we would infer anything known not to have any flights to be a domestic airport. (We could, however, define the intersection of such a definition and airport as being a domestic airport.)

Table 4.2: Ontology features for property axioms

Feature	Axiom	Condition (for all x_*, y_*, z_*)	Example
Sub-property	p –subp. of→ q	x–p→y implies x–q→y	venue –subp. of→ location
Domain	p –domain→ c	x–p→y implies x–type→c	venue –domain→ Event
Range	p –range→ c	x–p→y implies y–type→c	venue –range→ Venue
Equivalence	p –equiv. p.→ q	x–p→y iff x–q→y	start –equiv. p.→ begins
Inverse	p –inv. of→ q	x–p→y iff y–q→x	venue –inv. of→ hosts
Disjoint	p –disj. p.→ q	not x ⇄^q_p y	venue –disj. p.→ hosts
Transitive	p –type→ Transitive	x–p→y–p→z implies x–p→z	part of –type→ Transitive
Symmetric	p –type→ Symmetric	x–p→y iff y–p→x	nearby –type→ Symmetric
Asymmetric	p –type→ Asymmetric	not x ⇄^p_p y	capital –type→ Asymmetric
Reflexive	p –type→ Reflexive	x ↺ p	part of –type→ Reflexive
Irreflexive	p –type→ Irreflexive	not x ↺ p	flight –type→ Irreflexive
Functional	p –type→ Functional	y_1←p–x–p→y_2 implies y_1 = y_2	population –type→ Functional
Inv. Functional	p –type→ Inv. Functional	x_1–p→y←p–x_2 implies x_1 = x_2	capital –type→ Inv. Functional
Key	c –key→ $p_1 \vdots p_n$	x_1 ... y_1 ... x_2 implies x_1 = x_2	City –key→ lat long
Chain	p –chain→ $q_1 \vdots q_n$	x–q_1→y_1→...→y_{n-1}–q_n→z implies x–p→z	location –chain→ location part of

Table 4.3, we use the notation "#{ⓐ | ϕ}" to count distinct entities satisfying ϕ in the interpretation. These features can then be combined to create more complex classes, where combining the examples for INTERSECTION and HAS SELF in Table 4.3 gives the definition: *self-driving taxis are taxis having themselves as a driver.*

Other Features

OWL supports other language features not previously discussed, including: *annotation properties*, which provide metadata about ontologies, such as versioning info; *datatype vs. object properties*, which distinguish properties that take datatype values from those that do not; and *datatype facets*,

Table 4.3: Ontology features for class axioms and definitions

Feature	Axiom	Condition (for all x_*, y_*, z_*)	Example
Sub-class	c -subc. of- d	x -type- c implies x -type- d	City -subc. of- Place
Equivalence	c -equiv. c.- d	x -type- c iff x -type- d	Human -equiv. c.- Person
Disjoint	c -disj. c.- d	not c -type- x -type- d	City -disj. c.- Region
Complement	c -comp.- d	x -type- c iff not x -type- d	Dead -comp.- Alive
Union	c -union- $d_1 \vdots d_n$	x -type- c iff x -type- d_1 or x -type- $\ldots$ or x -type- d_n	Flight -union- DomesticFlight InternationalFlight
Intersection	c -inter.- $d_1 \vdots d_n$	x -type- c iff x -type- type- d_1 $\ldots$ type- d_n	SelfDrivingTaxi -inter.- Taxi SelfDriving
Enumeration	c -one of- $x_1 \vdots x_n$	x -type- c iff $x \in \{ x_1, \ldots, x_n \}$	EUState -one of- Austria $\vdots$ Sweden
Some values	c -prop- p -some- d	x -type- c iff there exists a such that x -p- a -type- d	EUCitizen -prop- nationality -some- EUState
All values	c -prop- p -all- d	x -type- c iff for all a with x -p- a it holds that a -type- d	Weightless -prop- has part -all- Weightless
Has value	c -prop- p -value- y	x -type- c iff x -p- y	ChileanCitizen -prop- nationality -value- Chile
Has self	c -prop- p -self- true	x -type- c iff x -p- x	SelfDriving -prop- driver -self- true
Cardinality $\star \in \{=, \leq, \geq\}$	c -prop- p -$\star$- n	x -type- c iff $\# \{ a \mid x$ -p- $a \} \star n$	Polyglot -prop- fluent -$\geq$- 2
Qualified Cardinality $\star \in \{=, \leq, \geq\}$	c -prop- p -class- d -$\star$- n	x -type- c iff $\# \{ a \mid x$ -p- a -type- $d \} \star n$	BinaryStarSystem -prop- body -class- Star -=- 2

which allow for defining new datatypes by applying restrictions to existing datatypes, such as to define that places in Chile must have a *float between -66.0 and -110.0* as their value for the (datatype) property latitude. For more details we refer to the OWL 2 standard [Hitzler et al., 2012]. We will further discuss methodologies for the creation of ontologies in Section 6.5.

Models Under Semantic Conditions

Each axiom described by the previous tables, when added to a graph, enforces some condition(s) on the models of the graph. If we were to consider only the base condition of the ASSERTION feature in Table 4.1, for example, then the models of a graph would be any interpretation such that for every edge (x)–y→(z) in the graph, there exists a relation (x)–y→(z) in the model. Given that there may be other relations in the model (under the OWA), the number of models of any such graph is infinite. Furthermore, given that we can map multiple nodes in the graph to one entity in the model (under the NUNA), any interpretation with (for example) the relation (a)–a→(a) is a model of any graph so long as for every edge (x)–y→(z) in the graph, it holds that (x) = (y) = (z) = (a) in the interpretation (in other words, the interpretation maps everything to (a)). As we add axioms with their associated conditions to the graph, we restrict models for the graph; for example, considering a graph with two edges—(x)–y→(z) and (y)–type→(Irreflexive)—the interpretation with (a)–a→(a), (x) = (y) = ... = (a) is no longer a model as it breaks the condition for the irreflexive axiom. In this way, we can define a precise model-theoretic semantics for graphs based on how the aforementioned ontological features used in the graph restrict the models of that graph.

We define models under semantics conditions.

Definition 4.3 Semantic condition.   Let 2^G denote the set of all (directed edge-labeled) graphs. A *semantic condition* is a mapping $\phi : 2^G \rightarrow \{\text{true}, \text{false}\}$. An interpretation $I = (\Gamma, \cdot^I)$ is a model of G under ϕ if and only if I is a model of G and $\phi(\Gamma)$. Given a set of semantic conditions Φ, we say that I is a model of G if and only if I is a model of G and for all $\phi \in \Phi$, $\phi(\Gamma)$ is true.

We do not restrict the language used to define semantic conditions, but, for example, we can define the HAS VALUE semantic condition of Table 4.3 in FOL as:

$$\forall c, p, y\Big(\big(\Gamma(c, \text{prop}^I, p) \wedge \Gamma(c, \text{value}^I, y)\big) \leftrightarrow \forall x\big(\Gamma(x, \text{type}^I, c) \leftrightarrow \Gamma(x, p, y)\big)\Big).$$

Here, we overload Γ as a ternary predicate to capture the edges of Γ. The other semantic conditions enumerated in Tables 4.1–4.3 can be defined in a similar way [Schneider and Sutcliffe, 2011].[a] This FOL formula defines an if-and-only-if version of the semantic condition for HAS VALUE (described in Section 4.1.4).

[a]Although these tables consider axioms originating in the data graph, it suffices to check their image in the domain graph since I only satisfies G if the edges of G defining the axioms are reflected in the domain graph of I per Definition 4.2. This then simplifies the definitions considerably.

4.1.3 ENTAILMENT

The conditions listed in the previous tables give rise to *entailments*, where, for example, in reference to the SYMMETRIC feature of Table 4.2, the definition (nearby)—type→(Symmetric) and edge (Santiago)—nearby→(Santiago Airport) entail the edge (Santiago Airport)—nearby→(Santiago) according to the condition given for that feature. We now describe how these conditions lead to entailments.

We say that one graph *entails* another if and only if any model of the former graph is also a model of the latter graph. Intuitively this means that the latter graph says nothing new over the former graph and thus holds as a logical consequence of the former graph. For example, consider the graph (Santiago)—type→(City)—subc. of→(Place) and the graph (Santiago)—type→(Place). All models of the latter must have that (Santiago)—type→(Place), but so must all models of the former, which must have (Santiago)—type→(City)—subc. of→(Place) and further must satisfy the condition for SUB-CLASS, which requires that (Santiago)—type→(Place) also hold. Hence, we conclude that any model of the former graph must be a model of the latter graph, or, in other words, the former graph entails the latter graph.

We now formally define entailment under semantic conditions.

Definition 4.4 Graph entailment. Letting G_1 and G_2 denote two (directed edge-labeled) graphs, and Φ a set of semantic conditions, we say that G_1 *entails* G_2 *under* Φ—denoted $G_1 \models_\Phi G_2$—if and only if any model of G_1 under Φ is also a model of G_2 under Φ.

An example of entailment is discussed in Section 4.1.3.[a]

[a]Here we have defined entailment under OWA. To define entailment under CWA, let $G \models_\Phi (s, p, o)$ denote that G entails the edge (s, p, o) under Φ (a slight abuse of notation). Under CWA, we make the additional assumption that if $G \not\models_\Phi e$, where e is an edge (strictly speaking, a *positive* edge), then $G \models_\Phi \neg e$; in other words, under CWA we assume that any (positive) edges that G does not entail under Φ can be assumed false according to G and Φ. However, note that in FOL, the CWA only applies to positive *facts*, whereas edges in a graph can be used to represent other FOL formulae. If one wished to maintain FOL-compatibility under CWA, additional restrictions on the types of edge e may be needed.

4.1.4 IF-THEN vs. IF-AND-ONLY-IF SEMANTICS

Consider the graph (nearby)—type→(Symmetric) and the graph (nearby)—inv. of→(nearby). Both of these graphs result in the same semantic conditions being applied in the domain graph, but does one entail the other? The answer depends on the semantics applied. Considering the axioms and conditions of Table 4.1, we can consider two semantics. Under *if*–*then* semantics—*if* **Axiom** matches the data graph *then* **Condition** holds in domain graph—the graphs do not entail each other: though both graphs give rise to the same condition, this condition is not translated back into the axioms that describe it.[5] Conversely, under *if-and-only-if* semantics—**Axiom** matches data graph *if-and-only-if* **Condition** holds in domain graph—the graphs entail each other: both graphs give rise to the same condition, which is translated back into all possible axioms that describe it. Hence, if-and-only-if semantics allows for entailing more axioms in the ontology language than if—then semantics. OWL generally applies an if-and-only-if semantics in order to enable richer entailments [Hitzler et al., 2012].

4.2   REASONING

Unfortunately, given two graphs, deciding if the first entails the second—per the notion of entailment we have defined and for all of the ontological features listed in Tables 4.1–4.3—is *undecidable*: no (finite) algorithm for such entailment can exist that halts on all inputs with the correct `true`/`false` answer [Hitzler et al., 2010]. However, we can provide practical reasoning algorithms for ontologies that (1) halt on any pair of input ontologies but may miss entailments, returning `false` instead of `true` in some cases, (2) always halt with the correct answer but only accept input ontologies with restricted features, or (3) only return correct answers for any pair of input ontologies but may never halt on certain inputs. Though option (3) has been explored using, e.g., theorem provers for First-Order-Logic (FOL) [Schneider and Sutcliffe, 2011], options (1) and (2) are more commonly pursued using rules and/or Description Logics. Option (1) generally allows for more efficient and scalable reasoning algorithms and is useful where data are incomplete and having some entailments is valuable. Option (2) may be a better choice in domains—such as medical ontologies—where missing entailments may have undesirable outcomes.

4.2.1   RULES

A straightforward way to provide automated access to the knowledge that can be deduced through (ontological or other forms of) entailments is through *inference rules* (or simply *rules*) encoding IF–THEN-style consequences. A rule is composed of a *body* (IF) and a *head* (THEN). Both the body and head are given as graph patterns. A rule indicates that if we can replace the variables of the body with terms from the data graph and form a sub-graph of a given data graph, then using the same replacement of variables in the head will yield a valid entailment. The head must typically use a subset of the variables appearing in the body to ensure that the conclusion leaves no variables unreplaced. Rules of this form correspond to (positive) Datalog [Ceri et al., 1989] in Databases, Horn clauses [Lloyd, 2012] in Logic Programming, etc.

Rules can capture entailments under ontological conditions. In Table 4.4, we list some example rules for sub-class, sub-property, domain, and range features [Mu noz et al., 2009];

---

[5]Here, nearby ⟵type⟶ Symmetric is a model of the first graph but not the second, while nearby ⟵inv. of⟶ nearby is a model of the second graph but not the first. Hence, neither graph entails the other.

Table 4.4: Example rules for sub-class, sub-property, domain, and range features

Feature	Body	⇒	Head
Sub-class (I)	?x —type→ ?c —subc. of→ ?d	⇒	?x —type→ ?d
Sub-class (II)	?c —subc. of→ ?d —subc. of→ ?e	⇒	?c —subc. of→ ?e
Sub-property (I)	?x —?p→ ?y , ?q (subp. of)	⇒	?x —?q→ ?y
Sub-property (II)	?p —subp. of→ ?q —subp. of→ ?r	⇒	?p —subp. of→ ?r
Domain	?x —?p→ ?y , ?c (domain)	⇒	?x —type→ ?c
Range	?x —?p→ ?y , ?c (range)	⇒	?y —type→ ?c

these rules may be considered incomplete, not capturing, for example, that every class is a sub-class of itself, that every property is a sub-property of itself, etc. A more comprehensive set of rules for the OWL features of Tables 4.1–4.3 have been defined as OWL 2 RL/RDF [Motik et al., 2012]; these rules are likewise incomplete as such rules cannot fully capture negation (e.g., COMPLEMENT), existentials (e.g., SOME VALUES), universals (e.g., ALL VALUES), or counting (e.g., CARDINALITY and QUALIFIED CARDINALITY). Other rule languages have, however, been proposed to support additional such features, including existentials (see, e.g., Datalog$^\pm$ [Bellomarini et al., 2018]), disjunction (see, e.g., Disjunctive Datalog [Rudolph et al., 2008]), etc.

Rules can be leveraged for reasoning in a number of ways. *Materialization* refers to the idea of applying rules recursively to a graph, adding the conclusions generated back to the graph until a fixpoint is reached and nothing more can be added. The materialized graph can then be treated as any other graph. Although the efficiency and scalability of materialization can be enhanced through optimizations like Rete networks [Forgy, 1982], or using distributed frameworks like MapReduce [Urbani et al., 2012], depending on the rules and the data, the materialized graph may become unfeasibly large to manage. Another strategy is to use rules for *query rewriting*, which given a query, will automatically extend the query in order to find solutions entailed by a set of rules; for example, taking the schema graph in Figure 3.2 and the rules in Table 4.4, the (sub-)pattern ?x —type→ Event in a given input query would be rewritten to the following disjunctive pattern evaluated on the original graph:

$$?x \text{ —type→ } \boxed{\text{Event}} \; \cup \; ?x \text{ —type→ } \boxed{\text{Festival}} \; \cup \; ?x \text{ —type→ } \boxed{\text{Periodic Market}} \; \cup \; ?x \text{ —venue→ } ?y$$

Figure 4.2 provides a more complete example of an ontology that is used to rewrite the query of Figure 4.1; if evaluated over the graph of Figure 2.1, Nam will be returned as a solution. However, not all of the aforementioned features of OWL can be supported in this manner. The OWL 2

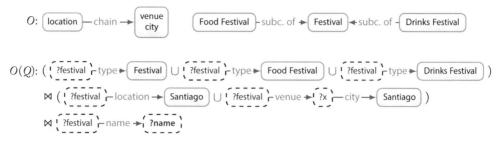

Figure 4.2: Query rewriting example for the query Q of Figure 4.1.

QL profile [Motik et al., 2012] is a subset of OWL designed specifically for query rewriting of this form [Artale et al., 2009].

While rules can be used to (partially) capture ontological entailments, they can also be defined independently of an ontology language, capturing entailments for a given domain. In fact, some rules—such as the following—cannot be captured by the ontology features previously seen, as they do not support ways to infer relations from cyclical graph patterns (for computability reasons):

$$\{?x\}\!\!-\!\text{flight}\!\rightarrow\!\{?y\}\!\!-\!\text{country}\!\rightarrow\!\{?z\} \;\Rightarrow\; \{?x\}\!\!-\!\text{domestic flight}\!\rightarrow\!\{?y\}$$

Various languages allow for expressing rules over graphs—independently or alongside of an ontology language—including: Notation3 (N3) [Berners-Lee and Connolly, 2011], Rule Interchange Format (RIF) [Kifer and Boley, 2013], Semantic Web Rule Language (SWRL) [Horrocks et al., 2004], and SPARQL Inferencing Notation (SPIN) [Knublauch et al., 2011], among others.

Given a graph pattern Q—be it a directed edge-labeled graph pattern per Definition 2.9 or a property graph pattern per Definition 2.11—recall that $\mathbf{Var}(Q)$ denotes the variables appearing in Q. We now define rules for graphs.

Definition 4.5 Rule.   A *rule* is a pair $R = (B, H)$ such that B and H are graph patterns and $\mathbf{Var}(H) \subseteq B$. The graph pattern B is called the *body* of the rule while H is called the *head* of the rule.

This definition of a rule applies for directed edge-labeled graphs and property graphs by considering the corresponding type of graph pattern. The head is considered to be a conjunction of edges. Given a graph G, a rule is *applied* by computing the mappings from the body to the graph and then using those mappings to substitute the variables in H. The restriction $\mathbf{Var}(H) \subseteq B$ ensures that the results of this substitution is a graph, with no variables in H left unsubstituted.

Definition 4.6 Rule application.   Given a rule $R = (B, H)$ and a graph G, we define the *application of R over G* as the graph $R(G) = \bigcup_{\mu \in B(G)} \mu(H)$.

Given a set of rules $\mathcal{R} = \{R_1, \ldots, R_n\}$ and a knowledge graph G, toward defining the set of inferences given by the rules over the graph, we denote by $\mathcal{R}(G) = \bigcup_{R \in \mathcal{R}} R(G)$ the union of the application of all rules of $\mathcal{R}$ over G, and we denote by $\mathcal{R}^+(G) = \mathcal{R}(G) \cup G$ the extension of G with respect to the application of $\mathcal{R}$. Finally, we denote by $\mathcal{R}^k(G)$ (for $k \in \mathbb{N}^+$) the recursive application of $\mathcal{R}^+(G)$, where $\mathcal{R}^1(G) = \mathcal{R}^+(G)$, and $\mathcal{R}^{i+1}(G) = \mathcal{R}^+(\mathcal{R}^i(G))$. We are now ready to define the *least model*, which captures the inferences possible for $\mathcal{R}$ over G.

Definition 4.7 Least model.   The *least model* of $\mathcal{R}$ over G is defined as $\mathcal{R}^*(G) = \bigcup_{k \in \mathbb{N}} (R^k(G))$.

At some point $R^{k'}(G) = R^{k'+1}(G)$: the rule applications reach a fixpoint and we have the least model. Once the least model $\mathcal{R}^*(G)$ is computed, the entailed data can be treated as any other data.

Rules can support graph entailments of the form $G_1 \models_\Phi G_2$. We say that a set of rules $\mathcal{R}$ is *correct* for Φ if, for any graph G, $G \models_\Phi \mathcal{R}^*(G)$. We say that $\mathcal{R}$ is *complete* for Φ if, for any graph G, there does not exist a graph $G' \not\subseteq \mathcal{R}^*(G)$ such that $G \models_\Phi G'$. Table 4.4 exemplifies a correct but incomplete set of rules for the semantic conditions of the RDFS standard [Brickley and Guha, 2014].

Alternatively, rather than supporting ontology-based graph entailments, rules can be directly specified in a rule language such as Notation3 (N3) [Berners-Lee and Connolly, 2011], Rule Interchange Format (RIF) [Kifer and Boley, 2013], Semantic Web Rule Language (SWRL) [Horrocks et al., 2004], or SPARQL Inferencing Notation (SPIN) [Knublauch et al., 2011]. Languages such as SPIN represent rules as graphs, allowing the rules of a knowledge graph to be embedded in the data graph. Taking advantage of this fact, we can then consider a form of graph entailment $G_1 \cup \gamma(\mathcal{R}) \models_\Phi G_2$, where by $\gamma(\mathcal{R})$ we denote the graph representation of rules $\mathcal{R}$. If the set of rules $\mathcal{R}$ is correct and complete for Φ, we may simply write $G_1 \cup \gamma(\mathcal{R}) \models G_2$, indicating that Φ captures the same semantics for $\gamma(\mathcal{R})$ as applying the rules in $\mathcal{R}$. Rules thus offer another form of graph entailment.

4.2.2 DESCRIPTION LOGICS

Description Logics (DLs) were initially introduced as a way to formalize the meaning of *frames* [Minsky, 1974] and *semantic networks* [Quillian, 1963]. Since semantic networks are an early version of knowledge graphs, and DLs have heavily influenced the OWL, DLs thus hold an important place in the logical formalization of knowledge graphs. DLs form a family of logics rather than a particular logic. Initially, DLs were restricted fragments of FOL that permit decidable reasoning tasks, such as entailment checking [Baader et al., 2017]. Different DLs strike different balances between expressive power and computational complexity of reasoning. DLs were later extended with features beyond FOL that are useful in the context of modeling graph data, such as transitive closure, datatypes, etc.

DLs are based on three types of elements: *individuals*, such as `Santiago`; *classes* (aka *concepts*) such as `City`; and *properties* (aka *roles*) such as `flight`. DLs then allow for making claims, known as *axioms*, about these elements. *Assertional axioms* can be either unary class relations on individuals, such as `City(Santiago)`, or binary property relations on individuals, such as `flight(Santiago,Arica)`. Such axioms form the *Assertional Box* (*A-Box*). DLs further introduce logical symbols to allow for defining *class axioms* (forming the *Terminology Box*, or *T-Box* for short), and *property axioms* (forming the *Role Box*, *R-Box*); for example, the class axiom `City ⊑ Place` states that the former class is a sub-class of the latter one, while the property axiom `flight ⊑ connectsTo` states that the former property is a sub-property of the latter one. DLs may then introduce a rich set of logical symbols, not only for defining class and property axioms, but also defining new classes based on existing terms; as an example of the latter, we can define a class `∃nearby.Airport` as the class of individuals that have some airport nearby. Noting that the symbol ⊤ is used in DLs to denote the class of all individuals, we can then add a class axiom `∃flight.⊤ ⊑ ∃nearby.Airport` to state that individuals with an outgoing flight must have some airport nearby. Noting that the symbol ⊔ can be used in DL to define that a class is the union of other classes, we can further define, for example, that `Airport ⊑ DomesticAirport ⊔ InternationalAirport`, i.e., that an airport is either a domestic airport or an international airport (or both).

The similarities between DL features and the OWL features seen previously are not coincidental: the OWL standard was heavily influenced by DLs, where, for example, the OWL 2 DL language is a fragment of OWL restricted so that entailment becomes decidable, where the restrictions are inspired by those defined for DLs. To exemplify a restriction, `DomesticAirport ⊑ = 1 destination ∘ country.⊤` defines in DL syntax that domestic airports have flights destined to precisely one country (where p ∘ q denotes a chain of properties). However, counting chains (in this case with = 1 `destination ∘ country`) is often disallowed in DLs to ensure decidability.

Expressive DLs support complex entailments involving existentials, universals, counting, etc. A common strategy for deciding such entailments is to reduce entailment to *satisfiability*, which decides if an ontology is consistent or not [Horrocks and Patel-Schneider, 2004].[6] Thereafter methods such as *tableau* can be used to check satisfiability, cautiously constructing models by completing them along similar lines to the materialization strategy previously described, but additionally branching models in the case of disjunction, introducing new elements to represent existentials, etc. If any model is successfully "completed," the process concludes that the original

---

[6]G entails G' if and only if $G \cup \text{not}(G')$ is not satisfiable, i.e., it has no model.

definitions are satisfiable (see, e.g., Motik et al. [2009]). Due to their prohibitive computational complexity [Motik et al., 2012]—where for example, disjunction may lead to an exponential number of branching possibilities—such reasoning strategies are not typically applied in the case of large-scale data, though they may be useful when modeling complex domains for knowledge graphs.

A DL knowledge base consists of an A-Box, T-Box, and R-Box.

Definition 4.8 DL knowledge base. A *DL knowledge base* K is defined as a tuple (A, T, R), where A is the *A-Box*: a set of assertional axioms; T is the *T-Box*: a set of class (aka concept/terminological) axioms; and R is the *R-Box*: a set of relation (aka property/role) axioms.

Table 4.5 provides definitions for all of the constructs typically found in Description Logics. The syntax column denotes how the construct is expressed in DL. The semantics column defines the meaning of axioms using *interpretations*, which are defined in a slightly different way to those seen previously for graphs.

Definition 4.9 DL interpretation. A *DL interpretation* I is defined as a pair $(\Delta^I, \cdot^I)$, where Δ^I is the *interpretation domain*, and $\cdot^I$ is the *interpretation function*. The interpretation domain is a set of individuals. The interpretation function accepts a definition of either an individual a, a class C, or a relation R, mapping them, respectively, to an element of the domain ($a^I \in \Delta^I$), a subset of the domain ($C^I \subseteq \Delta^I$), or a set of pairs from the domain ($R^I \subseteq \Delta^I \times \Delta^I$).

An interpretation I *satisfies* a knowledge-base K if and only if, for all of the syntactic axioms in K, the corresponding semantic conditions in Table 4.5 hold for I. In this case, we call I a *model* of K.

Example 4.10 For K = (A, T, R), let:

- A = {City(Arica), City(Santiago), flight(Arica, Santiago)};

- T = {City $\sqsubseteq$ Place, $\exists$flight.$\top$ $\sqsubseteq$ $\exists$nearby.Airport};

- R = {flight $\sqsubseteq$ connectsTo}.

For $I = (\Delta^I, \cdot^I)$, let:

- $\Delta^I = \{⚓, ◣, ✈\}$;

- Arica^I = ⚓, Santiago^I = ◣, AricaAirport^I = ✈;

- $\mathtt{City}^I = \{⚓, 🔺\}$, $\mathtt{Airport}^I = \{✈\}$;

- $\mathtt{flight}^I = \{(⚓, 🔺)\}$, $\mathtt{connectsTo}^I = \{(⚓, 🔺)\}$, $\mathtt{sells}^I = \{(✈, ☕)\}$.

The interpretation I is not a model of K since it does not have that ⚓ is nearby some Airport, nor that ⚓ and 🔺 are in the class Place. However, if we *extend* the interpretation I with the following:

- $\mathtt{Place}^I = \{⚓, 🔺\}$;

- $\mathtt{nearby}^I = \{(⚓, ✈)\}$.

Now I is a model of K. Note that although K does not imply that $\mathtt{sells}(\mathtt{Arica},\mathtt{coffee})$ while I indicates that ✈ does indeed sell ☕, I is still a model of K since K is not assumed to be a complete description, per the OWA.

Finally, the notion of a model gives rise to the notion of entailment, which tells us which knowledge bases hold as a logical consequence of which others.

Definition 4.11   Given two DL knowledge bases K_1 and K_2, we define that K_1 entails K_2, denoted $K_1 \models K_2$, if and only if any model of K_1 is a model of K_2.

Example 4.12   Let K_1 denote the knowledge base K from the Example 4.10, and define a second knowledge base $K_2 = (\{\mathtt{connectsTo}(\mathtt{Arica},\mathtt{Santiago})\}, \{\}, \{\})$ with one assertion. Though K_1 does not assert this axiom, it does entail K_2: to be a model of K_2, an interpretation must have that $(\mathtt{Arica}^I, \mathtt{Santiago}^I) \in \mathtt{connectsTo}^I$, but this must also be the case for any interpretation that satisfies K_1 since it must have that $(\mathtt{Arica}^I, \mathtt{Santiago}^I) \in \mathtt{flight}^I$ and $\mathtt{flight}^I \subseteq \mathtt{connectsTo}^I$. Hence, any model of K_1 must also be a model of K_2, and $K_1 \models K_2$ holds.

Unfortunately, the problem of deciding entailment for knowledge bases expressed in the DL composed of the unrestricted use of all of the axioms of Table 4.5 is undecidable since we could reduce instances of the Halting Problem to such entailment. Hence, DLs in practice restrict use of the features listed in Table 4.5. Different DLs apply different restrictions, implying different trade-offs for expressivity and the complexity of entailment. Most DLs are founded on one of the following base DLs (we use indentation to denote derivation):

ALC (*Attributive Language with Complement* [Schmidt-Schauß and Smolka, 1991]), supports atomic classes, the top and bottom classes, class intersection, class union, class negation, universal restrictions, and existential restrictions. Relation and class assertions are also supported.

$\mathcal{S}$ extends $\mathcal{ALC}$ with transitive closure.

These base languages can be extended as follows:

$\mathcal{H}$ adds relation inclusion.

$\mathcal{R}$ adds (limited) complex relation inclusion, relation reflexivity, relation irreflexivity, relation disjointness and the universal relation.

$\mathcal{O}$ adds (limited) nomimals.

$\mathcal{I}$ adds inverse relations.

$\mathcal{F}$ adds (limited) functional properties.

$\mathcal{N}$ adds (limited) number restrictions (covering $\mathcal{F}$ with $\top$).

$\mathcal{Q}$ adds (limited) qualified number restrictions (covering $\mathcal{N}$ with $\top$).

We use "(limited)" to indicate that such features are often only allowed under certain restrictions to ensure decidability; for example, complex relations (chains) typically cannot be combined with cardinality restrictions. DLs are then typically named per the following scheme, where $[a|b]$ denotes an alternative between a and b and $[c][d]$ denotes a concatenation cd:

$$[\mathcal{ALC}|\mathcal{S}][\mathcal{H}|\mathcal{R}][\mathcal{O}][\mathcal{I}][\mathcal{F}|\mathcal{N}|\mathcal{Q}]$$

Examples include $\mathcal{ALCO}$, $\mathcal{ALCHI}$, $\mathcal{SHIF}$, $\mathcal{SROIQ}$, etc. These languages often apply additional restrictions on class and property axioms to ensure decidability, which we do not discuss here. For further details on DLs, we refer to the recent book by Baader et al. [2017].

As mentioned in the body of the survey, DLs have been very influential in the definition of OWL, where the OWL 2 DL fragment (roughly) corresponds to the DL $\mathcal{SROIQ}$. For example, the axiom (venue)—domain→(Event) in OWL can be translated to $\exists$venue.$\top \sqsubseteq$ Event, meaning that the class of individuals with some value for venue (in any class) is a sub-class of the class Event. We leave other translations from the OWL axioms of Tables 4.1–4.3 to DL as an exercise.[a] Note, however, that axioms like (sub-taxon of)—subp. of→(subc. of)—which given a graph such as (Fred)—type→(Homo sapiens)—sub-taxon of→(Hominini) entails the edge (Fred)—type→(Hominini)— cannot be expressed in DL: "subTaxonOf $\sqsubseteq$ $\sqsubseteq$" is not syntactically valid. Hence, only a subset of graphs can be translated into well-formed DL ontologies; we refer to the OWL standard for details [Hitzler et al., 2012].

[a]Though not previously mentioned, OWL additionally defines the classes Thing and Nothing that correspond to $\top$ and $\bot$, respectively.

Table 4.5: Description Logic semantics (such that $x, y, z, a^I, a_1^I, \ldots a_n^I, b^I$ are in Δ^I)

Name	Syntax	Semantics ($\cdot^I$)
Class Definitions		
Atomic Class	A	A^I (a subset of Δ^I)
Top Class	$\top$	Δ^I
Bottom Class	$\bot$	$\emptyset$
Class Negation	$\neg C$	$\Delta^I \setminus C^I$
Class Intersection	$C \sqcap D$	$C^I \cap D^I$
Class Union	$C \sqcup D$	$C^I \cup D^I$
Nominal	$\{a_1, \ldots, a_n\}$	$\{a_1^I, \ldots, a_n^I\}$
Existential Restriction	$\exists R.C$	$\{x \mid \exists y : (x, y) \in R^I \text{ and } y \in C^I\}$
Universal Restriction	$\forall R.C$	$\{x \mid \forall y : (x, y) \in R^I \text{ implies } y \in C^I\}$
Self Restriction	$\exists R.\mathsf{Self}$	$\{x \mid (x, x) \in R^I\}$
Number Restriction	$\star\, n\, R$ (where $\star \in \{\geq, \leq, =\}$)	$\{x \mid \#\{y : (x, y) \in R^I\} \star n\}$
Qualified Number Restriction	$\star\, n\, R.C$ (where $\star \in \{\geq, \leq, =\}$)	$\{x \mid \#\{y : (x, y) \in R^I \text{ and } y \in C^I\} \star n\}$
Class Axioms (T-Box)		
Class Inclusion	$C \sqsubseteq D$	$C^I \subseteq D^I$
Relation Definitions		
Relation	R	R^I (a subset of $\Delta^I \times \Delta^I$)
Inverse Relation	R^-	$\{(y, x) \mid (x, y) \in R^I\}$
Universal Relation	U	$\Delta^I \times \Delta^I$
Relation Axioms (R-Box)		
Relation Inclusion	$R \sqsubseteq S$	$R^I \subseteq S^I$
Complex Relation Inclusion	$R_1 \circ \ldots \circ R_n \sqsubseteq S$	$R_1^I \circ \ldots \circ R_n^I \subseteq S^I$
Transitive Relations	$\mathsf{Trans}(R)$	$R^I \circ R^I \subseteq R^I$
Functional Relations	$\mathsf{Func}(R)$	$\{(x, y), (x, z)\} \subseteq R^I \text{ implies } y = z$
Reflexive Relations	$\mathsf{Ref}(R)$	for all $x : (x, x) \in R^I$
Irreflexive Relations	$\mathsf{Irref}(R)$	for all $x : (x, x) \notin R^I$
Symmetric Relations	$\mathsf{Sym}(R)$	$R^I = (R^-)^I$
Asymmetric Relations	$\mathsf{Asym}(R)$	$R^I \cap (R^-)^I = \emptyset$
Disjoint Relations	$\mathsf{Disj}(R, S)$	$R^I \cap S^I = \emptyset$
Assertional Definitions		
Individual	a	a^I
Assertional Axioms (A-Box)		
Relation Assertion	$R(a, b)$	$(a^I, b^I) \in R^I$
Negative Relation Assertion	$\neg R(a, b)$	$(a^I, b^I) \notin R^I$
Class Assertion	$C(a)$	$a^I \in C^I$
Equality	$a = b$	$a^I = b^I$
Inequality	$a \neq b$	$a^I \neq b^I$

CHAPTER 5

Inductive Knowledge

While deductive knowledge is characterized by precise logical consequences, inductively acquiring knowledge involves generalizing patterns from a given set of input observations, which can then be used to generate novel but potentially imprecise predictions. For example, from a large data graph with geographical and flight information, we may observe the pattern that almost all capital cities of countries have international airports serving them, and hence predict that if Santiago is a capital city, it *likely* has an international airport serving it; however, the predictions drawn from this pattern do not hold for certain, where, e.g., Vaduz, the capital city of Liechtenstein, has no (international) airport serving it. Hence, predictions will often be associated with a level of confidence; for example, we may say that a capital has an international airport in $\frac{187}{195}$ of cases, offering a confidence of 0.959 for predictions made with that pattern. We then refer to knowledge acquired inductively as *inductive knowledge*, which includes both the models used to encode patterns, as well as the predictions made by those models. Though fallible, inductive knowledge can be highly valuable.

In Figure 5.1 we provide an overview of the inductive techniques typically applied to knowledge graphs. In the case of unsupervised methods, there is a rich body of work on *graph analytics*, which uses well-known functions/algorithms to detect communities or clusters, find central nodes and edges, etc., in a graph. Alternatively, *knowledge graph embeddings* can use self-supervision to learn a low-dimensional numeric model of a knowledge graph that (typically) maps input edges to an output *plausibility score* indicating the likelihood of the edge being true. The structure of graphs can also be directly leveraged for supervised learning, as explored in the context of *graph neural networks*. Finally, while the aforementioned techniques learn numerical models, *symbolic learning* can learn symbolic models—i.e., logical formulae in the form of rules or axioms—from a graph in a self-supervised manner. We now discuss each of the aforementioned techniques in turn.

5.1   GRAPH ANALYTICS

Analytics is the process of discovering, interpreting, and communicating meaningful patterns inherent to (typically large) data collections. Graph analytics is then the application of analytical processes to (typically large) graph data. The nature of graphs naturally lends itself to certain types of analytics that derive conclusions about nodes and edges based on the *topology* of the graph, i.e., how the nodes of the graph are connected. Graph analytics draws upon techniques from related areas, such as graph theory and network analysis, which have been used to study

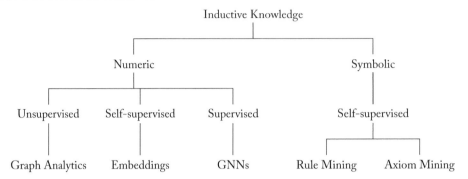

Figure 5.1: Conceptual overview of popular inductive techniques for knowledge graphs in terms of type of representation generated (Numeric/Symbolic) and type of paradigm used (Unsupervised/Self-supervised/Supervised).

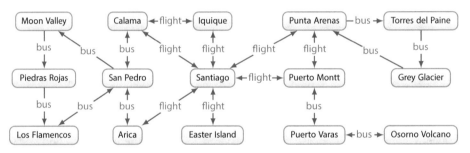

Figure 5.2: Data graph representing transport routes in Chile.

graphs representing social networks, the Web, internet routing, transport networks, ecosystems, protein—protein interactions, linguistic cooccurrences, and more besides [Estrada, 2011].

Returning to the domain of our running example, the tourism board could use graph analytics to extract knowledge about, for instance: key transport hubs that serve many tourist attractions (centrality); groupings of attractions visited by the same tourists (community detection); attractions that may become unreachable in the event of strikes or other route failures (connectivity), or pairs of attractions that are similar to each other (node similarity). Given that such analytics will require a complex, large-scale graph, for the purposes of illustration, in Figure 5.2 we present a more concise example of some transportation connections in Chile directed toward popular tourist destinations. We first introduce a selection of key techniques that can be applied for graph analytics. We then discuss frameworks and languages that can be used to compute such analytics in practice. Given that many traditional graph algorithms are defined for unlabeled graphs, we then describe ways in which analytics can be applied over directed edge-labeled graphs. Finally, we discuss the potential connections between graph analytics and querying and reasoning.

5.1.1   TECHNIQUES

A wide variety of techniques can be applied for graph analytics. In the following, we will enumerate some of the main techniques—as recognized, for example, by the survey of Iosup et al. [2016]—that can be invoked in this setting.

- *Centrality:* aims to identify the most important (aka *central*) nodes or edges of a graph. Specific node centrality measures include *degree, betweenness, closeness, Eigenvector, PageRank, HITS, Katz*, among others. Betweenness centrality can also be applied to edges. For example, a node centrality measure might predict transport hubs in Figure 5.2, while edge centrality might predict traffic by finding connections on which many shortest routes depend.

- *Community detection:* aims to identify *communities* in a graph, i.e., sub-graphs that are more densely connected internally than to the rest of the graph. Community detection algorithms, such as *minimum-cut algorithms, label propagation, Louvain modularity*, among others, can discover such communities. Community detection applied to Figure 5.2 may, for example, detect a community to the left (the north of Chile), to the right (the south of Chile), and perhaps also the center (Chilean cities with airports).

- *Connectivity:* aims to estimate how well-connected the graph is, revealing, for instance, the resilience and (un)reachability of elements of the graph. Specific techniques include measuring *graph density* or *k-connectivity*, detecting *strongly connected components* and *weakly connected components*, computing *spanning trees* or *minimum cuts*, etc. In the context of Figure 5.2, such analysis may tell us that routes to (Grey Glacier), (Osorno Volcano) and (Piedras Rojas) are the most "brittle," becoming disconnected if one of two bus routes fails.

- *Node (or vertex) similarity:* aims to find nodes that are similar to other nodes by virtue of how they are connected within their neighborhood. Node similarity metrics may be computed using *structural equivalence, random walks, diffusion kernels*, etc. These methods provide an understanding of what connects nodes, and, thereafter, in what ways they are similar. In the context of Figure 5.2, such analysis may tell us that (Calama) and (Arica) are similar nodes based on both having return flights to (Santiago) and return buses to (San Pedro).

While the previous techniques accept a graph alone as input,[1] other forms of graph analytics may further accept a node, a pair of nodes, etc., along with the graph.

- *Path finding:* aims to find paths in a graph, typically between pairs of nodes given as input. Various technical definitions exist that restrict the set of valid paths between such

---

[1]Node similarity can be run over an entire graph to find the k most similar nodes for each node, or can also be run for a specific node to find its most similar nodes. There are also measures for graph similarity (based on, e.g., frequent item-sets [Maillot and Bobed, 2018]) that accept multiple graphs as input.

nodes, including simple paths that do not visit the same node twice, shortest paths that visit the fewest number of edges, or—as previously discussed in Section 4.2.2—regular path queries that restrict the labels of edges that can be traversed by the path according to a regular expression [Angles et al., 2017]. We could use such algorithms to find, for example, the shortest path(s) in Figure 5.2 from ⬭Torres del Paine⬭ to ⬭Moon Valley⬭.

Most of the aforementioned techniques for graph analytics were originally proposed and studied for simple graphs or directed graphs without edge labels. We will discuss their application to more complex graph models—and how they can be combined with other techniques such as reasoning and querying—later in Section 5.1.3.

5.1.2   FRAMEWORKS

Various frameworks have been proposed for large-scale graph analytics, often in a distributed (cluster) setting. Among these we can mention Apache Spark (GraphX) [Dave et al., 2016, Xin et al., 2013a], GraphLab [Low et al., 2012], Pregel [Malewicz et al., 2010], Signal-Collect [Stutz et al., 2016], Shark [Xin et al., 2013b], etc. These *graph parallel frameworks* apply a *systolic abstraction* [Kung, 1982] based on a directed graph, where nodes are seen as processors that can send messages to other nodes along edges. Computation is then iterative, where in each iteration, each node reads messages received through inward edges (and possibly its own previous state), performs a computation, and then sends messages through outward edges based on the result. These frameworks then define the systolic computational abstraction on top of the data graph being processed: nodes and edges in the data graph become nodes and edges in the systolic graph.

To take an example, assume we wish to compute the places that are most (or least) easily reached by the routes shown in the graph of Figure 5.2. A good way to measure this is using centrality, where we choose PageRank [Page et al., 1999], which computes the probability of a tourist randomly following the routes shown in the graph being at a particular place after a given number of "hops." We can implement PageRank on large graphs using a graph parallel framework. In Figure 5.3, we provide an example of an iteration of PageRank for an illustrative sub-graph of Figure 5.2. The nodes are initialized with a score of $\frac{1}{|V|} = \frac{1}{6}$, where we assume the tourist to have an equal chance of starting at any point. In the *message phase* (MSG), each node v passes a score of $\frac{d R_i(v)}{|E(v)|}$ on each of its outgoing edges, where we denote by d a constant damping factor used to ensure convergence (typically $d = 0.85$, indicating the probability that a tourist randomly "jumps" to any place), by $R_i(v)$ the score of node v in iteration i (the probability of the tourist being at node v after i hops), and by $|E(v)|$ the number of outgoing edges of v. The aggregation phase (AGG) for v then sums all incoming messages received along with its constant share of the damping factor ($\frac{1-d}{|V|}$) to compute $R_{i+1}(v)$. We then proceed to the message phase of the next iteration, continuing until some termination criterion is reached (e.g., iteration count or residual threshold, etc.) and final scores are output.

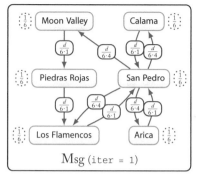
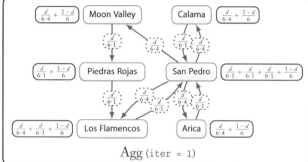

Figure 5.3: Example of a systolic iteration of PageRank on a sub-graph of Figure 5.2.

While the given example is for PageRank, the systolic abstraction is general enough to support a wide variety of graph analytics, including those previously mentioned. An algorithm in this framework consists of the functions to compute message values in the *message phase* (MSG), and to accumulate the messages in the aggregation phase (AGG). The framework will take care of distribution, message passing, fault tolerance, etc. However, such frameworks—based on message passing between neighbors—have limitations: not all types of analytics can be expressed in such frameworks [Xu et al., 2019].[2] Hence, frameworks may allow additional features, such as a *global step* that performs a global computation on all nodes, making the result available to each node [Malewicz et al., 2010]; or a *mutation step* that allows for adding or removing nodes and edges during processing [Malewicz et al., 2010].

Before defining a graph parallel framework, in the interest of generality, we first define a directed graph labeled with feature vectors, which captures the type of input that such a framework can accept, with vectors on both nodes and edges.

Definition 5.1 Directed vector-labeled graph. We define a *directed vector-labeled graph* $G = (V, E, F, \lambda)$, where V is a set of nodes, $E \subseteq V \times V$ is a set of edges, F is a set of feature vectors, and $\lambda : V \cup E \to F$ labels each node and edge with a feature vector.

A directed-edge labeled graph or property graph may be encoded as a directed vector-labeled graph in a number of ways. The type of node and/or a selection of its attributes may be encoded in the node feature vectors, while the label of an edge and/or a selection of its attributes may be encoded in the edge feature vector (including, for example, weights

---

[2]Formally Xu et al. [2019] have shown that such frameworks are as powerful as the (incomplete) Weisfeiler–Lehman (WL) graph isomorphism test for distinguishing graphs. This test involves nodes recursively hashing together hashes of local information received from neighbors, and passing these hashes to neighbors.

applied to edges). Typically, node feature vectors will all have the same dimensionality, as will edge feature vectors.

Example 5.2   We define a directed vector-labeled graph in preparation for later computing PageRank using a graph parallel framework. Let $G = (V, E, L)$ denote a directed edge-labeled graph. Let $|E(u)|$ denote the outdegree of node $u \in V$. We then initialize a directed vector-labeled graph $G' = (V, E', F, \lambda)$ such that $E' = \{(x, z) \mid \exists y : (x, y, z) \in E\}$, and for all $u \in V$, we define $\lambda(u) = \begin{bmatrix} \frac{1}{|V|} \\ |E'(u)| \\ |V| \end{bmatrix}$, and $\lambda(u, v) = []$, with $F = \{\lambda(u) \mid u \in V\} \cup \{\lambda(u, v) \mid (u, v) \in E'\}$, assigning each node a vector containing its initial PageRank score, the outdegree of the node, and the number of nodes in the graph. Conversely, edge-vectors are not used in this case.

We now define a graph parallel framework, where we use $\{\cdot\}$ to denote a multiset, $2^{S \to \mathbb{N}}$ to denote the set of all multisets containing (only) elements from the set S, and $\mathbb{R}^a$ to denote the set of all vectors of dimension a (i.e., the set of all vectors containing a real-valued elements).

Definition 5.3   Graph parallel framework.   A *graph parallel framework* (*GPF*) is a triple of functions $\mathfrak{G} = (\textsc{Msg}, \textsc{Agg}, \textsc{End})$ such that (with $a, b, c \in \mathbb{N}$):

- $\textsc{Msg} : \mathbb{R}^a \times \mathbb{R}^b \to \mathbb{R}^c$

- $\textsc{Agg} : \mathbb{R}^a \times 2^{\mathbb{R}^c \to \mathbb{N}} \to \mathbb{R}^a$

- $\textsc{End} : 2^{\mathbb{R}^a \to \mathbb{N}} \to \{\text{true}, \text{false}\}$

The function $\textsc{Msg}$ defines what message (i.e., vector) must be passed from a node to a neighboring node along a particular edge, given the current feature vectors of the node and the edge; the function $\textsc{Agg}$ is used to compute a new feature vector for a node, given its previous feature vector and incoming messages; the function $\textsc{End}$ defines a condition for termination of vector computation. The integers a, b, and c denote the dimensions of node feature vectors, edge feature vectors, and message vectors, respectively; we assume that a and b correspond with the dimensions of input feature vectors for nodes and edges. Given a GPF $\mathfrak{G} = (\textsc{Msg}, \textsc{Agg}, \textsc{End})$, a directed vector-labeled graph $G = (V, E, F, \lambda)$, and a node $u \in V$, we define the output vector assigned to node u in G by $\mathfrak{G}$ (written $\mathfrak{G}(G, u)$) as follows. First, let $\mathbf{n}_u^{(0)} = \lambda(u)$. For all $i \geq 1$, let:

$$M_u^{(i)} = \left\{ \text{Msg}\left(\mathbf{n}_v^{(i-1)}, \lambda(v, u) \right) \mid (v, u) \in E \right\}$$
$$\mathbf{n}_u^{(i)} = \text{Agg}\left(\mathbf{n}_u^{(i-1)}, M_u^{(i)} \right)$$

where $M_u^{(i)}$ is the multiset of messages received by node u during iteration i, and $\mathbf{n}_u^{(i)}$ is the state (vector) of node u at the end of iteration i. If j is the smallest integer for which $\text{End}(\{ \mathbf{n}_u^{(j)} \mid u \in V \})$ is true, then $\mathfrak{G}(G, u) = \mathbf{n}_u^{(j)}$.

This particular definition assumes that vectors are dynamically computed for nodes, and that messages are passed only to outgoing neighbors, but the definitions can be readily adapted to consider dynamic vectors for edges, or messages being passed to incoming neighbors, etc. We now provide an example instantiating a GPF to compute PageRank over a directed graph.

Example 5.4   We take as input the directed vector labeled graph $G' = (V, E, F, \lambda)$ from Example 5.2 for a PageRank GPF. First we define the messages passed from u to v:

$$\text{Msg}\left(\mathbf{n}_v, \lambda(v, u) \right) = \left[\frac{d(\mathbf{n}_v)_1}{(\mathbf{n}_v)_2} \right]$$

where d denotes PageRank's constant dampening factor (typically $d = 0.85$) and $(\mathbf{n}_v)_k$ denotes the kth element of the $\mathbf{n}_v$ vector. In other words, v will pass to u its PageRank score multiplied by the dampening factor and divided by its out-degree (we do not require $\lambda(v, u)$ in this particular example). Next, we define the function for u to aggregate the messages it receives from other nodes:

$$\text{Agg}\left(\mathbf{n}_u, M_u \right) = \begin{bmatrix} \frac{1-d}{(\mathbf{n}_u)_3} + \sum_{\mathbf{m} \in M_u} (\mathbf{m})_1 \\ (\mathbf{n}_u)_2 \\ (\mathbf{n}_u)_3 \end{bmatrix}$$

Here, we sum the scores received from other nodes along with its share of rank from the dampening factor, copying over the node's degree and the total number of nodes for future use. Finally, there are a number of ways that we could define the termination condition; here we simply define:

$$\text{End}(\{ \mathbf{n}_u^{(i)} \mid u \in V \}) = (i \geq z)$$

where z is a fixed number of iterations, at which point the process stops.

We may note in this example that the total number of nodes is duplicated in the vector for each node of the graph. Part of the benefit of GPFs is that only local information in the neighborhood of the node is required for each computation step. In practice, such frameworks may allow additional features, such as global computation steps whose results are made available to all nodes [Malewicz et al., 2010], operations that dynamically modify the graph [Malewicz et al., 2010], etc.

5.1.3   ANALYTICS ON DATA GRAPHS

As aforementioned, most analytics presented thus far are, in their "native" form, applicable for undirected or directed graphs without the *edge metadata*—i.e., edge labels or property-value pairs—typical of graph data models.[3] A number of strategies can be applied to make data graphs subject to analytics of this form.

- *Projection* involves simply "projecting" an undirected or directed graph by optionally selecting a sub-graph from the data graph from which all edge meta-data are dropped; for example, the graph of Figure 5.3 may be the result of extracting the sub-graph induced by the edge labels bus and flight from a larger data graph, where the labels are then dropped to create a directed graph.

- *Weighting* involves converting edge meta-data into numerical values according to some function. Many of the aforementioned techniques are easily adapted to the case of weighted (directed) graphs; for example, we could consider weights on the graph of Figure 5.3 denoting trip duration (or price, traffic, etc.), and then compute the shortest (weighted) paths considering time by adding the duration of each leg of the respective journey.[4] In the absence of external weights, we may rather map edge labels to weights, assigning the same weight to all flight edges, to all bus edges, etc., based on some criteria.

- *Transformation* involves transforming the graph to a lower arity model. A transformation may be *lossy*, meaning that the original graph cannot be recovered; or *lossless*, meaning that the original graph can be recovered. Figure 5.4 provides an example of a lossy and lossless transformation from a directed edge-labeled graph to directed graphs. In the lossy transformation, we cannot tell, for example, if the original graph contained the edge (Iquique)–flight→(Santiago), or rather the edge (Iquique)–flight→(Arica), or both. The lossless transformation must introduce new nodes (similar to reification) to maintain information about directed labeled edges. Both transformed graphs further attempt to preserve the directionality of the original graph.

- *Customization* involves changing the analytical procedure to incorporate edge meta-data, such as was the case for path finding based on path expressions. Other examples might include structural measures for node similarity that not only consider common neighbors, but also common neighbors connected by edges with the same label, or aggregate centrality measures that capture the importance of edges grouped by label, etc.

---

[3]We remark that in the case of property graphs, property-value pairs on nodes can be converted by mapping values to nodes and properties to edges with the corresponding label.

[4]Other forms of analytics are possible if we assume the graph is weighted; for example, if we annotated the graph of Figure 5.3 with probabilities of tourists moving from one place to the next, we could leverage *Markov processes* to understand features such as reducibility, periodicity, transience, recurrence, ergodicity, steady states, etc., of the routes [Dynkin, 1965].

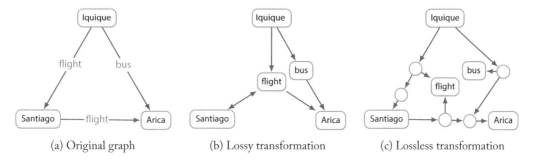

(a) Original graph   (b) Lossy transformation   (c) Lossless transformation

Figure 5.4: Transformations from a directed edge-labeled graph to a directed graph.

The results of an analytical process may change drastically depending on which of the previous strategies are chosen to prepare the graph for analysis. The choice of strategy may be a non-trivial one to make *a priori* and may require empirical validation. More study is required to more generally understand the effects of such strategies on the results of different analytical techniques over different graph models.

5.1.4 ANALYTICS WITH QUERIES

As discussed in Section 2.2, various languages for querying graphs have been proposed down through the years [Angles et al., 2017]. One may consider a variety of ways in which query languages and analytics can complement each other. First, we may consider using query languages to project or transform a graph suitable for a particular analytical task, such as to extract the graph of Figure 5.2 from a larger data graph. Query languages such as SPARQL [Harris et al., 2013], Cypher [Francis et al., 2018], and G-CORE [Angles et al., 2018] allow for outputting graphs, where such queries can be used to select sub-graphs for analysis. These languages can also express some limited (non-recursive) analytics, where aggregations can be used to compute degree centrality, for example; they may also have some built-in analytical support, where, for example, Cypher [Francis et al., 2018] allows for finding shortest paths. In the other direction, analytics can contribute to the querying process in terms of *optimizations*, where, for example, analysis of connectivity may suggest how to better distribute a large data graph over multiple machines for querying using, e.g., *minimum cuts* [Akhter et al., 2018, Janke et al., 2018]. Analytics have also been used to *rank* query results over large graphs [Fan et al., 2013, Wagner et al., 2012], selecting the most important results for presentation to the user.

In some use-cases we may further wish to interleave querying and analytical processes. For example, from the full data graph collected by the tourist board, consider an upcoming airline strike where the board wishes to find *the events during the strike with venues in cities unreachable from Santiago by public transport due to the strike*. Hypothetically, we could use a query to extract the transport network excluding the airline's routes (assuming, per Figure 2.3a that the airline information is available), use analytics to extract the strongly connected component containing

Santiago, and finally use a query to find events in cities not in the Santiago component on the given dates.[5] While one could solve this task using an imperative language such as Gremlin [Rodriguez, 2015], GraphX [Xin et al., 2013a], or R [The R. Foundation, 1992], more declarative languages are also being explored to express such tasks, with proposals including the extension of graph query languages with recursive capabilities [Bischof et al., 2012, Hogan et al., 2020, Reutter et al., 2015],[6] combining linear algebra with relational (query) algebra [Hutchison et al., 2017], and so forth.

5.1.5   ANALYTICS WITH ENTAILMENT

Knowledge graphs are often associated with a semantic schema or ontology that defines the semantics of domain terms, giving rise to entailments (per Chapter 4). Applying analytics with or without such entailments—e.g., before or after materialization—may yield radically different results. For example, observe that an edge Santa Lucía –hosts→ EID15 is semantically equivalent to an edge EID15 –venue→ Santa Lucía once the inverse axiom hosts –inv. of→ venue is invoked; however, these edges are far from equivalent from the perspective of analytical techniques that consider edge direction, for which including one type of edge, or the other, or both, may have a major bearing on the final results. To the best of our knowledge, the combination of analytics and entailment has not been well-explored, leaving open interesting research questions. Along these lines, it may be of interest to explore *semantically-invariant analytics* that yield the same results over semantically-equivalent graphs (i.e., graphs that entail one another), thus analyzing the semantic content of the knowledge graph rather than simply the topological features of the data graph; for example, semantically-invariant analytics would yield the same results over a graph containing the inverse axiom hosts –inv. of→ venue and a number of hosts edges, the same graph but where every hosts edge is replaced by an inverse venue edge, and the union of both graphs.

5.2   KNOWLEDGE GRAPH EMBEDDINGS

Methods for machine learning have gained significant attention in recent years. In the context of knowledge graphs, machine learning can either be used for directly *refining* a knowledge graph [Paulheim, 2017] (discussed further in Chapter 8), or for *downstream tasks* using the knowledge graph, such as recommendation [Zhang et al., 2016], information extraction [Vashishth et al., 2018], question answering [Huang et al., 2019], query relaxation [Wang et al., 2018], query approximation [Hamilton et al., 2018], etc. (discussed further in Chapter 10). However, many traditional machine learning techniques assume dense numeric input representations in the form of vectors, which is quite distinct from how graphs are usually expressed. So how can graphs—or nodes, edges, etc., thereof—be encoded as numeric vectors?

---

[5]Such a task could not be solved in a single query using regular path queries as such expressions would not be capable of filtering edges representing flights of a particular airline.

[6]Recursive query languages become Turing complete if one can also express operations on binary arrays.

A first attempt to represent a graph using vectors would be to use a *one-hot encoding*, generating a vector for each node of length $|L| \cdot |V|$—with $|V|$ the number of nodes in the input graph and $|L|$ the number of edge labels—placing a one at the corresponding index to indicate the existence of the respective edge in the graph, or zero otherwise. Such a representation will, however, typically result in large and sparse vectors, which will be detrimental for most machine learning models.

The main goal of knowledge graph embedding techniques is to create a dense representation of the graph (i.e., *embed* the graph) in a continuous, low-dimensional vector space that can then be used for machine learning tasks. The dimensionality d of the embedding is fixed and usually low (often, e.g., $50 \geq d \geq 1000$). Typically, the graph embedding is composed of an *entity embedding* for each node: a vector with d dimensions that we denote by $\mathbf{e}$; and a *relation embedding* for each edge label: (typically) a vector with d dimensions that we denote by $\mathbf{r}$. The overall goal of these vectors is to abstract and preserve latent structures in the graph. There are many ways in which this notion of an embedding can be instantiated. Most commonly, given an edge ⓢ-ₚ►ⓞ, a specific embedding approach defines a *scoring function* that accepts $\mathbf{e}_s$ (the entity embedding of node ⓢ), $\mathbf{r}_p$ (the entity embedding of edge label p) and $\mathbf{e}_o$ (the entity embedding of node ⓞ) and computes the *plausibility* of the edge, which estimates how likely it is to be true. Given a data graph, the goal is then to compute the embeddings of dimension d that maximize the plausibility of positive edges (typically edges in the graph) and minimize the plausibility of negative examples (typically edges in the graph with a node or edge label changed such that they are no longer in the graph) according to the given scoring function. The resulting embeddings can then be seen as models learned through self-supervision that encode (latent) features of the graph, mapping input edges to output plausibility scores.

Embeddings can then be used for a number of low-level tasks involving the nodes and edge-labels of the graph from which they were computed. First, we can use the plausibility scoring function to assign a confidence to edges that may, for example, have been extracted from an external source (discussed later in Chapter 6). Second, the plausibility scoring function can be used to complete edges with missing nodes/edge labels for the purposes of link prediction (discussed later in Chapter 8); for example, in Figure 5.2, we might ask which nodes in the graph are likely to complete the edge Grey Glacier —bus►⟨?⟩, where—aside from Punta Arenas, which is already given—we might intuitively expect Torres del Paine to be a plausible candidate. Third, embedding models will typically assign similar vectors to similar nodes and similar edge-labels, and thus they can be used as the basis of similarity measures, which may be useful for finding duplicate nodes that refer to the same entity, or for the purposes of providing recommendations (discussed later in Chapter 10).

A wide range of knowledge graph embedding techniques have been proposed by Wang et al. [2017]. Our goal here is to provide a high-level introduction to some of the most popular techniques proposed thus far. We first discuss *tensor-based approaches* that include three different sub-approaches using linear/tensor algebra to compute embeddings. We then discuss *language models* that leverage existing word embedding techniques, proposing ways of generating graph-like analogues for their expected (textual) inputs. Finally, we discuss *entailment-aware models* that can take into account the semantics of the graph, when available.

5.2.1   TENSOR-BASED MODELS

We first discuss tensor-based models, which we sub-divide into three categories: *translational models* that adopt a geometric perspective whereby relation embeddings translate subject entities to object entities; *tensor decomposition models* that extract latent factors approximating the graph's structure; and *neural models* that use neural networks to train embeddings that provide accurate plausibility scores.

Translational Models

Translational models interpret edge labels as transformations from subject nodes (aka the *source* or *head*) to object nodes (aka the *target* or *tail*); for example, in the edge (San Pedro)—bus→(Moon Valley), the edge label bus is seen as transforming (San Pedro) to (Moon Valley), and likewise for other bus edges. The most elementary approach in this family is TransE [Bordes et al., 2013]. Over all positive edges (s)-p→(o), TransE learns vectors $\mathbf{e}_s$, $\mathbf{r}_p$, and $\mathbf{e}_o$ aiming to make $\mathbf{e}_s + \mathbf{r}_p$ as close as possible to $\mathbf{e}_o$. Conversely, if the edge is a negative example, TransE attempts to learn a representation that keeps $\mathbf{e}_s + \mathbf{r}_p$ away from $\mathbf{e}_o$. To illustrate, Figure 5.5 provides a toy example of two-dimensional ($d = 2$) entity and relation embeddings computed by TransE. We keep the orientation of the vectors similar to the original graph for clarity. For any edge (s)-p→(o) in the original graph, adding the vectors $\mathbf{e}_s + \mathbf{r}_p$ should approximate $\mathbf{e}_o$. In this toy example, the vectors correspond precisely where, for instance, adding the vectors for (Licantén) ($\mathbf{e}_L$.) and west of ($\mathbf{r}_{wo.}$) gives a vector corresponding to (Curico) ($\mathbf{e}_C$.). We can use these embeddings to predict edges (among other tasks); for example, in order to predict which node in the graph is most likely to be west of (Antofagasta) ($A.$), by computing $\mathbf{e}_{A.} + \mathbf{r}_{wo.}$ we find that the resulting vector (dotted in Figure 5.5c) is closest to $\mathbf{e}_{T.}$, thus predicting (Toconao) ($T.$) to be the most *plausible* such node.

Aside from this toy example, TransE can be too simplistic; for example, in Figure 5.2, bus not only transforms (San Pedro) to (Moon Valley), but also to (Arica), (Calama), and so forth. TransE will, in this case, aim to give similar vectors to all such target locations, which may not be feasible given other edges. TransE will also tend to assign cyclical relations a zero vector, as the directional components will tend to cancel each other out. To resolve such issues, many variants of TransE have been investigated. Among these, for example, TransH [Wang et al., 2014] represents different relations using distinct hyperplanes, where for the edge (s)-p→(o), (s) is first projected onto the hyperplane of p before the translation to (o) is learned (uninfluenced by edges with other labels for (s) and for (o)). TransR [Lin et al., 2015] generalizes this approach by projecting (s) and (o) into a vector space specific to p, which involves multiplying the entity embeddings for (s) and (o) by a projection matrix specific to p. TransD [Ji et al., 2015] simplifies TransR by associating entities and relations with a second vector, where these secondary vectors are used to project the

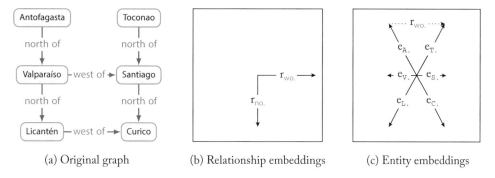

(a) Original graph   (b) Relationship embeddings   (c) Entity embeddings

Figure 5.5: Toy example of two-dimensional relation and entity embeddings learned by TransE; the entity embeddings use abbreviations and include an example of vector addition to predict what is west of Antofagasta.

entity into a relation-specific vector space. Recently, RotatE [Sun et al., 2019] proposes translational embeddings in complex space, which allows to capture more characteristics of relations, such as direction, symmetry, inversion, antisymmetry, and composition. Embeddings have also been proposed in non-Euclidean space; for example, MuRP [Balazevic et al., 2019a] uses relation embeddings that transform entity embeddings in the hyperbolic space of the Poincaré ball mode, whose curvature provides more "space" to separate entities with respect to the dimensionality. For discussion of other translational models, we refer to the surveys by Wang et al. [2017] and Cai et al. [2018].

Tensor Decomposition Models
A second approach to derive graph embeddings is to apply methods based on *tensor decomposition*. A *tensor* is a multidimensional numeric field that generalizes scalars (0-order tensors), vectors (1-order tensors) and matrices (2-order tensors) toward arbitrary dimension/order. Tensors have become a widely used abstraction for machine learning [Rabanser et al., 2017]. Tensor decomposition involves decomposing a tensor into more "elemental" tensors (e.g., of lower order) from which the original tensor can be recomposed (or approximated) by a fixed sequence of basic operations over the output tensors. These elemental tensors can be viewed as capturing *latent factors* underlying the information contained in the original tensor. There are many approaches to tensor decomposition, where we will now briefly introduce the main ideas behind *rank decompositions* [Rabanser et al., 2017].

Leaving aside graphs momentarily, consider an (a, b)-matrix (i.e., a 2-order tensor) $\mathbf{C}$, where a is the number of cities in Chile, b is the number of months in a year, and each element $(\mathbf{C})_{ij}$ denotes the average temperature of the ith city in the jth month. Noting that Chile is a long, thin country—ranging from subpolar climates in the south, to a desert climate in the north—we may find a decomposition of $\mathbf{C}$ into two vectors representing latent factors—

specifically $\mathbf{x}$ (with a elements) giving lower values for cities with lower latitude, and $\mathbf{y}$ (with b elements), giving lower values for months with lower temperatures—such that computing the outer product[7] of the two vectors approximates $\mathbf{C}$ reasonably well: $\mathbf{x} \otimes \mathbf{y} \approx \mathbf{C}$. In the (unlikely) case that there exist vectors $\mathbf{x}$ and $\mathbf{y}$ such that $\mathbf{C}$ is precisely the outer product of two vectors ($\mathbf{x} \otimes \mathbf{y} = \mathbf{C}$) we call $\mathbf{C}$ a rank-1 matrix; we can then precisely encode $\mathbf{C}$ using $a + b$ values rather than $a \times b$ values. Most times, however, to get precisely $\mathbf{C}$, we need to sum multiple rank-1 matrices, where the rank r of $\mathbf{C}$ is the minimum number of rank-1 matrices that need to be summed to derive precisely $\mathbf{C}$, such that $\mathbf{x}_1 \otimes \mathbf{y}_1 + \ldots \mathbf{x}_r \otimes \mathbf{y}_r = \mathbf{C}$. In the temperature example, $\mathbf{x}_2 \otimes \mathbf{y}_2$ might correspond to a correction for altitude, $\mathbf{x}_3 \otimes \mathbf{y}_3$ for higher temperature variance further south, etc. A (low) rank decomposition of a matrix then sets a limit d on the rank and computes the vectors $(\mathbf{x}_1, \mathbf{y}_1, \ldots, \mathbf{x}_d, \mathbf{y}_d)$ such that $\mathbf{x}_1 \otimes \mathbf{y}_1 + \ldots + \mathbf{x}_d \otimes \mathbf{y}_d$ gives the best d-rank approximation of $\mathbf{C}$. Noting that to generate n-order tensors we need to compute the outer product of n vectors, we can generalize this idea toward low-rank decomposition of tensors; this method is called Canonical Polyadic (CP) decomposition [Hitchcock, 1927]. For example, a 3-order tensor $\mathcal{C}$ containing monthly temperatures for Chilean cities *at four different times of day* could be approximated with $\mathbf{x}_1 \otimes \mathbf{y}_1 \otimes \mathbf{z}_1 + \ldots \mathbf{x}_d \otimes \mathbf{y}_d \otimes \mathbf{z}_d$ (e.g., $\mathbf{x}_1$ might be a latitude factor, $\mathbf{y}_1$ a monthly variation factor, and $\mathbf{z}_1$ a daily variation factor, and so on). Various algorithms exist to compute (approximate) CP decompositions, including Alternating Least Squares, Jennrich's Algorithm, and the Tensor Power method [Rabanser et al., 2017].

Returning to graphs, similar principles can be used to decompose a graph into vectors, thus yielding embeddings. In particular, a graph can be encoded as a one-hot 3-order tensor $\mathcal{G}$ with $|V| \times |L| \times |V|$ elements, where the element $(\mathcal{G})_{ijk}$ is set to one if the ith node links to the kth node with an edge having the jth label, or zero otherwise. As previously mentioned, such a tensor will typically be very large and sparse, where rank decompositions are thus applicable. A CP decomposition [Hitchcock, 1927] would compute a sequence of vectors $(\mathbf{x}_1, \mathbf{y}_1, \mathbf{z}_1, \ldots, \mathbf{x}_d, \mathbf{y}_d, \mathbf{z}_d)$ such that $\mathbf{x}_1 \otimes \mathbf{y}_1 \otimes \mathbf{z}_1 + \ldots + \mathbf{x}_d \otimes \mathbf{y}_d \otimes \mathbf{z}_d \approx \mathcal{G}$. We illustrate this scheme in Figure 5.6. Letting $\mathbf{X}, \mathbf{Y}, \mathbf{Z}$ denote the matrices formed by $\begin{bmatrix} \mathbf{x}_1 & \cdots & \mathbf{x}_d \end{bmatrix}$, $\begin{bmatrix} \mathbf{y}_1 & \cdots & \mathbf{y}_d \end{bmatrix}$, $\begin{bmatrix} \mathbf{z}_1 & \cdots & \mathbf{z}_d \end{bmatrix}$, respectively, with each vector forming a column of the corresponding matrix, we could then extract the ith row of $\mathbf{Y}$ as an embedding for the ith relation, and the jth rows of $\mathbf{X}$ and $\mathbf{Z}$ as *two* embeddings for the jth entity. However, knowledge graph embeddings typically aim to assign *one* vector to each entity.

DistMult [Yang et al., 2015] is a seminal method for computing knowledge graph embeddings based on rank decompositions, where each entity and relation is associated with a vector of dimension d, such that for an edge ⓢ-ₚ▸◯, a plausibility scoring function $\sum_{i=1}^{d} (\mathbf{e}_\mathrm{s})_i (\mathbf{r}_\mathrm{p})_i (\mathbf{e}_\mathrm{o})_i$ is defined, where $(\mathbf{e}_\mathrm{s})_i$, $(\mathbf{r}_\mathrm{p})_i$ and $(\mathbf{e}_\mathrm{o})_i$ denote the ith elements of vectors $\mathbf{e}_\mathrm{s}$, $\mathbf{r}_\mathrm{p}$, $\mathbf{e}_\mathrm{o}$, respectively. The goal, then, is to learn vectors for each node and edge label that maximize the plausibility of positive edges and minimize the plausibility of negative edges. This approach equates to a

---

[7]The outer product of two (column) vectors $\mathbf{x}$ of length a and $\mathbf{y}$ of length b, denoted $\mathbf{x} \otimes \mathbf{y}$, is defined as $\mathbf{xy}^\mathrm{T}$, yielding an (a, b)-matrix $\mathbf{M}$ such that $(\mathbf{M})_{ij} = (\mathbf{x})_i \cdot (\mathbf{y})_j$. Analogously, the outer product of k vectors is a k-order tensor.

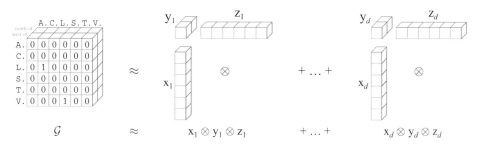

Figure 5.6: Abstract illustration of a CP d-rank decomposition of a tensor representing the graph of Figure 5.5a.

CP decomposition of the graph tensor $\mathcal{G}$, but where entities have one vector that is used twice: $\mathbf{x}_1 \otimes \mathbf{y}_1 \otimes \mathbf{x}_1 + \ldots + \mathbf{x}_d \otimes \mathbf{y}_d \otimes \mathbf{x}_d \approx \mathcal{G}$. A weakness of this approach is that per the scoring function, the plausibility of ⓢ-ᵖ→ⓞ will always be equal to that of ⓞ-ᵖ→ⓢ; in other words, Dist-Mult does not consider edge direction.

Rather than use a vector as a relation embedding, RESCAL [Nickel and Tresp, 2013] uses a matrix, which allows for combining values from $\mathbf{e}_s$ and $\mathbf{e}_o$ across all dimensions, and thus can capture, e.g., edge direction. However, RESCAL incurs a higher cost in terms of space and time than DistMult. HolE [Nickel et al., 2016b] uses vectors for relation and entity embeddings, but proposes to use the *circular correlation operator*—which takes sums along the diagonals of the outer product of two vectors—to combine them. This operator is not commutative, and can thus consider edge direction. ComplEx [Trouillon et al., 2016], on the other hand, uses a complex vector (i.e., a vector containing complex numbers) as a relational embedding, which similarly allows for breaking the aforementioned symmetry of DistMult's scoring function while keeping the number of parameters low. SimplE [Kazemi and Poole, 2018] rather proposes to compute a standard CP decomposition computing two initial vectors for entities from $\mathbf{X}$ and $\mathbf{Z}$ and then averaging terms across $\mathbf{X}$, $\mathbf{Y}$, $\mathbf{Z}$ to compute the final plausibility scores. TuckER [Balazevic et al., 2019b] employs a different type of decomposition—called a Tucker Decomposition [Tucker, 1964], which computes a smaller "core" tensor $\mathcal{T}$ and a sequence of three matrices $\mathbf{A}$, $\mathbf{B}$, and $\mathbf{C}$, such that $\mathcal{G} \approx \mathcal{T} \otimes \mathbf{A} \otimes \mathbf{B} \otimes \mathbf{C}$—where entity embeddings are taken from $\mathbf{A}$ and $\mathbf{C}$, while relation embeddings are taken from $\mathbf{B}$. Of these approaches, TuckER [Balazevic et al., 2019b] currently provides state-of-the-art results on standard benchmarks.

Neural Models

A limitation of the aforementioned approaches is that they assume either linear (preserving addition and scalar multiplication) or bilinear (e.g., matrix multiplication) operations over embeddings to compute plausibility scores. Other approaches rather use neural networks to learn embeddings with non-linear scoring for plausibility.

One of the earliest proposals of a neural model was Semantic Matching Energy (SME) [Glorot et al., 2013], which learns parameters (aka weights: $\mathbf{w}$, $\mathbf{w}'$) for two functions—$f_{\mathbf{w}}(\mathbf{e}_s, \mathbf{r}_p)$ and $g_{\mathbf{w}'}(\mathbf{e}_o, \mathbf{r}_p)$—such that the dot product of the result of both functions—$f_{\mathbf{w}}(\mathbf{e}_s, \mathbf{r}_p) \cdot g_{\mathbf{w}'}(\mathbf{e}_o, \mathbf{r}_p)$—gives the plausibility score. Both linear and bilinear variants of $f_{\mathbf{w}}$ and $g_{\mathbf{w}'}$ are proposed. Another early proposal was Neural Tensor Networks (NTN) [Socher et al., 2013], which proposes to maintain a tensor $\mathcal{W}$ of internal weights, such that the plausibility score is computed by a complex function that combines the outer product $\mathbf{e}_s \otimes \mathcal{W} \otimes \mathbf{e}_o$ with a standard neural layer over $\mathbf{e}_s$ and $\mathbf{e}_o$, which in turn is combined with $\mathbf{r}_p$, to produce a plausibility score. The tensor $\mathcal{W}$ results in a high number of parameters, limiting scalability [Wang et al., 2017]. Multi-Layer Perceptron (MLP) [Dong et al., 2014] is a simpler model, where $\mathbf{e}_s$, $\mathbf{r}_p$, and $\mathbf{e}_o$ are concatenated and fed into a hidden layer to compute plausibility scores.

A number of more recent approaches have proposed using convolutional kernels in their models. ConvE [Dettmers et al., 2018] proposes to generate a matrix from $\mathbf{e}_s$ and $\mathbf{r}_p$ by "wrapping" each vector over several rows and concatenating both matrices. The concatenated matrix serves as the input for a set of (2D) convolutional layers, which returns a feature map tensor. The feature map tensor is vectorized and projected into d dimensions using a parameterized linear transformation. The plausibility score is then computed based on the dot product of this vector and $\mathbf{e}_o$. A disadvantage of ConvE is that by wrapping vectors into matrices, it imposes an artificial two-dimensional structure on the embeddings. HypER [Balazevic et al., 2019c] is a similar model using convolutions, but avoids the need to wrap vectors into matrices. Instead, a fully connected layer (called the "hypernetwork") is applied to $\mathbf{r}_p$ and used to generate a matrix of relation-specific convolutional filters. These filters are applied directly to $\mathbf{e}_s$ to give a feature map, which is vectorized. The same process is then applied as in ConvE: the resulting vector is projected into d dimensions, and a dot product applied with $\mathbf{e}_o$ to produce the plausibility score. The resulting model is shown to outperform ConvE on standard benchmarks [Balazevic et al., 2019c].

The presented approaches strike different balances in terms of expressivity and the number of parameters that need to be trained. While more expressive models, such as NTN, may better fit more complex plausibility functions over lower dimensional embeddings by using more hidden parameters, simpler models, such as that proposed by Dong et al. [Dong et al., 2014], and convolutional networks [Balazevic et al., 2019c, Dettmers et al., 2018] that enable parameter sharing by applying the same (typically small) kernels over different regions of a matrix, require handling fewer parameters overall and are more scalable.

Survey and Definition of Tensor-Based Approaches
We now formally define and survey the aforementioned tensor-based approaches. For simplicity, we will consider directed edge-labeled graphs.

Before defining embeddings, we first introduce tensors.

Definition 5.5   Vector, matrix, tensor, order, mode.   For any positive integer a, a *vector* of dimension a is a family of real numbers indexed by integers in $\{1, \ldots, a\}$. For a and b positive integers, an (a, b)-matrix is a family of real numbers indexed by pairs of integers in $\{1, \ldots, a\} \times \{1, \ldots, b\}$. A tensor is a family of real numbers indexed by a finite sequence of integers such that there exist positive numbers $a_1, \ldots, a_n$ such that the indices are all the tuples of numbers in $\{1, \ldots, a_1\} \times \ldots \times \{1, \ldots, a_n\}$. The number n is called the *order* of the tensor, the subindices $i \in \{1, \ldots, n\}$ indicate the *mode* of a tensor, and each a_i defines the dimension of the ith mode. A 1-order tensor is a vector and a 2-order tensor is a matrix. We denote the set of all tensors as $\mathbb{T}$.

For specific dimensions $a_1, \ldots, a_n$ of modes, a tensor is an element of $(\cdots (\mathbb{R}^{a_1})^{\cdots})^{a_n}$ but we write $\mathbb{R}^{a_1, \ldots, a_n}$ to simplify the notation. We use lowercase bold font to denote vectors ($\mathbf{x} \in \mathbb{R}^a$), upper-case bold font to denote matrices ($\mathbf{X} \in \mathbb{R}^{a,b}$) and calligraphic font to denote tensors ($\mathcal{X} \in \mathbb{R}^{a_1, \ldots, a_n}$).

Now we are ready to abstractly define knowledge graph embeddings.

Definition 5.6   Knowledge graph embedding.   Given a directed edge-labeled graph $G = (V, E, L)$, a *knowledge graph embedding of* G is a pair of mappings (ε, ρ) such that $\varepsilon : V \to \mathbb{T}$ and $\rho : L \to \mathbb{T}$.

In the most typical case, ε and ρ map nodes and edge-labels, respectively, to vectors of fixed dimension. In some cases, however, they may map to matrices. Given this abstract notion of a knowledge graph embedding, we can then define a plausibility scoring function.

Definition 5.7   Plausibility scores.   A *plausibility scoring function* is a partial function $\phi : \mathbb{T} \times \mathbb{T} \times \mathbb{T} \to \mathbb{R}$. Given a directed edge-labeled graph $G = (V, E, L)$, an edge $(s, p, o) \in V \times L \times V$, and a knowledge graph embedding (ε, ρ) of G, the plausibility of (s, p, o) is given as $\phi(\varepsilon(s), \rho(p), \varepsilon(o))$.

Edges with higher scores are considered more plausible. Given a graph $G = (V, E, L)$, we assume a set of positive edges E^+ and a set of negative edges E^-. Positive edges are often simply the edges in the graph: $E^+ = E$. Negative edges use the vocabulary of G (i.e., $E^- \subseteq V \times L \times V$) and are typically defined by taking edges (s, p, o) from E and changing one term of each edge—often one of the nodes—such that the edge is no longer in E. Given sets of positive and negative edges, and a plausibility scoring function, the objective is to find the embedding that maximizes the plausibility of edges in E^+ while minimizing the plausibility of edges in E^-. Specific knowledge graph embeddings then instantiate the type of embedding considered and the plausibility scoring function in various ways.

In Table 5.1, we define the plausibility scoring function and types of embeddings used by different knowledge graph embeddings. To simplify the definitions, we use $\mathbf{e}_x$ to denote $\varepsilon(x)$ when it is a vector, $\mathbf{r}_y$ to denote $\rho(y)$ when it is a vector, and $\mathbf{R}_y$ to denote $\rho(y)$ when it is a matrix. Some models involve learned parameters (aka weights) for computing plausibility. We denote these as $\mathbf{v}, \mathbf{V}, \mathcal{V}, \mathbf{w}, \mathbf{W} \ \mathcal{W}$ (for vectors, matrices or tensors). We use d_e and d_r to denote the dimensionality chosen for entity embeddings and relation embeddings, respectively. Often it is assumed that $d_e = d_r$, in which case we will write d. Weights may have their own dimensionality, which we denote w. The embeddings in Table 5.1 use a variety of operators on vectors, matrices and tensors, which will be defined later.

The embeddings defined in Table 5.1 vary in complexity, where a trade-off exists between the number of parameters used, and the expressiveness of the model in terms of its capability to capture latent features of the graph. To increase expressivity, many of the models in Table 5.1 use additional parameters beyond the embeddings themselves. A possible formal guarantee of such models is *full expressiveness*, which, given any disjoint sets of positive edges E^+ and negative edges E^-, asserts that the model can always correctly partition those edges. On the one hand, for example, DistMult [Yang et al., 2015] cannot distinguish an edge ⓢ–ᴘ►ⓞ from its inverse ⓞ–ᴘ►ⓢ, so by adding an inverse of an edge in E^+ to E^-, we can show that it is *not* fully expressive. On the other hand, models such as ComplEx [Trouillon et al., 2016], SimplE [Kazemi and Poole, 2018], and TuckER [Balazevic et al., 2019b] have been proven to be fully expressive given sufficient dimensionality; for example, TuckER [Balazevic et al., 2019b] with dimensions $d_r = |L|$ and $d_e = |V|$ trivially satisfies full expressivity since its core tensor $\mathcal{W}$ then has sufficient capacity to store the full one-hot encoding of any graph. This formal property is useful to show that the model does not have built-in limitations for numerically representing a graph, though of course in practice the dimensions needed to reach full expressivity are often impractical/undesirable.

We continue by first defining the conventions used in Table 5.1.

- We use $(\mathbf{x})_i$, $(\mathbf{X})_{ij}$, and $(\mathcal{X})_{i_1 \dots i_n}$ to denote elements of vectors, matrices, and tensors, respectively. If a vector $\mathbf{x} \in \mathbb{R}^a$ is used in a context that requires a matrix, the vector is interpreted as an $(a, 1)$-matrix (i.e., a column vector) and can be turned into a row vector (i.e., a $(1, a)$-matrix) using the transpose operation $\mathbf{x}^T$. We use $\mathbf{x}^D \in \mathbb{R}^{a,a}$ to denote the diagonal matrix with the values of the vector $\mathbf{x} \in \mathbb{R}^a$ on its diagonal. We denote the identity matrix by $\mathbf{I}$ such that if $j = k$, then $(\mathbf{I})_{jk} = 1$; otherwise $(\mathbf{I})_{jk} = 0$.

- We denote by $\begin{bmatrix} \mathbf{X}_1 \\ \vdots \\ \mathbf{X}_n \end{bmatrix}$ the vertical stacking of matrices $\mathbf{X}_1, \dots, \mathbf{X}_n$ with the same number of columns. Given a vector $\mathbf{x} \in \mathbb{R}^{ab}$, we denote by $\mathbf{x}^{[a,b]} \in \mathbb{R}^{a,b}$ the "reshaping" of $\mathbf{x}$ into an (a, b)-matrix such that $(\mathbf{x}^{[a,b]})_{ij} = (\mathbf{x})_{(i+a(j-1))}$. Conversely, given a matrix $\mathbf{X} \in \mathbb{R}^{a,b}$, we denote by $\text{vec}(\mathbf{X}) \in \mathbb{R}^{ab}$ the *vectorization* of $\mathbf{X}$ such that $\text{vec}(\mathbf{X})_k = (\mathbf{X})_{ij}$ where $i = ((k-1) \bmod m) + 1$ and $j = \frac{k-i}{m} + 1$ (observe that $\text{vec}(\mathbf{x}^{[a,b]}) = \mathbf{x}$).

- Given a tensor $\mathcal{X} \in \mathbb{R}^{a,b,c}$, we denote by $\mathcal{X}^{[i::]} \in \mathbb{R}^{b,c}$, the ith *slice* of tensor $\mathcal{X}$ along the first mode; for example, given $\mathcal{X} \in \mathbb{R}^{5,2,3}$, then $\mathcal{X}^{[4::]}$ returns the $(2, 3)$- matrix consisting of the elements $\begin{bmatrix} (\mathcal{X})_{411} & (\mathcal{X})_{412} & (\mathcal{X})_{413} \\ (\mathcal{X})_{421} & (\mathcal{X})_{422} & (\mathcal{X})_{423} \end{bmatrix}$. Analogously, we use $\mathcal{X}^{[:i:]} \in \mathbb{R}^{a,c}$ and $\mathcal{X}^{[::i]} \in \mathbb{R}^{b,c}$ to indicate the ith slice along the second and third modes of $\mathcal{X}$, respectively.

- We denote by $\psi(\mathcal{X})$ the element-wise application of a function ψ to the tensor $\mathcal{X}$, such that $(\psi(\mathcal{X}))_{in_1...i_n} = \psi(\mathcal{X}_{i_1...i_n})$. Common choices for ψ include a sigmoid function (e.g., the logistic function $\psi(x) = \frac{1}{1+e^{-x}}$ or the hyperbolic tangent function $\psi(x) = \tanh x = \frac{e^x - e^{-x}}{e^x + e^{-x}}$), the rectifier ($\psi(x) = \max(0, x)$), softplus ($\psi(x) = \ln(1 + e^x)$), etc.

We now define the operators used in Table 5.1, where the first and most elemental operation we consider is that of matrix multiplication.

Definition 5.8 Matrix multiplication. The *multiplication of matrices* $\mathbf{X} \in \mathbb{R}^{a,b}$ and $\mathbf{Y} \in \mathbb{R}^{b,c}$ is a matrix $\mathbf{XY} \in \mathbb{R}^{a,c}$ such that $(\mathbf{XY})_{ij} = \sum_{k=1}^{b}(\mathbf{X})_{ik}(\mathbf{Y})_{kj}$. The matrix multiplication of two tensors $\mathcal{X} \in \mathbb{R}^{a_1,...,a_m,c}$ and $\mathcal{Y} \in \mathbb{R}^{c,b_1,...,b_n}$ is a tensor $\mathcal{XY} \in \mathbb{R}^{a_1,...,a_m,b_1,...,b_n}$ such that $(\mathcal{XY})_{i_1...i_m i_{m+1}...i_{m+n}} = \sum_{k=1}^{c}(\mathcal{X})_{i_1...i_m k}(\mathcal{Y})_{k i_{m+1} i_{m+n}}$.

For convenience, we may implicitly add or remove modes with dimension 1 for the purposes of matrix multiplication and other operators; for example, given two vectors $\mathbf{x} \in \mathbb{R}^a$ and $\mathbf{y} \in \mathbb{R}^a$, we denote by $\mathbf{x}^\mathsf{T}\mathbf{y}$ (aka the dot or inner product) the multiplication of matrix $\mathbf{x}^\mathsf{T} \in \mathbb{R}^{1,a}$ with $\mathbf{y} \in \mathbb{R}^{a,1}$ such that $\mathbf{x}^\mathsf{T}\mathbf{y} \in \mathbb{R}^{1,1}$ (i.e., a scalar in $\mathbb{R}$); conversely, $\mathbf{xy}^\mathsf{T} \in \mathbb{R}^{a,a}$ (the outer product).

Constraints on embeddings are sometimes given as norms, defined next.

Definition 5.9 L^p-norm, $L^{p,q}$-norm. For $p \in \mathbb{R}$, the L^p-*norm* of a vector $\mathbf{x} \in \mathbb{R}^a$ is the scalar $\|\mathbf{x}\|_p = (|(\mathbf{x})_1|^p + \ldots + |(\mathbf{x})_a|^p)^{\frac{1}{p}}$, where $|(\mathbf{x})_i|$ denotes the absolute value of the ith element of $\mathbf{x}$. For $p, q \in \mathbb{R}$, the $L^{p,q}$-*norm* of a matrix $\mathbf{X} \in \mathbb{R}^{a,b}$ is the scalar $\|\mathbf{X}\|_{p,q} = \left(\sum_{j=1}^{b}\left(\sum_{i=1}^{a}|(\mathbf{X})_{ij}|^p\right)^{\frac{q}{p}}\right)^{\frac{1}{q}}$.

The L^1 norm (i.e., $\|\mathbf{x}\|_1$) is thus simply the sum of the absolute values of $\mathbf{x}$, while the L^2 norm (i.e., $\|\mathbf{x}\|_2$) is the (Euclidean) length of the vector. The Frobenius norm of the matrix $\mathbf{X}$ then equates to $\|\mathbf{X}\|_{2,2} = \left(\sum_{j=1}^{b} \left(\sum_{i=1}^{a} |(\mathbf{X})_{ij}|^2 \right) \right)^{\frac{1}{2}}$; i.e., the square root of the sum of the squares of all elements.

Another type of product used by embedding techniques is the Hadamard product, which multiplies tensors of the same dimension and computes their product in an element-wise manner.

Definition 5.10   Hadamard product.   Given two tensors $\mathcal{X} \in \mathbb{R}^{a_1,\dots,a_n}$ and $\mathcal{Y} \in \mathbb{R}^{a_1,\dots,a_n}$, the *Hadamard product* $\mathcal{X} \odot \mathcal{Y}$ is defined as a tensor in $\mathbb{R}^{a_1,\dots,a_n}$, with each element computed as $(\mathcal{X} \odot \mathcal{Y})_{i_1 \dots i_n} = (\mathcal{X})_{i_1 \dots i_n} (\mathcal{Y})_{i_1 \dots i_n}$.

Other embedding techniques—namely RotatE [Sun et al., 2019] and ComplEx [Trouillon et al., 2016]—uses *complex space* based on complex numbers. With a slight abuse of notation, the definitions of vectors, matrices and tensors can be modified by replacing the set of real numbers $\mathbb{R}$ by the set of complex numbers $\mathbb{C}$, giving rise to complex vectors, complex matrices, and complex tensors. In this case, we denote by $\mathrm{Re}(\cdot)$ the real part of a complex number. Given a complex vector $\mathbf{x} \in \mathbb{C}^I$, we denote by $\bar{\mathbf{x}}$ its complex conjugate (swapping the sign of the imaginary part of each element). Complex analogues of the aforementioned operators can then be defined by replacing the multiplication and addition of real numbers with the analogous operators for complex numbers, where RotatE [Sun et al., 2019] uses the complex Hadamard product, and ComplEx [Trouillon et al., 2016] uses complex matrix multiplication.

One embedding technique—MuRP [Balazevic et al., 2019a]—uses hyperbolic space, specifically based on the Poincaré ball. As this is the only embedding we cover that uses this space, and the formalisms are lengthy (covering the Poincaré ball, Möbius addition, Möbius matrix—vector multiplication, logarithmic maps, exponential maps, etc.), we rather refer the reader to the paper for further details [Balazevic et al., 2019a].

As discussed in Section 5.2, tensor decompositions are used for many embeddings, and at the heart of such decompositions is the tensor product, which is often used to reconstruct (an approximation of) the original tensor.

Definition 5.11   Tensor product.   Given two tensors $\mathcal{X} \in \mathbb{R}^{a_1,\dots,a_m}$ and $\mathcal{Y} \in \mathbb{R}^{b_1,\dots,b_n}$, the *tensor product* $\mathcal{X} \otimes \mathcal{Y}$ is defined as a tensor in $\mathbb{R}^{a_1,\dots,a_m,b_1,\dots,b_n}$, with each element computed as $(\mathcal{X} \otimes \mathcal{Y})_{i_1 \dots i_m j_1 \dots j_n} = (\mathcal{X})_{i_1 \dots i_m} (\mathcal{Y})_{j_1 \dots j_n}$.[a]

Example 5.12   Assume that $\mathcal{X} \in \mathbb{R}^{2,3}$ and $\mathcal{Y} \in \mathbb{R}^{3,4,5}$. Then $\mathcal{X} \otimes \mathcal{Y}$ will be a tensor in $\mathbb{R}^{2,3,3,4,5}$. Element $(\mathcal{X} \otimes \mathcal{Y})_{12345}$ will be the product of $(\mathcal{X})_{12}$ and $(\mathcal{Y})_{345}$.

An n-mode product is used by other embeddings to transform elements along a given mode of a tensor by computing a product with a given matrix along that particular mode of the tensor.

Definition 5.13 n-mode product. For a positive integer n, a tensor $\mathcal{X} \in \mathbb{R}^{a_1,\ldots,a_{n-1},a_n,a_{n+1},\ldots,a_m}$ and matrix $\mathbf{Y} \in \mathbb{R}^{b,a_n}$, the *n-mode product* of $\mathcal{X}$ and $\mathbf{Y}$ is the tensor $\mathcal{X} \otimes_n \mathbf{Y} \in \mathbb{R}^{a_1,\ldots,a_{n-1},b,a_{n+1},\ldots,a_m}$ such that $(\mathcal{X} \otimes_n \mathbf{Y})_{i_1\ldots i_{n-1} j i_{n+1}\ldots i_m} = \sum_{k=1}^{a_n} (\mathcal{X})_{i_1\ldots i_{n-1} k i_{n+1}\ldots i_m} (\mathbf{Y})_{jk}$.

Example 5.14 Let us assume that $\mathcal{X} \in \mathbb{R}^{2,3,4}$ and $\mathbf{Y} \in \mathbb{R}^{5,3}$. The result of $\mathcal{X} \otimes_2 \mathbf{Y}$ will be a tensor in $\mathbb{R}^{2,5,4}$, where, for example, $(\mathcal{X} \otimes_2 \mathbf{Y})_{142}$ will be given as $(\mathcal{X})_{112}(\mathbf{Y})_{41} + (\mathcal{X})_{122}(\mathbf{Y})_{42} + (\mathcal{X})_{132}(\mathbf{Y})_{43}$. Observe that if $\mathbf{y} \in \mathbb{R}^{a_n}$—i.e., if $\mathbf{y}$ is a (column) vector—then the n-mode tensor product $\mathcal{X} \otimes_n \mathbf{y}^\mathsf{T}$ "flattens" the nth mode of $\mathcal{X}$ to one dimension, effectively reducing the order of $\mathcal{X}$ by one.

One embedding technique—HolE [Nickel et al., 2016b]—uses the circular correlation operator $\mathbf{x} \star \mathbf{y}$, where each element is the sum of elements along a diagonal of the outer product $\mathbf{x} \otimes \mathbf{y}$ that "wraps" if not the primary diagonal.

Definition 5.15   Circular correlation. The *circular correlation* of vector $\mathbf{x} \in \mathbb{R}^a$ with $\mathbf{y} \in \mathbb{R}^a$ is the vector $\mathbf{x} \star \mathbf{y} \in \mathbb{R}^a$ such that $(\mathbf{x} \star \mathbf{y})_k = \sum_{i=1}^a (\mathbf{x})_i (\mathbf{y})_{(((k+i-2) \bmod a)+1)}$.

Example 5.16 Assuming $a = 5$, then $(\mathbf{x} \star \mathbf{y})_1 = (\mathbf{x})_1(\mathbf{y})_1 + (\mathbf{x})_2(\mathbf{y})_2 + (\mathbf{x})_3(\mathbf{y})_3 + (\mathbf{x})_4(\mathbf{y})_4 + (\mathbf{x})_5(\mathbf{y})_5$, or a case that wraps: $(\mathbf{x} \star \mathbf{y})_4 = (\mathbf{x})_1(\mathbf{y})_4 + (\mathbf{x})_2(\mathbf{y})_5 + (\mathbf{x})_3(\mathbf{y})_1 + (\mathbf{x})_4(\mathbf{y})_2 + (\mathbf{x})_5(\mathbf{y})_3$.

Finally, a couple of neural models that we include—namely ConvE [Dettmers et al., 2018] and HypER [Balazevic et al., 2019c]—are based on convolutional architectures using the convolution operator.

Definition 5.17   Convolution. Given two matrices $\mathbf{X} \in \mathbb{R}^{a,b}$ and $\mathbf{Y} \in \mathbb{R}^{e,f}$, the *convolution* of $\mathbf{X}$ and $\mathbf{Y}$ is the matrix $\mathbf{X} * \mathbf{Y} \in \mathbb{R}^{(a+e-1),(b+f-1)}$ such that $(\mathbf{X} * \mathbf{Y})_{ij} = \sum_{k=1}^a \sum_{l=1}^b (\mathbf{X})_{kl}(\mathbf{Y})_{(i+k-a)(j+l-b)}$.[b] In cases where $(i+k-a) < 1$, $(j+l-b) < 1$, $(i+k-a) > e$ or $(j+l-b) > f$ (i.e., where $(\mathbf{Y})_{(i+k-a)(j+l-b)}$ lies outside the bounds of $\mathbf{Y}$), we say that $(\mathbf{Y})_{(i+k-a)(j+l-b)} = 0$.

Intuitively speaking, the convolution operator overlays $\mathbf{X}$ in every possible way over $\mathbf{Y}$ such that at least one pair of elements $(\mathbf{X})_{ij}, (\mathbf{Y})_{lk}$ overlaps, summing the products of pairs of overlapping elements to generate an element of the result. Elements of $\mathbf{X}$ extending beyond $\mathbf{Y}$ are ignored (equivalently we can consider $\mathbf{Y}$ to be "zero-padded" outside its borders).

Example 5.18   Given $\mathbf{X} \in \mathbb{R}^{3,3}$ and $\mathbf{Y} \in \mathbb{R}^{4,5}$, then $\mathbf{X} * \mathbf{Y} \in \mathbb{R}^{6,7}$, where, for example, $(\mathbf{X} * \mathbf{Y})_{11} = (\mathbf{X})_{33}(\mathbf{Y})_{11}$ (with the bottom right corner of $\mathbf{X}$ overlapping the top left corner of $\mathbf{Y}$), while $(\mathbf{X} * \mathbf{Y})_{34} = (\mathbf{X})_{11}(\mathbf{Y})_{12} + (\mathbf{X})_{12}(\mathbf{Y})_{13} + (\mathbf{X})_{13}(\mathbf{Y})_{14} + (\mathbf{X})_{21}(\mathbf{Y})_{22} + (\mathbf{X})_{22}(\mathbf{Y})_{23} + (\mathbf{X})_{23}(\mathbf{Y})_{24} + (\mathbf{X})_{31}(\mathbf{Y})_{32} + (\mathbf{X})_{32}(\mathbf{Y})_{33} + (\mathbf{X})_{33}(\mathbf{Y})_{34}$ (with $(\mathbf{X})_{22}$—the center of $\mathbf{X}$—overlapping $(\mathbf{Y})_{23}$).[c]

In a convolution $\mathbf{X} * \mathbf{Y}$, the matrix $\mathbf{X}$ is often called the "kernel" (or "filter"). Often several kernels are used in order to apply multiple convolutions. Given a tensor $\mathcal{X} \in \mathbb{R}^{c,a,b}$ (representing c (a, b)-kernels) and a matrix $\mathbf{Y} \in \mathbb{R}^{e,f}$, we denote by $\mathcal{X} * \mathbf{Y} \in \mathbb{R}^{c,(a+e-1),(b+f-1)}$ the result of the convolutions of the c first-mode slices of $\mathcal{X}$ over $\mathbf{Y}$ such that $(\mathcal{X} * \mathbf{Y})^{[i::]} = \mathcal{X}^{[i::]} * \mathbf{Y}$ for $1 \leq i \leq c$, yielding a tensor of results for c convolutions.

[a]Please note that "⊗" is used here in an unrelated sense to its use in Definition 3.13.

[b]We define the convolution operator per the widely used convention for convolutional neural networks. Strictly speaking, the operator should be called *cross-correlation*, where traditional convolution requires the matrix $\mathbf{X}$ to be initially "rotated" by $180°$. Since in our settings the matrix $\mathbf{X}$ is learned, rather than given, the rotation is redundant, and hence the distinction is not important.

[c]Models applying convolutions may differ regarding how edge cases are handled, or on the "stride" of the convolution applied, where, for example, a stride of 3 for $(\mathbf{X} * \mathbf{Y})$ would see the kernel $\mathbf{X}$ centered only on elements $(\mathbf{Y})_{ij}$ such that $i \bmod 3 = 0$ and $j \bmod 3 = 0$, reducing the number of output elements by a factor of 9. We do not consider such details here.

5.2.2   LANGUAGE MODELS

Embedding techniques were first explored as a way to represent natural language within machine learning frameworks, with word2vec [Mikolov et al., 2013] and GloVe [Pennington et al., 2014] being two seminal approaches. Both approaches compute embeddings for words based on large corpora of text such that words used in similar contexts (e.g., "frog," "toad") have similar vectors. Word2vec uses neural networks trained either to predict the current word from surrounding words (*continuous bag of words*), or to predict the surrounding words given the current word (*continuous skip-gram*). GloVe rather applies a regression model over a matrix of co-occurrence probabilities of word pairs. Embeddings generated by both approaches have become widely used in natural language processing tasks.

Another approach for graph embeddings is thus to leverage proven approaches for language embeddings. However, while a graph consists of an unordered set of sequences of three terms (i.e., a set of edges), text in natural language consists of arbitrary-length sequences of terms (i.e., sentences of words). RDF2Vec [Ristoski and Paulheim, 2016] thus performs (biased [Cochez et al., 2017a]) random walks on the graph and records the paths (the se-

Table 5.1: Details for selected knowledge graph embeddings, including the plausibility scoring function $\phi(\varepsilon(s), \rho(p), \varepsilon(o))$ for edge $\circledcirc\text{-}p\text{-}\blacktriangleright\circledcirc$, and other conditions

Model	$\phi(\varepsilon(s), \rho(p), \varepsilon(o))$	Conditions (for all $x \in V, y \in L$)
TransE	$-\|\mathbf{e}_s + \mathbf{r}_p - \mathbf{e}_o\|_q$	$\mathbf{e}_x \in \mathbb{R}^d, \mathbf{r}_y \in \mathbb{R}^d, q \in \{1, 2\}, \|\mathbf{e}_x\|_2 = 1$
TransH	$-\|(\mathbf{e}_s - (\mathbf{e}_s^\mathsf{T}\mathbf{w}_p)\mathbf{w}_p) + \mathbf{r}_p - (\mathbf{e}_o - (\mathbf{e}_o^\mathsf{T}\mathbf{w}_p)\mathbf{w}_p)\|_2^2$	$\mathbf{e}_x \in \mathbb{R}^d, \mathbf{r}_y \in \mathbb{R}^d, \mathbf{w}_y \in \mathbb{R}^d, \|\mathbf{w}_y\|_2 = 1,$ $\dfrac{\mathbf{w}_y^\mathsf{T}\mathbf{r}_y}{\|\mathbf{r}_y\|_2} \approx 0, \|\mathbf{e}_x\|_2 \leq 1$
TransR	$-\|\mathbf{W}_p\mathbf{e}_s + \mathbf{r}_p - \mathbf{W}_p\mathbf{e}_o\|_2^2$	$\mathbf{e}_x \in \mathbb{R}^{d_e}, \mathbf{r}_y \in \mathbb{R}^{d_r}, \mathbf{w}_y \in \mathbb{R}^{d_r, d_e}, \|\mathbf{e}_x\|_2 \leq 1,$ $\|\mathbf{r}_y\|_2 \leq 1, \|\mathbf{W}_y\mathbf{e}_x\|_2 \leq 1$
TransD	$-\|(\mathbf{w}_p \otimes \mathbf{w}_s + \mathbf{I})\mathbf{e}_s + \mathbf{r}_p - (\mathbf{w}_p \otimes \mathbf{w}_o + \mathbf{I})\mathbf{e}_o\|_2^2$	$\mathbf{e}_x \in \mathbb{R}^{d_e}, \mathbf{r}_y \in \mathbb{R}^{d_r}, \mathbf{w}_x \in \mathbb{R}^{d_e}, \mathbf{w}_y \in \mathbb{R}^{d_r},$ $\|\mathbf{e}_x\|_2 \leq 1, \|\mathbf{r}_y\|_2 \leq 1, \|(\mathbf{w}_y \otimes \mathbf{w}_x + \mathbf{I})\mathbf{e}_x\|_2 \leq 1$
RotatE	$-\|\mathbf{e}_s \odot \mathbf{r}_p - \mathbf{e}_o\|_2$	$\mathbf{e}_x \in \mathbb{C}^d, \mathbf{r}_y \in \mathbb{C}^d, \|\mathbf{r}_y\|_2 = 1$
RESCAL	$\mathbf{e}_s^\mathsf{T}\mathbf{R}_p\mathbf{e}_o$	$\mathbf{e}_x \in \mathbb{R}^d, \mathbf{R}_y \in \mathbb{R}^{d,d}, \|\mathbf{e}_x\|_2 \leq 1, \|\mathbf{R}_y\|_{2,2} \leq 1$
DistMult	$\mathbf{e}_s^\mathsf{T}\mathbf{r}_p^\mathrm{D}\mathbf{e}_o$	$\mathbf{e}_x \in \mathbb{R}^d, \mathbf{r}_y \in \mathbb{R}^d, \|\mathbf{e}_x\|_2 = 1, \|\mathbf{r}_y\|_2 \leq 1$
HolE	$\mathbf{e}_p^\mathsf{T}(\mathbf{e}_s \star \mathbf{e}_o)$	$\mathbf{e}_x \in \mathbb{R}^d, \mathbf{r}_y \in \mathbb{R}^d, \|\mathbf{e}_x\|_2 \leq 1, \|\mathbf{r}_y\|_2 \leq 1$
ComplEx	$\mathrm{Re}(\mathbf{e}_s^\mathsf{T}\mathbf{r}_p^\mathrm{D}\bar{\mathbf{e}}_o)$	$\mathbf{e}_x \in \mathbb{C}^d, \mathbf{r}_y \in \mathbb{C}^d, \|\mathbf{e}_x\|_2 \leq 1, \|\mathbf{r}_y\|_2 \leq 1$
SimplE	$\dfrac{\mathbf{e}_s^\mathsf{T}\mathbf{r}_p^\mathrm{D}\mathbf{w}_o + \mathbf{e}_o^\mathsf{T}\mathbf{w}_p^\mathrm{D}\mathbf{w}_s}{2}$	$\mathbf{e}_x \in \mathbb{R}^d, \mathbf{r}_y \in \mathbb{R}^d, \mathbf{w}_x \in \mathbb{R}^d, \mathbf{w}_y \in \mathbb{R}^d,$ $\|\mathbf{e}_x\|_2 \leq 1, \|\mathbf{w}_x\|_2 \leq 1, \|\mathbf{r}_y\|_2 \leq 1, \|\mathbf{w}_y\|_2 \leq 1$
TuckER	$\mathcal{W} \otimes_1 \mathbf{e}_s^\mathsf{T} \otimes_2 \mathbf{r}_p^\mathsf{T} \otimes_3 \mathbf{e}_o^\mathsf{T}$	$\mathbf{e}_x \in \mathbb{R}^{d_e}, \mathbf{r}_y \in \mathbb{R}^{d_r}, \mathcal{W} \in \mathbb{R}^{d_e, d_r, d_e}$
SME L.	$(\mathbf{V}\mathbf{e}_s + \mathbf{V}'\mathbf{r}_p + \mathbf{v})^\mathsf{T}(\mathbf{W}\mathbf{e}_o + \mathbf{W}'\mathbf{r}_p + \mathbf{w})$	$\mathbf{e}_x \in \mathbb{R}^d, \mathbf{r}_y \in \mathbb{R}^d, \mathbf{v} \in \mathbb{R}^w, \mathbf{w} \in \mathbb{R}^w, \|\mathbf{e}_x\|_2 = 1,$ $\mathbf{V} \in \mathbb{R}^{w,d}, \mathbf{V}' \in \mathbb{R}^{w,d}, \mathbf{W} \in \mathbb{R}^{w,d}, \mathbf{W}' \in \mathbb{R}^{w,d}$
SME Bi.	$((\mathcal{V} \otimes_3 \mathbf{r}_p^\mathsf{T})\mathbf{e}_s + \mathbf{v})^\mathsf{T}(\mathcal{W} \otimes_3 \mathbf{r}_p^\mathsf{T})\mathbf{e}_o + \mathbf{w})$	$\mathbf{e}_x \in \mathbb{R}^d, \mathbf{r}_y \in \mathbb{R}^d, \mathbf{v} \in \mathbb{R}^w, \mathbf{w} \in \mathbb{R}^w, \|\mathbf{e}_x\|_2 = 1,$ $\mathcal{V} \in \mathbb{R}^{w,d,d}, \mathcal{W} \in \mathbb{R}^{w,d,d}$
NTN	$\mathbf{r}_p^\mathsf{T}\psi\left(\mathbf{e}_s^\mathsf{T}\mathcal{W}\mathbf{e}_o + \mathbf{W}\begin{bmatrix}\mathbf{e}_s\\\mathbf{e}_o\end{bmatrix} + \mathbf{w}\right)$	$\mathbf{e}_x \in \mathbb{R}^d, \mathbf{r}_y \in \mathbb{R}^d, \mathbf{w} \in \mathbb{R}^w, \mathbf{W} \in \mathbb{R}^{w,2d},$ $\mathcal{W} \in \mathbb{R}^{d,w,d}, \|\mathbf{e}_x\|_2 \leq 1, \|\mathbf{r}_y\|_2 \leq 1, \|\mathbf{w}\|_2 \leq 1,$ $\|\mathbf{W}\|_{2,2} \leq 1, \|\mathcal{W}_{1 \leq i \leq w}^{[:,i,:]}\|_{2,2} \leq 1$
MLP	$\mathbf{v}^\mathsf{T}\psi\left(\mathbf{W}\begin{bmatrix}\mathbf{e}_s\\\mathbf{r}_p\\\mathbf{e}_o\end{bmatrix} + \mathbf{w}\right)$	$\mathbf{e}_x \in \mathbb{R}^d, \mathbf{r}_y \in \mathbb{R}^d, \mathbf{v} \in \mathbb{R}^w, \mathbf{w} \in \mathbb{R}^w, \mathbf{W} \in \mathbb{R}^{w,3d},$ $\|\mathbf{e}_x\|_2 \leq 1, \|\mathbf{r}_y\|_2 \leq 1$
ConvE	$\psi\left(\mathrm{vec}\left(\psi\left(\mathcal{W} * \begin{bmatrix}\mathbf{e}_s^{[a,b]}\\\mathbf{r}_p^{[a,b]}\end{bmatrix}\right)\right)^\mathsf{T}\mathbf{W}\right)\mathbf{e}_o$	$\mathbf{e}_x \in \mathbb{R}^d, \mathbf{r}_y \in \mathbb{R}^d, d = ab,$ $\mathbf{W} \in \mathbb{R}^{w_1(w_2+2a-1)(w_3+b-1),d}, \mathcal{W} \in \mathbb{R}^{w_1,w_2,w_3}$
HypER	$\psi(\mathrm{vec}\,(\mathbf{r}_p^\mathsf{T}\mathcal{W} * \mathbf{e}_s)^\mathsf{T}\mathbf{W})\mathbf{e}_o$	$\mathbf{e}_x \in \mathbb{R}^{d_e}, \mathbf{r}_y \in \mathbb{R}^{d_r}, \mathbf{W} \in \mathbb{R}^{w_2(w_1+d_e-1),d_e},$ $\mathcal{W} \in \mathbb{R}^{d_r,w_1,w_2}$

quence of nodes and edge labels traversed) as "sentences," which are then fed as input into the word2vec [Mikolov et al., 2013] model. An example of such a path extracted from Figure 5.2 might be, for example, (San Pedro)—bus→(Calama)—flight→(Iquique)—flight→(Santiago), where the paper experiments with 500 paths of length 8 per entity. RDF2Vec also proposes a second mode where sequences are generated for nodes from canonically-labeled sub-trees of which they are a root node, where sub-trees of depth 1 and 2 are used for experiments. KGloVe [Cochez et al., 2017b] is rather based on GloVe. Given that the original GloVe model [Pennington et al., 2014] considers words that co-occur frequently in windows of text to be more related, KGloVe uses personalized PageRank[8] to determine the most related nodes to a given node, which are fed into the GloVe model.

5.2.3 ENTAILMENT-AWARE MODELS

The embeddings thus far consider the data graph alone. But what if an ontology or set of rules is provided? Such deductive knowledge could be used to improve the embeddings. One approach is to use constraint rules to refine the predictions made by embeddings; for example, Wang et al. [2015] use functional and inverse-functional definitions as constraints (under UNA) such that, for example, if we define that an event can have at most one value for venue, this is used to lower the plausibility of edges that would assign multiple venues to an event.

More recent approaches rather propose joint embeddings that consider both the data graph and rules when computing embeddings. KALE [Guo et al., 2016] computes entity and relation embeddings using a translational model (specifically TransE) that is adapted to further consider rules using *t-norm fuzzy logics*. With reference to Figure 5.2, consider a simple rule (?x)—bus→(?y) $\Rightarrow$ (?x)—connects to→(?y). We can use embeddings to assign plausibility scores to new edges, such as e_1: (Piedras Rojas)—bus→(Moon Valley). We can further apply the previous rule to generate a new edge e_2: (Piedras Rojas)—connects to→(Moon Valley) from the predicted edge e_1. But what plausibility should we assign to this second edge? Letting p_1 and p_2 be the current plausibility scores of e_1 and e_2 (initialized using the standard embedding), then t-norm fuzzy logics suggests that the plausibility be updated as $p_1 p_2 - p_1 + 1$. Embeddings are then trained to jointly assign larger plausibility scores to positive examples versus negative examples of both edges and *ground rules*. An example of a positive ground rule based on Figure 5.2 would be (Arica)—bus→(San Pedro) $\Rightarrow$ (Arica)—connects to→(San Pedro). Negative ground rules randomly replace the relation in the head of the rule; for example, (Arica)—bus→(San Pedro) $\nRightarrow$ (Arica)—flight→(San Pedro). Guo et al. [2018] later propose RUGE, which uses a joint model over ground rules (possibly soft rules with confidence scores) and plausibility scores to align both forms of scoring for unseen edges.

Generating ground rules can be costly. An alternative approach, called FSL [Demeester et al., 2016], observes that in the case of a simple rule, such as (?x)—bus→(?y) $\Rightarrow$ (?x)—connects to→(?y), the

---

[8]Intuitively speaking, personalized PageRank starts at a given node and then determines the probability of a random walk being at a particular node after a given number of steps. A higher number of steps converges toward standard PageRank emphasizing global node centrality in the graph, while a lower number emphasizes proximity/relatedness to the starting node.

relation embedding bus should always return a lower plausibility than connects to. Thus, for all such rules, FSL proposes to train relation embeddings while avoiding violations of such inequalities. While relatively straightforward, FSL only supports simple rules, while KALE also supports more complex rules.

These works exemplify how deductive and inductive forms of knowledge—in this case rules and embeddings—can interplay and complement each other.

5.3   GRAPH NEURAL NETWORKS

While embeddings aim to provide a dense numerical representation of graphs suitable for use within existing machine learning models, another approach is to build custom machine learning models adapted for graph-structured data. Most custom learning models for graphs are based on (artificial) neural networks [Wu et al., 2019], exploiting a natural correspondence between both: a neural network already corresponds to a weighted, directed graph, where nodes serve as artificial neurons, and edges serve as weighted connections (axons). However, the typical topology of a traditional neural network—more specifically, a fully-connected feed-forward neural network—is quite homogeneous, being defined in terms of sequential layers of nodes where each node in one layer is connected to all nodes in the next layer. Conversely, the topology of a data graph is quite heterogeneous, being determined by the relations between entities that its edges represent.

A *graph neural network* (GNN) [Scarselli et al., 2009] builds a neural network based on the topology of the data graph, i.e., nodes are connected to their neighbors per the data graph. Typically a model is then learned to map input features for nodes to output features in a supervised manner; output features of the example nodes used for training may be manually labeled, or may be taken from the knowledge graph. Unlike knowledge graph embeddings, GNNs support end-to-end supervised learning for specific tasks: given a set of labeled examples, GNNs can be used to classify elements of the graph or the graph itself. GNNs have been used to perform classification over graphs encoding compounds, objects in images, documents, etc.; as well as to predict traffic, build recommender systems, verify software, etc. [Wu et al., 2019]. Given labeled examples, GNNs can even replace graph algorithms; for example, GNNs have been used to find central nodes in knowledge graphs in a supervised manner [Park et al., 2019, 2020, Scarselli et al., 2009].

We now discuss the ideas underlying two main flavors of GNN, specifically, *recursive GNNs* and *non-recursive GNNs*.

5.3.1   RECURSIVE GRAPH NEURAL NETWORKS

Recursive graph neural networks (RecGNNs) are the seminal approach to graph neural networks [Scarselli et al., 2009, Sperduti and Starita, 1997]. The approach is conceptually similar to the systolic abstraction illustrated in Figure 5.3, where messages are passed between neighbors toward recursively computing some result. However, rather than define the functions used to decide the messages to pass, we rather label the output of a training set of nodes and let the framework learn the functions that generate the expected output, thereafter applying them to label other examples.

In a seminal paper, Scarselli et al. [2009] proposed what they generically call a graph neural network (GNN), which takes as input a directed graph where nodes and edges are associated with *feature vectors* that can capture node and edge labels, weights, etc. These feature vectors remain fixed throughout the process. Each node in the graph is also associated with a *state vector*, which is recursively updated based on information from the node's neighbors—i.e., the feature and state vectors of the neighboring nodes and the feature vectors of the edges extending to/from them—using a parametric function, called the *transition function*. A second parametric function, called the *output function*, is used to compute the final output for a node based on its own feature and state vector. These functions are applied recursively up to a fixpoint. Both parametric functions can be implemented using neural networks where, given a partial set of *supervised nodes* in the graph—i.e., nodes labeled with their desired output—parameters for the transition and output functions can be learned that best approximate the supervised outputs. The result can thus be seen as a recursive neural network architecture.[9] To ensure convergence up to a fixpoint, certain restrictions are applied, namely that the transition function be a *contractor*, meaning that upon each application of the function, points in the numeric space are brought closer together (intuitively, in this case, the numeric space "shrinks" upon each application, ensuring convergence to a unique fixpoint).

To illustrate, consider, for example, that we wish to find priority locations for creating new tourist information offices. A good strategy would be to install them in hubs from which many tourists visit popular destinations. Along these lines, in Figure 5.7 we illustrate the GNN architecture proposed by Scarselli et al. [2009] for a sub-graph of Figure 5.2, where we highlight the neighborhood of (Punta Arenas). In this graph, nodes are annotated with feature vectors ($\mathbf{n}_x$) and hidden states at step t ($\mathbf{h}_x^{(t)}$), while edges are annotated with feature vectors ($\mathbf{a}_{xy}$). Feature vectors for nodes may, for example, one-hot encode the type of node (*City*, *Attraction*, etc.), directly encode statistics such as the number of tourists visiting per year, etc. Feature vectors for edges may, for example, one-hot encode the edge label (the type of transport), directly encode statistics such as the distance or number of tickets sold per year, etc. Hidden states can be randomly initialized. The right-hand side of Figure 5.7 provides the GNN transition and output functions, where $\mathrm{N}(x)$ denotes the neighboring nodes of x, $f_{\mathbf{w}}(\cdot)$ denotes the transition function with parameters $\mathbf{w}$, and $g_{\mathbf{w}'}(\cdot)$ denotes the output function with parameters $\mathbf{w}'$. An example is also provided for Punta Arenas ($x = 1$). These functions will be recursively applied until a fixpoint is reached. To train the network, we can label examples of places that already have (or should have) tourist offices and places that do (or should) not have tourist offices. These labels may be taken from the knowledge graph, or may be added manually. The GNN can then learn parameters $\mathbf{w}$

---

[9]Some authors refer to such architectures as *recurrent graph neural networks*, observing that the internal state maintained for nodes can be viewed as a form of recurrence over a sequence of transitions.

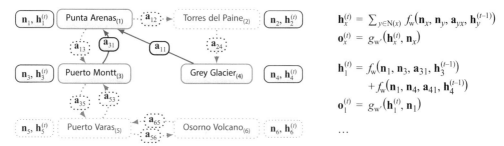

$$\mathbf{h}_x^{(t)} = \sum_{y \in \mathrm{N}(x)} f_\mathbf{w}(\mathbf{n}_x, \mathbf{n}_y, \mathbf{a}_{yx}, \mathbf{h}_y^{(t-1)})$$
$$\mathbf{o}_x^{(t)} = g_{\mathbf{w}'}(\mathbf{h}_x^{(t)}, \mathbf{n}_x)$$

$$\mathbf{h}_1^{(t)} = f_\mathbf{w}(\mathbf{n}_1, \mathbf{n}_3, \mathbf{a}_{31}, \mathbf{h}_3^{(t-1)})$$
$$\qquad + f_\mathbf{w}(\mathbf{n}_1, \mathbf{n}_4, \mathbf{a}_{41}, \mathbf{h}_4^{(t-1)})$$
$$\mathbf{o}_1^{(t)} = g_{\mathbf{w}'}(\mathbf{h}_1^{(t)}, \mathbf{n}_1)$$

...

Figure 5.7: On the left, a sub-graph of Figure 5.2 highlighting the neighborhood of Punta Arenas, where nodes are annotated with feature vectors ($\mathbf{n}_x$) and hidden states at step t ($\mathbf{h}_x^{(t)}$), and edges are annotated with feature vectors ($\mathbf{a}_{xy}$); on the right, the GNN transition and output functions proposed by Scarselli et al. [2009] and an example for Punta Arenas ($x = 1$), where $\mathrm{N}(x)$ denotes the neighboring nodes of x, $f_\mathbf{w}(\cdot)$ denotes the transition function with parameters $\mathbf{w}$ and $g_{\mathbf{w}'}(\cdot)$ denotes the output function with parameters $\mathbf{w}'$.

and $\mathbf{w}'$ that give the expected output for the labeled examples, which can subsequently be used to label other nodes.

This GNN model is flexible and can be adapted in various ways [Scarselli et al., 2009]: we may define neighboring nodes differently, for example to include nodes for outgoing edges, or nodes one or two hops away; we may allow pairs of nodes to be connected by multiple edges with different vectors; we may consider transition and output functions with distinct parameters for each node; we may add states and outputs for edges; we may change the sum to another aggregation function; etc.

We now define a recursive graph neural network. We assume that the GNN accepts a directed vector-labeled graph as input (see Definition 5.1).

Definition 5.19   Recursive graph neural network.   A *recursive graph neural network* (*RecGNN*) is a pair of functions $\mathfrak{R} = (\textsc{Agg}, \textsc{Out})$, such that (with $a, b, c \in \mathbb{N}$):

- $\textsc{Agg} : \mathbb{R}^a \times 2^{(\mathbb{R}^a \times \mathbb{R}^b) \to \mathbb{N}} \to \mathbb{R}^a$

- $\textsc{Out} : \mathbb{R}^a \to \mathbb{R}^c$

The function $\textsc{Agg}$ computes a new feature vector for a node, given its previous feature vector and the feature vectors of the nodes and edges forming its neighborhood; the function $\textsc{Out}$ transforms the final feature vector computed by $\textsc{Agg}$ for a node to the output vector for that node. We assume that a and b correspond to the dimensions of the input node and edge vectors, respectively, while c denotes the dimension of the output vector for each node.

Given a RecGNN $\mathfrak{R} = (\textsc{Agg}, \textsc{Out})$, a directed vector-labeled graph $G = (V, E, F, \lambda)$, and a node $u \in V$, we define the output vector assigned to node u in G by $\mathfrak{R}$ (written $\mathfrak{R}(G, u)$) as follows. First, let $\mathbf{n}_u^{(0)} = \lambda(u)$. For all $i \geq 1$, let:

$$\mathbf{n}_u^{(i)} = \textsc{Agg}\left(\mathbf{n}_u^{(i-1)}, \{(\mathbf{n}_v^{(i-1)}, \lambda(v, u)) \mid (v, u) \in E\}\right).$$

If $j \geq 1$ is an integer such that $\mathbf{n}_u^{(j)} = \mathbf{n}_u^{(j-1)}$ for all $u \in V$, then $\mathfrak{R}(G, u) = \textsc{Out}(\mathbf{n}_u^{(j)})$.

In a RecGNN, the same aggregation function (\textsc{Agg}) is applied recursively until a fixpoint is reached, at which point an output function (\textsc{Out}) creates the final output vector for each node. While in practice RecGNNs will often consider a static feature vector and a dynamic state vector [Scarselli et al., 2009], we can more concisely encode this as one vector, where part may remain static throughout the aggregation process representing input features, and part may be dynamically computed representing the state. In practice, \textsc{Agg} and \textsc{Out} are often based on parametric combinations of vectors, with the parameters learned based on a sample of output vectors for labeled nodes.

Example 5.20   The aggregation function for the GNN of Scarselli et al. [2009] is given as:

$$\textsc{Agg}(\mathbf{n}_u, N) = \sum_{(\mathbf{n}_v, \mathbf{a}_{vu}) \in N} f_\mathbf{w}(\mathbf{n}_u, \mathbf{n}_v, \mathbf{a}_{vu})$$

where $f_\mathbf{w}(\cdot)$ is a contraction function with parameters $\mathbf{w}$. The output function is defined as:

$$\textsc{Out}(\mathbf{n}_u) = g_{\mathbf{w}'}(\mathbf{n}_u)$$

where again $g_{\mathbf{w}'}(\cdot)$ is a function with parameters $\mathbf{w}'$. Given a set of nodes labeled with their expected output vectors, the parameters $\mathbf{w}$ and $\mathbf{w}'$ are learned.

There are notable similarities between graph parallel frameworks (GPFs; see Definition 5.3) and RecGNNs. While we defined GPFs using separate \textsc{Msg} and \textsc{Agg} functions, this is not essential: conceptually they could be defined in a similar way to RecGNN, with a single \textsc{Agg} function that "pulls" information from its neighbors (we maintain \textsc{Msg} to more closely reflect how GPFs are defined/implemented in practice). The key difference between GPFs and GNNs is that in the former, the functions are defined by the user, while in the latter, the functions are generally learned from labeled examples. Another difference arises from the termination condition present in GPFs, though often the GPF's termination condition will—like in RecGNNs—reflect convergence to a fixpoint.

5.3.2 NON-RECURSIVE GRAPH NEURAL NETWORKS

GNNs can also be defined in a non-recursive manner, where a fixed number of layers are applied over the input in order to generate the output. A benefit of this approach is that we do not need to worry about convergence since the process is non-recursive. Also, each layer will often have independent parameters, representing different transformation steps. Naively, a downside is that adding many layers could give rise to a high number of parameters. Addressing this problem, a popular approach for non-recursive GNNs is to use convolutional neural networks.

Convolutional neural networks (CNNs) have gained a lot of attention, in particular, for machine learning tasks involving images [Krizhevsky et al., 2017]. The core idea in the image setting is to train and apply small kernels (aka filters) over localized regions of an image using a convolution operator to extract features from that local region. When applied to all local regions, the convolution outputs a feature map of the image. Since the kernels are small, and are applied multiple times to different regions of the input, the number of parameters to train is reduced. Typically multiple kernels can thus be applied, forming multiple convolutional layers.

One may note that in GNNs and CNNs, operators are applied over local regions of the input data. In the case of GNNs, the transition function is applied over a node and its neighbors in the graph. In the case of CNNs, the convolution is applied on a pixel and its neighbors in the image. Following this intuition, a number of *convolutional graph neural networks (ConvGNNs)* [Bruna et al., 2014, Kipf and Welling, 2017, Wu et al., 2019] have been proposed, where the transition function is implemented by means of convolutions. A key consideration for ConvGNNs is how regions of a graph are defined. Unlike the pixels of an image, nodes in a graph may have varying numbers of neighbors. This creates a challenge: a benefit of CNNs is that the same kernel can be applied over all the regions of an image, but this requires more careful consideration in the case of ConvGNNs since neighborhoods of different nodes can be diverse. Approaches to address these challenges involve working with spectral (e.g., Bruna et al. [2014], Kipf and Welling [2017]) or spatial (e.g., Monti et al. [2017]) representations of graphs that induce a more regular structure from the graph. An alternative is to use an attention mechanism [Velickovic et al., 2018] to *learn* the nodes whose features are most important to the current node.

Next, we abstractly define a non-recursive GNN.

Definition 5.21 Non-recursive graph neural network. A *non-recursive graph neural network* (NRecGNN) with l layers is an l-tuple of functions $\mathfrak{N} = (\text{Agg}^{(1)}, \ldots, \text{Agg}^{(l)})$, such that, for $1 \leq k \leq l$ (with $a_0, \ldots a_l, b \in \mathbb{N}$), $\text{Agg}^{(k)} : \mathbb{R}^{a_{k-1}} \times 2^{(\mathbb{R}^{a_{k-1}} \times \mathbb{R}^b) \to \mathbb{N}} \to \mathbb{R}^{a_k}$.

Each function $\text{Agg}^{(k)}$ (as before) computes a new feature vector for a node, given its previous feature vector and the feature vectors of the nodes and edges forming its neighborhood. We assume that a_0 and b correspond to the dimensions of the input node and edge vectors, respectively, where each function $\textsc{Agg}^{(k)}$ for $2 \leq k \leq l$ accepts as input node vectors of the same dimension as the output of the function $\textsc{Agg}^{(k-1)}$. Given an NRecGNN $\mathfrak{N} = (\textsc{Agg}^{(1)}, \ldots, \textsc{Agg}^{(l)})$, a directed vector-labeled graph $G = (V, E, F, \lambda)$, and a node $u \in V$, we define the output vector assigned to node u in G by $\mathfrak{N}$ (written $\mathfrak{N}(G, u)$) as follows. First let $\mathbf{n}_u^{(0)} = \lambda(u)$. For all $i \geq 1$, let:

$$\mathbf{n}_u^{(i)} = \textsc{Agg}^{(i)} \left(\mathbf{n}_u^{(i-1)}, \{\!\!\{ (\mathbf{n}_v^{(i-1)}, \lambda(v, u)) \mid (v, u) \in E \}\!\!\} \right)$$

Then $\mathfrak{N}(G, u) = \mathbf{n}_u^{(l)}$.

In an l-layer NRecGNN, a different aggregation function can be applied at each step (i.e., in each layer), up to a fixed number of steps l. We do not consider a separate Out function as it can be combined with the final aggregation function $\textsc{Agg}^{(l)}$. When the aggregation functions use a convolutional operator based on kernels learned from labeled examples, we call the result a *convolutional graph neural network* (*ConvGNN*). We refer to the survey by Wu et al. [2019] for discussion of ConvGNNs proposed in the literature.

We have considered GNNs that define the neighborhood of a node based on its incoming edges. These definitions can be adapted to also consider outgoing neighbors by either adding inverse edges to the directed vector-labeled graph in pre-processing, or by adding outgoing neighbors as arguments to the $\textsc{Agg}(\cdot)$ function. More generally, GNNs (and indeed GPFs) relying solely on the neighborhood of each node have limited expressivity in terms of their ability to distinguish nodes and graphs [Xu et al., 2019]; for example, Barceló et al. [2020] show that such NRecGNNs have a similar expressiveness for classifying nodes as the $\mathcal{ALCQ}$ Description Logic discussed in Section 4.2.2. More expressive GNN variants have been proposed that allow the aggregation functions to access and update a globally shared vector [Barceló et al., 2020]. We refer to the papers by Xu et al. [2019] and Barceló et al. [2020] for further discussion.

5.4   SYMBOLIC LEARNING

The supervised techniques discussed thus far—namely knowledge graph embeddings and graph neural networks—learn numerical models over graphs. However, such models are often difficult to explain or understand. For example, taking the graph of Figure 5.8, knowledge graph embeddings might predict the edge $\boxed{\text{SCL}}\!-\!\text{flight}\!\rightarrow\!\boxed{\text{ARI}}$ as being highly plausible, but they will not provide an interpretable model to help understand why this is the case: the reason for the result may lie in a matrix of parameters learned to fit a plausibility score on training data. Such approaches also suffer from the *out-of-vocabulary* problem, where they are unable to provide results for edges involving previously unseen nodes or edges; for example, if we add an edge $\boxed{\text{SCL}}\!-\!\text{flight}\!\rightarrow\!\boxed{\text{CDG}}$, where $\boxed{\text{CDG}}$ is new to the graph, a knowledge graph embedding will not have the entity embed-

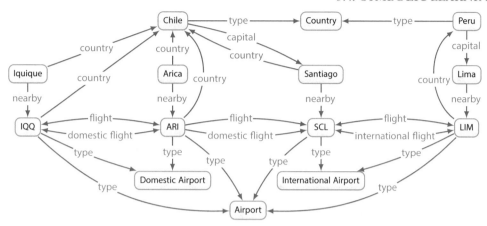

Figure 5.8: A directed edge-labeled graph describing flights between airports.

ding for (CDG) and would need to be retrained in order to estimate the plausibility of an edge
(CDG)—flight→(SCL).

An alternative (sometimes complementary) approach is to adopt *symbolic learning* in order to learn *hypotheses* in a symbolic (logical) language that "explain" a given set of positive
and negative edges. These edges are typically generated from the knowledge graph in an automatic manner (similar to the case of knowledge graph embeddings). The hypotheses then
serve as interpretable models that can be used for further deductive reasoning. Given the graph
of Figure 5.8, we may, for example, learn the rule (?x)—flight→(?y) ⇒ (?y)—flight→(?x) from observing
that flight routes tend to be return routes. Alternatively, rather than learn rules, we might learn
a DL axiom from the graph stating that airports are either domestic, international, or both:
Airport ⊑ DomesticAirport ⊔ InternationalAirport. Such rules and axioms can then be
used for deductive reasoning, and offer an interpretable model for new knowledge that is en-
tailed/predicted; for example, from the aforementioned rule for return flights, one can interpret
why a novel edge (SCL)—flight→(ARI) is predicted. This further offers domain experts the opportunity
to verify the models—e.g., the rules and axioms—derived by such processes. Finally, rules/ax-
ioms are quantified (*all* flights have a return flight, *all* airports are domestic or international,
etc.), so they can be applied to unseen examples (e.g., with the aforementioned rule, we can
derive (CDG)—flight→(SCL) from a new edge (SCL)—flight→(CDG) with the unseen node (CDG)).

In this section, we discuss two forms of symbolic learning: *rule mining*, which learns rules,
and *axiom mining*, which learns other forms of logical axioms.

5.4.1   RULE MINING

Rule mining, in the general sense, refers to discovering meaningful patterns in the form of
rules from large collections of background knowledge. In the context of knowledge graphs, we

assume a set of positive and negative edges as given. Typically, positive edges are observed edges (i.e., those given or entailed by a knowledge graph) while negative edges are defined according to a given assumption of completeness (discussed later). The goal of rule mining is to identify new rules that entail a high ratio of positive edges from other positive edges, but entail a low ratio of negative edges from positive edges. The types of rules considered may vary from more simple cases, such as $\langle ?x \rangle$–flight→$\langle ?y \rangle$ ⇒ $\langle ?y \rangle$–flight→$\langle ?x \rangle$ mentioned previously, to more complex rules, such as $\langle ?x \rangle$–capital→$\langle ?y \rangle$–nearby→$\langle ?z \rangle$–type→(Airport) ⇒ $\langle ?z \rangle$–type→(International Airport), based on observing in the graph that airports near capitals tend to be international airports; or $\langle ?x \rangle$–flight→$\langle ?y \rangle$–country→$\langle ?z \rangle$

⇒ $\langle ?x \rangle$–domestic flight→$\langle ?y \rangle$, indicating that flights within the same country denote domestic flights (as seen previously in Section 4.2.1).

Per the example inferring that airports near capital cities are international airports, rules are not assumed to hold in all cases, but rather are associated with measures of how well they conform to the positive and negative edges. In more detail, we call the edges entailed by a rule and the set of positive edges (not including the entailed edge itself), the *positive entailments* of that rule. The number of entailments that are positive is called the *support* for the rule, while the ratio of a rule's entailments that are positive is called the *confidence* for the rule [Suchanek et al., 2019]. Support and confidence indicate, respectively, the number and ratio of entailments "confirmed" to be true for the rule, where the goal is to identify rules that have both high support and high confidence. Techniques for rule mining in relational settings have long been explored in the context of *Inductive Logic Programming* (*ILP*) [Raedt, 2008]. However, knowledge graphs present novel challenges due to the scale of the data and the frequent assumption of incomplete data (OWA), where dedicated techniques have been proposed to address these issues [Galárraga et al., 2013].

When dealing with an incomplete knowledge graph, it is not immediately clear how to define negative edges. A common heuristic—also used for knowledge graph embeddings—is to adopt a Partial Completeness Assumption (PCA) [Galárraga et al., 2013], which considers the set of positive edges to be those contained in the data graph, and the set of negative examples to be the set of all edges (x)–p→(y') not in the graph but where there exists a node (y) such that (x)–p→(y) is in the graph. Taking Figure 5.8, an example of a negative edge under PCA would be (SCL)–flight→(ARI) (given the presence of (SCL)–flight→(LIM)); conversely, (SCL)–domestic flight→(ARI) is neither positive nor negative. The PCA confidence measure is then the ratio of the support to the number of entailments in the positive or negative set [Galárraga et al., 2013]. For example, the support for the rule $\langle ?x \rangle$–domestic flight→$\langle ?y \rangle$ ⇒ $\langle ?y \rangle$–domestic flight→$\langle ?x \rangle$ is 2 (since it entails (IQQ)–domestic flight→(ARI) and (ARI)–domestic flight→(IQQ) in the graph, which are thus positive edges), while the confidence is $\frac{2}{2} = 1$ (noting that (SCL)–domestic flight→(ARI), though entailed, is neither positive nor negative, and is thus ignored by the measure). The support for the rule $\langle ?x \rangle$–flight→$\langle ?y \rangle$ ⇒ $\langle ?y \rangle$–flight→$\langle ?x \rangle$ is analogously 4, while the confidence is $\frac{4}{5} = 0.8$ (noting that (SCL)–flight→(ARI) is a negative edge).

The goal then, is to find rules satisfying given support and confidence thresholds. An influential rule-mining system for graphs is AMIE [Galárraga et al., 2015, Galárraga et al., 2013], which adopts the PCA measure of confidence, and builds rules in a top-down fashion [Suchanek et al., 2019] starting with rule heads of the form $\Rightarrow$ (?x)—country→(?y). For each such rule head (one for each edge label), three types of *refinements* are considered, each of which adds a new edge to the body of the rule. This new edge takes an edge label from the graph and may otherwise use *fresh variables* not appearing previously in the rule, *existing variables* that already appear in the rule, or nodes from the graph. The three refinements may then:

1. add an edge with one existing variable and one fresh variable; for example, refining the aforementioned rule head might give: (?z)—flight→(?x) $\Rightarrow$ (?x)—country→(?y);

2. add an edge with an existing variable and a graph node; for example, refining the above rule might give: (Domestic Airport)←type—(?z)—flight→(?x) $\Rightarrow$ (?x)—country→(?y); and

3. add an edge with two existing variables; for example, refining the above rule might give: (Domestic Airport)←type—(?z)—flight→(?x) (?y) $\Rightarrow$ (?x)—country→(?y), with country edge.

These refinements can be combined arbitrarily, which gives rise to a potentially exponential search space, where rules meeting given thresholds for support and confidence are maintained. To improve efficiency, the search space can be pruned; for example, these three refinements always decrease support, so if a rule does not meet the support threshold, there is no need to explore its refinements. Further restrictions are imposed on the types of rules generated. First, only rules up to a certain fixed size are considered. Second, a rule must be *closed*, meaning that each variable appears in at least two edges of the rule, which ensures that rules are *safe*, meaning that each variable in the head appears in the body; for example, the rules produced by the first and second refinements in the example are neither closed (variable (y) appears once) nor safe (variable (y) appears only in the head).[10] The third refinement is thus applied until a rule is closed. For further discussion of possible optimizations based on pruning and indexing, we refer to the paper by [Galárraga et al., 2015].

Later works have built on these techniques for mining rules from knowledge graphs. Gad-Elrab et al. [2016] propose a method to learn non-monotonic rules—rules with negated edges in the body—in order to capture exceptions to base rules; for example, the rule (International Airport)←¬ type··(?z)—flight→(?x) (?y) $\Rightarrow$ (?x)—country→(?y) may be learned, indicating that flights are within the same country *except* when the (departure) airport is international, where the exception is shown dotted and we use ¬ to negate an edge (representing an exception). The RuLES system [Ho et al., 2018]—which is also capable of learning non-monotonic rules—proposes to mitigate the limitations of the PCA heuristic by extending the confidence measure

---

[10]Safe rules like (?x)—capital→(?y)—nearby→(?z)—type→(Airport) $\Rightarrow$ (?z)—type→(International Airport) are not closed as (?x) appears only in one edge. The condition that rules are closed is strictly stronger than the safety condition.

to consider the plausibility scores of knowledge graph embeddings for entailed edges not appearing in the graph. Where available, explicit statements about the completeness of the knowledge graph (such as expressed in shapes; see Section 3.1.2) can be used in lieu of PCA for identifying negative edges. Along these lines, CARL [Pellissier Tanon et al., 2017] exploits additional knowledge about the cardinalities of relations to refine the set of negative examples and the confidence measure for candidate rules. Alternatively, where available, ontologies can be used to derive logically certain negative edges under OWA through, for example, disjointness axioms. The system proposed by d'Amato et al. [2016a,b] leverages ontologically-entailed negative edges for determining the confidence of rules generated through an evolutionary algorithm.

While the previous works involve discrete expansions of candidate rules for which a fixed confidence scoring function is applied, another line of research is on a technique called *differentiable rule mining* [Rocktäschel and Riedel, 2017, Sadeghian et al., 2019, Yang et al., 2017], which allows end-to-end learning of rules. The core idea is that the joins in rule bodies can be represented as matrix multiplication. More specifically, we can represent the relations of an edge label p by the adjacency matrix $\mathbf{A}_p$ (of size $|V| \times |V|$) such that the value on the ith row of the jth column is 1 if there is an edge labeled p from the ith entity to the jth entity; otherwise, the value is 0. Now we can represent a join in a rule body as matrix multiplication; for example, given $(\underline{?x})$—domestic flight→$(\underline{?y})$—country→$(\underline{?z})$ $\Rightarrow$ $(\underline{?x})$—country→$(\underline{?z})$, we can denote the body by the matrix multiplication $\mathbf{A}_{df} \mathbf{A}_{c.}$, which gives an adjacency matrix representing entailed country edges, where we should expect the 1's in $\mathbf{A}_{df} \mathbf{A}_{c.}$ to be covered by the head's adjacency matrix $\mathbf{A}_{c.}$. Since we are given adjacency matrices for all edge labels, we are left to learn confidence scores for individual rules, and to learn rules (of varying length) with a threshold confidence. Along these lines, NeuralLP [Yang et al., 2017] uses an *attention mechanism* to select a variable-length sequence of edge labels for path-like rules of the form $(\underline{?x})$—p_1→$(\underline{?y_1})$—p_2→ ... —p_n→$(\underline{?y_n})$—p_{n+1}→$(\underline{?z})$ $\Rightarrow$ $(\underline{?x})$—p→$(\underline{?z})$, for which confidences are likewise learned. DRUM [Sadeghian et al., 2019] also learns path-like rules, where, observing that some edge labels are more/less likely to follow others in the rules—for example, flight will not be followed by capital in the graph of Figure 5.2 as the join will be empty—the system uses bidirectional recurrent neural networks (a popular technique for learning over sequential data) to learn sequences of relations for rules, and their confidences. These differentiable rule mining techniques are, however, currently limited to learning path-like rules.

5.4.2   AXIOM MINING

More general forms of axioms beyond rules—expressed in logical languages such as DLs (see Section 4.2.2)—can be mined from knowledge graphs. We divide these approaches into two: those mining specific axioms and more general axioms.

Among systems mining specific types of axioms, disjointness axioms are a popular target; for example, DomesticAirport ⊓ InternationalAirport ≡ ⊥ states that the two classes are disjoint by equivalently stating that the intersection of the two classes is equivalent to the empty class, or in simpler terms, no node can be simultaneously of type (Domestic Airport) and (International Airport).

The system proposed by Völker et al. [2015] extracts disjointness axioms based on (negative) *association rule mining* [Agrawal et al., 1993], which finds pairs of classes where each has many instances in the knowledge graph but there are relatively few (or no) instances of both classes. Töpper et al. [2012] rather extract disjointness for pairs of classes that have a cosine similarity below a fixed threshold. For computing this cosine similarity, class vectors are computed using a TF–IDF analogy, where the "document" of each class is constructed from all of its instances, and the "terms" of this document are the properties used on the class instances (preserving multiplicities). While the previous two approaches find disjointness constraints between named classes (e.g., *city* is disjoint with *airport*), Rizzo et al. [2017, 2021] proposed an approach that can capture disjointness constraints between class descriptions (e.g., *city without an airport nearby* is disjoint with *city that is the capital of a country*). The approach first clusters similar nodes of the knowledge base. Next, a *terminological cluster tree* is extracted, where each leaf node indicates a cluster extracted previously, and each internal (non-leaf) node is a class definition (e.g., *cities*) where the left child is either a cluster having all nodes in that class or a sub-class description (e.g., *cities without airports*) and the right child is either a cluster having no nodes in that class or a disjoint-class description (e.g., *non-cities with events*). Finally, candidate disjointness axioms are proposed for pairs of class descriptions in the tree that are not entailed to have a sub-class relation.

Other systems propose methods to learn more general axioms. One of the first proposals in this direction is the DL-FOIL system [Fanizzi et al., 2008, Rizzo et al., 2020], which is based on algorithms for *class learning* (aka *concept learning*), whereby given a set of positive nodes and negative nodes, the goal is to find a logical class description that divides the positive and negative sets. For example, given {(Iquique), (Arica)} as the positive set and {(Santiago)} as the negative set, we may learn a (DL) class description $\exists$nearby.Airport $\sqcap \neg(\exists$capital$^-$.$\top)$, denoting entities near to an airport that are not capitals, of which all positive nodes are instances and no negative nodes are instances. Such class descriptions are learned in an analogous manner to how aforementioned systems like AMIE learn rules, with a refinement operator used to move from more general classes to more specific classes (and vice-versa), a confidence scoring function, and a search strategy. Another prominent such system is DL-Learner [Bühmann et al., 2016], which further supports learning more general axioms through a scoring function that uses count queries to determine what ratio of expected edges—edges that would be entailed were the axiom true—are indeed found in the graph; for example, to score the axiom $\exists$flight$^-$.DomesticAirport $\sqsubseteq$ InternationalAirport over Figure 5.8, we can use a graph query to count how many nodes have incoming flights from a domestic airport (there are 3), and how many nodes have incoming flights from a domestic airport *and* are international airports (there is 1), where the greater the difference between both counts, the weaker the evidence for the axiom.

5.4.3   HYPOTHESIS MINING

We now provide some abstract formal definitions for the tasks of *rule mining* and *axiom mining* over graphs, which we generically refer to as *hypothesis mining*.

First, we introduce *hypothesis induction*: a task that captures a more abstract (ideal) case for hypothesis mining. For simplicity, we focus on directed edge-labeled graphs. With a slight abuse of notation, we may interpret a set of edges E as the graph with precisely those edges and with no nodes or labels without edges. We may also interpret an edge e as the graph formed by $\{e\}$.

Definition 5.22   Hypothesis induction.   The task of *hypothesis induction* assumes a particular graph entailment relation $\models_\Phi$ (see Definition 4.4; hereafter simply $\models$). Given *background knowledge* in the form of a knowledge graph G (a directed edge-labeled graph, possibly extended with rules or ontologies), a set of *positive edges* E^+ such that G does not entail any edge in E^+ (i.e., for all $e^+ \in E^+$, $G \not\models e^+$) and E^+ does not contradict G (i.e., there is a model of $G \cup E^+$), and a set of *negative edges* E^- such that G does not entail any edge in E^- (i.e., for all $e^- \in E^-$, $G \not\models e^-$), the task is to find a set of *hypotheses* (i.e., a set of directed edge-labeled graphs) Ψ such that:

- $G \not\models \psi$ for all $\psi \in \Psi$ (the background knowledge does not entail any hypothesis directly);

- $G \cup \Psi^* \models E^+$ (the background knowledge and hypotheses together entail all positive edges);

- for all $e^- \in E^-$, $G \cup \Psi^* \not\models e^-$ (the background knowledge and hypotheses together do not entail any negative edge);

- $G \cup \Psi^* \cup E^+$ has a model (the background knowledge, hypotheses, and positive edges taken together do not contain a contradiction); and

- for all $e^+ \in E^+$, $\Psi^* \not\models e^+$ (the hypotheses alone do not entail a positive edge).

where by $\Psi^* = \cup_{\psi \in \Psi} \psi$ we denote the union of all graphs in Ψ.

Example 5.23   Let us assume ontological entailment $\models$ with semantic conditions Φ as defined in Tables 4.1–4.3. Given the graph of Figure 5.8 as the background knowledge G, along with

- a set of positive edges $E^+ = \{$ SCL —flight→ ARI , SCL —domestic flight→ ARI $\}$, and

- a set of negative edges $E^- = \{$ ARI —flight→ LIM , SCL —domestic flight→ LIM $\}$, then a set of hypotheses $\Psi = \{$ flight —type→ Symmetric , domestic flight —type→ Symmetric $\}$ are not entailed by G, entail all positive edges in E^+ and no negative edges in E^- when combined with G, do not contradict $G \cup E^+$, and do not entail a positive edge without G. Thus, Ψ satisfies the conditions for hypothesis induction.

This task represents a somewhat idealized case. Often there is no set of positive edges distinct from the background knowledge itself. Furthermore, hypotheses not entailing a few positive edges, or entailing a few negative edges, may still be useful. The task of *hypothesis mining* rather accepts as input the background knowledge G and a set of negative edges E^- (such that for all $e^- \in E^-$, $G \not\models e^-$), and attempts to *score* individual hypotheses ψ (such that $G \not\models \psi$) per their ability to "explain" G while minimizing the number of elements of E^- entailed by G and ψ. We can now abstractly define the task of hypothesis mining.

Definition 5.24 Hypothesis mining.   Given a knowledge graph G, a set of negative edges E^-, a scoring function σ, and a threshold $\min_\sigma$, the goal of *hypothesis mining* is to identify a set of hypotheses $\{\psi \mid G \not\models \psi$ and $\sigma(\psi, G, E^-) \geq \min_\sigma\}$.

There are two scoring functions that are frequently used for σ in the literature: *support* and *confidence*.

Definition 5.25   Hypothesis support and confidence.   Given a knowledge graph $G = (V, E, L)$ and a hypothesis ψ, the *positive support* of ψ is defined as:

$$\sigma^+(\psi, G) = |\{e \in E \mid G' \not\models e \text{ and } G' \cup \psi \models e\}|$$

where G' denotes G with the edge e removed. Further given a set of negative edges E^-, the *negative support* of ψ is defined as:

$$\sigma^-(\psi, G, E^-) = |\{e^- \in E^- \mid G \cup \psi \models e^-\}|$$

Finally, the *confidence* of ψ is defined as $\sigma^\pm(\psi, G, E^-) = \frac{\sigma^+(\psi,G)}{\sigma^+(\psi,G)+\sigma^-(\psi,G,E^-)}$.

We have yet to define how the set of negative edges are defined, which, in the context of a knowledge graph G, depends on which assumption is applied:

- *Closed world assumption (CWA):* For any (positive) edge e, $G \not\models e$ if and only if $G \models \neg e$. Under CWA, any edge e not entailed by G can be considered a negative edge.

- *Open world assumption:* For a (positive) edge e, $G \not\models e$ does not necessarily imply $G \models \neg e$. Under OWA, the negation of an edge must be entailed by G for it to be considered negative.

- *Partial completeness assumption (PCA)*: If there exists an edge (s, p, o) such that $G \models (s, p, o)$, then for all o' such that $G \not\models (s, p, o')$, it is assumed that $G \models \neg(s, p, o')$. Under PCA, if G entails some outgoing edge(s) labeled p from a node s, then such edges are assumed to be complete, and any edge (s, p, o') not entailed by G can be considered a negative edge.

Knowledge graphs are generally incomplete—in fact, one of the main applications of hypothesis mining is to try to improve the completeness of the knowledge graph—and thus it would appear unwise to assume that any edge that is not currently entailed is false/negative. We can thus rule out CWA. Conversely, under OWA, potentially few (or no) negative edges might be entailed by the given ontologies/rules, and thus hypotheses may end up having low negative support despite entailing many edges that do not make sense in practice. Hence, the PCA can be adopted as a heuristic to increase the number of negative edges and apply more sensible scoring of hypotheses. We remark that one can adapt PCA to define negative triples by changing the subject or predicate instead of the object.

Different implementations of hypothesis mining may consider different logical languages. Rule mining, for example, mines hypotheses expressed either as monotonic rules (with positive edges) or non-monotonic edges (possibly with negated edges). On the other hand, axiom mining considers hypotheses expressed in a logical language such as Description Logics. Particular implementations may, for practical reasons, impose further syntactic restrictions on the hypotheses generated, such as to impose thresholds on their length, on the symbols they use, or on other structural properties (such as "closed rules" in the case of the AMIE rule mining system [Galárraga et al., 2013]; see Section 5.4). Systems may further implement different search strategies for hypotheses. Systems such as DL-FOIL [Fanizzi et al., 2008, Rizzo et al., 2020], AMIE [Galárraga et al., 2013], RuLES [Ho et al., 2018], CARL [Pellissier Tanon et al., 2017], DL-Learner [Bühmann et al., 2016], etc., propose *discrete mining* that recursively generates candidate formulae through refinement/genetic operators that are then scored and checked for threshold criteria. On the other hand, systems such as NeuralLP [Yang et al., 2017] and DRUM [Sadeghian et al., 2019] apply *differentiable mining* that allows for learning (path-like) rules and their scores in a more continuous fashion (e.g., using gradient descent). We refer to Section 5.4 for further discussion and examples of such techniques for mining hypotheses.

CHAPTER 6

Creation and Enrichment

In this chapter, we discuss the principal techniques by which knowledge graphs can be created and subsequently enriched from diverse sources of legacy data that range from plain text to structured formats (and anything in between). The appropriate methodology to follow when creating a knowledge graph depends on the actors involved, the domain, the envisaged applications, the available data sources, etc. Generally speaking, however, the flexibility of knowledge graphs lends itself to starting with an initial core that can be incrementally enriched from other sources as required (typically following an Agile [Hunt and Thomas, 2003] or "pay-as-you-go" [Sequeda et al., 2019] methodology). For our running example, we assume that the tourism board decides to build a knowledge graph from scratch, aiming to initially describe the main tourist attractions—places, events, etc.—in Chile in order to help visiting tourists identify those that most interest them. The board decides to postpone adding further data, like transport routes, reports of crime, etc., for a later date.

6.1   HUMAN COLLABORATION

One approach for creating and enriching knowledge graphs is to solicit direct contributions from human editors. Such editors may be found in-house (e.g., employees of the tourist board), using crowd-sourcing platforms, through feedback mechanisms (e.g., tourists adding comments on attractions), through collaborative-editing platforms (e.g., an attractions wiki open to public edits), etc. Though human involvement incurs high costs [Paulheim, 2018], some prominent knowledge graphs have been primarily based on direct contributions from human editors [He et al., 2016, Vrandečić and Krötzsch, 2014]. Depending on how the contributions are solicited, however, the approach has a number of key drawbacks, due primarily to human error [Pellissier Tanon et al., 2016], disagreement [Yasseri et al., 2012], bias [Janowicz et al., 2018], vandalism [Heindorf et al., 2016], etc. Successful collaborative creation further raises challenges concerning licensing, tooling, and culture [Pellissier Tanon et al., 2016]. Humans are sometimes rather employed to verify and curate additions to a knowledge graph extracted by other means [Pellissier Tanon et al., 2016] (through, e.g., video games with a purpose [Jurgens and Navigli, 2014]), to define high-quality mappings from other sources [Das et al., 2012], to define appropriate high-level schema [Keet, 2018, Labra Gayo et al., 2017], and so forth.

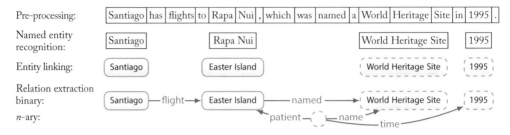

Figure 6.1: Text extraction example; dashed nodes are new to the knowledge graph.

6.2 TEXT SOURCES

Text corpora—such as sourced from newspapers, books, scientific articles, social media, emails, web crawls, etc.—are an abundant source of rich information [Hellmann et al., 2013, Rospocher et al., 2016]. However, extracting such information with high precision and recall for the purposes of creating or enriching a knowledge graph is a non-trivial challenge. To address this, techniques from Natural Language Processing (NLP) [Jurafsky and Martin, 2019, Maynard et al., 2016] and Information Extraction (IE) [Grishman, 2012, Martínez-Rodríguez et al., 2020, Weikum and Theobald, 2010] can be applied. Though processes vary considerably across text extraction frameworks, in Figure 6.1 we illustrate four core tasks for text extraction on a sample sentence. We will discuss these tasks in turn.

6.2.1 PRE-PROCESSING

The pre-processing task may involve applying various techniques to the input text, where Figure 6.1 illustrates *Tokenization*, which parses the text into atomic terms and symbols. Other pre-processing tasks applied to a text corpus may include: *Part-of-Speech (POS) tagging* [Jurafsky and Martin, 2019, Maynard et al., 2016] to identify terms representing verbs, nouns, adjectives, etc.; *Dependency Parsing*, which extracts a grammatical tree structure for a sentence where leaf nodes indicate individual words that together form phrases (e.g., noun phrases, verb phrases) and eventually clauses and sentences [Jurafsky and Martin, 2019, Maynard et al., 2016]; and *Word Sense Disambiguation (WSD)* [Navigli, 2009] to identify the meaning (aka *sense*) in which a word is used, linking words with a lexicon of senses (e.g., WordNet [Miller and Fellbaum, 2007] or BabelNet [Navigli and Ponzetto, 2012]), where, for instance, the term flights may be linked with the WordNet sense "an instance of traveling by air" rather than "a stairway between one floor and the next." The appropriate type of pre-processing to apply often depends on the requirements of later tasks in the pipeline.

6.2.2   NAMED ENTITY RECOGNITION (NER)

The NER task identifies mentions of named entities in a text [Nadeau and Sekine, 2007, Ratinov and Roth, 2009], typically targeting mentions of people, organizations, locations, and potentially other types [Ling and Weld, 2012, Nakashole et al., 2013, Yogatama et al., 2015]. A variety of NER techniques exist, with many modern approaches based on learning frameworks that leverage lexical features (e.g., POS tags, dependency parse trees, etc.) and gazetteers (e.g., lists of common first names, last names, countries, prominent businesses, etc.). Supervised methods [Bikel et al., 1999, Finkel et al., 2005, Lample et al., 2016] require manually labeling all entity mentions in a training corpus, whereas *bootstrapping*-based approaches [Collins and Singer, 1999, Etzioni et al., 2004, Gupta and Manning, 2014, Nakashole et al., 2013] rather require a small set of *seed examples* of entity mentions from which patterns can be learned and applied to unlabeled text. *Distant supervision* [Ling and Weld, 2012, Ren et al., 2015, Yogatama et al., 2015] uses known entities in a knowledge graph as seed examples through which similar entities can be detected. Aside from learning-based frameworks, traditional approaches based on manually crafted rules [Chiticariu et al., 2018, Kluegl et al., 2009] are still sometimes used due to their more controllable and predictable behavior [Chiticariu et al., 2013]. The named entities identified by NER may be used to generate new candidate nodes for the knowledge graph (known as *emerging entities*, shown dashed in Figure 6.1), or may be linked to existing nodes per the Entity Linking task described in the following.

6.2.3   ENTITY LINKING (EL)

The EL task associates mentions of entities in a text with the existing nodes of a target knowledge graph, which may be the nucleus of a knowledge graph under creation, or an external knowledge graph [Wu et al., 2018]. In Figure 6.1, we assume that the nodes (Santiago) and (Easter Island) already exist in the knowledge graph (possibly extracted from other sources). EL may then link the given mentions to these nodes. The EL task presents two main challenges. First, there may be multiple ways to mention the same entity, as in the case of [Rapa Nui] and [Easter Island]; if we created a node (Rapa Nui) to represent that mention, we would split the information available under both mentions across different nodes, where it is thus important for the target knowledge graph to capture the various aliases and multilingual labels by which one can refer to an entity [Moro et al., 2014]. Second, the same mention in different contexts can refer to distinct entities; for instance, [Santiago] can refer to cities in Chile, Cuba, Spain, among others. The EL task thus considers a *disambiguation phase* wherein mentions are associated to candidate nodes in the knowledge graph, the candidates are ranked, and the most likely node being mentioned is chosen [Wu et al., 2018]. Context can be used in this phase; for example, if (Easter Island) is a likely candidate for the corresponding mention alongside [Santiago], we may boost the probability that this mention refers to the Chilean capital as both candidates are located in Chile. Other heuristics for disambiguation consider a prior probability, where for example, [Santiago] most often refers to the Chilean capital (being, e.g., the largest city with that name); centrality measures on the knowledge graph can be used for such purposes [Wu et al., 2018].

6.2.4   RELATION EXTRACTION (RE)

The RE task extracts relations between entities in the text [Bach and Badaskar, 2007, Zhou et al., 2005]. The simplest case is that of extracting binary relations in a *closed setting* wherein a fixed set of relation types are considered. While traditional approaches often relied on manually-crafted patterns [Hearst, 1992], modern approaches rather tend to use learning-based frameworks [Roller et al., 2018], including supervised methods over manually-labeled examples [Bunescu and Mooney, 2005, Zhou et al., 2005]. Other learning-based approaches again use bootstrapping [Bunescu and Mooney, 2007, Etzioni et al., 2004] and distant supervision [Hoffmann et al., 2011, Mintz et al., 2009, Riedel et al., 2010, Smirnova and Cudré-Mauroux, 2019, Surdeanu et al., 2012, Xu et al., 2013] to forgo the need for manual labeling; the former requires a subset of manually-labeled seed examples, while the latter finds sentences in a large corpus of text mentioning pairs of entities with a known relation/edge, which are used to learn patterns for that relation. Binary RE can also be applied using unsupervised methods in an open setting—often referred to as *Open Information Extraction* (*OIE*) [Banko et al., 2007, Etzioni et al., 2011, Fader et al., 2011, Mausam, 2016, Mausam et al., 2012, Mitchell et al., 2018]—whereby the set of target relations is not pre-defined but rather extracted from text based on, for example, dependency parse trees from which relations are taken.

A variety of RE methods have been proposed to extract n-ary relations that capture further context for how entities are related. In Figure 6.1, we see how an n-ary relation captures additional temporal context, denoting when Rapa Nui was named a World Heritage site; in this case, an anonymous node is created to represent the higher-arity relation in the directed-labeled graph. Various methods for n-ary RE are based on *frame semantics* [Fillmore, 1976], which, for a given verb (e.g., "*named*"), captures the entities involved and how they may be interrelated. Resources such as FrameNet [Baker et al., 1998] then define frames for words, which, for example, may identify that the semantic frame for "*named*" includes a *speaker* (the person naming something), an *entity* (the thing named) and a *name*. Optional frame elements are an *explanation*, a *purpose*, a *place*, a *time*, etc., that may add context to the relation. Other RE methods are rather based on *Discourse Representation Theory* (*DRT*) [Kamp, 1981], which considers a logical representation of text based on existential events. Under this theory, for example, the naming of Easter Island as a World Heritage Site is considered to be an (existential) event where Easter Island is the *patient* (the entity affected), leading to the logical (neo-Davidsonian) formula:

$$\exists e : \big(\mathrm{naming}(e), \mathrm{patient}(e, \boxed{\text{Easter Island}}), \mathrm{name}(e, \boxed{\text{World Heritage Site}})\big)$$

Such a formula is analogous to reification, as discussed previously in Section 3.3, where e is an existential term that refers to the n-ary relation being extracted.

Finally, while relations extracted in a closed setting are typically mapped directly to a knowledge graph, relations that are extracted in an open setting may need to be aligned with the knowledge graph; for example, if an OIE process extracts a binary relation ⟨Santiago⟩—has flights to→⟨Easter Island⟩, it may be the case that the knowledge graph does not have other edges labeled has flights to, where alignment may rather map such a relation to the edge ⟨Santiago⟩—flight→⟨Easter Island⟩ assuming flight is used in the knowledge graph. A variety of methods have been applied for performing such alignments, including mappings [Corcoglioniti et al., 2016, Gangemi et al., 2017] and rules [Rouces et al., 2015] for aligning n-ary relations; distributional and dependency-based similarities [Moro and Navigli, 2013], association rule mining [Dutta et al., 2014], Markov clustering [Dutta et al., 2015] and linguistic techniques [Martínez-Rodríguez et al., 2018] for aligning OIE relations; among others.

6.2.5   JOINT TASKS

Having presented the four main tasks for building knowledge graphs from text, it is important to note that frameworks do not always follow this particular sequence of tasks. A common trend, for example, is to combine interdependent tasks, jointly performing WSD and EL [Moro et al., 2014], or NER and EL [Luo et al., 2015, Nguyen et al., 2016], or NER and RE [Ren et al., 2017, Zheng et al., 2017], etc., in order to mutually improve the performance of multiple tasks. For further details on extracting knowledge graphs from text we refer to the book by Maynard et al. [2016] and the recent survey by Martínez-Rodríguez et al. [2020].

6.3   MARKUP SOURCES

The Web was founded on interlinking *markup documents* wherein markers (aka *tags*) are used to separate elements of the document (typically for formatting purposes). Most documents on the Web use the HyperText Markup Language (HTML). Figure 6.2 presents an example HTML webpage about World Heritage Sites in Chile. Other formats of markup include Wikitext used by Wikipedia, TeX for typesetting, Markdown used by Content Management Systems, etc. One approach for extracting information from markup documents—in order to create and/or enrich a knowledge graph—is to strip the markers (e.g., HTML tags), leaving only plain text upon which the techniques from the previous section can be applied. However, markup can be useful for extraction purposes, where variations of the aforementioned tasks for text extraction have been adapted to exploit such markup [Lockard et al., 2018, Lu et al., 2013, Martínez-Rodríguez et al., 2020]. We can divide extraction techniques for markup documents into three main categories: general approaches that work independently of the markup used in a particular format, often based on *wrappers* that map elements of the document to the output; focussed approaches that target specific forms of markup in a document, most typically *web tables* (but sometimes also lists, links, etc.); and form-based approaches that extract the data underlying a webpage, per the notion of the *Deep Web*. These approaches can often benefit from the regularities shared by webpages of a given website; for example, intuitively speaking, while the webpage of Figure 6.2

```
<html>
 <head><title>UNESCO World Heritage Sites</title></head>
 <body>
  <h1>World Heritage Sites</h1>
  <h2>Chile</h2>
  <p>Chile has 6 UNESCO World Heritage Sites.</p>
  <table border="1">
   <tr><th>Place</th><th>Year</th><th>Criteria</th></tr>
   <tr><td>Rapa Nui</td><td>1995</td>
       <td rowspan="6">Cultural</td></tr>
   <tr><td>Churches of Chiloé</td><td>2000</td></tr>
   <tr><td>Historical Valparaíso</td><td>2003</td></tr>
   <tr><td>Saltpeter Works</td><td>2005</td></tr>
   <tr><td>Sewell Mining Town</td><td>2006</td></tr>
   <tr><td>Qhapaq Ñan</td><td>2014</td></tr>
  </table>
 </body>
</html>
```

Figure 6.2: Example markup document (HTML) with source-code (left) and formatted document (right).

is about Chile, we will likely find pages for other countries following the same structure on the same website.

6.3.1   WRAPPER-BASED EXTRACTION

Many general approaches are based on *wrappers* that locate and extract the useful information directly from the markup document. While the traditional approach was to define such wrappers manually—a task for which a variety of declarative languages and tools have been defined—such approaches are brittle to changes in a website's layout [Ferrara et al., 2014]. Hence other approaches allow for (semi-)automatically *inducing* wrappers [Flesca et al., 2004]. A modern such approach—used to enrich knowledge graphs in systems such as LODIE [Gentile et al., 2014]—is to apply distant supervision, whereby EL is used to identify and link entities in the webpage to nodes in the knowledge graph such that paths in the markup that connect pairs of nodes for known edges can be extracted, ranked, and applied to other examples. Taking Figure 6.2, for example, distant supervision may link Rapa Nui and World Heritage Sites to the nodes Easter Island and World Heritage Site in the knowledge graph using EL, and given the edge Easter Island –named→ World Heritage Site in the knowledge graph (extracted per Figure 6.1), identify the candidate path $(x, \mathtt{td}[1]^- \cdot \mathtt{tr}^- \cdot \mathtt{table}^- \cdot \mathtt{h1}, y)$ as reflecting edges of the form x –named→ y, where $t[n]$ indicates the nth child of tag t, t^- its inverse, and $t_1 \cdot t_2$ concatenation. Finally, paths with high confidence (e.g., ones "witnessed" by many known edges in the knowledge graph) can then be used to extract novel edges, such as Qhapaq Ñan –named→ World Heritage Site , both on this page and on related pages of the website with similar structure (e.g., for world heritage sites of other countries).

6.3.2   WEB TABLE EXTRACTION

Other approaches target specific types of markup, most commonly *web tables* embedded in HTML webpages. However, web tables are designed to enhance human rather than machine readability. Many web tables are used for layout and page structure (e.g., navigation bars). Those that contain data may follow different formats, such as relational tables, listings, attribute-value tables, and matrices [Cafarella et al., 2008, Crestan and Pantel, 2011]. A first step is to classify tables to find ones appropriate for the given extraction mechanism(s) [Crestan and Pantel, 2011, Eberius et al., 2015]. Next, web tables may contain column spans, row spans, inner tables, or may be split vertically to improve human aesthetics. Table normalization merges split tables, un-nests tables, transposes tables, etc. [Cafarella et al., 2008, Crestan and Pantel, 2011, Deng et al., 2013, Ermilov and Ngonga Ngomo, 2016, Lehmberg et al., 2016, Pivk et al., 2007]. Some approaches then identify the table *protagonist* [Crestan and Pantel, 2011, Mu noz et al., 2014]—the main entity that the table describes—often found elsewhere in the webpages; for example, though not mentioned by the table of Figure 6.1, World Heritage Sites is its protagonist. Finally, extraction processes may associate cells with entities [Limaye et al., 2010, Mulwad et al., 2013], columns with types [Deng et al., 2013, Limaye et al., 2010, Mulwad et al., 2013], and column pairs with relations [Limaye et al., 2010, Mu noz et al., 2014]. When enriching knowledge graphs, recent approaches apply distant supervision, linking cells to knowledge graph nodes in order to generate candidates for type and relation extraction [Limaye et al., 2010, Mulwad et al., 2013, Mu noz et al., 2014]. Statistical distributions can also help to link numerical columns [Neumaier et al., 2016]. Specialized table extraction frameworks have also been proposed for specific websites, where prominent knowledge graphs, such as DBpedia [Lehmann et al., 2015] and YAGO [Suchanek et al., 2008], focus on extraction from info-box tables in Wikipedia.

6.3.3   DEEP WEB CRAWLING

The *Deep Web* presents a rich source of information accessible only through searches on web forms, thus requiring *Deep Web crawling* techniques to access [Madhavan et al., 2008]. Systems have been proposed to extract knowledge graphs from Deep Web sources [Collarana et al., 2016, Geller et al., 2008, Lehmann et al., 2012]. Approaches typically attempt to generate sensible form inputs—which may be based on a user query or generated from reference knowledge—and then extract data from the generated responses (markup documents) using the aforementioned techniques [Collarana et al., 2016, Geller et al., 2008, Lehmann et al., 2012].

6.4   STRUCTURED SOURCES

Much of the legacy data available within organizations and on the Web is represented in structured formats, primarily tables—in the form of relational databases, CSV files, etc.—but also tree-structured formats such as JSON, XML etc. Unlike text and markup documents, structured sources can often be *mapped* to knowledge graphs whereby the structure is (precisely)

Report

crime	claimant	station	date
Pickpocketing	XY12SDA	Viña del Mar	2019-04-12
Assault	AB9123N	Arica	2019-04-12
Pickpocketing	XY12SDA	Rapa Nui	2019-04-12
Fraud	FI92HAS	Arica	2019-04-13

Claimant

id	name	country
XY12SDA	John Smith	U.S.
AB9123N	Joan Dubois	France
XI92HAS	Jorge Hernández	Chile

Figure 6.3: Relational database instance with two tables describing crime data.

Figure 6.4: Direct mapping result for the first rows of both tables in Figure 6.3.

transformed according to a mapping rather than (imprecisely) extracted. The mapping process involves two steps: (1) create a mapping from the source to a graph, and (2) use the mapping in order to materialize the source data as a graph or to virtualize the source (creating a graph view over the legacy data).

6.4.1 MAPPING FROM TABLES

Tabular sources of data are prevalent; for example, the structured content underlying many organizations and websites are housed in relational databases. In Figure 6.3, we present an example of a relational database instance that we wish to integrate into our knowledge graph. There are then two approaches for mapping content from tables to knowledge graphs: a *direct mapping* and a *custom mapping*.

A direct mapping automatically generates a graph from a table. We present in Figure 6.4 the result of a standard direct mapping [Arenas et al., 2012], which creates an edge (x)-$y$$\rightarrow$$(z)$ for each (non-header, non-empty, non-NULL) cell of the table, such that (x) represents the row of the cell, y the column name of the cell, and (z) the value of the cell. In particular, (x) typically encodes the values of the primary key for a row (e.g., **Claimant.id**); otherwise, if no primary key is defined (e.g., per the **Report** table), (x) can be an anonymous node or a node based on the row number. The node (x) and edge label y further encode the name of the table to avoid clashes across tables that have the same column names used with different meanings. For each row (x), we may add a type edge based on the name of its table. The value (z) may be mapped to datatype values in the corresponding graph model based on the source domain (e.g., a value in an SQL column of type `Date` can be mapped to `xsd:date` in the RDF data model). If the value is NULL (or empty), typically the corresponding edge will be omitted.[1] With respect to Figure 6.4, we highlight the difference between the nodes (Claimant-XY12SDA) and (XY12SDA), where the former denotes the row (or entity) identified by the latter primary key value. In case of a foreign key between two tables—such as **Report.claimant** referencing **Claimant.id**—we can link, for example, to (Claimant-XY12SDA) rather than (XY12SDA), where the former node also has the name and country of the claimant. A direct mapping along these lines has been standardized for mapping relational databases to RDF [Arenas et al., 2012], where Stoica et al. [2019] have recently proposed an analogous direct mapping for property graphs. Another direct mapping has been defined for CSV and other tabular data [Tandy et al., 2015] that further allows for specifying column names, primary/foreign keys, and data types—which are often missing in such data formats—as part of the mapping itself.

Although a direct mapping can be applied automatically on tabular sources of data and preserve the information of the original source—i.e., allowing a deterministic inverse mapping that reconstructs the tabular source from the output graph [Sequeda et al., 2012]—in many cases it is desirable to customize a mapping, such as to align edge labels or nodes with a knowledge graph under enrichment, etc. Along these lines, declarative mapping languages allow for manually defining custom mappings from tabular sources to graphs. A standard language along these lines is the RDB2RDF Mapping Language (R2RML) [Das et al., 2012], which allows for mapping from individual rows of a table to one or more custom edges, with nodes and edges defined either as constants, as individual cell values, or using templates that concatenate multiple cell values from a row and static substrings into a single term; for example, a template `{id}-{country}` may produce nodes such as (XY12SDA-U.S.) from the **Claimant** table. In case that the desired output edges cannot be defined from a single row, R2RML allows for (SQL) queries to generate tables from which edges can be extracted where, for example, edges such as (U.S.)—crimes→(2) can be generated by defining the mapping with respect to an SQL query that joins the `Report` and `Claimant` tables on `claimant=id`, grouping by `country`, and applying a count for each country group. A mapping can then be defined on the results table such that the source node denotes the value of `country`, the edge label is the constant crimes, and the target node is the count value. An analogous standard also exists for mapping CSV and other tabular data to RDF graphs, again allowing keys, column names, and datatypes to be chosen as part of the mapping [Tennison and Kellogg, 2015].

Once the mappings have been defined, one option is to use them to *materialize* graph data following an *Extract-Transform-Load* (*ETL*) approach, whereby the tabular data are transformed and explicitly serialized as graph data using the mapping. A second option is to use *virtualization* through a *Query Rewriting* (*QR*) approach, whereby queries on the graph (using, e.g., SPARQL, Cypher, etc.) are translated to queries over the tabular data (typically using

---

[1]One might consider representing NULLs with anonymous/blank nodes. However, NULLs in SQL can be used to mean that there is no such value, which conflicts with the existential semantics of such nodes (e.g., in RDF).

SQL). Comparing these two options, ETL allows the graph data to be used as if they were any other data in the knowledge graph. However, ETL requires updates to the underlying tabular data to be explicitly propagated to the knowledge graph, whereas a QR approach only maintains one copy of data to be updated. The area of *Ontology-Based Data Access* (*OBDA*) [Xiao et al., 2018] is concerned with QR approaches that support ontological entailments as seen in Chapter 4. Although most QR approaches only support non-recursive entailments expressible as a single (non-recursive) query, some QR approaches support recursive entailments through rewritings to recursive queries [Sequeda et al., 2014].

6.4.2   MAPPING FROM TREES

A number of popular data formats are based on trees, including XML and JSON. While one could imagine—leaving aside issues such as the ordering of children in a tree—a trivial direct mapping from trees to graphs by simply creating edges of the form x–child→y for each node y that is a child of x in the source tree, such an approach is not typically used, as it represents the literal structure of the source data. Instead, the content of tree-structured data can be more naturally represented as a graph using a custom mapping. Along these lines, the GRDLL standard [Connolly, 2007] allows for mapping from XML to (RDF) graphs, the JSON-LD standard [Sporny et al., 2014] allows for mapping from JSON to (RDF) graphs, while languages such as RML allow for mapping from a variety of formats, including XML and JSON, to (RDF) graphs [Dimou et al., 2014]. In contrast, hybrid query languages such as XSPARQL [Bischof et al., 2012] allow for querying XML and RDF in unison, thus supporting both materialization and virtualization of graphs over tree-structured sources of legacy data.

6.4.3   MAPPING FROM OTHER KNOWLEDGE GRAPHS

We may also leverage existing knowledge graphs in order to construct or enrich another knowledge graph. For example, a large number of points of interest for the Chilean tourist board may be available in existing knowledge graphs such as BabelNet [Navigli and Ponzetto, 2012], DBpedia [Lehmann et al., 2015], LinkedGeoData [Stadler et al., 2012], Wikidata [Vrandečić and Krötzsch, 2014], YAGO [Hoffart et al., 2011], etc. However, not all entities and/or relations may be of interest. A standard option to extract a relevant sub-graph of data is to use construct queries that generate graphs as output [Neumaier and Polleres, 2019]. Entity and schema alignment between the knowledge graphs may be further necessary to better integrate (parts of) external knowledge graphs, using linking tools for graphs [Ngonga Ngomo and Auer, 2011, Volz et al., 2009], external identifiers [Pellissier Tanon et al., 2016], or indeed may be done manually [Pellissier Tanon et al., 2016]. For instance, Wikidata [Vrandečić and Krötzsch, 2014] uses Freebase [Bollacker et al., 2007a, Pellissier Tanon et al., 2016] as a source; Gottschalk and Demidova [2018] extract an event-centric knowledge graph from Wikidata, DBpedia and YAGO; while Neumaier and Polleres [2019] construct a spatio-temporal knowledge graph from Geonames, Wikidata, and PeriodO [Golden and Shaw, 2016] (as well as tabular data).

6.5   SCHEMA/ONTOLOGY CREATION

The discussion thus far has focussed on extracting *data* from external sources in order to create and enrich a knowledge graph. In this section, we discuss some of the principal methods for generating a schema based on external sources of data, including human knowledge. For discussion on extracting a schema from the knowledge graph itself, we refer back to Section 3.1.3. In general, much of the work in this area has focussed on the creation of ontologies using either ontology engineering methodologies, and/or ontology learning. We discuss these two approaches in turn.

6.5.1   ONTOLOGY ENGINEERING

Ontology engineering refers to the development and application of methodologies for building ontologies, proposing principled processes by which better quality ontologies can be constructed and maintained with less effort. Early methodologies [Fernández et al., 1997, Grüninger and Fox, 1995a, Noy and McGuinness, 2001] were often based on a waterfall-like process, where requirements and conceptualization were fixed before starting to define the ontology, using, for example, an ontology engineering tool [Gómez-Pérez et al., 2006, Keet, 2018, Kendall and McGuinness, 2019]. However, for situations involving large or ever-evolving ontologies, more iterative and agile ways of building and maintaining ontologies have been proposed.

DILIGENT [Pinto et al., 2009] was an early example of an agile methodology for ontology engineering, proposing a complete process for ontology life-cycle management and knowledge evolution, as well as separating local changes (local views on knowledge) from global updates of the core part of the ontology, using a review process to authorize the propagation of changes from the local to the global level. This methodology is similar to how, for instance, the large clinical reference terminology SNOMED CT [Int, 2019] (also available as an ontology) is maintained and evolved, where the (international) core terminology is maintained based on global requirements, while national or local extensions to SNOMED CT are maintained based on local requirements. A group of authors then decides which national or local extensions to propagate to the core terminology. More modern agile methodologies include eXtreme Design (XD) [Blomqvist et al., 2016b, Presutti et al., 2009], Modular Ontology modeling (MOM) [Hitzler and Krisnadhi, 2018, Krisnadhi and Hitzler, 2016b], Simplified Agile Methodology for Ontology Development (SAMOD) [Peroni, 2016], and more besides. Such methodologies typically include two key elements: *ontology requirements* and (more recently) *ontology design patterns*.

Ontology requirements specify the intended task of the resulting ontology, or of the knowledge graph itself in conjunction with the new ontology. A common way to express ontology requirements is through *Competency Questions (CQ)* [Grüninger and Fox, 1995b], which are natural language questions illustrating the typical information needs that one would require the ontology (or the knowledge graph) to respond to. Such CQs can then be complemented with additional restrictions, and reasoning requirements, in case that the ontology should also contain restrictions and general axioms for inferring new knowledge or checking data consistency. A common way of testing ontologies (or knowledge graphs based on them) is then to formalize the CQs as queries over some test set of data, and make sure the expected results are entailed [Blomqvist et al., 2012, Keet and Ławrynowicz, 2016]. We may, for example, consider the CQ "*What are all the events happening in Santiago?*," which can be represented as a graph query (Event)←type—(?event)—location→(Santiago). Taking the data graph of Figure 2.1 and the axioms of Figure 3.2, we can check to see if the expected result (EID15) is entailed by the ontology and the data, and since it is not, we may consider expanding the axioms to assert that (location)—type→(Transitive).

Ontology Design Patterns (ODPs) are another common feature of modern methodologies [Blomqvist and Sandkuhl, 2005, Gangemi, 2005], specifying generalisable ontology modeling patterns that can be used as inspiration for modeling similar patterns, as modeling templates [Ega na et al., 2008, Skjæveland et al., 2018], or as directly reusable components [Daga et al., 2008, Shimizu et al., 2019]. Several pattern libraries have been made available online, ranging from carefully curated ones [Aranguren et al., 2008, Shimizu et al., 2019] to open and community moderated ones [Daga et al., 2008]. As an example, to model events in our scenario, we may adopt the Core Event ontology pattern proposed by Krisnadhi and Hitzler [2016a], which specifies a spatio-temporal extent, sub-events, and participants of an event, along with competency questions, formal definitions, etc., to support this pattern.

6.5.2 ONTOLOGY LEARNING

The previous methodologies outline methods by which ontologies can be built and maintained manually. Ontology learning, in contrast, can be used to (semi-)automatically extract information from text that is useful for the ontology engineering process [Buitelaar et al., 2005, Cimiano, 2006]. Early methods focussed on extracting terminology from text that may represent the relevant domain's classes; for example, from a collection of text documents about tourism, a terminology extraction tool—using measures of *unithood* that determine how cohesive an n-gram is as a unitary phrase, and *termhood* that determine how relevant the phrase is to a domain [Martínez-Rodríguez et al., 2018]—may identify n-grams such as "visitor visa," "World Heritage Site," "off-peak rate," etc., as terminology of particular importance to the tourist domain that thus may merit inclusion in such an ontology. Ontological axioms may also be extracted from text. A common target is to extract sub-class axioms from text, leveraging patterns based on modifying nouns and adjectives that incrementally specialize concepts (e.g., extracting (Visitor Visa)—subc. of→(Visa) from the noun phrase "visitor visa" and isolated appearances of "visa" elsewhere), or using Hearst patterns [Hearst, 1992] (e.g., extracting (Off-Peak Rate)—subc. of→(Discount) from "many discounts, such as off-peak rates, are available" based on the pattern "X, such as Y"). Textual definitions can also be harvested from large texts to extract hypernym relations and induce a taxonomy from scratch [Velardi et al., 2013]. More recent works aim to extract more expressive axioms from text, including disjointness axioms [Völker et al., 2015]; and axioms involving the union and intersection of classes, along with existential, universal, and qualified-cardinality restrictions [Petrucci et al., 2016]. The results of an ontology learning process can then serve as input to a more general ontology engineering methodology, allowing us to validate the terminological coverage of an ontology, to identify new classes and axioms, etc.

CHAPTER 7

Quality Assessment

Independent of the (kinds of) source(s) from which a knowledge graph is created, the resulting initial knowledge graph will usually be incomplete, and will often contain duplicate, contradictory or even incorrect statements, especially when taken from multiple sources. After the initial creation and enrichment of a knowledge graph from external sources, a crucial step is thus to assess the *quality* of the resulting knowledge graph. By quality, we here refer to *fitness for purpose*. Quality assessment then helps to ascertain for which purposes a knowledge graph can be reliably used. Take, for instance, the sample of an initial knowledge graph created by the tourist board shown in Figure 7.1. Is this knowledge graph of good quality? Does it exhibit issues that might limit the applications for which it is fit for purpose? Can we define and detect such issues? These questions are crucial to address before the knowledge graph is deployed, but they are also challenging to address in a general way.

This chapter discusses (sometimes overlapping) *quality dimensions* that capture qualitative aspects of the multifaceted notion of data quality; some of these dimensions apply more generally to databases [Batini et al., 2015], while others are more specific to knowledge graphs [Zaveri et al., 2016]. We further discuss *quality metrics* that provide ways to measure quantitative aspects of these dimensions. We group dimensions and metrics in a manner inspired by Batini and Scannapieco [2016].

7.1 ACCURACY

Accuracy refers to the extent to which entities and relations—encoded by nodes and edges in the graph—correctly represent real-life phenomena. Accuracy can be divided into three dimensions: *syntactic accuracy*, *semantic accuracy*, and *timeliness*.

7.1.1 SYNTACTIC ACCURACY

Syntactic accuracy is the degree to which the data are accurate with respect to the grammatical rules defined for the domain and/or data model. A prevalent example of syntactic inaccuracy occurs with datatype nodes, which may be incompatible with a defined range or be malformed. For example, assuming that a property start is defined with the range xsd:dateTime, the value `March 22, 2019` in Figure 7.1 would be incompatible with the defined range, while a value `"March 22, 2019"^^xsd:dateTime` would be malformed (a value such as `"2019-03-22T20:00:00"^^xsd:dateTime` is rather expected). A corresponding metric for syntactic accuracy is the ratio between the number of invalid values of a given property and the total number of values for the same property [Zaveri et al.,

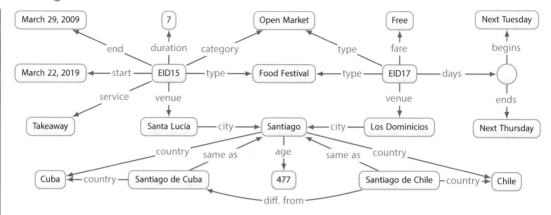

Figure 7.1: **A newly created knowledge graph about events and their venues.**

2016]. Such forms of syntactic accuracy can typically be assessed using validation tools [Fürber and Hepp, 2011, Hogan et al., 2010].

7.1.2 SEMANTIC ACCURACY

Semantic accuracy is the degree to which data values correctly represent real-world phenomena, which may be affected by imprecise extraction results, untrustworthy sources, vandalism, etc. For instance, in Figure 7.1, the start of the (EID15) event comes after the end of the event, possibly due to a typo in the year. While such a case could potentially be identified using, for example, shape-based validation, other cases might be more difficult to detect; for example, if we were to accidentally (and incorrectly) swap the venues for (EID15) and (EID17), there might be no indication whatsoever in the knowledge graph that the venues are incorrect, even if we have additional schemata/ontologies/rules available. Assessing the level of semantic inaccuracy is challenging. While one option is to apply manual verification, an automatic option may be to check the stated relation against several sources [Esteves et al., 2018, Lei et al., 2007]. An alternative is to validate the quality of the processes used to generate the knowledge graph, based on measures such as precision, possibly with the help of human experts or gold standards [Martínez-Rodríguez et al., 2020].

7.1.3 TIMELINESS

Timeliness is the degree to which the knowledge graph is kept up-to-date with the real-world state [Käfer et al., 2013]. A knowledge graph may be semantically accurate now, but may quickly become inaccurate (outdated) if no procedures are in place to keep it up-to-date in a timely manner. Considering Figure 7.1, the events appear to be from years ago, and if not updated, then the knowledge graph will not be suitable for applications that wish to recommend upcoming events to users. Additionally, the meaning of some values in the graph, such as (Next Tuesday) or

(Next Thursday) (which may have been extracted from the text of a news article, for example), will change over time, and become semantically inaccurate in the future. Similarly, the age of Santiago will quickly become outdated, where instead representing the year that the city was founded would facilitate timeliness. Timeliness can be assessed based on how frequently the knowledge graph is updated with respect to underlying sources [Käfer et al., 2013, Rula et al., 2014], which can be done using temporal annotations of changes in the knowledge graph [Rula et al., 2012, 2019], as well as contextual representations that capture the temporal validity of data (see Section 3.3).

7.2   COVERAGE

Coverage refers to avoiding the omission of domain-relevant elements, which otherwise may yield incomplete query results or entailments, biased models, etc.

7.2.1   COMPLETENESS

Completeness refers to the degree to which all required information is present in a particular dataset. Completeness comprises the following aspects: (i) *schema completeness* refers to the degree to which the classes and properties of a schema are represented in the data graph; (ii) *property completeness* refers to the ratio of missing values for a specific property; (iii) *population completeness* refers to the percentage of all real-world entities of a particular type that are represented in the datasets; and (iv) *linkability completeness* refers to the degree to which instances in the data set are interlinked. Taking some examples from Figure 7.1, the lack of information about the fare for (EID15) might be seen as a form of property incompleteness, while missing events held in Chile around the same time might lead to population incompleteness. Measuring completeness is non-trivial as it assumes knowledge of a hypothetical *ideal knowledge graph* [Darari et al., 2018] that contains all the elements that the knowledge graph in question *should* have. Concrete strategies may involve comparison with gold standards that provide samples of the ideal knowledge graph (possibly based on *completeness statements* [Darari et al., 2018]), or measuring the recall of extraction methods from complete sources [Martínez-Rodríguez et al., 2020].

7.2.2   REPRESENTATIVENESS

Representativeness is a related dimension that, instead of focusing on the ratio of domain-relevant elements that are missing, rather focuses on assessing high-level *biases* in what is included/excluded from the knowledge graph [Baeza-Yates, 2018]. As such, this dimension assumes that the knowledge graph is incomplete—i.e., that it is a sample of the ideal knowledge graph— and asks how biased this sample is. Biases may occur in the data, in the schema, or during reasoning [Janowicz et al., 2018]. Examples of data biases include geographic biases that underrepresent entities/relations from certain parts of the world [Janowicz et al., 2018], linguistic biases that under-represent multilingual resources (e.g., labels and descriptions) for certain lan-

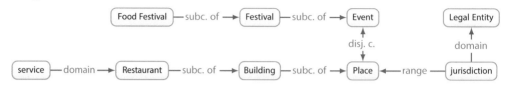

Figure 7.2: An ontology for the knowledge graph of Figure 7.1.

guages [Kaffee et al., 2017], social biases that under-represent people of particular genders or races [Wagner et al., 2016], and so forth. In contrast, schema biases may result from high-level definitions extracted from biased data [Janowicz et al., 2018], semantic definitions that do not cover uncommon cases, etc. Unrecognized biases may lead to adverse effects; for example, if the knowledge graph of Figure 7.1 has a geographic bias toward events and attractions close to Santiago city—due perhaps to the sources used for creation, the employment of curators from the city, etc.—then this may lead to tourism in and around Santiago being disproportionately promoted to the detriment of tourism elsewhere in Chile. Measures of representativeness may involve comparing known statistical distributions with those of the knowledge graph, for example, comparing geolocated entities with known population densities [Janowicz et al., 2018], linguistic distributions with known distributions of speakers [Kaffee et al., 2017], etc. Another more general option is to compare the knowledge graph with general statistical laws, where Soulet et al. [2018] use (non-)conformance with Benford's law[1] to measure representativeness in knowledge graphs.

7.3   COHERENCY

Coherency refers to how well the knowledge graph conforms to—or is coherent with—the formal semantics and constraints defined at the schema-level.

7.3.1   CONSISTENCY

Consistency means that a knowledge graph is free of contradictions (i.e., inconsistencies) with respect to the particular logical entailment considered. For example, if we apply the entailments defined in Table 4.1 over the graph of Figure 7.1, we see that the edge (Santiago de Chile)—same as→(Santiago de Cuba) is inferred from both entities being the same as (Santiago), which generates an inconsistency with the edge (Santiago de Chile)—diff. from→(Santiago de Cuba) as stated in the graph. While in this case it is evident that (Santiago de Cuba)—same as→(Santiago) is semantically inaccurate (considering that the venues connected to (Santiago) are in Chile), in other cases there may not be an obvious inaccuracy. Take, for example, the ontology defined in Figure 7.2, combined with the graph of Figure 7.1, and the ontological entailments of Tables 4.1–4.3. Noting that the food festival (EID15) offers a takeaway service, according to the ontology, this entails that (EID15) is a

---

[1]Benford's law states that the leading significant digit in many collections of numbers is more likely to be small.

restaurant, a building, and a place, which is disjoint with event. However, (EID15) is also entailed to be a festival, and then an event, generating an inconsistency. In this case, there is no clear individual "error" leading to an inconsistency. Possibly the graph of Figure 7.1 should not use the property service for a food event (though it seems a "good fit"), or perhaps the ontology of Figure 7.2 should not define the domain of the property service to be a restaurant. Any ontological features in Tables 4.1–4.3 with a "not" condition can give rise to inconsistencies if the negated condition is entailed. A measure of consistency can be the number of inconsistencies found in a knowledge graph, possibly sub-divided into the number of such inconsistencies identified by each semantic feature [Bonatti et al., 2011].

7.3.2   VALIDITY

Validity means that the knowledge graph is free of constraint violations, such as captured by shape expressions [Thornton et al., 2019] (see Section 3.1.2). We may, for example, specify a shape [CITY] whose target nodes have at most one country. Then, taking the edges (Chile)←country—(Santiago)—country→(Cuba) from Figure 7.1, and assuming that (Santiago) becomes a target of [CITY], we have a constraint violation. Conversely, even if we defined analogous cardinality restrictions in an ontology (e.g., even if we defined that country was functional), this would not necessarily cause an inconsistency since, without UNA, we would first infer that (Chile) and (Cuba) refer to the same entity. Similarly, using shapes, we can more easily detect missing data; for example, we can define a shape [EVENT], and require that it have at least one value for the property fare. Now, if (EID15) becomes targetted by [EVENT], then we will have a constraint violation as the node has no value for fare. Conversely, even if we defined analogous cardinality restrictions in an ontology (e.g., we defined that events have a minimum cardinality of 1 for fare), this would not cause an inconsistency since, under the OWA, we would rather entail that the event (EID15) has some fair (that is not described in the graph). Consistency and validity can thus indicate different types of issues. A straightforward measure of validity is to count the number of violations per constraint.

7.4   SUCCINCTNESS

Succinctness refers to the inclusion only of relevant content (avoiding "information overload") that is represented in a concise and intelligible manner.

7.4.1   CONCISENESS

Conciseness refers to avoiding schema and data elements that are irrelevant to the domain. Mendes et al. [2012b] distinguish *intensional conciseness* (schema level), which refers to the case when the data do not contain redundant schema elements (properties, classes, shapes, etc.), and *extensional conciseness* (data level), where the data do not describe redundant entities and relations. For example, the inclusion of a property and class for modeling jurisdictions and legal entities in the ontology of Figure 7.2 may affect the intensional conciseness of the ontology in the context of a knowledge graph about tourist events. Similarly, the inclusion of data about (Santiago de Cuba) in our knowledge graph dedicated to tourism in Chile may affect the extensional conciseness of the knowledge graph, potentially returning irrelevant results for the given domain. In general, conciseness can be measured in terms of the ratio of properties, classes, shapes, entities, relations, etc., of relevance to the domain, which may in turn require a gold standard, or measures of domain-relevance.

7.4.2 REPRESENTATIONAL CONCISENESS

Representational conciseness refers to the extent to which content is compactly represented in the knowledge graph, which may again be intensional or extensional [Zaveri et al., 2016]. For example, having two properties category and type serving the same purpose would negatively affect the intensional form of representational conciseness, while having two nodes (Santiago) and (Santiago de Chile) that split the data available about the capital of Chile would affect the extensional form of representational conciseness. Another example of poor representational conciseness is the unnecessary use of complex modeling constructs, such as using reification unnecessarily, or using linked lists when the order of elements is not important [Hogan et al., 2012a]. An example of this is the anonymous node used in Figure 7.1 to represent the days on which (EID17) starts and ends, which could rather be directly associated with the event (at least if we assume that events have one start and one end moment in time). A different example is the specification of the duration of (EID15), which could be calculated from the start and end values (assuming the correct datatypes were used). Though representational conciseness is challenging to assess, measures such as the number of redundant nodes can be used [Fürber and Hepp, 2011].

7.4.3 UNDERSTANDABILITY

Understandability refers to the ease with which data can be interpreted without ambiguity by human users, which involves—at least—the provision of human-readable labels and descriptions (preferably in different languages [Kaffee et al., 2017]) that allow such beings to understand what is being spoken about [Hogan et al., 2012a]. Referring back to Figure 7.1, though the nodes (EID15) and (EID17) are used to ensure unique identifiers for events, they should also be associated with labels, such as (Ñam). Ideally the human readable information is sufficient to disambiguate a particular node, such as associating a description ("Santiago, the capital of Chile"@en) with (Santiago) to disambiguate the city from synonymous ones. Measures of understandability may include the ratio of nodes with human-readable labels and descriptions, the uniqueness of such labels and descriptions, the languages supported, etc.

7.5   OTHER QUALITY DIMENSIONS

The list of quality dimensions provided here should be considered illustrative rather than complete. Further dimensions may be pertinent in the context of specific domains, applications, or graph data models. For more discussion, we refer to the survey by Zaveri et al. [2016] and to the book by Batini and Scannapieco [2016].

CHAPTER 8

Refinement

Beyond assessing the quality of a knowledge graph, there exist techniques to *refine* the knowledge graph, in particular to (semi-)automatically complete and correct the knowledge graph [Paulheim, 2017], aka *knowledge graph completion* and *knowledge graph correction*, respectively. As distinguished from the creation and enrichment tasks outlined in Chapter 6, refinement typically does not involve applying extraction or mappings over external sources in order to ingest their content into the local knowledge graph. Instead, refinement typically targets improvement of a given knowledge graph (potentially using external sources to verify its content).

8.1 COMPLETION

Knowledge graphs are characterized by incompleteness [West et al., 2014]. As such, knowledge graph completion aims at filling in the *missing edges* (aka *missing links*) of a knowledge graph, i.e., edges that are deemed correct but are neither given nor entailed by the knowledge graph. This task is often addressed with *link prediction* techniques proposed in the area of *Statistical Relational Learning* [Getoor and Taskar, 2007], which predict the existence—or sometimes more generally, predict the probability of correctness—of missing edges. For instance, one might predict that the edge (Moon Valley)─bus→(San Pedro) is a probable missing edge for the graph of Figure 5.2, given that most bus routes observed are return services (i.e., bus is typically symmetric). Link prediction may target three settings: *general links* involving edges with arbitrary labels, e.g., bus, flight, type, etc.; *type links* involving edges with label type, indicating the type of an entity; and *identity links* involving edges with label same as, indicating that two nodes refer to the same entity (cf. Section 3.2.2). While type and identity links can be addressed using general link prediction techniques, the particular semantics of type and identity links can be addressed with custom techniques. (The related task of generating links across knowledge graphs—referred to as *link discovery* [Nentwig et al., 2017]—will be discussed later in Section 9.1.)

8.1.1 GENERAL LINK PREDICTION

Link prediction, in the general case, is often addressed with inductive techniques as discussed in Chapter 5, and in particular, knowledge graph embeddings and rule/axiom mining. For example, given Figure 5.2, using knowledge graph embeddings, we may detect that given an edge of the form (x)─bus→(y), a (missing) edge (y)─bus→(x) has high plausibility, while using symbol-based approaches, we may learn the high-level rule (?x)─bus→(?y) ⇒ (?y)─bus→(?x) that may infer/predict new bus links. Either approach would help us to predict the missing link (Moon Valley)─bus→(San Pedro).

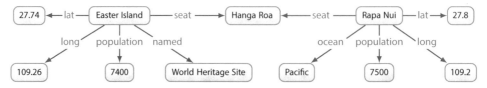

Figure 8.1: Identity linking example: (Easter Island) and (Rapa Nui) denote the same place.

8.1.2   TYPE-LINK PREDICTION

Type links are of particular importance to a knowledge graph, where dedicated techniques can be leveraged taking into account the specific semantics of such links. In the case of type prediction, there is only one edge label (type) and typically fewer distinct values (classes) than in other cases, such that the task can be reduced to a traditional classification task [Paulheim, 2017], training models to identify each semantic class based on features such as outgoing and/or incoming edge labels on their instances in the knowledge graph [Paulheim and Bizer, 2013, Sleeman and Finin, 2013]. For example, assume that in Figure 5.2 we also know that (Arica), (Calama), (Puerto Montt), (Punta Arenas), and (Santiago) are of type (City). We may then predict that (Iquique) and (Easter Island) are also of type (City) based on the presence of edges labeled flight to/from these nodes, which (we assume) are learned to be a good feature for prediction of that class (the former prediction is correct, while the latter is incorrect). Graph neural networks (see Section 5.3) can also be used for node classification/type prediction.

8.1.3   IDENTITY-LINK PREDICTION

Predicting identity links involves searching for nodes that refer to the same entity, but are not stated or entailed to be the same; this is analogous to the task of *entity matching* (aka record linkage, deduplication, etc.) considered in more general data integration settings [Köpcke and Rahm, 2010]. Such techniques are generally based on two types of *matchers*: *value matchers* determine how similar the values of two entities on a given property are, which may involve similarity metrics on strings, numbers, dates, etc.; while *context matchers* consider the similarity of entities based on various nodes and edges [Köpcke and Rahm, 2010]. An illustrative example is given in Figure 8.1, where value matchers will compute similarity between values such as (7400) and (7500), while context matchers will compute similarity between (Easter Island) and (Rapa Nui) based on their surrounding information, such as similar latitudes, longitudes, populations, and the same seat (conversely, a value matcher on this pair of nodes would measure string similarity between "Easter Island" and "Rapa Nui").

   A major challenge in this setting is efficiency, where pairwise matching would require $O(n^2)$ comparisons for n the number of nodes. To address this issue, *blocking* can be used to group similar entities into (possibly overlapping, possibly disjoint) "blocks" based on similarity-preserving keys, with matching performed within each block [Draisbach and Naumann, 2011,

Isele et al., 2011, Köpcke and Rahm, 2010]; for example, if matching places based on latitude/-longitude, blocks may represent geographic regions. An alternative to discrete blocking is to use *windowing* over entities in a similarity-preserving ordering [Draisbach and Naumann, 2011], or to consider searching for similar entities within *multi-dimensional spaces* (e.g., spacetime [Santipantakis et al., 2019], spaces with Minkowski distances [Ngonga Ngomo, 2012], orthodromic spaces [Ngonga Ngomo, 2013], etc. [Sherif and Ngonga Ngomo, 2018]). The results can either be pairs of nodes with a computed confidence of them referring to the same entity, or crisp identity links extracted based on a fixed threshold, or binary classification [Köpcke and Rahm, 2010]. For confident identity links, the nodes' edges may then be *consolidated* [Hogan et al., 2012b]; for example, we may select ⬭Easter Island⬭ as the canonical node and merge the edges of ⬭Rapa Nui⬭ onto it, enabling us to find, e.g., *World Heritage Sites in the Pacific Ocean* from Figure 8.1 based on the (consolidated) sub-graph ⬭World Heritage Site⬭◄–named–⬭Easter Island⬭–ocean►⬭Pacific⬭.

8.2   CORRECTION

As opposed to completion—which finds new edges in a knowledge graph—correction identifies and removes existing incorrect edges in the knowledge graph. We here divide the principal approaches for knowledge graph correction into two main lines: *fact validation*, which assigns a plausibility score to a given edge, typically in reference to external sources; and *inconsistency repairs*, which aim to resolve inconsistencies found in the knowledge graph through ontological axioms.

8.2.1   FACT VALIDATION

The task of *fact validation* (aka *fact checking*) [Bordes et al., 2013, Esteves et al., 2018, Gerber et al., 2015, Shi and Weninger, 2016, Shiralkar et al., 2017, Socher et al., 2013, Syed et al., 2018, 2019, Yin et al., 2008] involves assigning plausibility or *veracity* scores to facts/edges, typically between 0 and 1. An ideal fact-checking function assumes a hypothetical reference universe (an ideal knowledge graph) and would return 1 for the fact ⬭Santa Lucía⬭–city►⬭Santiago⬭ (being true) while returning 0 for ⬭Sotomayor⬭–city►⬭Santiago⬭ (being false). There is a clear relation between fact validation and link prediction—with both relying on assessing the plausibility of edges/facts/links—and indeed the same numeric- and symbol-based techniques can be applied for both cases. However, fact validation often considers online assessment of edges given as input, whereas link prediction is often an offline task that generates novel candidate edges to be assessed from the knowledge graph. Furthermore, works on fact validation are characterized by their consideration of external reference sources, which may be *unstructured sources* [Gerber et al., 2015, Samadi et al., 2016, Syed et al., 2018, Yin et al., 2008] or *structured sources* [Bordes et al., 2013, Shi and Weninger, 2016, Shiralkar et al., 2017, Socher et al., 2013, Syed et al., 2019].

Approaches based on unstructured sources assume that they are given a *verbalization function*—using, for example, rule-based approaches [Ell et al., 2014, Ngonga Ngomo et al., 2013], encoder-decoder architectures [Gardent et al., 2017], etc.—that is able to translate edges into natural language. Thereafter, approaches for computing the plausibility of facts in natural language—called *fact finders* [Pasternack and Roth, 2010, 2011]—can be directly employed. Many fact finding algorithms construct an *n*-partite (often bipartite) graph whose nodes are facts and sources, where a source is connected to a fact if the source "evidences" the fact, i.e., if it contains a text snippet that matches—with sufficient confidence—the verbalization of the input edge. Two mutually-dependent scores, namely the trustworthiness of sources and the plausibility of facts, are then calculated based on this graph, where fact finders differ on how they compute these scores [Pasternack and Roth, 2011]. Here we mention three scores proposed by Pasternack and Roth [2010].

- *Sums* [Pasternack and Roth, 2010] adapts the classical HITS centrality algorithm [Kleinberg, 1999] by defining sources as hubs (with 0 authority score) and facts as authorities (with 0 hub score).

- *Average Log* [Pasternack and Roth, 2010] extends HITS with a normalization factor that prevents a single source from receiving a high trustworthiness score by evidencing many facts (that may be false).

- *Investment* [Pasternack and Roth, 2010] lets the scores of facts grow with a non-linear function based on "investments" coming from the connected sources. The score a source receives from a fact is based on the individual facts in this particular source compared to the other connected sources.

Pasternack and Roth [2011] then show that these three algorithms can be generalized into a single multi-layered graph-based framework within which (1) a source can support a fact with a weight expressing uncertainty, (2) similar facts can support each other, and (3) sources can be grouped together leading to an implicit support between sources of the same group. Other approaches for fact checking of knowledge graphs later extended this framework [Galland et al., 2010, Samadi et al., 2016]. Alternative approaches based on machine learning classifiers have also emerged, where commonly-used features include trust scores for information sources, co-occurrences of facts in sources, and so forth [Gerber et al., 2015, Syed et al., 2018].

Approaches for fact validation based on structured data typically assume external knowledge graphs as reference sources and are based on finding paths that support the edge being validated. Unsupervised approaches search for undirected [Ciampaglia et al., 2015, Shiralkar et al., 2017] or directed [Syed et al., 2019] paths up to a given threshold length that support the input edge. The relatedness between input edges and paths is computed using a mutual information function, such as normalized pointwise mutual information [Bouma, 2009]. Supervised approaches rather extract features for input edges from external knowledge graphs [Lao and Cohen, 2010, Sun et al., 2011, Zhao et al., 2015] and train a classification model to label the edges as true or false. An important set of features are *metapaths*, which encode sequences of predicates that correlate positively with the edge label of the input edge. Among such works, PredPath [Shi and Weninger, 2016] automatically extracts metapaths based on type information. Several approaches rather encode the reference nodes and edges using graph embeddings (see Section 5.2), which are then used to estimate the plausibility of the input edge being validated.

8.2.2 INCONSISTENCY REPAIRS

Ontologies can contain axioms—such as disjointness—that lead to inconsistencies. While such axioms can be provided by experts, they can also be derived through symbolic learning, as discussed in Section 5.4. Such axioms can then be used to detect inconsistencies. With respect to correcting a knowledge graph, however, detecting inconsistencies is not enough: techniques are also required to *repair* such inconsistencies, which itself is not a trivial task. In the simplest case, we may have an instance of two disjoint classes, such as that (Santiago) is of type (City) and (Airport), which are stated or found to be disjoint. To repair the inconsistency, it would be preferable to remove only the "incorrect" class, but which should we remove? This is not a trivial question, particularly if we consider that one edge can be involved in many inconsistencies, and one inconsistency can involve many edges. The issue of computing repairs becomes more complex when entailment is considered, where we not only need to remove the stated type, but also all of the ways in which it might be entailed; for example, removing the edge (Santiago)–type→(Airport) is insufficient if we further have an edge (Arica)–flight→(Santiago) combined with an axiom (flight)–range→(Airport). Töpper et al. [2012] suggest potential repairs for such violations—remove a domain/range constraint, remove a disjointness constraint, remove a type edge, or remove an edge with a domain/range constraint—where one is chosen manually. In contrast, Bonatti et al. [2011] propose an automated method to repair inconsistencies based on *minimal hitting sets* [Reiter, 1987], where each set is a minimal explanation for an inconsistency. The edges to remove are chosen based on scores of the trustworthiness of their sources and how many minimal hitting sets they are either elements of or help to entail an element of, where the knowledge graph is revised to avoid re-entailment of the removed edges. Rather than repairing the data, another option is to evaluate queries under inconsistency-aware semantics, such as returning *consistent answers* valid under every possible repair [Lukasiewicz et al., 2013].

8.3 OTHER REFINEMENT TASKS

In comparison to the quality clusters discussed in Chapter 7, the refinement methods discussed herein address particular aspects of the accuracy, coverage, and coherency dimensions. Beyond these, one could conceive of further refinement methods to address further quality issues of knowledge graphs, such as succinctness. In general, however, the refinement tasks of *knowledge graph completion* and *knowledge graph correction* have received the majority of attention until now. For further details on knowledge graph refinement, we refer to the survey by Paulheim [2017].

CHAPTER 9

Publication

While it may not always be desirable to publish knowledge graphs (for example, those that offer a competitive advantage to a company [Noy et al., 2019]), it may be desirable or even required to publish other knowledge graphs, such as those produced by volunteers [Lehmann et al., 2015, Mahdisoltani et al., 2015, Vrandečić and Krötzsch, 2014], by publicly-funded research [Callahan et al., 2013, Groth et al., 2014, The UniProt Consortium, 2014], or by governmental organizations [Hendler et al., 2012, Shadbolt and O'Hara, 2013]. Publishing refers to making the knowledge graph (or part thereof) accessible to the public, often on the Web. Knowledge graphs published as open data are called open knowledge graphs (discussed in Section 10.1).

In the following, we first discuss two sets of principles that have been proposed to guide the publication of data on the Web. We next discuss access protocols by which the public can interact with the content of a knowledge graph. Finally, we consider techniques to restrict the access or usage of (parts of) a knowledge graph.

9.1 BEST PRACTICES

We now discuss two key sets of publishing principles: the FAIR Principles [Wilkinson et al., 2016] and the Linked Data Principles [Berners-Lee, 2006].

9.1.1 FAIR PRINCIPLES

The FAIR Principles were originally proposed in the context of publishing scientific data [Wilkinson et al., 2016]—particularly motivated by maximising the impact of publicly-funded research—but the principles generally apply to other situations where data are to be published in a manner that facilitates their re-use by external agents, with particular emphasis on machine-readability.

FAIR itself is an acronym for four foundational principles, each with particular goals [Wilkinson et al., 2016], that may apply to *data*, *metadata*, or both—the latter being denoted *(meta)data*.[1] We now describe the FAIR principles (slightly rephrasing the original wording in some cases for brevity [Wilkinson et al., 2016]).

- *Findability* refers to the ease with which external agents who might benefit from the dataset can initially locate the dataset. Four sub-goals should be met:

---

[1]Metadata are data about data. The distinction is often important in observational sciences, where in astronomy, for example, data may include raw image data, while metadata may include coordinates and time.

– F1: (meta)data are assigned a globally unique and persistent identifier.

– F2: data are described with rich metadata (see R1).

– F3: metadata explicitly include the identifier of the data they describe.

– F4: (meta)data are registered or indexed in a searchable resource.

• *Accessibility* refers to the ease with which external agents can access the dataset (after locating it). Two goals are defined, the first with two sub-goals:

– A1: (meta)data are retrievable by their identifier via a standard protocol.

  ○ A1.1: the protocol is open, free, and universally implementable.

  ○ A1.2: the protocol uses authentication and authorization if suitable.

– A2: metadata are accessible, even when the data are no longer available.

• *Interoperability* refers to the ease with which the dataset can be exploited (in unison with other datasets) using standard tools. Three goals are defined:

– I1: (meta)data use an accessible, agreed-upon, and general knowledge representation formalism.

– I2: (meta)data use vocabularies that follow FAIR principles.

– I3: (meta)data include qualified references to other (meta)data.

• *Reusability* refers to the ease with which the dataset can be re-used in conjunction with other datasets. One goal is defined (with three sub-goals):

– R1: meta(data) are richly described with accurate and relevant attributes.

  ○ R1.1. (meta)data are released with a clear and accessible license.

  ○ R1.2. (meta)data are associated with detailed provenance.

  ○ R1.3. (meta)data meet domain-relevant community standards.

In the context of knowledge graphs, a variety of vocabularies, tools, and services have been proposed that both directly and indirectly help to satisfy the FAIR principles. In terms of *Findability*, as discussed in Chapter 2, IRIs are built into the RDF model, providing a general schema for global identifiers. In addition, resources such as the Vocabulary of Interlinked Datasets (VoID) [Alexander et al., 2009] allow for representing metadata about graphs, while services such as DataHub [Bhardwaj et al., 2015] provide a central repository of such dataset descriptions. Access protocols that enable *Accessibility* will be discussed in Section 9.2, while mechanisms for authorization will be discussed in Section 9.3. With respect to *Interoperability*, as discussed in Chapter 4, ontologies serve as a general knowledge representation formalism, and can in turn be used to describe vocabularies that follow FAIR principles. Regarding *Reusability*, licensing will be discussed in Section 9.3, while the *PROV Data Model* [Gil et al., 2013], discussed in Chapter 3, can encode provenance in detail.

Various knowledge graphs have been published using FAIR principles, where Wilkinson et al. [2016] explicitly mention Open PHACTS [Groth et al., 2014], a data integration platform for drug discovery, and UniProt [The UniProt Consortium, 2014], a large collection of protein sequence and annotation data, as conforming to FAIR principles. Both datasets offer graph views of their content through RDF.

9.1.2 LINKED DATA PRINCIPLES

Wilkinson et al. [2016] state that FAIR Principles "precede implementation choices," meaning that the principles do not cover *how* they can or should be achieved. Preceding the FAIR Principles by almost a decade are the Linked Data Principles, proposed by Berners-Lee [2006], which provide a technical basis for one way in which these FAIR Principles can be achieved. These Linked Data Principles are as follows.

1. Use IRIs as names for things.

2. Use HTTP IRIs so those names can be looked up.

3. When a HTTP IRI is looked up, provide useful content about the entity that the IRI names using standard data formats.

4. Include links to the IRIs of related entities in the content returned.

These principles were proposed in a Semantic Web setting, where for principle (3), the standards based on RDF (including RDFS, OWL, etc.) are currently recommended for use, particularly because they allow for naming entities using HTTP IRIs, which further paves the way for satisfying all four principles. As such, these principles outline a way in which (RDF) graph-structured data can be published on the Web such that these graphs are interlinked to form what Berners-Lee [2006] calls a "Web of Data," whose goal is to increase automation on the Web by making content available not only in (HTML) documents intended for human consumption, but also as (RDF) structured data that machines can locate, retrieve, combine, validate, reason over, query over, etc., toward solving tasks automatically [Hogan, 2020b]. Conceptually, the Web of Data is then composed of graphs of data published on individual web-pages, where one can click on a node or edge-label—or more precisely perform a HTTP lookup on an IRI of the graph—to be transported to another graph elsewhere on the Web with relevant content for that node or edge-label, and so on recursively.

Figure 9.1 provides a small example with two Linked Data documents published on the Web, with each containing an RDF graph. As discussed in Section 3.2, terms such as `clv:Concert`, `wd:Q142701`, `rdfs:label`, etc. are abbreviations for IRIs, where, for example, `wd:Q142701` expands to http://www.wikidata.org/entity/Q142701. Prefixes beginning with `cl` are fictitious prefixes we assume to have been created by the Chilean tourist board. The IRIs prefixed with ↪🏠 indicate the document returned if the node is looked up. The leftmost document is published by the tourist board and describes Lollapalooza 2018 (identified by the node

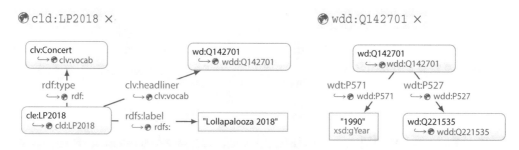

Figure 9.1: Two example Linked Data documents from two websites, each containing an RDF graph, where wd:Q142701 refers to Pearl Jam in Wikidata while wdd:Q142701 refers to the RDF graph about Pearl Jam, and where wd:Q221535 refers to Eddie Vedder while wdd:Q221535 refers to the RDF graph about Eddie Vedder; the edge-label wdt:571 refers to "inception" in Wikidata, while wdt:527 refers to "has part."

(cle:LP2018)), which links to the headlining act Pearl Jam ((wd:Q142701)) described by an external knowledge graph, namely Wikidata. By looking up the node (wd:Q142701) in the leftmost graph, the IRI *dereferences* (i.e., returns via HTTP) the document with the RDF graph on the right describing that entity in more detail. From the rightmost document, the node (wd:Q221535) can be looked up, in turn, to find a graph about Eddie Vedder (not shown in the example). The IRIs for entities and documents are distinguished to ensure that we do not confuse data about the entity and the document; for example, while wd:Q221535 refers to Eddie Vedder, the IRI wdd:Q221535 refers to the document about Eddie Vedder; if we were to assign a last-modified date to the document, we should use (wdd:Q221535) not (wd:Q221535). In Figure 9.1, we can further observe that edge labels (which are also IRIs) and nodes representing classes (e.g., (clv:Concert)) can also be dereferenced, typically returning semantic definitions of the respective terms.

A key challenge is posed by the fourth principle—include links to related entities—as illustrated in Figure 9.1, where (wd:Q221535) in the leftmost graph constitutes a link to related content about Pearl Jam in an external knowledge graph. Specifically, the *link discovery* task considers adding such links from one knowledge graph to another, which may involve inclusion of IRIs that dereference to external graphs (per Figure 9.1), or links with special semantics such as identity links. In comparison with the link prediction task discussed in Section 8.1, which is used to complete links within a knowledge graph, link discovery aims to discover links across knowledge graphs, which involves unique aspects: first, link discovery typically considers disjoint sets of source (local) nodes and target (remote) nodes; second, the knowledge graphs may often use different vocabularies; and third, while in link prediction there already exist local examples of the links to predict, in link discovery, there are often no existing links between knowledge graphs to learn from. A common technique is to define manually-crafted linkage rules (aka link specifications) that apply heuristics for defining links that potentially incorporate similarity mea-

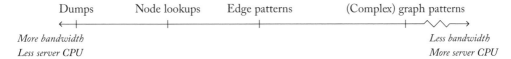

Figure 9.2: Access protocols for knowledge graphs, from simple protocols (left) to more complex protocols (right).

sures [Ngonga Ngomo and Auer, 2011, Volz et al., 2009]. Link discovery is greatly expedited by the provision of standard identifier schemes within knowledge graphs, such as ISBNs for books, alpha-2 and alpha-3 codes for countries (e.g., CL, CLP), or even links to common knowledge graphs such as DBpedia [Lehmann et al., 2015] or Wikidata [Vrandečić and Krötzsch, 2014] (that themselves include standard identifiers). We refer to the survey on link discovery by Nentwig et al. [2017] for more details.

More finer-grained recommendations for publishing Linked Data have also been proposed, relating to how best implement dereferencing, what kinds of links to include, how to publish and interlink vocabularies, among other considerations [Heath and Bizer, 2011, Janowicz et al., 2014]. We refer to the book by Heath and Bizer [2011] for more discussion on how to publish Linked Data on the Web.

9.2   ACCESS PROTOCOLS

Publishing involves giving access to the public to interact with the knowledge graph, which implies the provision of *access protocols* that define the requests that agents can make and the response that they can expect as a result. Per the *Accessibility* principle of FAIR (specifically A1.1), this protocol should be open, free, and universally implementable. In the context of knowledge graphs, as shown in Figure 9.2, there are a number of access protocols to choose from, varying from simple protocols that allow users to simply download all content, toward protocols that accept and evaluate increasingly complex requests. While simpler protocols require less computation on the server that publishes the data, more complex protocols allow agents to request more specific data, thus reducing bandwidth. A knowledge graph may also offer a variety of access protocols catering to different agents with different requirements [Verborgh et al., 2014]. We now discuss such access protocols.

9.2.1   DUMPS

A dump is a file or collection of files containing the content of the knowledge graph available for download. The request in this case is for the file(s) and the response is the content of the file(s). In order to publish dumps, first of all, concrete—and ideally standard—syntaxes are required to serialize the graph. While for RDF graphs there are various standard syntaxes available based on XML [Gandon and Schreiber, 2014], JSON [Sporny et al., 2014], custom syntaxes [Prud'hommeaux and Carothers, 2014], and more besides, currently there are only non-standard syntaxes available for property graphs [Tomaszuk et al., 2019]. Second, to reduce bandwidth, compression methods can be applied. While standard compression such as GZIP or BZip2 can be straightforwardly applied on any file, custom compression methods have been proposed for graphs that not only offer better compression ratios than these standard methods, but also offer additional functionalities, such as compact indexes for performing efficient lookups once the file is downloaded [Fernández et al., 2013]. Finally, to further reduce bandwidth, when the knowledge graph is updated, "diffs" can be computed and published to obviate the need for agents to download all data from scratch (see Ahn et al. [2015], Papavasileiou et al. [2013], Tummarello et al. [2007]). Still, however, dumps are only suited to certain use-cases, in particular for agents that wish to maintain a full local copy of a knowledge graph. If an agent were rather only interested in, for example, all food festivals in Santiago, downloading the entire dump may require transferring and processing a lot of irrelevant data.

9.2.2   NODE LOOKUPS

Protocols for performing node lookups accept a node (id) request (e.g., cle:LP2018 in Figure 9.1) and return a (sub-)graph describing that node (e.g., the document cld:LP2018). Such a protocol is the basis for the Linked Data principles outlined previously, whereby node lookups are implemented through HTTP dereferencing, which further allows nodes in remote graphs to be referenced from across the Web. Although there are varying definitions on what content should be returned for a node [Stickler, 2005], a common convention is to return a sub-graph containing either all outgoing edges for that node or all incident edges (both outgoing and incoming) for that node [Hogan et al., 2012a]. Though simple, mechanisms for evaluating graph patterns can be implemented on top of a node lookup interface by traversing from node to node per the particular graph pattern [Hartig et al., 2009]; for example, to find all food festivals in Santiago—represented by the graph pattern Food Festival ←type— ?ff —location→ Santiago —we may perform a node lookup for Santiago, subsequently performing a node lookup for each node connected by a location edge to Santiago, returning those nodes declared to be of type Food Festival. However, such an approach may not be feasible if no starting node is declared (e.g., if all nodes are variables), if the node lookup service does not return incoming edges, etc. The client agent may also need to request more data than necessary; for example, the document returned for Santiago may return a lot of data irrelevant to the query, and nodes with a location in Santiago that are not instances of Food Festival still need to be looked up to check their type. Node lookups are relatively inexpensive for servers to support in terms of CPU, but may again waste bandwidth due to transferring irrelevant data.

9.2.3   EDGE PATTERNS

Edge patterns—also known as *triple patterns* in the case of directed, edge-labeled graphs—are singleton graph patterns, i.e., graph patterns with a single edge. Examples of edge patterns are

[?ff ⊢type→ Food Festival] or [?ff ⊢location→ Santiago], etc., where any term can be a variable or a constant. A protocol for edge patterns accepts such a pattern and returns all solutions for the pattern. Edge patterns provide more flexibility than node lookups, where graph patterns are more readily decomposed into edge patterns than node lookups. With respect to the agent interested in food festivals in Santiago, they can first, for example, request solutions for the edge pattern [?ff ⊢location→ Santiago] and locally join/intersect these solutions with those of [?ff ⊢type→ Food Festival]. Given that some edge patterns (e.g., [?x ⊢?y→ ?z]) can return many solutions, protocols for edge patterns may offer additional practical features such as iteration or pagination over results [Verborgh et al., 2016]. Much like node lookups, the server cost of responding to a request is relatively low and easy to predict. However, the server may often need to transfer irrelevant intermediate results to the client, which in the previous example may involve returning nodes located in Santiago that are not food festivals. This issue is further aggravated if the client does not have access to statistics about the knowledge graph in order to plan how to best perform the join; for example, if there are relatively few food festivals but many things located in Santiago, rather than intersecting the solutions of the two aforementioned edge patterns, it should be more efficient to send a request for each food festival to see if it is in Santiago, but deciding this requires statistics about the knowledge graph. Extensions to the edge-pattern protocol have thus been proposed to allow for more efficient joins [Hartig et al., 2017], such as allowing batches of solutions to be sent alongside the edge pattern to only return solutions compatible with the solutions in the request [Hartig and Buil-Aranda, 2016] (e.g., sending a batch of solutions for [?ff ⊢type→ Food Festival] to join with the solutions for the request [?ff ⊢location→ Santiago]).

9.2.4   (COMPLEX) GRAPH PATTERNS

Another alternative is to let client agents make requests based on (complex) graph patterns (see Section 2.2), with the server returning (only) the final solutions. In our running example, this involves the client issuing a request for [Food Festival ←type─ ?ff ⊢location→ Santiago] and directly receiving the relevant results. Compared with the previous protocols, this protocol is much more efficient in terms of bandwidth: it allows clients to make more specific requests and the server to return more specific responses. However, this reduction in bandwidth use comes at the cost of the server having to evaluate much more complex requests, where, furthermore, the costs of a single request are much more difficult to anticipate. While a variety of optimized engines exist for evaluating (complex) graph patterns (e.g., Erling [2012], Miller [2013], Thompson et al. [2014] among many others), the problem of evaluating such queries is known to be intractable [Angles et al., 2017]. Perhaps for this reason, public services offering such a protocol (most often supporting SPARQL queries [Harris et al., 2013]) have been found to often exhibit downtimes, timeouts, partial results, slow performance, etc. [Buil-Aranda et al., 2013b]. Even considering such issues, however, popular services continue to receive—and successfully evaluate—millions of requests/queries per day [Malyshev et al., 2018, Saleem et al., 2015], with difficult (worst-case) instances being rare in practice [Bonifati et al., 2017].

9.2.5 OTHER PROTOCOLS

While Figure 9.2 makes explicit reference to some of the most commonly-encountered access protocols found for knowledge graphs in practice, one may of course imagine other protocols lying almost anywhere on the spectrum from more simple to more complex interfaces. To the right of (Complex) Graph Patterns, one could consider supporting even more complex requests, such as queries with entailments [Glimm, 2011], queries that allow recursion [Reutter et al., 2015], federated queries that can join results from remote services [Buil-Aranda et al., 2013a], or even (hypothetically) supporting Turing-complete requests that allow running arbitrary procedural code on a knowledge graph. As mentioned at the outset, a server may also choose to support multiple, complementary protocols [Verborgh et al., 2014].

9.3 USAGE CONTROL

Considering our hypothetical tourism knowledge graph, at first glance, one might assume that the knowledge required to deliver the envisaged services is public and thus can be used both by the tourism board and the tourists. On closer inspection, however, we may see the need for usage control in various forms:

1. both the tourist board and its partners should associate an appropriate license with knowledge that they contribute to the knowledge graph, such that the terms of use are clear to all interested parties;

2. a tourist might opt to install an app on their mobile phone that could be used to recommend tourist attractions based on their location, bringing with it potential privacy concerns regarding who has access to their location;

3. the tourist board may be required to report criminal activities to the police services and thus may need to encrypt personal information; and

4. the tourist board could potentially share information relating to tourism demographics in an anonymous format to allow for other agencies and companies to anticipate demand and improve transport infrastructure on strategic routes.

Thus, in this section, we examine the state of the art in terms of knowledge graph licensing, usage policies, encryption, and anonymization.

9.3.1 LICENSING

When it comes to associating machine readable licenses with knowledge graphs, the W3C Open Digital Rights Language (ODRL) [Iannella and Villata, 2018] provides an information model and related vocabularies that can be used to specify permissions, duties, and prohibitions with respect to actions relating to assets. ODRL supports fine-grained descriptions of digital rights

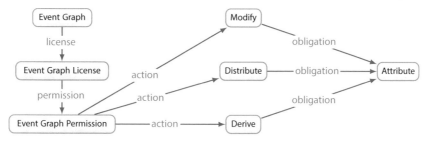

Figure 9.3: A license for event data, along with permissions, actions, and obligations.

that are represented as—and thus can be embedded within—graphs. Figure 9.3 illustrates a license granting the assignee the permission to (Modify), (Distribute), and (Derive) work from the (Event Graph) (e.g., Figure 2.1); however, the assignee is obliged to (Attribute) the copyright holder. From a modeling perspective, ODRL can be used to model several well-known license families, for instance Apache, Creative Commons (CC), and Berkeley Software Distribution (BSD), to name but a few [Cabrio et al., 2014, Panasiuk et al., 2018]. Additionally, Cabrio et al. [2014] propose methods to automatically extract machine-readable licenses from unstructured text. From a reasoning perspective, license compatibility validation and composition techniques [Governatori et al., 2013, Moreau et al., 2019, Villata and Gandon, 2012] can be used to combine knowledge graphs that are governed by different licenses. Such techniques are employed by the Data Licenses Clearance Center (DALICC), which includes a library of standard machine readable licenses, and tools that enable users both to compose arbitrary custom licenses and also to verify the compatibility of different licenses [Pellegrini et al., 2019].

9.3.2   USAGE POLICIES

Access control policies based on edge patterns can be used to restrict access to parts of a knowledge graph [Flouris et al., 2010, Kirrane et al., 2013, Reddivari et al., 2005]. WebAccessControl (WAC)[2] is an access control framework for graphs that uses WebID for authentication and provides a vocabulary for specifying access control policies. Extensions of this WAC vocabulary have been proposed to capture privacy preferences [Sacco and Passant, 2011] and to cater for contextual constraints [Costabello et al., 2012, Villata et al., 2011]. Although ODRL is primarily used to specify licenses, profiles to additionally specify access policies [Steyskal and Polleres, 2014] and regulatory obligations [Agarwal et al., 2018, De Vos et al., 2019] have also been proposed in recent years, as discussed in the survey by Kirrane et al. [2017].

As a generalization of access policies, usage policies specify how data can be used: what kinds of processing can be applied, by whom, for what purpose, etc. The example usage policy presented in Figure 9.4 states that the process (Analyse) of (Location Graph) can be performed on (Internal Servers) by members of (Company Staff) in order to provide (Event Recommendations). Vocabularies for us-

[2]WAC, http://www.w3.org/wiki/WebAccessControl.

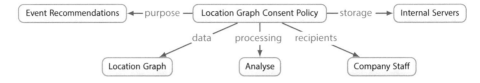

Figure 9.4: A policy for usage of a sub-graph of location data in the knowledge graph.

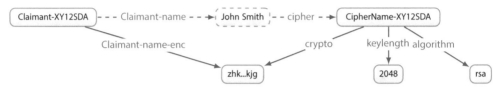

Figure 9.5: Directed edge-labeled graph with the name of the claimant encrypted; plaintext elements are dashed and may be omitted from published data (possibly along with encryption details).

age policies have been proposed by the SPECIAL H2020 project [Bonatti et al., 2019] and the W3C Data Privacy Vocabularies and Controls Community Group (DPVCG) [Bonatti and Kirrane, 2019, Pandit et al., 2019]. Once specified in these vocabularies, usage policies can then be used to verify that data processing conforms to legal norms and to the consent provided by subjects [Bonatti and Kirrane, 2019, Delanaux et al., 2018].

9.3.3   ENCRYPTION

Rather than internally controlling usage, the tourist board could use encryption mechanisms on parts of the published knowledge graph, for example relating to reports of crimes, and provide keys to partners who should have access to the plaintext. While a straightforward approach is to encrypt the entire graph (or sub-graphs) with one key, more fine-grained encryption can be performed for individual nodes or edge-labels in a graph, potentially providing different clients access to different information through different keys [Giereth, 2005]. The CryptOntology [Gerbracht, 2008] can further be used to embed details about the encryption mechanism used within the knowledge graph. Figure 9.5 illustrates how this could be used to encrypt the names of claimants from Figure 6.4, storing the ciphertext (zhk...kjg), as well as the key-length and encryption algorithm used. In order to grant access to the plaintext, one approach is to encrypt individual edges with symmetric keys so as to allow specific types of edge patterns to only be executed by clients with the appropriate key [Kasten et al., 2013]. This approach can be used, for example, to allow clients who know a claimant ID (e.g., (Claimant-XY12SDA)) and have the appropriate key to find (only) the name of the claimant through an edge pattern (Claimant-XY12SDA)—Claimant-name→(?name). A key limitation of this approach, however, is that it requires attempting to decrypt all edges to find all possible solutions. A more efficient alternative is to combine functional encryption

Figure 9.6: Anonymized sample of a directed edge-labeled graph describing a passenger (dashed) of a flight.

and specialized indexing to retrieve solutions from the encrypted graph without attempting to decrypt all edges [Fernández et al., 2017].

9.3.4   ANONYMIZATION

Consider that the tourist board acquires information on transport taken by individuals within the country, which can be used—not only by the board, but potentially other stakeholders, such as travel companies—to understand trajectories taken by tourists. However, from a data-protection perspective, it would be advisable to anonymise the knowledge graph to avoid leaking the personal travel history of individuals.

A first approach to anonymization is to suppress and generalize knowledge in a graph such that individuals cannot be identified, based on k-anonymity [Samarati and Sweeney, 1998],[3] l-diversity [Li et al., 2007][4], etc. Approaches that apply k-anonymity on graphs identify and suppress "quasi-identifiers" that would allow a given individual to be distinguished from fewer than $k - 1$ other individuals [Heitmann et al., 2017, Radulovic et al., 2015]. Figure 9.6 illustrates a possible result of k-anonymization for a sub-graph describing a flight passenger, where quasi-identifiers (passport, plane ticket) have been converted into blank nodes, ensuring that the passenger (the dashed blank node) cannot be distinguished from $k - 1$ other individuals. In the context of a graph, however, *neighborhood attacks* [Zhou and Pei, 2011]—using information about neighbors—can also break k-anonymity, where we also suppress the day and time of the flight, which, though not sensitive information per se, could otherwise break k-anonymity for passengers (if, for example, a particular flight had fewer than k males from the U.S. onboard). The graph shown in Figure 9.6 then offers k-anonymity for the particular individual assuming that at least k male passengers from the U.S. flew during December 2018 from Arica to Santiago.

More complex neighborhood attacks may rely on more abstract graph patterns, observing that individuals can be deanonymized purely from knowledge of the graph structure, even if all nodes and edge labels are left blank; for example, if we know that a team of $k - 1$ players

---

[3]k-anonymity guarantees that the data of an individual is indistinguishable from at least $k - 1$ other individuals.

[4]l-diversity guarantees that sensitive data fields have at least l diverse values within each group of individuals; this avoids leaks such as that all tourists from Austria (a group of individuals) in the data have been pick-pocketed (a sensitive attribute), which would reveal sensitive information about individuals from Austria.

take flights together for a particular number of away games, we could use this information for a neighborhood attack that reveals the set of players in the graph. Hence, a number of guarantees specific to graphs have been proposed, including k-degree anonymity [Liu and Terzi, 2008], which ensures that individuals cannot be deanonymized by attackers with knowledge of the degree of particular individuals. The approach is based on minimally modifying the graph to ensure that each node has at least $k - 1$ other nodes with the same degree. A stronger guarantee, called k-isomorphic neighbor anonymity [Zhou and Pei, 2008], avoids neighborhood attacks where an attacker knows how an individual is connected to nodes in their neighborhood; this is done by modifying the graph to ensure that for each node, there exist at least $k - 1$ nodes with isomorphic (i.e., identically structured) neighborhoods elsewhere in the graph. Both approaches only protect against attackers with knowledge of bounded neighborhoods. An even stronger notion is that of k-automorphism [Zou et al., 2009], which ensures that for every node, it is structurally indistinguishable from $k - 1$ other nodes, thus avoiding any attack based on structural information (as a trivial example, a k-clique or a k-cycle satisfy k-automorphism). Many of these techniques for anonymization of graph data were motivated by social networks [Narayanan and Shmatikov, 2009], though they can also be applied to knowledge graphs, per the work of Lin and Tripunitara [2017], who adapt k-automorphism for directed edge-labeled graphs (specifically RDF graphs).

While the aforementioned approaches anonymize data, a second approach is to apply anonymization when answering queries, such as adding noise to the solutions in a way that preserves privacy. One approach is to apply ε-differential privacy [Dwork, 2006][5] for querying graphs [Silva et al., 2017]. Such mechanisms are typically used for aggregate (e.g., count) queries, where noise is added to avoid leaks about individuals. To illustrate, differential privacy may allow for counting the number of passengers of specified nationalities taking specified flights, adding (just enough) random noise to the count to ensure that we cannot tell, within a certain probability (controlled by ε), whether or not a particular individual took a flight, where, intuitively speaking, we would require (proportionally) less noise for nationalities with many passengers in the data, but more noise to "hide" passengers from more uncommon nationalities.

These approaches require information loss for stronger guarantees of privacy. Which to choose is thus heavily application dependent. If the anonymized data are to be published in their entirety as a "dump," then an approach based on k-anonymity can be used to protect individuals, while l-diversity can be used to protect groups. On the other hand, if the data are to be made available, in part, through a query interface, then ε-differential privacy is a more suitable framework.

---

[5]ε-differential privacy ensures that the probability of a given result from a process (e.g., query) applied to data, to which random noise is added, differs no more than e^{ε} when the data includes or excludes any individual.

CHAPTER 10

Knowledge Graphs in Practice

In this chapter, we discuss some of the most prominent knowledge graphs that have emerged in the past years. We begin by discussing open knowledge graphs, most of which have been published on the Web per the guidelines and protocols described in Chapter 9. We later discuss enterprise knowledge graphs that have been created by companies from diverse industries for a wide range of applications.

10.1   OPEN KNOWLEDGE GRAPHS

By *open knowledge graphs*, we refer to knowledge graphs published under the Open Data philosophy, namely that *"open means anyone can freely access, use, modify, and share for any purpose (subject, at most, to requirements that preserve provenance and openness)."*[1] Many open knowledge graphs have been published in the form of *Linked Open Datasets* [Heath and Bizer, 2011], which are (RDF) graphs published under the Linked Data principles (see Section 9.1.2) following the Open Data philosophy. Many of the most prominent open knowledge graphs—including DBpedia [Lehmann et al., 2015], YAGO [Suchanek et al., 2007], Freebase [Bollacker et al., 2007a], and Wikidata [Vrandečić and Krötzsch, 2014]—cover multiple domains, representing a broad diversity of entities and relationships; we first discuss these in turn. Later, we discuss some of the other (specific) domains for which open knowledge graphs are currently available. Most of the open knowledge graphs we discuss in this section are modeled in RDF, published following Linked Data principles, and offer access to their data through dumps (RDF), node lookups (Linked Data), graph patterns (SPARQL) and, in some cases, edge patterns (Triple Pattern Fragments).

10.1.1   DBPEDIA

The DBpedia project was developed to extract a graph-structured representation of the semi-structured data embedded in Wikipedia articles [Auer et al., 2007], enabling the integration, processing, and querying of these data in a unified manner. The resulting knowledge graph is further enriched by linking to external open resources, including images, webpages, and external datasets such as DailyMed, DrugBank, GeoNames, MusicBrainz, New York Times, and Word-Net [Lehmann et al., 2015]. The DBpedia extraction framework consists of several components, corresponding to abstractions of Wikipedia article sources, graph storage and serialization des-

---

[1]See http://opendefinition.org/.

tinations, wiki-markup extractors, parsers, and extraction managers [Bizer et al., 2009]. Specific extractors are designed to process labels, abstracts, interlanguage links, images, redirects, disambiguation pages, external links, internal pagelinks, homepages, categories, and geocoordinates. The content in the DBpedia knowledge graph is not only multidomain, but also multilingual: as of 2012, DBpedia contained labels and abstracts in up to 97 different languages [Mendes et al., 2012a]. Entities within DBpedia are classified using four different schemata in order to address varying requirements [Bizer et al., 2009]. These schemata include a Simple Knowledge Organization System (SKOS) representation of Wikipedia categories, a Yet Another Great Ontology (YAGO) classification schema (discussed presently), an Upper Mapping and Binding Exchange Layer (UMBEL) ontology categorization schema, and a custom schema called the DBpedia ontology with classes such as `Person`, `Place`, `Organisation`, and `Work` [Lehmann et al., 2015]. DBpedia also supports live synchronization in order to remain consistent with dynamic Wikipedia articles [Lehmann et al., 2015].

10.1.2   YET ANOTHER GREAT ONTOLOGY

YAGO likewise extracts graph-structured data from Wikipedia, which are then unified with the hierarchical structure of WordNet to create a *"light-weight and extensible ontology with high quality and coverage"* [Suchanek et al., 2007]. This knowledge graph aims to be applied for various information technology tasks, such as machine translation, word sense disambiguation, query expansion, document classification, data cleaning, information integration, etc. While earlier approaches automatically extracted structured knowledge from text using pattern matching, NLP, and statistical learning, the resulting content tended to lack in quality when compared with what was possible through manual construction [Suchanek et al., 2007]. However, manual construction is costly, making it challenging to achieve broad coverage and keep the data up-to-date. In order to extract data with high coverage and quality, YAGO (like DBpedia) mostly extracts data from Wikipedia infoboxes and category pages, which contain core entity information and lists of articles for a specific category, respectively. These, in turn, are unified with hierarchical concepts from WordNet [Suchanek et al., 2008]. A schema—called the YAGO model—provides a vocabulary defined in RDFS; this model allows for representing words as entities, capturing synonymy, and ambiguity [Suchanek et al., 2007]. The model further supports reification, n-ary relations, and data types [Suchanek et al., 2008]. Refinement mechanisms employed within YAGO include canonicalization, where each edge and node is mapped to a unique identifier and duplicate elements are removed, and type checking, where nodes that cannot be assigned to a class by deductive or inductive methods are eliminated [Suchanek et al., 2008]. YAGO would be extended in later years to support spatio-temporal context [Hoffart et al., 2011] and multilingual Wikipedias [Mahdisoltani et al., 2015].

10.1.3 FREEBASE

Freebase was a general-purpose, broad collection of human knowledge that aimed to address some of the large-scale information integration problems associated with the decentralized nature of the Semantic Web, such as uneven adoption, implementation challenges, and distributed query performance limitations [Bollacker et al., 2007b]. Unlike DBpedia and YAGO—which are mostly extracted from Wikipedia/WordNet—Freebase solicited contributions directly from human editors. Included in the Freebase platform were a scalable data store with versioning mechanisms; a large data object store (LOB) for the storage of text, image, and media files; an API that could be queried using the Metaweb Query Language (MQL); a Web user interface; and a lightweight typing system [Bollacker et al., 2007b]. The latter typing system was designed to support collaborative processes. Rather than forcing ontological correctness or logical consistency, the system was implemented as a loose collection of structuring mechanisms—based on datatypes, semantic classes, properties, schema definitions, etc.—that allowed for incompatible types and properties to coexist simultaneously [Bollacker et al., 2007b]. Content could be added to Freebase interactively through the Web user interface or in an automated way by leveraging the API's write functionality. Freebase had been acquired by Google in 2010, where the content of Freebase formed an important part of the Google Knowledge Graph announced in 2012 [Singhal, 2012]. When Freebase became read-only as of March 2015, the knowledge graph contained over three billion edges. Much of this content was subsequently migrated to Wikidata [Pellissier Tanon et al., 2016].

10.1.4 WIKIDATA

Wikipedia contains a wealth of semi-structured data embedded in info-boxes, lists, tables, etc., as exploited by DBpedia and YAGO. However, these data have traditionally been curated and updated manually across different articles and languages; for example, a goal scored by a Chilean football player may require manual updates in the player's article, the tournament article, the team article, lists of top scorers, and so forth, across hundreds of language versions. Manual curation has led to a variety of data quality issues, including contradictory data in different articles, languages, etc. The Wikimedia Foundation uses Wikidata as a centralized, collaboratively-edited knowledge graph to supply Wikipedia—and arbitrary other clients—with data. Under this vision, a fact could be added to Wikidata once, triggering the automatic update of potentially multitudinous articles in Wikipedia across different languages [Vrandečić and Krötzsch, 2014]. Like Wikipedia, Wikidata is also considered a secondary source containing *claims* that should reference primary sources, though claims can also be initially added without reference [Piscopo et al., 2017]. Wikidata further allows for different viewpoints in terms of potentially contradictory (referenced) claims [Vrandečić and Krötzsch, 2014]. Wikidata is multilingual, where nodes and edges are assigned language-agnostic Qxx and Pxx codes (see Figure 9.1) and are subsequently associated with labels, aliases, and descriptions in various languages [Kaffee et al., 2017], allowing claims to be surfaced in these languages. Collaborative editing is not only permitted on the data level, but also on the schema level, allowing users to add or modify lightweight semantic axioms [Piscopo and Simperl, 2018]—including sub-classes, sub-properties, inverse properties, etc.—as well as shapes [Boneva et al., 2019]. Wikidata offers various access protocols [Malyshev et al., 2018] and has received broad adoption, being used by Wikipedia to generate infoboxes in certain domains [Sáez and Hogan, 2018], being supported by Google [Pellissier Tanon et al., 2016], and having been used as a data source for prominent end-user applications such as Apple's Siri, among others [Malyshev et al., 2018].

10.1.5   OTHER OPEN CROSS-DOMAIN KNOWLEDGE GRAPHS

Aside from DBpedia, YAGO, Freebase, and Wikidata, a number of other cross-domain knowledge graphs have been developed down through the years. BabelNet [Navigli and Ponzetto, 2012], like YAGO, is based on unifying WordNet and Wikipedia, but with the integration of additional knowledge graphs such as Wikidata, and a focus on creating a knowledge graph of multilingual lexical forms (organized into multilingual synsets) by transforming lexicographic resources such as Wiktionary and OmegaWiki into knowledge graphs. Compared to other knowledge graphs, lexicalized knowledge graphs such as BabelNet bring together the encyclopedic information found in Wikipedia with the lexicographic information usually found in monolingual and bilingual dictionaries. The Cyc project [Lenat, 1995] aims to encode common-sense knowledge in a machine-readable way, where over 900 person-years of effort [Matuszek et al., 2006] have, since 1986, gone into the creation of 2.2 million facts and rules. Though Cyc is proprietary, an open subset called OpenCyc has been published, where we refer to the comparison by Färber et al. [2018] of DBpedia, Freebase, OpenCyc, and YAGO for further details. The Never Ending Language Learning (NELL) project [Mitchell et al., 2018] has, since 2010, extracted a graph of 120 million edges from the text of web pages using OIE methods (see Chapter 6). Each such open knowledge graph applies different combinations of the languages and techniques discussed in this book over different sources with differing results.

10.1.6   DOMAIN-SPECIFIC OPEN KNOWLEDGE GRAPHS

Open knowledge graphs have been published in a variety of specific domains. Schmachtenberg et al. [2014] identify the most prominent domains in the context of Linked Data as follows: *media*, relating to news, television, radio, etc. (e.g., the BBC World Service Archive [Raimond et al., 2014]); *government*, relating to the publication of data for transparency and development (e.g., by the U.S. [Hendler et al., 2012] and U.K. [Shadbolt and O'Hara, 2013] governments); *publications*, relating to academic literature in various disciplines (e.g., OpenCitations [Peroni et al., 2017], SciGraph [Iana et al., 2019], Microsoft Academic Knowledge Graph [Färber, 2019]); *geographic*, relating to places and regions of interest (e.g., LinkedGeoData [Stadler et al., 2012]); *life sciences*, relating to proteins, genes, drugs, diseases, etc. (e.g., Bio2RDF [Callahan et al., 2013]); and *user-generated content*, relating to reviews, open source projects, etc. (e.g., Revyu [Heath and Motta, 2008]). Open knowledge graphs have also been published in other domains, including *cultural heritage* [Hyvönen et al., 2009], *music* [Raimond et al., 2009], *law* [Montiel-Ponsoda et al., 2017], *theology* [Sherif and Ngonga Ngomo, 2015], and even *tourism* [Alonso Maturana et al., 2018, Kärle et al., 2018, Lu et al., 2016, Zhang et al., 2019]. The envisaged applications for such knowledge graphs are as varied as the domains from which they emanate, but often relate to integration [Callahan et al., 2013, Raimond et al., 2009], recommendation [Lu et al., 2016, Raimond et al., 2009], transparency [Hendler et al., 2012, Shadbolt and O'Hara, 2013], archiving [Hyvönen et al., 2009, Raimond et al., 2014], decentralization [Heath and Motta, 2008], multilingual support [Sherif and Ngonga Ngomo, 2015], regulatory compliance [Montiel-Ponsoda et al., 2017], etc.

10.2   ENTERPRISE KNOWLEDGE GRAPHS

A variety of companies have announced the creation of proprietary "enterprise knowledge graphs" with a variety of goals in mind, which include: improving search capabilities [Chang, 2018, Hamad et al., 2018, Krishnan, 2018, Shrivastava, 2017, Singhal, 2012], providing user recommendations [Chang, 2018, Hamad et al., 2018], implementing conversational/personal agents [Pittman et al., 2017], enhancing targeted advertising [He et al., 2016], empowering business analytics [He et al., 2016], connecting users [He et al., 2016, Noy et al., 2019], extending multilingual support [He et al., 2016], facilitating research and discovery [Bendtsen and Petrovski, 2019], assessing and mitigating risk [Dalgliesh, 2016, Tobin, 2017], tracking news events [Meij, 2019], and increasing transport automation [Henson et al., 2019], among (many) others. Though highly diverse, these enterprise knowledge graphs do follow some high-level trends, as reflected in the discussion by Noy et al. [2019]: (1) data are typically integrated into the knowledge graph from a variety of both external and internal sources (often involving text); (2) the enterprise knowledge graph is often very large, with millions or even billions of nodes and edges, posing challenges in terms of scalability; (3) refinement of the initial knowledge graph—adding new links, consolidating duplicate entities, etc.—is important to improve quality; (4) techniques to keep the knowledge graph up-to-date with the domain are often crucial; (5) a mix of ontological and machine learning representations are often combined or used in different situations in order to draw conclusions from the enterprise knowledge graph; and (6) the ontologies used tend to be lightweight, often simple taxonomies representing a hierarchy of classes or concepts. We now discuss the main industries in which enterprise knowledge graphs have been deployed.

10.2.1   WEB SEARCH

Web search engines have traditionally focused on matching a query string with sub-strings in web documents. The Google Knowledge Graph [Noy et al., 2019, Singhal, 2012] rather promoted a paradigm of "*things not strings*"—analogous to semantic search [Guha et al., 2003]—where the search engine would now try to identify the entities that a particular search may be expressing interest in. The knowledge graph itself describes these entities and how they interrelate. One of the main user-facing applications of the Google Knowledge Graph is the "Knowledge Panel," which presents a pane on the right-hand side of (some) search results describing the principal entity that the search appears to be seeking, including some images, attribute—value pairs, and a list of related entities that users also search for. The Google Knowledge Graph was key to popularizing the modern usage of the phrase "knowledge graph" (see Appendix A). Other major search engines, such as Microsoft Bing[2] [Shrivastava, 2017], would later announce knowledge graphs along similar lines.

10.2.2   COMMERCE

Enterprise knowledge graphs have also been announced by companies that are principally concerned with selling or renting goods and services. A prominent example of such a knowledge graph is that used by Amazon [Dong, 2019, Krishnan, 2018], which describes the products on sale in their online marketplace. One of the main stated goals of this knowledge graph is to enable more advanced (semantic) search features for products, as well as to improve product recommendations to users of its online marketplace. Another knowledge graph for commerce was announced by eBay [Pittman et al., 2017], which encodes product descriptions and shopping behavior patterns, and is used to power conversational agents that help users to find relevant products through a natural language interface. Airbnb [Chang, 2018] has also described a knowledge graph that encodes accommodation for rent, places, events, experiences, neighborhoods, users, tags, etc., on top of which a taxonomic schema is defined. This knowledge graph is used to offer potential clients recommendations of attractions, events, and activities available in the neighborhood of a particular home for rent. Uber [Hamad et al., 2018] has similarly announced a knowledge graph focused on food and restaurants for their "Uber Eats" delivery service. The goals are again to offer semantic search features and recommendations to users who are uncertain of precisely what kind of food they are looking for.

10.2.3   SOCIAL NETWORKS

Enterprise knowledge graphs have also emerged in the context of social networking services. Facebook [Noy et al., 2019] has gathered together a knowledge graph describing not only social data about users, but also the entities they are interested in, including celebrities, places, movies, music, etc., in order to connect people, understand their interests, and provide recommendations. LinkedIn [He et al., 2016] announced a knowledge graph containing users, jobs, skills, companies, places, schools, etc., on top of which a taxonomic schema is defined. The knowledge graph is used to provide multilingual translations of important concepts, to improve targeted advertising, to provide advanced features for job search and people search, and likewise to provide recommendations matching jobs to people (and vice versa). Another knowledge graph has been created by Pinterest [Gonçalves et al., 2019], describing users and their interests, the latter being organized into a taxonomy. The main use-cases for the knowledge graph are to help users

---

[2]Microsoft's Knowledge Graph was previously called "Satori" (meaning *understanding* in Japanese).

to more easily find content of interest to them, as well as to enhance revenue through targeted advertisements.

10.2.4   FINANCE

The financial sector has also seen deployment of enterprise knowledge graphs. Among these, Bloomberg [Meij, 2019] has proposed a knowledge graph that powers financial data analytics, including sentiment analysis for companies based on current news reports and tweets, a question answering service, as well as detecting emerging events that may affect stock values. Thomson Reuters (Refinitiv) [Tobin, 2017] has likewise announced a knowledge graph encoding "the financial ecosystem" of people, organizations, equity instruments, industry classifications, joint ventures and alliances, supply chains, etc., using a taxonomic schema to organize these entities. Some of the applications they mention for the knowledge graph include supply chain monitoring, risk assessment, and investment research. Knowledge graphs have also been used for deductive reasoning, with Banca d'Italia [Bellomarini et al., 2019] using rule-based reasoning to determine, for example, the percentage of ownership of a company by various stakeholders. Other companies exploring financial knowledge graphs include Accenture [Okorafor and Ray, 2019], Capital One [Branum and Sehon, 2019], Wells Fargo [Newman, 2019], among various others.

10.2.5   OTHER INDUSTRIES

Enterprises have also been actively developing knowledge graphs to enable novel applications in a variety of other industries, including: *health care*, where IBM are exploring use-cases for drug discovery [Noy et al., 2019] and information extraction from package inserts [Gentile et al., 2019], while AstraZeneca [Bendtsen and Petrovski, 2019] are using a knowledge graph to advance genomics research and disease understanding; *transport*, where Bosch are exploring a knowledge graph of scenes and locations for driving automation [Henson et al., 2019]; *oil & gas*, where Maana [Dalgliesh, 2016] are using knowledge graphs to perform data integration for risk mitigation regarding oil wells and drilling; and more.

C H A P T E R   11

Conclusions

We have provided a comprehensive introduction to knowledge graphs, which have been receiving more and more attention in recent years. Under the definition of a knowledge graph as *a graph of data intended to accumulate and convey knowledge of the real world, whose nodes represent entities of interest and whose edges represent relations between these entities*, we have discussed models by which data can be structured as graphs; representations of schema, identity and context; techniques for leveraging deductive and inductive knowledge; methods for the creation, enrichment, quality assessment and refinement of knowledge graphs; principles and standards for publishing knowledge graphs; and finally, we have discussed the adoption of both open and enterprise knowledge graphs in the real world.

In this final chapter, we provide some concluding remarks, and further offer some insights on potential future directions for research on knowledge graphs.

Concluding remarks Knowledge graphs have garnered significant attention not only from diverse organizations and industries, but also diverse research communities. This attention is due, in no small part, to the ubiquitous nature of the problem that knowledge graphs address: integrating and extracting value from diverse sources of data at large scale, be it in the context of a particular organization, community, or more general collections of human knowledge. The key insight of knowledge graphs is that graphs provide a simple, flexible, intuitive and yet powerful abstraction for representing and integrating diverse data at large scale. This insight is far from new (see Appendix A), but rather has finally come of age with the advent of knowledge graphs. Graphs have long been used to represent data and knowledge in areas such as Graph Algorithms and Theory, Graph Databases, Information Extraction, Knowledge Representation, Machine Learning, the Semantic Web, and more. The advances in these areas can now be unified and applied for knowledge graphs.

Thus, the decision to model data as a graph opens up a "tool-box" of languages, techniques and systems—stemming from diverse areas—that can be deployed in order to integrate and extract value from data at large scale, as follows:

- A variety of *graph query languages* are now available that (unlike other NoSQL alternatives) are fully featured, supporting not only the relational algebra, but also novel features such as navigational queries that can match paths of arbitrary length. A broad selection of graph databases and user interfaces supporting these query languages are now also available.

- Though graphs do not depend on a detailed (relational-like) schema to represent data, various notions of *graph schemata* have been proposed in order to validate, summarize and define the semantics of graphs.

- *Contextual frameworks for graphs* can be used to represent and reason about the scope of truth of knowledge in the graph—relating to the time, space, provenance, confidence level, etc., for which something is held true—including various alternatives for reification, annotated graph frameworks, etc.

- Deductive forms of reasoning can be enabled over graphs using *ontologies* and/or *rules*, which can not only encode a machine-readable consensus about the meaning of the graph, but also provide automated access to implicit knowledge entailed by a graph through materialization or query rewriting.

- *Graph algorithms*, such as centrality measures, community detection, clustering, etc., can be applied on the data to gain insights about influential entities or edges, close-knit sub-graphs of entities, and more besides, with *graph parallel frameworks* capable of applying such algorithms at large scale.

- Recent and continual advances in *knowledge graph embeddings* and *graph neural networks* have now opened up new possibilities for applying machine learning natively over graphs in the context of diverse tasks, including classification, question answering, recommendations, and more besides.

- *Rule and axiom mining* techniques allow for extracting formal, declarative hypotheses from a knowledge graph that encode high-level patterns and can be applied to derive new knowledge in a deductive, explainable manner.

- *Graph-based information extraction* can be applied to extract and/or enrich a knowledge graph from legacy sources of text and semi-structured data, while *graph-based mapping languages* facilitate integrating diverse sources of legacy structured data into the knowledge graph.

- Tools, techniques, and methodologies for *ontology engineering* and *ontology learning* can further guide the—potentially collaborative—creation of an ontology for the knowledge graph, encoding a consensus about its semantics, and enabling access to implicit knowledge through deductive reasoning.

- *Quality dimensions and metrics for knowledge graphs* allow for systematically assessing the readiness of the knowledge graph for its envisaged applications, in both a qualitative and quantitative manner, where a variety of tools and frameworks are available to help perform such assessments.

- Knowledge graphs that have been integrated from diverse sources are likely to be in-complete, or to encode incorrect data, where techniques and tools for *knowledge graph refinement* facilitate the automated completion and correction of knowledge graphs, thus improving its overall quality and usefulness.

- For the purposes of publishing open knowledge graphs, *principles & best practices* and *access protocols*, as well as techniques for *linking*, *licensing*, *access & usage control*, *encryp-tion*, and *anonymization*, can be leveraged to maximize their potential impact on society in an ethical way.

As we discussed in Chapter 10, the various components of this "knowledge graph tool-box" can already be found deployed in practice, having been applied—to varying degrees—in the context of numerous open and enterprise knowledge graphs. As adoption of knowledge graphs continues, work will also continue on improving and combining these tools, as well as on developing novel tools that help to better integrate and extract value from diverse sources of data at large scale.

Future directions   Research on knowledge graphs involves a confluence of techniques from different research areas with the common objective of maximizing the knowledge—and thus value—that can be distilled from diverse sources at large scale using a graph-based data abstrac-tion [Hogan, 2020a]. While advances within these individual disciplines are sure to continue and to generate further impact, particularly interesting research topics for knowledge graph arise from their intersections.

In the intersection of data graphs and deductive knowledge, we emphazise emerging topics such as *formal semantics for property graphs*, with languages that can take into account the mean-ing of labels and property—value pairs on nodes and edges [Krötzsch et al., 2018]; and *reasoning and querying over contextual data*, in order to derive conclusions and results valid in a particu-lar setting [Homola and Serafini, 2012, Schuetz et al., 2020, Zimmermann et al., 2012]. In the intersection of data graphs and inductive knowledge, we highlight topics such as *similarity-based query relaxation*, allowing to find approximate answers to exact queries based on numerical representations (e.g., embeddings) [Wang et al., 2018]; *shape induction*, in order to learn and formalize inherent patterns in the knowledge graph as constraints [Mihindukulasooriya et al., 2018]; and *contextual knowledge graph embeddings* that provide numeric representations of nodes and edges that vary with time, place, etc. [Kazemi et al., 2019]. In the intersection of deductive and inductive knowledge, we mention the topics of *entailment-aware knowledge graph embed-dings* [Demeester et al., 2016, Guo et al., 2016], that incorporate rules and/or ontologies when computing plausibility; *expressive graph neural networks* proven capable of complex classification analogous to expressive ontology languages [Barceló et al., 2020]; as well as further advances on *rule and axiom mining*, allowing to extract symbolic, deductive representations from the knowl-edge graphs [Bühmann et al., 2016, Galárraga et al., 2015]. Further challenges arise when con-sidering the creation, enrichment, refinement and publication of knowledge graphs, which call for further work on topics such as *automated quality assessment (and repair)*, *distantly supervised extraction frameworks*, *efficient access protocols*, and *anonymization*, to name but a few.

Aside from specific topics, more general challenges for knowledge graphs include: *scalability*, particularly for deductive and inductive reasoning; *quality*, not only in terms of data, but also the models induced from knowledge graphs; *diversity*, such as managing contextual or multi-modal data; *dynamicity*, considering temporal or streaming data; and finally *usability*, which is key to increasing adoption. Though techniques are continuously being proposed to address these challenges, they are unlikely to ever be completely "solved;" rather, they serve as dimensions along which knowledge graphs, and their techniques, tools, etc., will continue to mature.

Given the availability of open knowledge graphs whose quality continues to improve, as well as the growing adoption of enterprise knowledge graphs in various industries, future research on knowledge graphs has the potential to foster key advancements in broad aspects of society. Here we have highlighted just some examples of future research directions of importance to this pursuit.

APPENDIX A

Background

We now discuss the broader historical context that has paved the way for the modern advent of knowledge graphs, and the definitions of the notion of "knowledge graph" that have been proposed both before and after the announcement of the Google Knowledge Graph [Singhal, 2012]. We remark that the discussion presented here builds upon (but does not subsume) previous discussion by Ehrlinger and Wöß [2016] and Bergman [2019], which we refer to for further details. Though our goal is to be comprehensive, the list of historical references should not be considered exhaustive.

A.1   HISTORICAL PERSPECTIVE

The lineage of knowledge graphs can be traced back to the origins of diagrammatic forms of knowledge representation: a tradition going back at least as far as Aristotle (∼350 BC), followed by notions such as Euler circles and Venn diagrams that helped humans to reason through visual insights. Centuries later, a variety of researchers—particularly Sylvester [1878], Peirce [1878], and Frege [1879]—independently devised formal diagrammatic systems that not only facilitate reasoning, but also codify reasoning; in other words, their goal was to use diagrams as formal systems.

With the advent of digital computers, programs began to be used to perform formal reasoning and to code representations of knowledge. These developments can be traced back to works such as those of Ritchens [1956], Quillian [1963], and Travers and Milgram [1969], which focused on formal representations for natural language, information, and knowledge. These early works were limited (at least by modern standards) by the poor computational resources available. From the formal (logical) point of view, a number of influential developments took place in the 1970's, including the introduction of *frames* by Minsky [1974], the formalization of *semantic networks* by Brachman [1977] and Woods [1975], and the proposal of *conceptual graphs* by Sowa [1979]. These works tried to integrate formal logic with diagrammatic representations of knowledge by giving a (more-or-less) formal semantics to graph representations. But as Sowa [1987] later wrote in the entry "*Semantic networks*" of the Encyclopedia of Cognitive Science: "*Woods (1975) and McDermott (1976) observed, the semantic networks themselves have no well-defined semantics. Standard predicate calculus does have a precisely defined, model theoretic semantics; it is adequate for describing mathematical theories with a closed set of axioms. But the real world is messy, incompletely explored, and full of unexpected surprises.*"

From this era of exploration and attempts to define programs to simulate the visual and formal reasoning of humans, the following key notions were established that are still of relevance today:

- knowledge representation using diagrams (often graphs) and visual means;

- computational procedures and algorithms to perform formal reasoning;

- combinations of formal (logical) and statistical forms of reasoning; and

- relevance of diverse types of data (e.g., images, audio) as knowledge sources.

These works on conceptual graphs, semantic networks, and frames were direct predecessors of Description Logics, which aimed to give a well-defined semantics to these earlier notions toward building practical reasoning systems for decidable logics. Description Logics stem from the KL-ONE system proposed by Brachman and Schmolze [1985], and the "*attributive concept descriptions with complements*" language (aka $\mathcal{ALC}$) proposed by Schmidt-Schauß and Smolka [1991]. Description Logics would be further explored in later years (see Section 4.2.2) and formed the underpinnings of the Web Ontology Language (OWL) standard [Hitzler et al., 2012]. Together with the Resource Description Framework (RDF) [Cyganiak et al., 2014], OWL would become one of the main building blocks of the Semantic Web [Berners-Lee et al., 2001], within which many of the formative ideas and standards underlying knowledge graphs would later be developed, including not only RDF and OWL, but also RDFS [Brickley and Guha, 2014], SPARQL [Harris et al., 2013], Linked Data principles [Berners-Lee, 2006], Shape Expressions [Brickley and Guha, 2014, Thornton et al., 2019], and indeed, many of the other concepts, standards and techniques discussed in this book. Most of the open knowledge graphs discussed in Section 10.1—including BabelNet [Navigli and Ponzetto, 2012], DBpedia [Lehmann et al., 2015], Freebase [Bollacker et al., 2007b], Wikidata [Vrandečić and Krötzsch, 2014], YAGO [Suchanek et al., 2007], etc.—have either emerged from the Semantic Web community, or would later adopt the standards it proposes.

A.2   "KNOWLEDGE GRAPHS:" PRE-2012

Long before the 2012 announcement of the Google Knowledge Graph, various authors had used the phrase "knowledge graph" in publications stretching back to the 1940's, but with unrelated meaning. To the best of our knowledge, the first reference to a "knowledge graph" of relevance to the modern meaning was in a paper by Schneider [1973] in the area of computerized instructional systems for education, where a knowledge graph—in his case a directed graph whose nodes are units of knowledge (concepts) that a student should acquire, and whose edges denote dependencies between such units of knowledge—is used to represent and store an instructional course on a computer. An analogous notion of a "knowledge graph" was used by Marchi and Miguel [1974] to study paths through the knowledge units of an instructional course that yield the highest payoffs for teachers and students in a game-theoretic sense. Around the same time, in a paper on linguistics, Kümmel [1973] describes a numerical representation of knowledge, with "radicals"—referring to some symbol with meaning—forming the nodes of a knowledge graph.

Further authors were to define instantiations of knowledge graphs in the 1980's. Rada [1986] defines a knowledge graph in the context of medical expert systems, where domain knowledge is defined as a weighted graph, over which a "gradual" learning process is applied to refine knowledge by making small changes to weights. Bakker [1987] defines a knowledge graph with the purpose of cumulatively representing content gleaned from medical and sociological texts, with a focus on causal relationships. Work on knowledge graphs from the same group would continue over the years, with contributions by Stokman and de Vries [1988] further introducing mereological (*part of*) and instantiation (*is a*) relations to the knowledge graph, and thereafter by James [1992], Hoede [1995], Zhang [2002], Popping [2003], among others, in the decades that followed [Nurdiati and Hoede, 2012]. The notion of knowledge graph used in such works considered a fixed number of relations. Other authors pursued their own parallel notions of knowledge graphs toward the end of the 1980's. Rappaport and Gouyet [1988] described a user interface for visualizing a knowledge-base—composed of facts and rules—using a knowledge graph that connects related elements of the knowledge-base. Srikanth and Jarke [1989] used the notion of a knowledge graph to represent the entities and relations involved in projects, particularly software projects, where partitioning techniques are applied to the knowledge graph to modularize the knowledge required in the project.

Continuing to the 1990's, the notion of a "knowledge graph" would again arise in different, seemingly independent settings. De Raedt et al. [1990] proposed a knowledge graph as a directed graph composed of a taxonomy of instances being related with weighted edges to a taxonomy of classes; they use symbolic learning to extract such knowledge graphs from examples. Machado and Freitas da Rocha [1990] defined a knowledge graph as an acyclic, weighted *and—or* graph,[1] defining fuzzy dependencies that connect observations to hypotheses through intermediary nodes. These knowledge graphs are elicited from domain experts and can be used to generate neural networks for selecting hypotheses from input observations. Knowledge graphs were again later used by Dieng et al. [1992] to represent the results of knowledge acquisition from experts. Shimony et al. [1997] rather define a knowledge graph based on a *Bayesian knowledge base*—i.e., a Bayesian network that permits directed cycles—over which Bayesian inference can be applied. This definition was further built upon in a later work by Santos Jr. and Santos [1999].

Moving to the 2000's, Jiang and Ma [2002] introduce the notion of "plan knowledge graphs" where nodes represent goals and edges dependencies between goals, further encoding supporting degrees that can change upon further evidence. Search algorithms are then defined

---

[1] An *and—or* graph denotes dependency relations, where *and* denotes a conjunction of sub-goals on which a goal depends, while *or* denotes a disjunction of sub-goals.

on the graph to determine a plan for a particular goal. Helms and Buijsrogge [2005] proposed a knowledge graph to represent the flow of knowledge in an organization, with nodes representing knowledge actors (creators, sharers, users), edges representing knowledge flow from one actor to another, and edge weights indicating the "velocity" (delay of flow) and "viscosity" (the depth of knowledge transferred). Graph algorithms are then proposed to find bottlenecks in knowledge flow. Kasneci et al. [2008] proposed a search engine for knowledge graphs, defined to be weighted directed edge-labeled graphs, where weights denote confidence scores based on the centrality of source documents from which the edge/relation was extracted. From the same group, Elbassuoni et al. [2009] adopted a similar notion of a knowledge graph, adding edge attributes to include keywords from the source, a count of supporting sources, etc., showing how the graph can be queried. Coursey and Mihalcea [2009] constructed a knowledge graph from Wikipedia, where nodes represent Wikipedia articles and categories, while edges represent the proximity of nodes. Given an input text, entity linking and centrality measures are applied over the knowledge graph to determine relevant Wikipedia categories for the text.

Concluding with the 2010's (prior to 2012), Pechsiri and Piriyakul [2010] used knowledge graphs to capture "explanation knowledge"—the knowledge of why something is the way it is— by representing events as nodes and causal relationships as edges, claiming that this graphical notation offers more intuitive explanations to users; their work focuses on extracting such graphs from text. Corby and Faron-Zucker [2010] used the phrase "knowledge graph" in a general way to denote any graph encoding knowledge, proposing an abstract machine for querying such graphs.

Other phrases were used to represent similar notions by other authors, including "information graphs" [Kümmel, 1973], "information networks" [Sun et al., 2011], "knowledge networks" [Ciampaglia et al., 2015], as well as "semantic networks" [Brachman, 1977, Navigli and Ponzetto, 2012, Woods, 1975] and "conceptual graphs" [Sowa, 1979], as mentioned previously. Here, we exclusively considered works that (happen to) use the phrase "knowledge graph" prior to Google's announcement of their knowledge graph in 2012, where we see that many works had independently coined this phrase for different purposes. Similar to the current practice, all of the works of this period consider a knowledge graph to be formed of a set of nodes denoting entities of interest and a set of edges denoting relations between those entities, with different entities and relations being considered in different works. Some works add extra elements to these knowledge graphs, such as edge weights, edge labels, or other metadata [Elbassuoni et al., 2009]. Other trends include knowledge acquisition from experts [Dieng et al., 1992, Machado and Freitas da Rocha, 1990, Rada, 1986] and knowledge extraction from text [Bakker, 1987, Hoede, 1995, James, 1992, Stokman and de Vries, 1988], combinations of symbolic and inductive methods [De Raedt et al., 1990, Machado and Freitas da Rocha, 1990, Santos Jr. and Santos, 1999, Shimony et al., 1997], as well as the use of rules [Rappaport and Gouyet, 1988], ontologies [Hoede, 1995], graph analytics [Helms and Buijsrogge, 2005, Kasneci et al., 2008, Srikanth and Jarke, 1989], learning [De Raedt et al., 1990, Rada, 1986, Santos Jr. and Santos,

1999, Shimony et al., 1997], among other techniques. Later papers (2008–2010) by Kasneci et al. [2008], Elbassuoni et al. [2009], Coursey and Mihalcea [2009] and Corby and Faron-Zucker [2010] introduce notions of "knowledge graph" that are more similar to the current practice.

However, some trends are not reflected in current practice. Of note is that many of the knowledge graphs defined in this period consider edges as denoting a form of dependence or causality, where $x \rightarrow y$ may denote that x is a prerequisite for y [Jiang and Ma, 2002, Marchi and Miguel, 1974, Schneider, 1973] or that x leads to y [Bakker, 1987, Jiang and Ma, 2002, Machado and Freitas da Rocha, 1990, Rada, 1986, Rappaport and Gouyet, 1988, Shimony et al., 1997]. In some cases, *and–or* graphs are used to denote conjunctions or disjunctions of such relations [Machado and Freitas da Rocha, 1990], while in other cases edges are weighted to assign a belief to a relation [Jiang and Ma, 2002, Machado and Freitas da Rocha, 1990, Rada, 1986]. Papers from 1970–2000 tend to have worked with small graphs, which contrasts with modern practice where knowledge graphs can reach scales of millions or billions of nodes [Noy et al., 2019]: during this period, computational resources were more limited [Schneider, 1973], and fewer sources of structured data were readily available, meaning that the knowledge graphs were often sourced solely from human experts [Dieng et al., 1992, Machado and Freitas da Rocha, 1990, Rada, 1986] or from text [Bakker, 1987, Hoede, 1995, James, 1992, Stokman and de Vries, 1988].

A.3   "KNOWLEDGE GRAPHS:" 2012 ONWARD

The Google Knowledge Graph was announced in 2012 [Singhal, 2012]. This initial announcement was targeted at a broad audience, mainly motivating the knowledge graph and describing applications that it would enable, where the knowledge graph itself is described as "*[a graph] that understands real-world entities and their relationships to one another*" [Singhal, 2012]. Mentions of "knowledge graphs" gained momentum in the research literature from that point. As noted by Bergman [2019], this announcement by Google was a watershed moment for adopting the phrase "knowledge graph." However, given the informal nature of the announcement, a technical definition was lacking [Bonatti et al., 2018, Ehrlinger and Wöß, 2016].

Given that knowledge graphs were gaining more and more attention not only in practice, but also in the academic literature, formal definitions were becoming a necessity in order to precisely characterize what they were, how they were structured, how they could be used, etc., and more generally to facilitate their study in a precise manner. We can determine four general categories of definitions that have emerged.

Category I: The first category simply defines the knowledge graph as a graph where nodes represent entities, and edges represent relationships between those entities. Often a directed edge-labeled graph is assumed (or analogously, a set of named binary relations, or a set of triples). This simple definition was popularized by seminal papers on knowledge graph embeddings [Lin et al., 2015, Wang et al., 2014], being sufficient to represent the data model upon which these embeddings operate. As reflected in the later survey by Wang et al. [2017], the multitude of works that would follow on knowledge graph embeddings have continued to use this definition. Though simple, the *Category I* definition raised some doubts: How is a knowledge graph different from a graph (database)? Where does knowledge come into play?

Category II: A second common definition goes as follows: "*a knowledge graph is a graph-structured knowledge base.*" To the best of our knowledge, the earliest usages of this definition in the literature were by Nickel et al. [2016a] and Seufert et al. [2016] (interestingly in the formal notation of these initial papers, a knowledge graph is defined analogously to a directed edge-labeled graph). Such a definition raises the question: what, then, is a "knowledge base"? The phrase "knowledge base" was popularized in the 1970's (possibly earlier) in the context of rule-based expert systems [Buchanan and Feigenbaum, 1978], and later were used in the context of ontologies and other logical formalisms [Brachman and Schmolze, 1985]. The follow-up question then is: can we have a knowledge base (graph-structured or not) without a logical formalism while staying true to the original definitions? Looking in further detail, similar ambiguities have also existed regarding the definition of a "knowledge base" (KB). Of note: Brachman and Levesque [1986]—reporting after a workshop on this issue—state that "*if we ask what the KB tells us about the world, we are asking about its Knowledge Level.*"

Category III: The third category of definitions outline more specific technical characteristics that a "knowledge graph" should comply with.

– In an influential survey on knowledge graph refinement, Paulheim [2017] lists four criteria that characterize the knowledge graphs considered for the paper. Specifically, he puts forward that a knowledge graph "*mainly describes real world entities and their interrelations, organized in a graph; defines possible classes and relations of entities in a schema; allows for potentially interrelating arbitrary entities with each other; covers various topical domains;*" he thus rules out ontologies without instances (e.g., DOLCE) and graphs of word senses (e.g., WordNet) as not meeting the first two criteria, while relational databases do not meet the third criterion (due to schema restrictions), and domain-specific graphs (e.g., Geonames) are considered to not meet the fourth criterion; this leaves graphs such as DBpedia, YAGO, Freebase, etc.

– Ehrlinger and Wöß [2016] also review definitions of "knowledge graph," where they criticize the *Category II* definitions based on the argument that knowledge bases are often synonymous with ontologies,[2] while knowledge graphs are not; they further criticize Google for calling its knowledge graph a "knowledge base." After reviewing prior definitions of terms such as "knowledge base," "ontology,"

---

[2]Prior definitions of an ontology—such as by Guarino et al. [2009]—would seem to contradict this conclusion.

and "knowledge graph," they propose their definition: "*A knowledge graph acquires and integrates information into an ontology and applies a reasoner to derive new knowledge.*" In the subsequent discussion, they remark that a knowledge graph is distinguished from an ontology (considered synonymous with a knowledge base) by the provision of reasoning capabilities.

– One of the most detailed technical definitions for a "knowledge graph" is provided by Bellomarini et al. [2019], who state: "*A knowledge graph is a semi-structured data model characterized by three components: (i) a ground extensional component, that is, a set of relational constructs for schema and data (which can be effectively modeled as graphs or generalizations thereof); (ii) an intensional component, that is, a set of inference rules over the constructs of the ground extensional component; and (iii) a derived extensional component that can be produced as the result of the application of the inference rules over the ground extensional component (with the so-called "reasoning" process).*" They remark that ontologies and rules represent analogous structures, and that a knowledge graph is then a knowledge base extended with reasoning along similar lines to the definition provided by Ehrlinger and Wöß [2016].

We refer to Bergman [2019] for a list of further definitions that fit *Category III*. While having a specific, technical definition for knowledge graphs provides a more solid foundation for their study, as Bergman [2019] remarks, many such definitions do not seem to fit the current practice of knowledge graphs. For example, it is not clear which of these definitions the Google Knowledge Graph itself—responsible for popularizing the idea—would meet (if any). Many of the criteria proposed by such definitions are also orthogonal to the many works in the area of knowledge graph embeddings [Wang et al., 2017].

Category IV: While the previous three categories involve (sometimes conflicting) intensional definitions, the fourth category adopts an extensional definition of knowledge graphs, defining them in terms of prominent examples of knowledge graphs, such as DBpedia, Google's Knowledge Graph, Freebase, YAGO, among others [Bonatti et al., 2018]. Arguably this category avoids the issue of defining a knowledge graph, rather than actually defining them.

These categories refer to definitions that have appeared in the academic literature. In terms of enterprise knowledge graphs, an important reference is the paper of Noy et al. [2019], which has been co-authored by leaders of knowledge graph projects from eBay, Facebook, Google, IBM, and Microsoft, and thus can be seen as representing a form of consensus among these companies—who have played a key role in the popularization of knowledge graphs—on what a "knowledge graph" means in this setting. Specifically this paper states that "*a knowledge graph describes objects of interest and connections between them,*" and goes on to state that "*many practical implementations impose constraints on the links in knowledge graphs by defining a schema or ontology.*"

They later add "*Knowledge graphs and similar structures usually provide a shared substrate of knowledge within an organization, allowing different products and applications to use similar vocabulary and to reuse definitions and descriptions that others create. Furthermore, they usually provide a compact formal representation that developers can use to infer new facts and build up the knowledge.*" We interpret this definition as corresponding to *Category I*, but further acknowledging that while not a necessary condition for a knowledge graph, ontologies and formal representations *usually* play a key role. The definition we provide at the outset of the paper is largely compatible with that of Noy et al. [2019].

Bibliography

Karl Aberer, Key-Sun Choi, Natasha Fridman Noy, Dean Allemang, Kyung-Il Lee, Lyndon J. B. Nixon, Jennifer Golbeck, Peter Mika, Diana Maynard, Riichiro Mizoguchi, Guus Schreiber, and Philippe Cudré-Mauroux, Eds. *The Semantic Web, 6th International Semantic Web Conference, 2nd Asian Semantic Web Conference, ISWC + ASWC, Busan, Korea, November 11–15*, volume 4825 of *Lecture Notes in Computer Science*. Springer, 2007. DOI: 10.1007/978-3-540-76298-0 167, 222

Serge Abiteboul. Querying semi-structured data. In Foto N. Afrati and Phokion G. Kolaitis, Eds., *Database Theory—ICDT, 6th International Conference, Delphi, Greece, January 8–10, Proceedings*, volume 1186 of *Lecture Notes in Computer Science*, pages 1–18. Springer, 1997. DOI: 10.1007/3-540-62222-5_33 1

Sushant Agarwal, Simon Steyskal, Franjo Antunovic, and Sabrina Kirrane. Legislative compliance assessment: Framework, model and GDPR instantiation. In Manel Medina, Andreas Mitrakas, Kai Rannenberg, Erich Schweighofer, and Nikolaos Tsouroulas, Eds., *Privacy Technologies and Policy—6th Annual Privacy Forum, APF, Barcelona, Spain, June 13–14, Revised Selected Papers*, volume 11079 of *Lecture Notes in Computer Science*, pages 131–149. Springer, 2018. DOI: 10.1007/978-3-030-02547-2_8 141

Rakesh Agrawal, Tomasz Imieliński, and Arun Swami. Mining association rules between sets of items in large databases. In Peter Buneman and Sushil Jajodia, Eds., *Proc. of the ACM SIGMOD International Conference on Management of Data, Washington, DC, May 26–28*, pages 207–216. ACM Press, 1993. DOI: 10.1145/170036.170072 101

Jinhyun Ahn, Dong-Hyuk Im, Jae-Hong Eom, Nansu Zong, and Hong-Gee Kim. G-Diff: A grouping algorithm for RDF change detection on MapReduce. In Thepchai Supnithi, Takahira Yamaguchi, Jeff Z. Pan, Vilas Wuwongse, and Marut Buranarach, Eds., *Semantic Technology—4th Joint International Conference, JIST, Chiang Mai, Thailand, November 9-11. Revised Selected Papers*, volume 8943 of *Lecture Notes in Computer Science*, pages 230–235. Springer, 2015. DOI: 10.1007/978-3-319-15615-6_17 138

Adnan Akhter, Axel-Cyrille Ngonga Ngomo, and Muhammad Saleem. An empirical evaluation of RDF graph partitioning techniques. In Catherine Faron-Zucker, Chiara Ghidini, Amedeo Napoli, and Yannick Toussaint, Eds., *Knowledge Engineering and Knowledge Management—21st International Conference, EKAW, Nancy, France, November 12–16, Proceed-*

ings, volume 11313 of *Lecture Notes in Computer Science*, pages 3–18. Springer, 2018. DOI: 10.1007/978-3-030-03667-6_1 75

Harith Alani, Lalana Kagal, Achille Fokoue, Paul T. Groth, , Josian Xavier Parreira, Lora Aroyo, Natasha Fridman Noy, Christopher A. Welty, and Krzysztof Janowicz, Eds. *The Semantic Web—ISWC—12th International Semantic Web Conference, Sydney, NSW, Australia, October 21–25, Proceedings, Part I*, volume 8218 of *Lecture Notes in Computer Science*. Springer, 2013a. 197, 205, 206, 211

Harith Alani, Lalana Kagal, Achille Fokoue, Paul T. Groth, , Josian Xavier Parreira, Lora Aroyo, Natasha Fridman Noy, Christopher A. Welty, and Krzysztof Janowicz, Eds. *The Semantic Web—ISWC—12th International Semantic Web Conference, Sydney, NSW, Australia, October 21–25, Proceedings, Part II*, volume 8219 of *Lecture Notes in Computer Science*. Springer, 2013b. 173, 190, 208

Keith Alexander, Richard Cyganiak, Michael Hausenblas, and Jun Zhao. Describing linked datasets. In Christian Bizer, Tom Heath, Tim Berners-Lee, and Michael Hausenblas, Eds., *Proc. of the WWW Workshop on Linked Data on the Web, LDOW, Madrid, Spain, April 20*, volume 538 of *CEUR Workshop Proceedings*. Sun SITE Central Europe (CEUR), 2009. http://ceur-ws.org/Vol-538/ldow2009_paper20.pdf 134

Gustavo Alonso, José A. Blakeley, and Arbee L. P. Chen, Eds. *Proc. of the 24th International Conference on Data Engineering, ICDE, April 7–12, Cancún, Mexico*. IEEE Computer Society, 2008. 196, 227

Ricardo Alonso Maturana, Elena Alvarado-Cortes, Susana López-Sola, María Ortega Martínez-Losa, and Pablo Hermoso-González. La Rioja turismo: The construction and exploitation of a queryable tourism knowledge graph. In Cesare Pautasso, Fernando Sánchez-Figueroa, Kari Systä, and Juan Manuel Murillo Rodriguez, Eds., *Current Trends in Web Engineering—ICWE International Workshops, MATWEP, EnWot, KD-WEB, WEOD, TourismKG, Cáceres, Spain, June 5, Revised Selected Papers*, volume 11153 of *Lecture Notes in Computer Science*, pages 213–220. Springer, 2018. DOI: 10.1007/978-3-030-03056-8_20 3, 149

Renzo Angles. The property graph database model. In Dan Olteanu and Barbara Poblete, Eds., *Proc. of the 12th Alberto Mendelzon International Workshop on Foundations of Data Management, Cali, Colombia, May 21–25*, volume 2100 of *CEUR Workshop Proceedings*. Sun SITE Central Europe (CEUR), 2018. http://ceur-ws.org/Vol-2100/paper26.pdf 29

Renzo Angles and Claudio Gutiérrez. Survey of graph database models. *ACM Computing Surveys*, 40(1):1:1–1:39, 2008. DOI: 10.1145/1322432.1322433 1, 12, 13

Renzo Angles, Marcelo Arenas, Pablo Barceló, Aidan Hogan, Juan L. Reutter, and Domagoj Vrgoc. Foundations of modern query languages for graph databases. *ACM Computing Surveys*, 50(5):68:1–68:40, 2017. DOI: 10.1145/3104031 1, 6, 9, 11, 13, 14, 17, 19, 22, 70, 75, 139

Renzo Angles, Marcelo Arenas, Pablo Barceló, Peter A. Boncz, George H. L. Fletcher, Claudio Gutierrez, Tobias Lindaaker, Marcus Paradies, Stefan Plantikow, Juan F. Sequeda, Oskar van Rest, and Hannes Voigt. G-CORE: A core for future graph query languages. In Das et al. [2018], pages 1421–1432. DOI: 10.1145/3183713.3190654 13, 19, 22, 75

Renzo Angles, Harsh Thakkar, and Dominik Tomaszuk. RDF and property graphs interoperability: Status and issues. In Hogan and Milo [2019]. http://ceur-ws.org/Vol-2369/paper01.pdf 9

Mikel Ega na Aranguren, Erick Antezana, Martin Kuiper, and Robert Stevens. Ontology design patterns for bio-ontologies: A case study on the cell cycle ontology. *BMC Bioinformatics*, 9(5):S1, 2008. DOI: 10.1186/1471-2105-9-S5-S1 116

Marcelo Arenas, Alexandre Bertails, Eric Prud'hommeaux, and Juan Sequeda. A direct mapping of relational data to RDF, *W3C Recommendation, World Wide Web Consortium*, September 27, 2012. https://www.w3.org/TR/2012/REC-rdb-direct-mapping-20120927/ 112, 113

Marcelo Arenas, Bernardo Cuenca Grau, Evgeny Kharlamov, Sarunas Marciuska, and Dmitriy Zheleznyakov. Faceted search over RDF-based knowledge graphs. *Journal of Web Semantics*, 37–38:55–74, 2016. DOI: 10.1016/j.websem.2015.12.002 22

Alessandro Artale, Diego Calvanese, Roman Kontchakov, and Michael Zakharyaschev. The DL-lite family and relations. *Journal of Artificial Intelligence Research*, 36:1–69, 2009. DOI: 10.1613/jair.2820 59

Sören Auer, Christian Bizer, Georgi Kobilarov, Jens Lehmann, Richard Cyganiak, and Zachary Ives. DBpedia: A nucleus for a Web of open data. In Aberer et al. [2007], pages 722–735. DOI: 10.1007/978-3-540-76298-0_52 145

Franz Baader, Ian Horrocks, Carsten Lutz, and Ulrike Sattler. *An Introduction to Description Logic*. Cambridge University Press, Cambridge, UK, 2017. DOI: 10.1017/9781139025355 61, 64

Nguyen Bach and Sameer Badaskar. A review of relation extraction. *Technical Report*, Carnegie Mellon University, 2007. 108

Ricardo Baeza-Yates. Bias on the Web. *Communications of the ACM*, 61(6):54–61, 2018. DOI: 10.1145/3209581 121

Collin F. Baker, Charles J. Fillmore, and John B. Lowe. The Berkeley FrameNet project. In Christian Boitet and Pete Whitelock, Eds., *36th Annual Meeting of the Association for Computational Linguistics and 17th International Conference on Computational Linguistics, COLING-ACL, August 10–14, Université de Montréal, Montréal, Quebec, Canada. Proceedings of the Conference*, pages 86–90. Morgan Kaufmann, 1998. DOI: 10.3115/980845.980860 108

René Ronald Bakker. Knowledge graphs: Representation and structuring of scientific knowledge. Ph.D. thesis, University of Twente, 1987. 159, 160, 161

Ivana Balazevic, Carl Allen, and Timothy M. Hospedales. Multi-relational Poincaré graph embeddings. In Wallach et al. [2019], pages 4465–4475. http://papers.nips.cc/book/advances-in-neural-information-processing-systems-32-2019 6, 79, 86

Ivana Balazevic, Carl Allen, and Timothy M. Hospedales. TuckER: Tensor factorization for knowledge graph completion. In Kentaro Inui, Jing Jiang, Vincent Ng, and Xiaojun Wan, Eds., *Proc. of the Conference on Empirical Methods in Natural Language Processing and the 9th International Joint Conference on Natural Language Processing, EMNLP-IJCNLP, Hong Kong, China, November 3–7*, pages 5184–5193. The Association for Computational Linguistics, 2019b. https://aclweb.org/anthology/volumes/D19-1/ DOI: 10.18653/v1/d19-1522 81, 84

Ivana Balazevic, Carl Allen, and Timothy M. Hospedales. Hypernetwork knowledge graph embeddings. In Igor V. Tetko, Vera Kurková, Pavel Karpov, and Fabian J. Theis, Eds., *Artificial Neural Networks and Machine Learning—ICANN—28th International Conference on Artificial Neural Networks, Munich, Germany, September 17–19, Proceedings—Workshop and Special Sessions*, volume 11731 of *Lecture Notes in Computer Science*, pages 553–565. Springer, 2019c. DOI: 10.1007/978-3-030-30493-5_52 82, 87

Michele Banko, Michael J. Cafarella, Stephen Soderland, Matthew Broadhead, and Oren Etzioni. Open information extraction from the Web. In Manuela M. Veloso, Ed., *IJCAI, Proceedings of the 20th International Joint Conference on Artificial Intelligence, Hyderabad, India, January 6–12*, pages 2670–2676. AAAI Press, 2007. 108

Pablo Barceló, Egor V. Kostylev, Mikael Monet, Jorge Peréz, Juan Reutter, and Juan Pablo Silva. The logical expressiveness of graph neural networks. In *8th International Conference on Learning Representations, ICLR, Addis Ababa, Ethiopia, April 26–30*. OpenReview.net, 2020. https://openreview.net/forum?id=r1lZ7AEKvB 96, 155

Hannah Bast and Björn Buchhold. An index for efficient semantic full-text search. In Qi He, Arun Iyengar, Wolfgang Nejdl, Jian Pei, and Rajeev Rastogi, Eds., *22nd ACM International Conference on Information and Knowledge Management, CIKM'13, San Francisco, CA, October 27—November 1*, pages 369–378. ACM Press, 2013. DOI: 10.1145/2505515.2505689 22

Carlo Batini and Monica Scannapieco. *Data and Information Quality—Dimensions, Principles and Techniques*. Data-Centric Systems and Applications. Springer, 2016. DOI: 10.1007/978-3-319-24106-7 119, 125

Carlo Batini, Anisa Rula, Monica Scannapieco, and Gianluigi Viscusi. From data quality to big data quality. *Journal of Database Management*, 26(1):60–82, 2015. DOI: 10.4018/JDM.2015010103 119

Luigi Bellomarini, Emanuel Sallinger, and Georg Gottlob. The vadalog system: Datalog-based reasoning for knowledge graphs. *Proc. of the VLDB Endowment*, 11(9):975–987, 2018. DOI: 10.14778/3213880.3213888 58

Luigi Bellomarini, Daniele Fakhoury, Georg Gottlob, and Emanuel Sallinger. Knowledge graphs and enterprise AI: The promise of an enabling technology. In ICDE 2019, pages 26–37. DOI: 10.1109/icde.2019.00011 3, 151, 163

Claus Bendtsen and Slavé Petrovski. How data and AI are helping unlock the secrets of disease. AstraZeneca Blog, November 2019. https://www.astrazeneca.com/what-science-can-do/labtalk-blog/uncategorized/how-data-and-ai-are-helping-unlock-the-secrets-of-disease.html 149, 151

Samy Bengio, Hanna M. Wallach, Hugo Larochelle, Kristen Grauman, Nicolò Cesa-Bianchi, and Roman Garnett, Eds. *Advances in Neural Information Processing Systems 31: Annual Conference on Neural Information Processing Systems, NeurIPS: December 3–8, Montréal, Canada*, 2018. http://papers.nips.cc/book/advances-in-neural-information-processing-systems-31-2018 188, 196

Yoshua Bengio and Yann LeCun, Eds. *1st International Conference on Learning Representations, ICLR, Scottsdale, Arizona, May 2–4, Workshop Track Proceedings*. OpenReview.net, 2013. 186, 203

Michael K. Bergman. A common sense view of knowledge graphs. Adaptive Information, Adaptive Innovation, Adaptive Infrastructure Blog, July 2019. http://www.mkbergman.com/2244/a-common-sense-view-of-knowledge-graphs/ 2, 157, 161, 163

Tim Berners-Lee. Linked data. W3C Design Issues, July 2006. https://www.w3.org/DesignIssues/LinkedData.html 37, 133, 135, 158

Tim Berners-Lee and Dan Connolly. Notation3(N3): A readable RDF syntax. *W3C Team Submission, World Wide Web Consortium*, March 28, 2011. https://www.w3.org/TeamSubmission/2011/SUBM-n3-20110328/ 12, 59, 60

Tim Berners-Lee, James Hendler, and Ora Lassila. The semantic web. *Scientific American*, 284(5):34–43, May 2001. 158

Abraham Bernstein, David R. Karger, Tom Heath, Lee Feigenbaum, Diana Maynard, Enrico Motta, and Krishnaprasad Thirunarayan, Eds. *The Semantic Web—ISWC, 8th International Semantic Web Conference, ISWC, Chantilly, VA, October 25–29. Proceedings*, volume 5823 of *Lecture Notes in Computer Science*. Springer, 2009. 189, 223

Anant P. Bhardwaj, Souvik Bhattacherjee, Amit Chavan, Amol Deshpande, Aaron J. Elmore, Samuel Madden, and Aditya G. Parameswaran. DataHub: Collaborative data science and dataset version management at scale. In CIDR. http://cidrdb.org/cidr2015/Papers/ CIDR15_Paper18.pdf 134

Daniel M. Bikel, Richard M. Schwartz, and Ralph M. Weischedel. An algorithm that learns what's in a name. *Machine Learning*, 34(1–3):211–231, 1999. 107

Stefan Bischof, Stefan Decker, Thomas Krennwallner, Nuno Lopes, and Axel Polleres. Mapping between RDF and XML with XSPARQL. *Journal of Web Semantics*, 1(3):147–185, 2012. DOI: 10.1007/s13740-012-0008-7 76, 114

Christian Bizer, Jens Lehmann, Georgi Kobilarov, Sören Auer, Christian Becker, Richard Cyganiak, and Sebastian Hellmann. DBpedia—a crystallization point for the Web of data. *Journal of Web Semantics*, 7(3):154–165, 2009. DOI: 10.1016/j.websem.2009.07.002 146

Eva Blomqvist and Kurt Sandkuhl. Patterns in ontology engineering: Classification of ontology patterns. In Chin-Sheng Chen, Joaquim Filipe, Isabel Seruca, and José Cordeiro, Eds., *ICEIS, Proceedings of the 7th International Conference on Enterprise Information Systems, Miami, May 25–28*, 3:413–416, 2005. DOI: 10.5220/0002518804130416 116

Eva Blomqvist, Azam Seil Sepour, and Valentina Presutti. Ontology testing—methodology and tool. In Annette ten Teije, Johanna Völker, Siegfried Handschuh, Heiner Stuckenschmidt, Mathieu d'Aquin, Andriy Nikolov, Nathalie Aussenac-Gilles, and Nathalie Hernandez, Eds., *Knowledge Engineering and Knowledge Management—18th International Conference, EKAW, Galway City, Ireland, October 8–12. Proceedings*, volume 7603 of *Lecture Notes in Computer Science*, pages 216–226. Springer, 2012. DOI: 10.1007/978-3-642-33876-2_20 116

Eva Blomqvist, Paolo Ciancarini, Francesco Poggi, and Fabio Vitali, Eds. *Knowledge Engineering and Knowledge Management—20th International Conference, EKAW, Bologna, Italy, November 19–23, Proceedings*, volume 10024 of *Lecture Notes in Computer Science*. Springer, 2016a. 177, 181, 200, 209

Eva Blomqvist, Karl Hammar, and Valentina Presutti. Engineering ontologies with patterns—the eXtreme design methodology. In Pascal Hitzler, Aldo Gangemi, Krzysztof Janowicz, Adila Krisnadhi, and Valentina Presutti, Eds., *Ontology Engineering with Ontology Design Patterns*, volume 25 of *Studies on the Semantic Web*. IOS Press, 2016b. 115

Eva Blomqvist, Diana Maynard, Aldo Gangemi, Rinke Hoekstra, Pascal Hitzler, and Olaf Har-tig, Eds. *The Semantic Web—14th International Conference, ESWC, Portorož, Slovenia, May 28–June 1, Proceedings, Part I*, volume 10249 of *Lecture Notes in Computer Science*. Springer, 2017. 182, 185, 212

Kurt Bollacker, Robert Cook, and Patrick Tufts. Freebase: A shared database of structured general human knowledge. In *Proc. of the 22nd AAAI Conference on Artificial Intelligence, July 22–26, Vancouver, British Columbia, Canada*, pages 1962–1963. AAAI Press, 2007a. 114, 145

Kurt Bollacker, Patrick Tufts, Tomi Pierce, and Robert Cook. A platform for scalable, collab-orative, structured information integration. In Ullas Nambiar and Zaiqing Nie, Eds., *Intl. Workshop on Information Integration on the Web (IIWeb)*, 2007b. 3, 147, 158

Piero Bonatti, Sabrina Kirrane, Iliana Mineva Petrova, Luigi Sauro, and Eva Schlehahn. The SPECIAL usage policy language, V1.0. Draft, Vienna University of Economics and Business, December 31, 2019. https://ai.wu.ac.at/policies/policylanguage/ 142

Piero A. Bonatti and Sabrina Kirrane. Big data and analytics in the age of the GDPR. In Elisa Bertino, Carl K. Chang, Peter Chen, Ernesto Damiani, Michael Goul, and Katsunori Oyama, Eds., *IEEE International Congress on Big Data, BigData Congress, Milan, Italy, July 8–13*, pages 7–16. IEEE Computer Society, 2019. DOI: 10.1109/bigdatacongress.2019.00015 142

Piero A. Bonatti, Aidan Hogan, Axel Polleres, and Luigi Sauro. Robust and scalable linked data reasoning incorporating provenance and trust annotations. *Journal of Web Semantics*, 9(2):165–201, 2011. DOI: 10.1016/j.websem.2011.06.003 11, 123, 131

Piero Andrea Bonatti, Stefan Decker, Axel Polleres, and Valentina Presutti. Knowledge graphs: New directions for knowledge representation on the semantic web (Dagstuhl Seminar 18371). *Dagstuhl Reports*, 8(9):29–111, 2018. 2, 39, 161, 163

Iovka Boneva, Jose Emilio Labra Gayo, and Eric G. Prud'hommeaux. Semantics and validation of shapes schemas for RDF. In d'Amato et al. [2017], pages 104–120. DOI: 10.1007/978-3-319-68288-4_7 29

Iovka Boneva, Jérémie Dusart, Daniel Fernández-Álvarez, and José Emilio Labra Gayo. Shape designer for ShEx and SHACL constraints. In Suárez-Figueroa et al. [2019], pages 269–272. http://ceur-ws.org/Vol-2456 148

Angela Bonifati, Wim Martens, and Thomas Timm. An analytical study of large SPARQL query logs. *Proc. of the VLDB Endowment*, 11(2):149–161, 2017. DOI: 10.14778/3149193.3149196 139

Antoine Bordes, Nicolas Usunier, Alberto García-Durán, Jason Weston, and Oksana Yakhnenko. Translating embeddings for modeling multi-relational data. In Burges et al. [2013], pages 2787–2795. http://papers.nips.cc/book/advances-in-neural-information-processing-systems-26-2013 6, 78, 129

Gerlof Bouma. Normalized (pointwise) mutual information in collocation extraction. In Christian Chiarcos, Richard Eckart de Castilho, and Manfred Stede, Eds., *Von der Form zur Bedeutung: Texte automatisch verarbeiten—From Form to Meaning: Processing Texts Automatically, Proceedings of the Biennial GSCL Conference*, pages 31–40. Gunter Narr Verlag, 2009. 130

Jacqueline Bourdeau, Jim Hendler, Roger Nkambou, Ian Horrocks, and Ben Y. Zhao, Eds. *Proc. of the 25th International Conference on World Wide Web, WWW, Montreal, Canada, April 11–15, Companion Volume*. ACM Press, 2016. 199, 216

Ronald J. Brachman. A structural paradigm for representing knowledge. Ph.D. thesis, Harvard University, 1977. 157, 160

Ronald J. Brachman and Hector J. Levesque. The knowledge level of a KBMS. In Michael L. Brodie and John Mylopoulos, Eds., *On Knowledge Base Management Systems: Integrating Artificial Intelligence and Database Technologies, Book resulting from the Islamorada Workshop 1985 (Islamorada, FL,)*, Topics in Information Systems, pages 9–12. Springer, 1986. DOI: 10.1007/978-1-4612-4980-1_2 162

Ronald J. Brachman and James G. Schmolze. An overview of the KL-ONE knowledge representation system. *Cognitive Science*, 9(2):171–216, 1985. DOI: 10.1207/s15516709cog0902_1 158, 162

Patricia Branum and Bethany Sehon. Knowledge graph pilot improves data quality while providing a customer 360 view. In *Knowledge Graph Conference*, 2019. (Invited talk). 3, 151

Dan Brickley and R. V. Guha. RDF schema 1.1, *W3C Recommendation, World Wide Web Consortium*, February 25, 2014. https://www.w3.org/TR/2014/REC-rdf-schema-20140225/ 1, 26, 60, 158

Joan Bruna, Wojciech Zaremba, Arthur Szlam, and Yann LeCun. Spectral networks and locally connected networks on graphs. In Yoshua Bengio and Yann LeCun, Eds., *2nd International Conference on Learning Representations, ICLR, Banff, AB, Canada, April 14–16, Conference Track Proceedings*. OpenReview.net, 2014. https://openreview.net/group?id=ICLR.cc/2014 95

Bruce G. Buchanan and Edward A. Feigenbaum. Dendral and meta-dendral: Their applications dimension. *Artificial Intelligence*, 11(1–2):5–24, 1978. DOI: 10.1016/0004-3702(78)90010-3 162

Lorenz Bühmann, Jens Lehmann, and Patrick Westphal. DL-learner—a framework for inductive learning on the semantic web. *Journal of Web Semantics*, 39:15–24, 2016. DOI: 10.1016/j.websem.2016.06.001 101, 104, 155

Carlos Buil-Aranda, Marcelo Arenas, Óscar Corcho, and Axel Polleres. Federating queries in SPARQL 1.1: Syntax, semantics and evaluation. *Journal of Web Semantics*, 18(1):1–17, 2013a. DOI: 10.1016/j.websem.2012.10.001 140

Carlos Buil-Aranda, Aidan Hogan, Jürgen Umbrich, and Pierre-Yves Vandenbussche. SPARQL web-querying infrastructure: Ready for action? In Alani et al. [2013b], pages 277–293. DOI: 10.1007/978-3-642-41338-4_18 139

Paul Buitelaar, Philipp Cimiano, and Bernardo Magnini, Eds. *Ontology Learning from Text: Methods, Evaluation, and Applications*, volume 123 of *Frontiers in Artificial Intelligence and Applications*. IOS Press, July 2005. 116

Razvan C. Bunescu and Raymond J. Mooney. Subsequence kernels for relation extraction. In Christopher J. C. Burges, Léon Bottou, Zoubin Ghahramani, and Kilian Q. Weinberger, Eds., *Advances in Neural Information Processing Systems 18, Neural Information Processing Systems, NIPS, December 5–8, Vancouver, British Columbia, Canada*, pages 171–178, 2005. http://papers.nips.cc/book/advances-in-neural-information-processing-systems-18-2005 108

Razvan C. Bunescu and Raymond J. Mooney. Learning to extract relations from the Web using minimal supervision. In John A. Carroll, Antal van den Bosch, and Annie Zaenen, Eds., *ACL, Proceedings of the 45th Annual Meeting of the Association for Computational Linguistics, June 23-30, Prague, Czech Republic*, pages 576–583. The Association for Computational Linguistics, 2007. 108

Christopher J. C. Burges, Léon Bottou, Zoubin Ghahramani, and Kilian Q. Weinberger, Eds. *Advances in Neural Information Processing Systems 26: 27th Annual Conference on Neural Information Processing Systems. Proceedings of a meeting held December 5–8, Lake Tahoe, NV*, 2013. http://papers.nips.cc/book/advances-in-neural-information-processing-systems-26-2013 172, 218

Elena Cabrio, Alessio Palmero Aprosio, and Serena Villata. These are your rights—a natural language processing approach to automated RDF licenses generation. In Presutti et al. [2014], pages 255–269. DOI: 10.1007/978-3-319-07443-6_18 141

Michael J. Cafarella, Alon Y. Halevy, Daisy Zhe Wang, Eugene Wu, and Yang Zhang. WebTables: Exploring the power of tables on the Web. *Proc. of the VLDB Endowment*, 1(1):538–549, 2008. DOI: 10.14778/1453856.1453916 111

Hongyun Cai, Vincent W. Zheng, and Kevin Chen-Chuan Chang. A comprehensive survey of graph embedding: Problems, techniques, and applications. *IEEE Transactions on Knowledge and Data Engineering*, 30(9):1616–1637, 2018. DOI: 10.1109/TKDE.2018.2807452 79

Alison Callahan, Jose Cruz-Toledo, Peter Ansell, and Michel Dumontier. Bio2RDF release 2: Improved coverage, interoperability, and provenance of life science linked data. In Cimiano et al. [2013], pages 200–212. DOI: 10.1007/978-3-642-38288-8_14 3, 133, 148, 149

Nicholas J. Car, Paul J. Box, and Ashley Sommer. The location index: A semantic web spatial data infrastructure. In Hitzler et al. [2019], pages 543–557. DOI: 10.1007/978-3-030-21348-0_35 29

Šejla Čebirić, François Goasdoué, Haridimos Kondylakis, Dimitris Kotzinos, Ioana Manolescu, Georgia Troullinou, and Mussab Zneika. Summarizing semantic graphs: A survey. *The Very Large Data Base Journal*, 28(3):295–327, 2019. DOI: 10.1007/s00778-018-0528-3 32, 33, 34

Stefano Ceri, Georg Gottlob, and Letizia Tanca. What you always wanted to know about datalog (and never dared to ask). *IEEE Transactions on Knowledge and Data Engineering*, 1(1):146–166, 1989. DOI: 10.1109/69.43410 57

Pierre-Antoine Champin, Fabien L. Gandon, Mounia Lalmas, and Panagiotis G. Ipeirotis, Eds. *Proc. of the World Wide Web Conference on World Wide Web, WWW, Lyon, France, April 23–27.* ACM Press, 2018. 186, 222

Spencer Chang. Scaling knowledge access and retrieval at Airbnb. AirBnB Medium Blog, September 2018. https://medium.com/airbnb-engineering/scaling-knowledge-access-and-retrieval-at-airbnb-665b6ba21e95 1, 3, 149, 150

Laura Chiticariu, Yunyao Li, and Frederick R. Reiss. Rule-based information extraction is dead! Long live rule-based information extraction systems! In *Proc. of the Conference on Empirical Methods in Natural Language Processing, EMNLP, October 18–21, Grand Hyatt Seattle, Seattle, WA, a Meeting of SIGDAT, a Special Interest Group of the ACL*, pages 827–832. The Association for Computational Linguistics, 2013. https://www.aclweb.org/anthology/volumes/D13-1/ 107

Laura Chiticariu, Marina Danilevsky, Yunyao Li, Frederick Reiss, and Huaiyu Zhu. SystemT: Declarative text understanding for enterprise. In Srinivas Bangalore, Jennifer Chu-Carroll, and Yunyao Li, Eds., *Proc. of the Conference of the North American Chapter of the Association for Computational Linguistics: Human Language Technologies, NAACL-HLT, New Orleans, LA, June 1–6, Volume 3 (Industry Papers)*, pages 76–83. The Association for Computational Linguistics, 2018. DOI: 10.18653/v1/n18-3010 107

Chin-Wan Chung, Andrei Z. Broder, Kyuseok Shim, and Torsten Suel, Eds. *23rd International World Wide Web Conference, WWW, Seoul, Republic of Korea, April 7–11*. ACM Press, 2014. 206, 225

Giovanni Luca Ciampaglia, Prashant Shiralkar, Luis M. Rocha, Johan Bollen, Filippo Menczer, and Alessandro Flammini. Computational fact checking from knowledge networks. *PLOS One*, 10(6):e0128193, 2015. DOI: 10.1371/journal.pone.0128193 130, 160

CIDR. *CIDR, 7th Biennial Conference on Innovative Data Systems Research, Asilomar, CA, January 4–7, Online Proceedings*, 2015. www.cidrdb.org 170, 201

Philipp Cimiano. Ontology learning from text. In *Ontology Learning and Population from Text: Algorithms, Evaluation and Applications*, chapter 3, pages 19–34. Springer, 2006. DOI: 10.1007/978-0-387-39252-3_3 116

Philipp Cimiano, Óscar Corcho, Valentina Presutti, Laura Hollink, and Sebastian Rudolph, Eds. *The Semantic Web: Semantics and Big Data, 10th International Conference, ESWC, Montpellier, France, May 26–30. Proceedings*, volume 7882 of *Lecture Notes in Computer Science*. Springer, 2013. 174, 195

Aaron Clemmer and Stephen Davies. Smeagol: A specific-to-general semantic web query interface paradigm for novices. In Abdelkader Hameurlain, Stephen W. Liddle, Klaus-Dieter Schewe, and Xiaofang Zhou, Eds., *Database and Expert Systems Applications—22nd International Conference, DEXA Toulouse, France, August 29–September 2. Proceedings, Part I*, volume 6860 of *Lecture Notes in Computer Science*, pages 288–302. Springer, 2011. DOI: 10.1007/978-3-642-23088-2_21 22

Michael Cochez, Petar Ristoski, Simone Paolo Ponzetto, and Heiko Paulheim. Biased graph walks for RDF graph embeddings. In Rajendra Akerkar, Alfredo Cuzzocrea, Jannong Cao, and Mohand-Said Hacid, Eds., *Proc. of the 7th International Conference on Web Intelligence, Mining and Semantics, WIMS, Amantea, Italy, June 19–22*, page 21:1–21:12. ACM Press, 2017a. DOI: 10.1145/3102254.3102279 88

Michael Cochez, Petar Ristoski, Simone Paolo Ponzetto, and Heiko Paulheim. Global RDF vector space embeddings. In d'Amato et al. [2017], pages 190–207. DOI: 10.1007/978-3-319-68288-4_12 90

Diego Collarana, Mikhail Galkin, Christoph Lange, Irlán Grangel-González, Maria-Esther Vidal, and Sören Auer. FuhSen: A federated hybrid search engine for building a knowledge graph on-demand (short paper). In Debruyne et al. [2016], pages 752–761. DOI: 10.1007/978-3-319-48472-3_47 111

Michael Collins and Yoram Singer. Unsupervised models for named entity classification. In *Joint SIGDAT Conference on Empirical Methods in Natural Language Processing and Very Large*

Corpora, EMNLP, College Park, MD, June 21–22. The Association for Computational Linguistics, 1999. https://www.aclweb.org/anthology/W99-0613/ 107

Dan Connolly. Gleaning resource descriptions from dialects of languages (GRDDL), *W3C Recommendation, World Wide Web Consortium*, September 11, 2007. https://www.w3.org/TR/2007/REC-grddl-20070911/ 114

Mariano P. Consens and Alberto O. Mendelzon. GraphLog: A visual formalism for real life recursion. In Daniel J. Rosenkrantz and Yehoshua Sagiv, Eds., *Proc. of the 9th ACM SIGACT-SIGMOD-SIGART Symposium on Principles of Database Systems, April 2–4, Nashville, TN*, pages 404–416. ACM Press, 1990. DOI: 10.1145/298514.298591 13

Olivier Corby and Catherine Faron-Zucker. The KGRAM abstract machine for knowledge graph querying. In Jimmy Xiangji Huang, Irwin King, Vijay V. Raghavan, and Stefan Rueger, Eds., *IEEE/WIC/ACM International Conference on Web Intelligence, WI, Toronto, Canada, August 31–September 3, Main Conference Proceedings*, pages 338–341. IEEE Computer Society, 2010. DOI: 10.1109/wi-iat.2010.144 160, 161

Francesco Corcoglioniti, Marco Rospocher, and Alessio Palmero Aprosio. Frame-based ontology population with PIKES. *IEEE Transactions on Knowledge and Data Engineering*, 28(12):3261–3275, 2016. DOI: 10.1109/tkde.2016.2602206 109

Julien Corman, Juan L. Reutter, and Ognjen Savković. Semantics and validation of recursive SHACL. In Vrandečić et al. [2018], pages 318–336. DOI: 10.1007/978-3-030-00671-6_19 29, 31, 32

Julien Corman, Fernando Florenzano, Juan L. Reutter, and Ognjen Savkovic. Validating SHACL constraints over a SPARQL endpoint. In Ghidini et al. [2019a], pages 145–163. DOI: 10.1007/978-3-030-30793-6_9 32

Luca Costabello, Serena Villata, Nicolas Delaforge, and Fabien Gandon. Linked data access goes mobile: Context-aware authorization for graph stores. In Christian Bizer, Tom Heath, Tim Berners-Lee, and Michael Hausenblas, Eds., *WWW Workshop on Linked Data on the Web, Lyon, France, April 16*, volume 937 of *CEUR Workshop Proceedings*. Sun SITE Central Europe (CEUR), 2012. http://ceur-ws.org/Vol-937/ldow2012-paper-05.pdf 141

Kino Coursey and Rada Mihalcea. Topic identification using wikipedia graph centrality. In *Human Language Technologies: Conference of the North American Chapter of the Association of Computational Linguistics, Proceedings, May 31–June 5, Boulder, CO, Short Papers*, pages 117–120. The Association for Computational Linguistics, 2009. DOI: 10.3115/1620853.1620887 160, 161

Simon Cox, Chris Little, Jerry R. Hobbs, and Feng Pan. Time ontology in OWL. *W3C Recommendation/OGC 16-071r2, World Wide Web Consortium and Open Geospatial Consortium*, October 19, 2017. https://www.w3.org/TR/2017/REC-owl-time-20171019/ 40

Eric Crestan and Patrick Pantel. Web-scale table census and classification. In Irwin King, Wolfgang Nejdl, and Hang Li, Eds., *Proc. of the 4th International Conference on Web Search and Web Data Mining, WSDM, Hong Kong, China, February 9–12*, pages 545–554. ACM Press, 2011. DOI: 10.1145/1935826.1935904 111

Philippe Cudré-Mauroux, Jeff Heflin, Evren Sirin, Tania Tudorache, Jérôme Euzenat, Manfred Hauswirth, Josiane Xavier Parreira, Jim Hendler, Guus Schreiber, Abraham Bernstein, and Eva Blomqvist, Eds. *The Semantic Web—ISWC—11th International Semantic Web Conference, Boston, MA, November 11–15, Proceedings, Part I*, volume 7649 of *Lecture Notes in Computer Science*. Springer, 2012. 206, 214

Alfredo Cuzzocrea, James Allan, Norman W. Paton, Divesh Srivastava, Rakesh Agrawal, Andrei Z. Broder, Mohammed J. Zaki, K. Selçuk Candan, Alexandros Labrinidis, Assaf Schuster, and Haixun Wang, Eds. *Proc. of the 27th ACM International Conference on Information and Knowledge Management, CIKM, Torino, Italy, October 22–26*. ACM Press, 2018. 193, 220

Richard Cyganiak, David Wood, and Markus Lanthaler. RDF 1.1 concepts and abstract syntax. *W3C Recommendation, World Wide Web Consortium*, February 25, 2014. https://www.w3.org/TR/2014/REC-rdf11-concepts-20140225/ 6, 11, 39, 41, 158

Enrico Daga, Valentina Presutti, and Alberto Salvati. http://ontologydesignpatterns.org and evaluation WikiFlow. In Aldo Gangemi, Johannes Keizer, Valentina Presutti, and Heiko Stoermer, Eds., *Proc. of the 5th Workshop on Semantic Web Applications and Perspectives (SWAP), Rome, Italy, December 15–17*, volume 426 of *CEUR Workshop Proceedings*, pages 1–11. Sun SITE Central Europe (CEUR), 2008. http://ceur-ws.org/Vol-426 116

Jeff Dalgliesh. How the enterprise knowledge graph connects oil and gas data silos. Maana Blog, May 2016. https://www.maana.io/blog/enterprise-knowledge-graph-connects-oil-gas-data-silos/ 3, 149, 151

Claudia d'Amato, Steffen Staab, Andrea G. B. Tettamanzi, Duc Minh Tran, and Fabien L. Gandon. Ontology enrichment by discovering multi-relational association rules from ontological knowledge bases. In Sascha Ossowski, Ed., *Proc. of the 31st Annual ACM Symposium on Applied Computing, Pisa, Italy, April 4–8*, pages 333–338. ACM Press, 2016a. DOI: 10.1145/2851613.2851842 100

Claudia d'Amato, Andrea G. B. Tettamanzi, and Minh Duc Tran. Evolutionary discovery of multi-relational association rules from ontological knowledge bases. In Blomqvist et al. [2016a], pages 113–128. DOI: 10.1007/978-3-319-49004-5_8 100

Claudia d'Amato, Miriam Fernández, Valentina A. M. Tamma, Freddy Lécué, Philippe Cudré-Mauroux, Juan F. Sequeda, Christoph Lange, and Jeff Heflin, Eds. *The Semantic Web—ISWC—16th International Semantic Web Conference, Vienna, Austria, October 21–25, Proceedings, Part I*, volume 10587 of *Lecture Notes in Computer Science*. Springer, 2017. 171, 175, 189, 209, 210

Fariz Darari, Werner Nutt, Giuseppe Pirrò, and Simon Razniewski. Completeness management for RDF data sources. *ACM Transactions on the Web*, 12(3):18:1–18:53, 2018. DOI: 10.1145/3196248 121

Gautam Das, Christopher M. Jermaine, and Philip A. Bernstein, Eds. *Proc. of the International Conference on Management of Data, SIGMOD Conference, Houston, TX, June 10–15*. ACM Press, 2018. 167, 183

Souripriya Das, Seema Sundara, and Richard Cyganiak. R2RML: RDB to RDF mapping language. *W3C Recommendation, World Wide Web Consortium*, September 27, 2012. https://www.w3.org/TR/2012/REC-r2rml-20120927/ 105, 113

Ankur Dave, Alekh Jindal, Li Erran Li, Reynold Xin, Joseph Gonzalez, and Matei Zaharia. GraphFrames: An integrated API for mixing graph and relational queries. In Peter A. Boncz and Josep-Lluís Larriba-Pey, Eds., *Proc. of the 4th International Workshop on Graph Data Management Experiences and Systems, Redwood Shores, CA, June 24–24*, page 2. ACM Press, 2016. DOI: 10.1145/2960414.2960416 70

Gerard de Melo. Lexvo.org: Language-related information for the linguistic linked data cloud. *Semantic Web Journal*, 6(4):393–400, August 2015. DOI: 10.3233/sw-150171 39

Luc De Raedt, Bart Vandersmissen, Marc Denecker, and Maurice Bruynooghe. A hybrid approach to learning and its knowledge representation. In *Proc. of the 3rd COGNITIVA Symposium on at the Crossroads of Artificial Intelligence, Cognitive Science, and Neuroscience*, pages 409–416. Elsevier, 1990. 159, 160

Marina De Vos, Sabrina Kirrane, Julian Padget, and Ken Satoh. ODRL policy modelling and compliance checking. In Paul Fodor, Marco Montali, Diego Calvanese, and Dumitru Roman, Eds., *Rules and Reasoning—3rd International Joint Conference, RuleML+RR, Bolzano, Italy, September 16–19, Proceedings*, volume 11784 of *Lecture Notes in Computer Science*, pages 36–51. Springer, 2019. DOI: 10.1007/978-3-030-31095-0_3 141

Christophe Debruyne, Hervé Panetto, Robert Meersman, Tharam S. Dillon, eva Kühn, Declan O'Sullivan, and Claudio Agostino Ardagna, Eds. *On the Move to Meaningful Internet Systems: OTM Conferences—Confederated International Conferences: CoopIS, C&TC, and ODBASE, Rhodes, Greece, October 24–28, Proceedings*, volume 10033 of *Lecture Notes in Computer Science*. Springer, 2016. DOI: 10.1007/978-3-319-48472-3 175, 189

Remy Delanaux, Angela Bonifati, Marie-Christine Rousset, and Romuald Thion. Query-based linked data anonymization. In Vrandečić et al. [2018], pages 530–546. DOI: 10.1007/978-3-030-00671-6_31 142

Thomas Demeester, Tim Rocktäschel, and Sebastian Riedel. Lifted rule injection for relation embeddings. In Su et al. [2016], pages 1389–1399. DOI: 10.18653/v1/d16-1146 90, 155

Dong Deng, Yu Jiang, Guoliang Li, Jian Li, and Cong Yu. Scalable column concept determination for web tables using large knowledge bases. *Proc. of the VLDB Endowment*, 6(13):1606–1617, 2013. DOI: 10.14778/2536258.2536271 111

Tim Dettmers, Pasquale Minervini, Pontus Stenetorp, and Sebastian Riedel. Convolutional 2D knowledge graph embeddings. In McIlraith and Weinberger [2018], pages 1811–1818. 82, 87

Deepika Devarajan. Happy birthday Watson discovery. IBM Cloud Blog, December 2017. https://www.ibm.com/blogs/bluemix/2017/12/happy-birthday-watson-discovery/ 1

Gonzalo I. Diaz, Marcelo Arenas, and Michael Benedikt. SPARQLByE: Querying RDF data by example. *Proc. of the VLDB Endowment*, 9(13):1533–1536, 2016. DOI: 10.14778/3007263.3007302 23

Dennis Diefenbach, Andreas Both, Kamal Singh, and Pierre Maret. Towards a question answering system over the semantic web. *Semantic Web Journal*, 11(3):421–439, 2020. DOI: 10.3233/SW-190343 23

Rose Dieng, Alain Giboin, Paul-André Tourtier, and Olivier Corby. Knowledge acquisition for explainable, multi-expert, knowledge-based design systems. In Thomas Wetter, Klaus-Dieter Althoff, John H. Boose, Brian R. Gaines, and Marc Linster, Eds., *Current Developments in Knowledge Acquisition—EKAW, 6th European Knowledge Acquisition Workshop, Heidelberg and Kaiserslautern, Germany, May 18–22*, volume 599 of *Lecture Notes in Computer Science*, pages 298–317. Springer, 1992. DOI: 10.1007/3-540-55546-3_47 159, 160, 161

Anastasia Dimou, Miel Vander Sande, Jason Slepicka, Pedro A. Szekely, Erik Mannens, Craig A. Knoblock, and Rik Van de Walle. Mapping hierarchical sources into RDF using the RML mapping language. In *IEEE International Conference on Semantic Computing, Newport Beach, CA, June 16–18*, pages 151–158. IEEE Computer Society, 2014. DOI: 10.1109/icsc.2014.25 114

Renata Queiroz Dividino, Sergej Sizov, Steffen Staab, and Bernhard Schueler. Querying for provenance, trust, uncertainty and other meta knowledge in RDF. *Journal of Web Semantics*, 7(3):204–219, 2009. DOI: 10.1016/j.websem.2009.07.004 11, 42

Xin Dong, Evgeniy Gabrilovich, Geremy Heitz, Wilko Horn, Ni Lao, Kevin Murphy, Thomas Strohmann, Shaohua Sun, and Wei Zhang. Knowledge vault: A web-scale approach to probabilistic knowledge fusion. In Sofus A. Macskassy, Claudia Perlich, Jure Leskovec, Wei Wang, and Rayid Ghani, Eds., *The 20th ACM SIGKDD International Conference on Knowledge Discovery and Data Mining, KDD, New York, August 24–27*, pages 601–610. ACM Press, 2014. DOI: 10.1145/2623330.2623623 82

Xin Luna Dong. Building a broad knowledge graph for products. In ICDE 2019, pages 25–25. DOI: 10.1109/icde.2019.00010 3, 150

Uwe Draisbach and Felix Naumann. A generalization of blocking and windowing algorithms for duplicate detection. In Ji Zhang and Giovanni Livraga, Eds., *International Conference on Data and Knowledge Engineering, ICDKE, Milano, Italy, September 6*, pages 18–24. IEEE Computer Society, 2011. DOI: 10.1109/icdke.2011.6053920 128, 129

Martin Dürst and Michel Suignard. Internationalized resource identifiers (IRIs). RFC 3987, Internet Engineering Task Force, January 2005. http://www.ietf.org/rfc/rfc3987.txt DOI: 10.17487/rfc3987 6

Arnab Dutta, Christian Meilicke, and Heiner Stuckenschmidt. Semantifying triples from open information extraction systems. In Ulle Endriss and Jo ao Leite, Eds., *STAIRS, Proceedings of the 7th European Starting AI Researcher Symposium, Prague, Czech Republic, August 18–22*, volume 264 of *Frontiers in Artificial Intelligence and Applications*, pages 111–120. IOS Press, 2014. 109

Arnab Dutta, Christian Meilicke, and Heiner Stuckenschmidt. Enriching structured knowledge with open information. In Gangemi et al. [2015], pages 267–277. DOI: 10.1145/2736277.2741139 109

Cynthia Dwork. Differential privacy. In Michele Bugliesi, Bart Preneel, Vladimiro Sassone, and Ingo Wegener, Eds., *Automata, Languages and Programming, 33rd International Colloquium, ICALP, Venice, Italy, July 10–14, Proceedings, Part II*, volume 4052 of *Lecture Notes in Computer Science*, pages 1–12. Springer, 2006. DOI: 10.1007/11787006_1 144

Eugene Dynkin. *Markov Processes*. Springer, 1965. DOI: 10.1007/978-3-662-00031-1 74

Julian Eberius, Katrin Braunschweig, Markus Hentsch, Maik Thiele, Ahmad Ahmadov, and Wolfgang Lehner. Building the Dresden web table corpus: A classification approach. In Ioan Raicu, Omer F. Rana, and Rajkumar Buyya, Eds., *2nd IEEE/ACM International Symposium on Big Data Computing, BDC, Limassol, Cyprus, December 7–10*, pages 41–50. IEEE Computer Society, 2015. DOI: 10.1109/bdc.2015.30 111

Mikel Ega na, Alan Rector, Robert Stevens, and Erick Antezana. Applying ontology design patterns in bio-ontologies. In Aldo Gangemi and Jérôme Euzenat, Eds., *Knowledge Engineering: Practice and Patterns, 16th International Conference, EKAW, Acitrezza, Italy, September 29–October 2. Proceedings*, volume 5268 of *Lecture Notes in Computer Science*, pages 7–16. Springer, 2008. DOI: 10.1007/978-3-540-87696-0_4 116

Lisa Ehrlinger and Wolfram Wöß. Towards a definition of knowledge graphs. In Michael Martin, Martí Cuquet, and Erwin Folmer, Eds., *Joint Proceedings of the Posters and Demos Track of the 12th International Conference on Semantic Systems—SEMANTiCS and the 1st International Workshop on Semantic Change and Evolving Semantics (SuCCESS) Co-Located with the 12th International Conference on Semantic Systems (SEMANTiCS), Leipzig, Germany, September 12–15*, volume 1695 of *CEUR Workshop Proceedings*. Sun SITE Central Europe (CEUR), 2016. http://ceur-ws.org/Vol-1695/paper4.pdf 1, 2, 157, 161, 162, 163

Shady Elbassuoni, Maya Ramanath, Ralf Schenkel, Marcin Sydow, and Gerhard Weikum. Language-model-based ranking for queries on RDF-graphs. In David Wai-Lok Cheung, Il-Yeol Song, Wesley W. Chu, Xiaohua Hu, and Jimmy J. Lin, Eds., *Proc. of the 18th ACM Conference on Information and Knowledge Management, CIKM, Hong Kong, China, November 2–6*, pages 977–986. ACM Press, 2009. DOI: 10.1145/1645953.1646078 160, 161

Basil Ell, Andreas Harth, and Elena Simperl. SPARQL query verbalization for explaining semantic search engine queries. In Presutti et al. [2014], pages 426–441. DOI: 10.1007/978-3-319-07443-6_29 129

Orri Erling. Virtuoso, a hybrid RDBMS/graph column store. *IEEE Data Engineering Bulletin*, 35(1):3–8, 2012. 139

Ivan Ermilov and Axel-Cyrille Ngonga Ngomo. TAIPAN: Automatic property mapping for tabular data. In Blomqvist et al. [2016a], pages 163–179. DOI: 10.1007/978-3-319-49004-5_11 111

Diego Esteves, Anisa Rula, Aniketh Janardhan Reddy, and Jens Lehmann. Toward veracity assessment in RDF knowledge bases: An exploratory analysis. *Journal of Data and Information Quality*, 9(3):16:1–16:26, 2018. DOI: 10.1145/3177873 120, 129

Ernesto Estrada. *The Structure of Complex Networks: Theory and Applications*. Oxford University Press, Inc., 2011. DOI: 10.1093/acprof:oso/9780199591756.001.0001 68

Oren Etzioni, Michael J. Cafarella, Doug Downey, Stanley Kok, Ana-Maria Popescu, Tal Shaked, Stephen Soderland, Daniel S. Weld, and Alexander Yates. Web-scale information extraction in knowitall: (preliminary results). In Stuart I. Feldman, Mike Uretsky, Marc Najork, and Craig E. Wills, Eds., *Proc. of the 13th International Conference on World Wide Web, WWW, New York, May 17–20*, pages 100–110. ACM Press, 2004. DOI: 10.1145/988672.988687 107, 108

Oren Etzioni, Anthony Fader, Janara Christensen, Stephen Soderland, and Mausam. Open information extraction: The second generation. In Walsh [2011], pages 3–10. 108

Anthony Fader, Stephen Soderland, and Oren Etzioni. Identifying relations for open information extraction. In *Proc. of the Conference on Empirical Methods in Natural Language Processing, EMNLP, July 27–31, John McIntyre Conference Centre, Edinburgh, UK, a Meeting of SIGDAT, a Special Interest Group of the ACL*, pages 1535–1545. The Association for Computational Linguistics, 2011. https://www.aclweb.org/anthology/volumes/D11-1/ 108

Wenfei Fan, Xin Wang, and Yinghui Wu. Diversified top-k graph pattern matching. *Proc. of the VLDB Endowment*, 6(13):1510–1521, 2013. DOI: 10.14778/2536258.2536263 75

Nicola Fanizzi, Claudia d'Amato, and Floriana Esposito. DL-FOIL concept learning in description logics. In Filip Zelezný and Nada Lavrac, Eds., *Inductive Logic Programming, 18th International Conference, ILP, Prague, Czech Republic, September 10–12, Proceedings*, volume 5194 of *Lecture Notes in Computer Science*, pages 107–121. Springer, 2008. DOI: 10.1007/978-3-540-85928-4_12 101, 104

Michael Färber. The microsoft academic knowledge graph: A linked data source with 8 billion triples of scholarly data. In Ghidini et al. [2019b], pages 113–129. DOI: 10.1007/978-3-030-30796-7_8 148

Michael Färber, Frederic Bartscherer, Carsten Menne, and Achim Rettinger. Linked data quality of DBpedia, Freebase, OpenCyc, Wikidata, and YAGO. *Semantic Web Journal*, 9(1):77–129, 2018. DOI: 10.3233/sw-170275 148

Dieter Fensel, Umutcan Simsek, Kevin Angele, Elwin Huaman, Elias Kärle, Oleksandra Panasiuk, Ioan Toma, Jürgen Umbrich, and Alexander Wahler. *Knowledge Graphs—Methodology, Tools and Selected Use Cases*. Springer, 2020. DOI: 10.1007/978-3-030-37439-6 1

Javier D. Fernández, Miguel A. Martínez-Prieto, Claudio Gutiérrez, Axel Polleres, and Mario Arias. Binary RDF representation for publication and exchange (HDT). *Journal of Web Semantics*, 19:22–41, 2013. DOI: 10.1016/j.websem.2013.01.002 138

Javier D. Fernández, Sabrina Kirrane, Axel Polleres, and Simon Steyskal. Self-enforcing access control for encrypted RDF. In Blomqvist et al. [2017], pages 607–622. DOI: 10.1007/978-3-319-58068-5_37 143

Mariano Fernández, Asuncón Gómez-Pérez, and Natalia Juristo. Methontology: From ontological art towards ontological engineering. In *Proc. of the AAAI Spring Symposium Series on Ontological Engineering*, 1997. 115

Emilio Ferrara, Pasquale De Meo, Giacomo Fiumara, and Robert Baumgartner. Web data extraction, applications and techniques: A survey. *Knowledge-Based Systems*, 70:301–323, 2014. DOI: 10.1016/j.knosys.2014.07.007 110

Sébastien Ferré. Sparklis: An expressive query builder for SPARQL endpoints with guidance in natural language. *Semantic Web Journal*, 8(3):405–418, 2017. DOI: 10.3233/SW-150208 22

Charles J. Fillmore. Frame semantics and the nature of language. *Annals of the New York Academy of Sciences*, 280(1):20–32, 1976. DOI: 10.1111/j.1749-6632.1976.tb25467.x 108

Jenny Rose Finkel, Trond Grenager, and Christopher D. Manning. Incorporating non-local information into information extraction systems by Gibbs sampling. In Knight et al. [2005], pages 363–370. DOI: 10.3115/1219840.1219885 107

Sergio Flesca, Giuseppe Manco, Elio Masciari, Eugenio Rende, and Andrea Tagarelli. Web wrapper induction: A brief survey. *AI Communications*, 17(2):57–61, 2004. 110

Giorgos Flouris, Irini Fundulaki, Maria Michou, and Grigoris Antoniou. Controlling Access to RDF Graphs. In Arne-Jørgen Berre, Asunción Gómez-Pérez, Kurt Tutschku, and Dieter Fensel, Eds., *Future Internet—FIS—3rd Future Internet Symposium, Berlin, Germany, September 20–22. Proceedings*, volume 6369 of *Lecture Notes in Computer Science*, pages 107–117. Springer, 2010. DOI: 10.1007/978-3-642-15877-3_12 141

Charles Forgy. Rete: A fast algorithm for the many patterns/many objects match problem. *Artificial Intelligence*, 19(1):17–37, 1982. 58

Nadime Francis, Alastair Green, Paolo Guagliardo, Leonid Libkin, Tobias Lindaaker, Victor Marsault, Stefan Plantikow, Mats Rydberg, Petra Selmer, and Andrés Taylor. Cypher: An evolving query language for property graphs. In Das et al. [2018], pages 1433–1445. DOI: 10.1145/3183713.3190657 13, 17, 19, 75

Gottlob Frege. *Begriffsschrift*. Halle, 1879. 157

André Freitas, Jo ao Gabriel Oliveira, Seán O'Riain, Edward Curry, and Jo ao Carlos Pereira da Silva. Treo: Best-effort natural language queries over linked data. In Rafael Mu noz, Andrés Montoyo, and Elisabeth Métais, Eds., *Natural Language Processing and Information Systems—16th International Conference on Applications of Natural Language to Information Systems, NLDB, Alicante, Spain, June 28–30. Proceedings*, volume 6716 of *Lecture Notes in Computer Science*, pages 286–289. Springer, 2011. DOI: 10.1007/978-3-642-22327-3 23

Christian Fürber and Martin Hepp. SWIQA—a semantic web information quality assessment framework. In Virpi Kristiina Tuunainen, Matti Rossi, and Joe Nandhakumar, Eds., *19th European Conference on Information Systems, ECIS, Helsinki, Finland, June 9–11*, page 76, 2011. http://aisel.aisnet.org/ecis2011/ 120, 124

Mohamed H. Gad-Elrab, Daria Stepanova, Jacopo Urbani, and Gerhard Weikum. Exception-enriched rule learning from knowledge graphs. In Groth et al. [2016], pages 234–251. DOI: 10.1007/978-3-319-46523-4_15 99

Luis Galárraga, Chistina Teflioudi, Katja Hose, and Fabian M. Suchanek. Fast rule mining in ontological knowledge bases with AMIE+. *The Very Large Data Base Journal*, 24(6):707–730, 2015. DOI: 10.1007/s00778-015-0394-1 99, 155

Luis Antonio Galárraga, Christina Teflioudi, Katja Hose, and Fabian Suchanek. Amie: Association rule mining under incomplete evidence in ontological knowledge bases. In Schwabe et al. [2013], pages 413–422. DOI: 10.1145/2488388.2488425 98, 99, 104

Alban Galland, Serge Abiteboul, Amélie Marian, and Pierre Senellart. Corroborating Information from Disagreeing Views. In Brian D. Davison, Torsten Suel, Nick Craswell, and Bing Liu, Eds., *Proc. of the 3rd International Conference on Web Search and Web Data Mining, WSDM, New York, February 4–6*, pages 131–140. ACM Press, 2010. DOI: 10.1145/1718487.1718504 130

Fabien Gandon and Guus Schreiber. RDF 1.1 XML syntax. *W3C Recommendation, World Wide Web Consortium*, February 25, 2014. https://www.w3.org/TR/2014/REC-rdf-syntax-grammar-20140225/ 137

Aldo Gangemi. Ontology design patterns for semantic web content. In Gil et al. [2005], pages 262–276. DOI: 10.1007/11574620_21 116

Aldo Gangemi, Stefano Leonardi, and Alessandro Panconesi, Eds. *Proc. of the 24th International Conference on World Wide Web, WWW, Florence, Italy, May 18–22*, 2015. ACM Press. 180, 210

Aldo Gangemi, Valentina Presutti, Diego Reforgiato Recupero, Andrea Giovanni Nuzzolese, Francesco Draicchio, and Misael Mongiovì. Semantic web machine reading with FRED. *Semantic Web Journal*, 8(6):873–893, 2017. DOI: 10.3233/sw-160240 109

Claire Gardent, Anastasia Shimorina, Shashi Narayan, and Laura Perez-Beltrachini. The WebNLG challenge: Generating text from RDF data. In José M. Alonso, Alberto Bugarín, and Ehud Reiter, Eds., *Proc. of the 10th International Conference on Natural Language Generation, INLG, Santiago de Compostela, Spain, September 4–7*, pages 124–133. The Association for Computational Linguistics, 2017. DOI: 10.18653/v1/w17-3518 129

Michael Gelfond and Vladimir Lifschitz. The stable model semantics for logic programming. In Robert A. Kowalski and Kenneth A. Bowen, Eds., *Logic Programming, Proceedings of the 5th International Conference and Symposium, Seattle, WA, August 15–19, (2 Volumes)*, pages 1070–1080. The MIT Press, 1988. 29

James Geller, Soon Ae Chun, and Yoo Jung An. Toward the semantic deep web. *IEEE Computer*, 41(9):95–97, 2008. DOI: 10.1109/mc.2008.402 111

Anna Lisa Gentile, Ziqi Zhang, and Fabio Ciravegna. Self training wrapper induction with linked data. In Petr Sojka, Ales Horák, Ivan Kopecek, and Karel Pala, Eds., *Text, Speech and*

Dialogue—17th International Conference, TSD, Brno, Czech Republic, September 8–12. Proceedings, volume 8655 of *Lecture Notes in Computer Science*, pages 285–292. Springer, 2014. DOI: 10.1007/978-3-319-10816-2_35 110

Anna Lisa Gentile, Daniel Gruhl, Petar Ristoski, and Steve Welch. Personalized Knowledge Graphs for the Pharmaceutical Domain. In Ghidini et al. [2019b], pages 400–417. DOI: 10.1007/978-3-030-30796-7_25 151

Daniel Gerber, Diego Esteves, Jens Lehmann, Lorenz Bühmann, Ricardo Usbeck, Axel-Cyrille Ngonga Ngomo, and René Speck. DeFacto—temporal and multilingual deep fact validation. *Journal of Web Semantics*, 35:85–101, 2015. DOI: 10.1016/j.websem.2015.08.001 129, 130

Sabrina Gerbracht. Possibilities to encrypt an RDF-graph. In *3rd International Conference on Information and Communication Technologies: From Theory to Applications*. IEEE Computer Society, 2008. DOI: 10.1109/ictta.2008.4530288 142

Lise Getoor and Ben Taskar, Eds. *Introduction to Statistical Relational Learning*. The MIT Press, 2007. DOI: 10.7551/mitpress/7432.001.0001 127

Chiara Ghidini, Olaf Hartig, Maria Maleshkova, Vojtech Svátek, Isabel F. Cruz, Aidan Hogan, Jie Song, Maxime Lefrançois, and Fabien Gandon, Eds. *The Semantic Web—ISWC—18th International Semantic Web Conference, Auckland, New Zealand, October 26–30, Proceedings, Part I*, volume 11778 of *Lecture Notes in Computer Science*. Springer, 2019a. 176, 220, 222

Chiara Ghidini, Olaf Hartig, Maria Maleshkova, Vojtech Svátek, Isabel F. Cruz, Aidan Hogan, Jie Song, Maxime Lefrançois, and Fabien Gandon, Eds. *The Semantic Web—ISWC—18th International Semantic Web Conference, Auckland, New Zealand, October 26–30, Proceedings, Part II*, volume 11779 of *Lecture Notes in Computer Science*. Springer, 2019b. 182, 185, 186, 216

Mark Giereth. On partial encryption of RDF-graphs. In Gil et al. [2005], pages 308–322. DOI: 10.1007/11574620_24 142

Yolanda Gil, Enrico Motta, V. Richard Benjamins, and Mark A. Musen, Eds. *The Semantic Web—ISWC, 4th International Semantic Web Conference, ISWC, Galway, Ireland, November 6–10, Proceedings*, volume 3729 of *Lecture Notes in Computer Science*. Springer, 2005. 184, 185

Yolanda Gil, Simon Miles, Khalid Belhajjame, Daniel Garijo, Graham Klyne, Paolo Missier, Stian Soiland-Reyes, and Stephan Zednik. PROV model primer. *W3C Working Group Note. World Wide Web Consortium*, April 30, 2013. https://www.w3.org/TR/2013/NOTE-prov-primer-20130430/ 40, 134

José M. Giménez-García, Antoine Zimmermann, and Pierre Maret. NdFluents: An ontology for annotated statements with inference preservation. In Blomqvist et al. [2017], pages 638–654. DOI: 10.1007/978-3-319-58068-5_39 41

Birte Glimm. Using SPARQL with RDFS and OWL entailment. In Axel Polleres, Claudia d'Amato, Marcelo Arenas, Siegfried Handschuh, Paula Kroner, Sascha Ossowski, and Peter F. Patel-Schneider, Eds., *Reasoning Web. Semantic Technologies for the Web of Data—7th International Summer School, Galway, Ireland, August 23–27, Tutorial Lectures*, volume 6848 of *Lecture Notes in Computer Science*, pages 137–201. Springer, 2011. DOI: 10.1007/978-3-642-23032-5_3 140

Xavier Glorot, Antoine Bordes, Jason Weston, and Yoshua Bengio. A semantic matching energy function for learning with multi-relational data. In Bengio and LeCun [2013]. http://arxiv.org/abs/1301.3485 DOI: 10.1007/s10994-013-5363-6 82

Patrick Golden and Ryan B. Shaw. Nanopublication beyond the sciences: The periodO period gazetteer. *PeerJ Computer Science*, 2:e44, 2016. DOI: 10.7717/peerj-cs.44 114

Asunción Gómez-Pérez, Mariano Fernández-López, and Oscar Corcho. *Ontological Engineering: With Examples from the Areas of Knowledge Management, e-Commerce and the Semantic Web*. Springer, 2006. 115

Rafael S. Gonçalves, Matthew Horridge, Rui Li, Yu Liu, Mark A. Musen, Csongor I. Nyulas, Evelyn Obamos, Dhananjay Shrouty, and David Temple. Use of OWL and semantic web technologies at Pinterest. In Ghidini et al. [2019b], pages 418–435. DOI: 10.1007/978-3-030-30796-7_26 150

Larry González and Aidan Hogan. Modelling dynamics in semantic web knowledge graphs with formal concept analysis. In Champin et al. [2018], pages 1175–1184. DOI: 10.1145/3178876.3186016 34

Simon Gottschalk and Elena Demidova. EventKG: A multilingual event-centric temporal knowledge graph. In Aldo Gangemi, Roberto Navigli, Maria-Esther Vidal, Pascal Hitzler, Troncy Raphaël, Laura Hollink, Anna Tordai, and Mehwish Alam, Eds., *The Semantic Web—15th International Conference, ESWC, Heraklion, Crete, Greece, June 3–7, Proceedings*, volume 10843 of *Lecture Notes in Computer Science*, pages 272–287. Springer, 2018. DOI: 10.1007/978-3-319-93417-4_18 114

Guido Governatori, Ho-Pun Lam, Antonino Rotolo, Serena Villata, and Fabien Gandon. Heuristics for licenses composition. In Kevin D. Ashley, Ed., *Legal Knowledge and Information Systems—JURIX: The 26th Annual Conference, December 11–13, University of Bologna, Italy*, volume 259 of *Frontiers in Artificial Intelligence and Applications*, pages 77–86. IOS Press, 2013. 141

Ralph Grishman. Information extraction: Capabilities and challenges. *Technical Report*, NYU Dept. CS, 2012. Notes prepared for the 2012 International Winter School in Language and Speech Technologies. 106

Paul T. Groth, Antonis Loizou, Alasdair J. G. Gray, Carole A. Goble, Lee Harland, and Steve Pettifer. API-centric linked data integration: The open PHACTS discovery platform case study. *Journal of Web Semantics*, 29:12–18, 2014. DOI: 10.1016/j.websem.2014.03.003 133, 135

Paul T. Groth, Elena Simperl, Alasdair J. G. Gray, Marta Sabou, Markus Krötzsch, Freddy Lécué, Fabian Flöck, and Yolanda Gil, Eds. *The Semantic Web—ISWC—15th International Semantic Web Conference, Kobe, Japan, October 17–21, Proceedings, Part I*, volume 9981 of *Lecture Notes in Computer Science*. Springer, 2016. 183, 206, 212

Michael Grüninger and Mark S. Fox. Methodology for the design and evaluation of ontologies. In *Workshop on Basic Ontological Issues in Knowledge Sharing, IJCAI, Montreal*, 1995a. 115

Michael Grüninger and Mark S. Fox. The role of competency questions in enterprise engineering. In Asbjorn Rolstadas, Ed., *Benchmarking—Theory and Practice*, pages 22–31. Springer, 1995b. DOI: 10.1007/978-0-387-34847-6_3 115

Nicola Guarino, Daniel Oberle, and Steffen Staab. What is an ontology? In Staab and Studer [2009], pages 1–17. DOI: 10.1007/978-3-540-92673-3 162

Ramanathan V. Guha, Rob McCool, and Eric Miller. Semantic search. In Gusztáv Hencsey, Bebo White, Yih-Farn Robin Chen, László Kovács, and Steve Lawrence, Eds., *Proc. of the 12th International World Wide Web Conference, WWW, Budapest, Hungary, May 20–24*, pages 700–709. ACM Press, 2003. DOI: 10.1145/775152.775250 149

Ramanathan V. Guha, Rob McCool, and Richard Fikes. Contexts for the semantic web. In Frank van Harmelen, Sheila McIlraith, and Dimitri Plexousakis, Eds., *The Semantic Web—ISWC: 3rd International Semantic Web Conference, Hiroshima, Japan, November 7–11, Proceedings*, volume 3298 of *Lecture Notes in Computer Science*, pages 32–46. Springer, 2004. DOI: 10.1007/978-3-540-30475-3_4 40

Shu Guo, Quan Wang, Lihong Wang, Bin Wang, and Li Guo. Jointly embedding knowledge graphs and logical rules. In Su et al. [2016], pages 192–202. DOI: 10.18653/v1/d16-1019 90, 155

Shu Guo, Quan Wang, Lihong Wang, Bin Wang, and Li Guo. Knowledge graph embedding with iterative guidance from soft rules. In McIlraith and Weinberger [2018], pages 4816–4823. https://www.aaai.org/ocs/index.php/AAAI/AAAI18/paper/view/16369 90

Sonal Gupta and Christopher D. Manning. Improved pattern learning for bootstrapped entity extraction. In Roser Morante and Wen-tau Yih, Eds., *Proc. of the 18th Conference on Computational Natural Language Learning, CoNLL, Baltimore, MD, June 26–27*, pages 98–108. The Association for Computational Linguistics, 2014. DOI: 10.3115/v1/w14-1611 107

Claudio Gutiérrez, Carlos A. Hurtado, and Alejandro A. Vaisman. Introducing time into RDF. *IEEE Transactions on Knowledge and Data Engineering*, 19(2):207–218, 2007. DOI: 10.1109/tkde.2007.34 42

Isabelle Guyon, Ulrike von Luxburg, Samy Bengio, Hanna M. Wallach, Rob Fergus, S. V. N. Vishwanathan, and Roman Garnett, Eds. *Advances in Neural Information Processing Systems 30: Annual Conference on Neural Information Processing Systems: December 4–9, Long Beach, CA*, 2017. http://papers.nips.cc/book/advances-in-neural-information-processing-systems-30-2017 213, 226

Florian Haag, Steffen Lohmann, Stephan Siek, and Thomas Ertl. QueryVOWL: A visual query notation for linked data. In Fabien Gandon, Christophe Guéret, Serena Villata, John G. Breslin, Catherine Faron-Zucker, and Antoine Zimmermann, Eds., *The Semantic Web: ESWC Satellite Events—ESWC Satellite Events Portorož, Slovenia, May 31–June 4, Revised Selected Papers*, volume 9341 of *Lecture Notes in Computer Science*, pages 387–402. Springer, 2015. DOI: 10.1007/978-3-319-25639-9_51 22

Hisham M. Haddad, Roger L. Wainwright, and Richard Chbeir, Eds. *Proc. of the 33rd Annual ACM Symposium on Applied Computing, SAC, Pau, France, April 9–13*. ACM Press, 2018. DOI: 10.1145/3167132 201, 203

Juha Hakala. Persistent identifiers—an overview. *Persid Technical Report*, September 3, 2010. http://www.persid.org/downloads/PI-intro-2010-09-22.pdf 36

Ferras Hamad, Isaac Liu, and Xian Xing Zhang. Food discovery with uber eats: Building a query understanding engine. Uber Engineering Blog, June 2018. https://eng.uber.com/uber-eats-query-understanding/ 1, 3, 149, 150

William L. Hamilton, Payal Bajaj, Marinka Zitnik, Dan Jurafsky, and Jure Leskovec. Embedding logical queries on knowledge graphs. In Bengio et al. [2018], pages 2030–2041. http://papers.nips.cc/book/advances-in-neural-information-processing-systems-31-2018 76

Tony Hammond, Michele Pasin, and Evangelos Theodoridis. Data integration and disintegration: Managing springer nature SciGraph with SHACL and OWL. In Nadeschda Nikitina, Dezhao Song, Achille Fokoue, and Peter Haase, Eds., *Proc. of the ISWC Posters and Demonstrations and Industry Tracks co-located with 16th International Semantic Web Conference (ISWC), Vienna, Austria, October 23–25*, volume 1963 of *CEUR Workshop Proceedings*. Sun SITE Central Europe (CEUR), 2017. http://ceur-ws.org/Vol-1963/paper493.pdf 29

Steve Harris, Andy Seaborne, and Eric Prud'hommeaux. SPARQL 1.1 query language. *W3C Recommendation, World Wide Web Consortium*, March 21, 2013. https://www.w3.org/TR/2013/REC-sparql11-query-20130321/ 13, 17, 20, 21, 22, 75, 139, 158

Andreas Harth. Visinav: A system for visual search and navigation on web data. *Journal of Web Semantics*, 8(4):348–354, 2010. DOI: 10.1016/j.websem.2010.08.001 22

Olaf Hartig. Foundations of RDF* and SPARQL*—An alternative approach to statement-level metadata in RDF. In Juan L. Reutter and Divesh Srivastava, Eds., *Proc. of the 11th Alberto Mendelzon International Workshop on Foundations of Data Management and the Web, Montevideo, Uruguay, June 7–9*, volume 1912 of *CEUR Workshop Proceedings*. Sun SITE Central Europe (CEUR), 2017. http://ceur-ws.org/Vol-1912/paper12.pdf 41

Olaf Hartig and Carlos Buil-Aranda. Bindings-restricted triple pattern fragments. In Debruyne et al. [2016], pages 762–779. DOI: 10.1007/978-3-319-48472-3_48 139

Olaf Hartig and Bryan Thompson. Foundations of an alternative approach to reification in RDF. *CoRR*, 2014. http://arxiv.org/abs/1406.3399 12

Olaf Hartig, Christian Bizer, and Johann Christoph Freytag. Executing SPARQL queries over the Web of linked data. In Bernstein et al. [2009], pages 293–309. DOI: 10.1007/978-3-642-04930-9_19 138

Olaf Hartig, Ian Letter, and Jorge Pérez. A formal framework for comparing linked data fragments. In d'Amato et al. [2017], pages 364–382. DOI: 10.1007/978-3-319-68288-4_22 139

Qi He, Bee-Chung Chen, and Deepak Agarwal. Building the LinkedIn knowledge graph. LinkedIn Blog, October 2016. https://engineering.linkedin.com/blog/2016/10/building-the-linkedin-knowledge-graph 1, 3, 105, 149, 150

Marti A. Hearst. Automatic acquisition of hyponyms from large text corpora. In *14th International Conference on Computational Linguistics, COLING, Nantes, France, August 23–28*, pages 539–545, 1992. https://www.aclweb.org/anthology/volumes/C92-1/ DOI: 10.3115/992133.992154 108, 116

Tom Heath and Christian Bizer. *Linked Data: Evolving the Web into a Global Data Space (1st ed.)*, volume 1 of *Synthesis Lectures on the Semantic Web: Theory and Technology*. Morgan & Claypool, 2011. 37, 39, 137, 145

Tom Heath and Enrico Motta. Revyu: Linking reviews and ratings into the Web of data. *Journal of Web Semantics*, 6(4):266–273, 2008. DOI: 10.1016/j.websem.2008.09.003 148, 149

Stefan Heindorf, Martin Potthast, Benno Stein, and Gregor Engels. Vandalism detection in Wikidata. In Snehasis Mukhopadhyay, ChengXiang Zhai, Elisa Bertino, Fabio Crestani, Javed Mostafa, Jie Tang, Luo Si, Xiaofang Zhou, Yi Chang, Yunyao Li, and Parikshit Sondhi, Eds., *Proc. of the 25th ACM International Conference on Information and Knowledge Management, CIKM, Indianapolis, IN, October 24–28*, pages 327–336. ACM Press, 2016. DOI: 10.1145/2983323.2983740 105

Benjamin Heitmann, Felix Hermsen, and Stefan Decker. k-RDF-neighbourhood anonymity: Combining structural and attribute-based anonymisation for linked data. In Christopher Brewster, Michelle Cheatham, Mathieu d'Aquin, Stefan Decker, and Sabrina Kirrane, Eds., *Proc. of the 5th Workshop on Society, Privacy and the Semantic Web—Policy and Technology (PrivOn) Co-Located with 16th International Semantic Web Conference (ISWC), Vienna, Austria, October 22*, volume 1951 of *CEUR Workshop Proceedings*. Sun SITE Central Europe (CEUR), 2017. http://ceur-ws.org/Vol-1951/PrivOn2017_paper_3.pdf 143

Sebastian Hellmann, Jens Lehmann, Sören Auer, and Martin Brümmer. Integrating NLP using linked data. In Alani et al. [2013b], pages 98–113. DOI: 10.1007/978-3-642-41338-4_7 106

Remko Helms and Kees Buijsrogge. Knowledge network analysis: A technique to analyze knowledge management bottlenecks in organizations. In *16th International Workshop on Database and Expert Systems Applications (DEXA), August 22–26, Copenhagen, Denmark*, pages 410–414. IEEE Computer Society, 2005. https://ieeexplore.ieee.org/xpl/conhome/10080/proceeding DOI: 10.1109/dexa.2005.127 160

James A. Hendler, Jeanne Holm, Chris Musialek, and George Thomas. U.S. government linked open data: Semantic.data.gov. *IEEE Intelligent Systems*, 27(3):25–31, 2012. DOI: 10.1109/mis.2012.27 3, 133, 148, 149

Cory Henson, Stefan Schmid, Anh Tuan Tran, and Antonios Karatzoglou. Using a knowledge graph of scenes to enable search of autonomous driving data. In Suárez-Figueroa et al. [2019], pages 313–314. http://ceur-ws.org/Vol-2456 3, 149, 151

Daniel Hernández, Aidan Hogan, and Markus Krötzsch. Reifying RDF: What works well with Wikidata? In Thorsten Liebig and Achille Fokoue, Eds., *Proc. of the 11th International Workshop on Scalable Semantic Web Knowledge Base Systems co-located with 14th International Semantic Web Conference (ISWC), Bethlehem, PA, October 11*, volume 1457 of *CEUR Workshop Proceedings*, pages 32–47. Sun SITE Central Europe (CEUR), 2015. http://ceur-ws.org/Vol-1457/SSWS2015_paper3.pdf 9, 41

Frank L. Hitchcock. The expression of a tensor or a polyadic as a sum of products. *Journal of Mathematics and Physics*, 6(1–4):164–189, 1927. DOI: 10.1002/sapm192761164 80

Pascal Hitzler and Adila Krisnadhi. A tutorial on modular ontology modeling with ontology design patterns: The cooking recipes ontology. *CoRR*, 2018. http://arxiv.org/abs/1808.08433 115

Pascal Hitzler, Markus Krötzsch, and Sebastian Rudolph. *Foundations of Semantic Web Technologies*. Chapman and Hall/CRC Press, 2010. DOI: 10.1201/9781420090512 57

Pascal Hitzler, Markus Krötzsch, Bijan Parsia, Peter F. Patel-Schneider, and Sebastian Rudolph. OWL 2 web ontology language primer (2nd ed.). *W3C Recommendation, World Wide Web Consortium*, December 11, 2012. https://www.w3.org/TR/2012/REC-owl2-primer-20121211/ 1, 26, 49, 51, 55, 57, 64, 158

Pascal Hitzler, Miriam Fernández, Krzysztof Janowicz, Amrapali Zaveri, Alasdair J. G. Gray, Vanessa López, Armin Haller, and Karl Hammar, Eds. *The Semantic Web—16th International Conference, ESWC, Portorož, Slovenia, June 2–6, Proceedings*, volume 11503 of *Lecture Notes in Computer Science*. Springer, 2019. 174, 204, 221

Vinh Thinh Ho, Daria Stepanova, Mohamed H. Gad-Elrab, Evgeny Kharlamov, and Gerhard Weikum. Rule learning from knowledge graphs guided by embedding models. In Vrandečić et al. [2018], pages 72–90. DOI: 10.1007/978-3-030-00671-6_5 99, 104

Cornelis Hoede. On the ontology of knowledge graphs. In Gerard Ellis, Robert Levinson, William Rich, and John F. Sowa, Eds., *Conceptual Structures: Applications, Implementation and Theory, 3rd International Conference on Conceptual Structures, ICCS, Santa Cruz, CA, August 14–18, Proceedings*, volume 954 of *Lecture Notes in Computer Science*, pages 308–322. Springer, 1995. DOI: 10.1007/3-540-60161-9_46 159, 160, 161

Johannes Hoffart, Fabian M. Suchanek, Klaus Berberich, Edwin Lewis-Kelham, Gerard de Melo, and Gerhard Weikum. YAGO2: Exploring and querying world knowledge in time, space, context, and many languages. In Sadagopan Srinivasan, Krithi Ramamritham, Arun Kumar, M. P. Ravindra, Elisa Bertino, and Ravi Kumar, Eds., *Proc. of the 20th International Conference on World Wide Web, WWW, Hyderabad, India, March 28–April 1, (Companion Volume)*, pages 229–232. ACM Press, 2011. DOI: 10.1145/1963192.1963296 3, 114, 146

Raphael Hoffmann, Congle Zhang, Xiao Ling, Luke S. Zettlemoyer, and Daniel S. Weld. Knowledge-based weak supervision for information extraction of overlapping relations. In Dekang Lin, Yuji Matsumoto, and Rada Mihalcea, Eds., *The 49th Annual Meeting of the Association for Computational Linguistics: Human Language Technologies, Proceedings of the Conference, June 19–24, Portland, OR*, pages 541–550. The Association for Computational Linguistics, 2011. 108

Aidan Hogan. Canonical forms for isomorphic and equivalent RDF graphs: Algorithms for leaning and labelling blank nodes. *ACM Transactions on the Web*, 11(4):22:1–22:62, 2017. DOI: 10.1145/3068333 39

Aidan Hogan. Knowledge graphs: Research directions. In Marco Manna and Andreas Pieris, Eds., *Reasoning Web. Declarative Artificial Intelligence—16th International Summer School, Oslo, Norway, June 24–26, Tutorial Lectures*, volume 12258 of *Lecture Notes in Computer Science*, pages 223–253. Springer, 2020a. DOI: 10.1007/978-3-030-60067-9_8 155

Aidan Hogan. *The Web of Data*. Springer, 2020b. DOI: 10.1007/978-3-030-51580-5 135

Aidan Hogan and Tova Milo, Eds. *Proc. of the 13th Alberto Mendelzon International Workshop on Foundations of Data Management, Asunción, Paraguay, June 3–7*, volume 2369 of *CEUR Workshop Proceedings*. Sun SITE Central Europe (CEUR), 2019. 167, 219

Aidan Hogan, Andreas Harth, Alexandre Passant, Stefan Decker, and Axel Polleres. Weaving the pedantic web. In Christian Bizer, Tom Heath, Tim Berners-Lee, and Michael Hausenblas, Eds., *Proc. of the WWW Workshop on Linked Data on the Web, LDOW, Raleigh, April 27*, volume 628 of *CEUR Workshop Proceedings*. Sun SITE Central Europe (CEUR), 2010. http://ceur-ws.org/Vol-628/ldow2010_paper04.pdf 120

Aidan Hogan, Jürgen Umbrich, Andreas Harth, Richard Cyganiak, Axel Polleres, and Stefan Decker. An empirical survey of linked data conformance. *Journal of Web Semantics*, 14:14–44, 2012a. DOI: 10.1016/j.websem.2012.02.001 124, 138

Aidan Hogan, Antoine Zimmermann, Jürgen Umbrich, Axel Polleres, and Stefan Decker. Scalable and distributed methods for entity matching, consolidation and disambiguation over linked data corpora. *Journal of Web Semantics*, 10:76–110, 2012b. DOI: 10.1016/j.websem.2011.11.002 129

Aidan Hogan, Marcelo Arenas, Alejandro Mallea, and Axel Polleres. Everything you always wanted to know about blank nodes. *Journal of Web Semantics*, 27–28:42–69, 2014. DOI: 10.1016/j.websem.2014.06.004 39

Aidan Hogan, Juan L. Reutter, and Adrián Soto. In-database graph analytics with recursive SPARQL. In Jeff Z. Pan, Valentina A. M. Tamma, Claudia d'Amato, Krzysztof Janowicz, Bo Fu, Axel Polleres, Oshani Seneviratne, and Lalana Kagal, Eds., *The Semantic Web—ISWC—19th International Semantic Web Conference, Athens, Greece, November 2–6, Proceedings, Part I*, volume 12506 of *Lecture Notes in Computer Science*, pages 511–528. Springer, 2020. DOI: 10.1007/978-3-030-62419-4_29 76

Aidan Hogan, Eva Blomqvist, Michael Cochez, Claudia d'Amato, Gerard de Melo, Claudio Gutiérrez, Sabrina Kirrane, José Emilio Labra Gayo, Roberto Navigli, Sebastian Neumaier, Axel-Cyrille Ngonga Ngomo, Axel Polleres, Sabbir M. Rashid, Anisa Rula, Lukas Schmelzeisen, Juan F. Sequeda, Steffen Staab, and Antoine Zimmermann. Knowledge Graphs, *ACM Computing Surveys*, 54(4):1–37, 2021. DOI: 10.1145/3447772 xvi

Martin Homola and Luciano Serafini. Contextualized knowledge repositories for the semantic web. *Journal of Web Semantics*, 12:64–87, 2012. DOI: 10.1016/j.websem.2011.12.003 44, 45, 155

Ian Horrocks and Peter F. Patel-Schneider. Reducing OWL entailment to description logic satisfiability. *Journal of Web Semantics*, 1(4):345–357, 2004. DOI: 10.1016/j.websem.2004.06.003 61

Ian Horrocks, Peter F. Patel-Schneider, Harold Boley, Said Tabet, Benjamin Grosof, and Mike Dean. SWRL: A semantic web rule language combining OWL and RuleML. *W3C Member Submission*, May 21, 2004. https://www.w3.org/Submission/2004/SUBM-SWRL-20040521/ 1, 59, 60

Sen Hu, Lei Zou, Jeffrey Xu Yu, Haixun Wang, and Dongyan Zhao. Answering natural language questions by subgraph matching over knowledge graphs. *IEEE Transactions on Knowledge and Data Engineering*, 30(5):824–837, 2018. DOI: 10.1109/TKDE.2017.2766634 23

Xiao Huang, Jingyuan Zhang, Dingcheng Li, and Ping Li. Knowledge graph embedding based question answering. In J. Shane Culpepper, Alistair Moffat, Paul N. Bennett, and Kristina Lerman, Eds., *Proc. of the 12th ACM International Conference on Web Search and Data Mining, WSDM, Melbourne, VIC, Australia, February 11–15*, pages 105–113. ACM Press, 2019. DOI: 10.1145/3289600 76

Andy Hunt and Dave Thomas. The trip-packing dilemma. *IEEE Software*, 20(3):106–107, 2003. DOI: 10.1109/ms.2003.1196331 105

Rana Hussein, Dingqi Yang, and Philippe Cudré-Mauroux. Are meta-paths necessary?: Revisiting heterogeneous graph embeddings. In Cuzzocrea et al. [2018], pages 437–446. DOI: 10.1145/3269206.3271777 8

Dylan Hutchison, Bill Howe, and Dan Suciu. LaraDB: A minimalist kernel for linear and relational algebra computation. In Foto N. Afrati and Jacek Sroka, Eds., *Proc. of the 4th ACM SIGMOD Workshop on Algorithms and Systems for MapReduce and Beyond, BeyondMR@SIGMOD, Chicago, IL, May 19*, page 2:1–2:10. ACM Press, 2017. DOI: 10.1145/3070607.3070608 76

Eero Hyvönen, Eetu Mäkelä, Tomi Kauppinen, Olli Alm, Jussi Kurki, Tuukka Ruotsalo, Katri Seppälä, Joeli Takala, Kimmo Puputti, Heini Kuittinen, Kim Viljanen, Jouni Tuominen, Tuomas Palonen, Matias Frosterus, Reetta Sinkkilä, Panu Paakkarinen, Joonas Laitio, and Katariina Nyberg. CultureSampo: A national publication system of cultural heritage on the semantic web 2.0. In Lora Aroyo, Paolo Traverso, Fabio Ciravegna, Philipp Cimiano, Tom Heath, Eero Hyvönen, Riichiro Mizoguchi, Eyal Oren, Marta Sabou, and Elena Paslaru Bontas Simperl, Eds., *The Semantic Web: Research and Applications, 6th European Semantic Web Conference, ESWC, Heraklion, Crete, Greece, May 31–June 4, Proceedings*, 5554:851–856. Springer, 2009. DOI: 10.1007/978-3-642-02121-3_69 149

Andreea Iana, Steffen Jung, Philipp Naeser, Aliaksandr Birukou, Sven Hertling, and Heiko Paulheim. Building a conference recommender system based on SciGraph and WikiCFP.

In Maribel Acosta, Philippe Cudré-Mauroux, Maria Maleshkova, Tassilo Pellegrini, Harald Sack, and York Sure-Vetter, Eds., *Semantic Systems. The Power of AI and Knowledge Graphs—15th International Conference, SEMANTiCS, Karlsruhe, Germany, September 9–12, Proceedings*, volume 11702 of *Lecture Notes in Computer Science*, pages 117–123. Springer, 2019. DOI: 10.1007/978-3-030-33220-4_9 148

Renato Iannella and Serena Villata. ODRL information model 2.2. *W3C Recommendation, World Wide Web Consortium*, February 15, 2018. https://www.w3.org/TR/odrl-model/ 140

ICDE 2019. *35th IEEE International Conference on Data Engineering, ICDE, Macao, China, April 8–11*. IEEE Computer Society, 2019. 169, 180

SNOMED CT Editorial Guide. *International Health Terminology Standards Development Organisation*, July 31, 2019. https://confluence.ihtsdotools.org/display/DOCEG?preview=/71172150/94404969/SNOMED%20CT%20Editorial%20Guide-20190731.pdf 115

Alexandru Iosup, Tim Hegeman, Wing Lung Ngai, Stijn Heldens, Arnau Prat-Pérez, Thomas Manhardt, Hassan Chafi, Mihai Capota, Narayanan Sundaram, Michael J. Anderson, Ilie Gabriel Tanase, Yinglong Xia, Lifeng Nai, and Peter A. Boncz. LDBC graphalytics: A benchmark for large-scale graph on parallel and distributed platforms. *Proc. of the VLDB Endowment*, 9(13):1317–1328, 2016. 69

Robert Isele, Anja Jentzsch, and Christian Bizer. Efficient multidimensional blocking for link discovery without losing recall. In Amélie Marian and Vasilis Vassalos, Eds., *Proc. of the 14th International Workshop on the Web and Databases, WebDB, Athens, Greece, June 12*, 2011. 129

P. James. Knowledge graphs. *Linguistic Instruments in Knowledge Engineering*, 1992. 159, 160, 161

Daniel Janke and Steffen Staab. Storing and querying semantic data in the cloud. In Claudia d'Amato and Martin Theobald, Eds., *Reasoning Web. Learning, Uncertainty, Streaming, and Scalability—14th International Summer School, Esch-sur-Alzette, Luxembourg, September 22–26, Tutorial Lectures*, volume 11078 of *Lecture Notes in Computer Science*, pages 173–222. Springer, 2018. DOI: 10.1007/978-3-030-00338-8 13

Daniel Janke, Steffen Staab, and Matthias Thimm. Impact analysis of data placement strategies on query efforts in distributed RDF stores. *Journal of Web Semantics*, 50:21–48, 2018. DOI: 10.1016/j.websem.2018.02.002 75

Krzysztof Janowicz, Pascal Hitzler, Benjamin Adams, Dave Kolas, and Charles Vardeman. Five stars of linked data vocabulary use. *Semantic Web Journal*, 5(3):173–176, 2014. DOI: 10.3233/sw-140135 137

Krzysztof Janowicz, Bo Yan, Blake Regalia, Rui Zhu, and Gengchen Mai. Debiasing knowledge graphs: Why female presidents are not like female popes. In van Erp et al. [2018]. http://ceur-ws.org/Vol-2180/ISWC_2018_Outrageous_Ideas_paper_17.pdf 105, 121, 122

Nandish Jayaram, Sidharth Goyal, and Chengkai Li. VIIQ: Auto-suggestion enabled visual interface for interactive graph query formulation. *Proc. of the VLDB Endowment*, 8(12):1940–1943, 2015a. DOI: 10.14778/2824032.2824106 22

Nandish Jayaram, Arijit Khan, Chengkai Li, Xifeng Yan, and Ramez Elmasri. Querying knowledge graphs by example entity tuples. *IEEE Transactions on Knowledge and Data Engineering*, 27(10):2797–2811, 2015b. DOI: 10.1109/TKDE.2015.2426696 23

Guoliang Ji, Shizhu He, Liheng Xu, Kang Liu, and Jun Zhao. Knowledge graph embedding via dynamic mapping matrix. In *Proc. of the 53rd Annual Meeting of the Association for Computational Linguistics and the 7th International Joint Conference on NaturalLanguage Processing of the Asian Federation of Natural Language Processing, ACL, July 26–31, Beijing, China, Volume 1: Long Papers*, pages 687–696. The Association for Computational Linguistics, 2015. https://www.aclweb.org/anthology/volumes/P15-1/ DOI: 10.3115/v1/p15-1067 78

Yun-fei Jiang and Ning Ma. A plan recognition algorithm based on plan knowledge graph. *Journal of Software*, 13, 2002. 159, 161

Dan Jurafsky and James H. Martin. *Speech and Language Processing*, 2019. https://web.stanford.edu/jurafsky/slp3/ Draft chapters in progress. 106

David Jurgens and Roberto Navigli. It's all fun and games until someone annotates: Video games with a purpose for linguistic annotation. *Transactions of the Association for Computational Linguistics*, 2:449–464, 2014. DOI: 10.1162/tacl_a_00195 105

Tobias Käfer, Ahmed Abdelrahman, Jürgen Umbrich, Patrick O'Byrne, and Aidan Hogan. Observing linked data dynamics. In Cimiano et al. [2013], pages 213–227. DOI: 10.1007/978-3-642-38288-8_15 120, 121

Lucie-Aimée Kaffee, Alessandro Piscopo, Pavlos Vougiouklis, Elena Simperl, Leslie Carr, and Lydia Pintscher. A glimpse into babel: An analysis of multilinguality in Wikidata. In Lorraine Morgan, Ed., *Proc. of the 13th International Symposium on Open Collaboration, OpenSym, Galway, Ireland, August 23–25*, page 14:1–14:5. ACM Press, 2017. DOI: 10.1145/3125433.3125465 122, 124, 147

Hans Kamp. A theory of truth and semantic representation. In Paul H. Portner and Barbara H. Partee, Eds., *Formal Semantics—the Essential Readings*, pages 189–222. Blackwell, 1981. DOI: 10.1002/9780470758335.ch8 108

Elias Kärle, Umutcan Simsek, Oleksandra Panasiuk, and Dieter Fensel. Building an ecosystem for the Tyrolean tourism knowledge graph. *CoRR*, 2018. http://arxiv.org/abs/1805.05744 DOI: 10.1007/978-3-030-03056-8_25 3, 149

Gjergji Kasneci, Fabian M. Suchanek, Georgiana Ifrim, Maya Ramanath, and Gerhard Weikum. NAGA: Searching and ranking knowledge. In Alonso et al. [2008], pages 953–962. DOI: 10.1109/icde.2008.4497504 160, 161

Andreas Kasten, Ansgar Scherp, Frederik Armknecht, and Matthias Krause. Towards search on encrypted graph data. In Stefan Decker, Jim Hendler, and Sabrina Kirrane, Eds., *Proc. of the Workshop on Society, Privacy and the Semantic Web—Policy and Technology (PrivOn) Co-Located with the 12th International Semantic Web Conference (ISWC), Sydney, Australia, October 22*, volume 1121 of *CEUR Workshop Proceedings*, pages 46–57. Sun SITE Central Europe (CEUR), 2013. http://ceur-ws.org/Vol-1121/privon2013_paper5.pdf 142

Seyed Mehran Kazemi and David Poole. Simple embedding for link prediction in knowledge graphs. In Bengio et al. [2018], pages 4289–4300. http://papers.nips.cc/book/advances-in-neural-information-processing-systems-31-2018 81, 84

Seyed Mehran Kazemi, Rishab Goel, Kshitij Jain, Ivan Kobyzev, Akshay Sethi, Peter Forsyth, and Pascal Poupart. Relational representation learning for dynamic (knowledge) graphs: A survey. *CoRR*, 2019. http://arxiv.org/abs/1905.11485 155

C. Maria Keet. *An Introduction to Ontology Engineering*. College Publications, 2018. 105, 115

C. Maria Keet and Agnieszka Ławrynowicz. Test-driven development of ontologies. In Harald Sack, Eva Blomqvist, Mathieu d'Aquin, Chiara Ghidini, Simone Paolo Ponzetto, and Christoph Lange, Eds., *The Semantic Web. Latest Advances and New Domains—13th International Conference, ESWC, Heraklion, Crete, Greece, May 29–June 2, Proceedings*, volume 9678 of *Lecture Notes in Computer Science*, pages 642–657. Springer, 2016. DOI: 10.1007/978-3-319-34129-3_39 116

Mayank Kejriwal, Craig A. Knoblock, and Pedro Szekely, Eds. *Knowledge Graphs: Fundamentals, Techniques, and Applications*. The MIT Press, 2021. 1

Elisa F. Kendall and Deborah L. McGuinness. *Ontology Engineering*, volume 9 of *Synthesis Lectures on the Semantic Web: Theory and Technology*. Morgan & Claypool, 2019. 115

Michael Kifer and Harold Boley. RIF overview (2nd ed.). *W3C Working Group Note, World Wide Web Consortium*, February 5, 2013. https://www.w3.org/TR/2013/NOTE-rif-overview-20130205/ 1, 59, 60

Thomas N. Kipf and Max Welling. Semi-supervised classification with graph convolutional networks. In *5th International Conference on Learning Representations, ICLR, Toulon, France,*

April 24–26, Conference Track Proceedings. OpenReview.net, 2017. https://openreview.net/forum?id=SJU4ayYgl 95

Sabrina Kirrane, Ahmed Abdelrahman, Alessandra Mileo, and Stefan Decker. Secure manipulation of linked data. In Alani et al. [2013a], pages 248–263. DOI: 10.1007/978-3-642-41335-3_16 141

Sabrina Kirrane, Alessandra Mileo, and Stefan Decker. Access control and the resource description framework: A survey. *Semantic Web Journal*, 8(2):311–352, 2017. DOI: 10.3233/SW-160236 141

Jon M. Kleinberg. Hubs, authorities, and communities. *ACM Computing Surveys*, 31(4es):5, 1999. DOI: 10.1145/345966.345982 130

Peter Kluegl, Martin Atzmueller, and Frank Puppe. TextMarker: A tool for rule-based information extraction. In *UIMAGSCL Workshop*, pages 233–240, September 2009. 107

Kevin Knight, Hwee Tou Ng, and Kemal Oflazer, Eds. *ACL, 43rd Annual Meeting of the Association for Computational Linguistics, Proceedings of the Conference, June 25–30, University of Michigan.* The Association for Computational Linguistics, 2005. 183, 228

Holger Knublauch and Dimitris Kontokostas. Shapes constraint language (SHACL). *W3C Recommendation, World Wide Web Consortium*, June 20, 2017. https://www.w3.org/TR/2017/REC-shacl-20170720/ 27, 29, 30, 32

Holger Knublauch, James A. Hendler, and Kingsley Idehen. SPIN—Overview and motivation. *W3C Member Submission*, February 22, 2011. https://www.w3.org/Submission/2011/SUBM-spin-overview-20110222/ 59, 60

Hanna Köpcke and Erhard Rahm. Frameworks for entity matching: A comparison. *Data and Knowledge Engineering*, 69(2):197–210, 2010. DOI: 10.1016/j.datak.2009.10.003 128, 129

Arun Krishnan. Making search easier: How Amazon's product graph is helping customers find products more easily. Amazon Blog, August 2018. https://blog.aboutamazon.com/innovation/making-search-easier 1, 3, 149, 150

Adila Krisnadhi and Pascal Hitzler. A core pattern for events. In Karl Hammar, Pascal Hitzler, Adila Krisnadhi, Agnieszka Lawrynowicz, Andrea Giovanni Nuzzolese, and Monika Solanki, Eds., *Advances in Ontology Design and Patterns [revised and extended versions of the papers presented at the 7th ed., of the Workshop on Ontology and Semantic Web Patterns, WOP@ISWC, Kobe, Japan, October 18]*, volume 32 of *Studies on the Semantic Web*, pages 29–37. IOS Press, 2016a. 116

Adila Krisnadhi and Pascal Hitzler. Modeling with ontology design patterns: Chess games as a worked example. In Pascal Hitzler, Aldo Gangemi, Krysztof Janowicz, Adila Krisnadhi, and Valentina Presutti, Eds., *Ontology Engineering with Ontology Design Patterns: Foundations and Applications*, volume 25 of *Studies on the Semantic Web*, pages 3–21. IOS Press, 2016b. 115

Alex Krizhevsky, Ilya Sutskever, and Geoffrey E. Hinton. ImageNet classification with deep convolutional neural networks. *Communications of the ACM*, 60(6):84–90, 2017. DOI: 10.1145/3065386 95

Markus Krötzsch, Maximilian Marx, Ana Ozaki, and Veronika Thost. Attributed description logics: Reasoning on knowledge graphs. In Lang [2018], pages 5309–5313. DOI: 10.24963/i-jcai.2018/743 155

Peter Kümmel. An algorithm of limited syntax based on language universals. In Antonio Zampolli and Nicoletta Calzolari, Eds., *Computational and Mathematical Linguistics: Proceedings of the 5th International Conference on Computational Linguistics, COLING, Pisa, Italy, August 27–September 1*, pages 225–248. The Association for Computational Linguistics, 1973. https://www.aclweb.org/anthology/volumes/C73-1/ DOI: 10.3115/992567.992589 159, 160

H. T. Kung. Why systolic architectures? *IEEE Computer*, 15(1):37–46, 1982. DOI: 10.1109/mc.1982.1653825 70

Jose Emilio Labra Gayo, Eric Prud'hommeaux, Iovka Boneva, and Dimitris Kontokostas. *Validating RDF Data*, volume 7 of *Synthesis Lectures on the Semantic Web: Theory and Technology*. Morgan & Claypool, September 2017. DOI: 10.2200/s00786ed1v01y201707wbe016 27, 29, 105

Jose Emilio Labra Gayo, Herminio García-González, Daniel Fernández-Alvarez, and Eric Prud'hommeaux. Challenges in RDF validation. In Giner Alor-Hernández, José Luis Sánchez-Cervantes, Alejandro Rodríguez-González, and Rafael Valencia-García, Eds., *Current Trends in Semantic Web Technologies: Theory and Practice*, Studies in Computational Intelligence, pages 121–151. Springer, 2019. DOI: 10.1007/978-3-030-06149-4_6 29, 31, 32

Guillaume Lample, Miguel Ballesteros, Sandeep Subramanian, Kazuya Kawakami, and Chris Dyer. Neural architectures for named entity recognition. In Kevin Knight, Ani Nenkova, and Owen Rambow, Eds., *NAACL HLT, The Conference of the North American Chapter of the Association for Computational Linguistics: Human Language Technologies, San Diego California, June 12–17*, pages 260–270. The Association for Computational Linguistics, 2016. DOI: 10.18653/v1/n16-1030 107

Jérôme Lang, Ed. *Proc. of the 27th International Joint Conference on Artificial Intelligence, IJCAI, July 13–19, Stockholm, Sweden*. IJCAI/AAAI, 2018. 198, 225

Ni Lao and William W. Cohen. Relational retrieval using a combination of path-constrained random walks. *Machine Learning*, 81(1):53–67, 2010. DOI: 10.1007/s10994-010-5205-8 130

Jens Lehmann, Tim Furche, Giovanni Grasso, Axel-Cyrille Ngonga Ngomo, Christian Schall-hart, Andrew Jon Sellers, Christina Unger, Lorenz Bühmann, Daniel Gerber, Konrad Höffner, David Liu, and Sören Auer. DEQA: Deep web extraction for question answering. In Philippe Cudré-Mauroux, Jeff Heflin, Evren Sirin, Tania Tudorache, Jérôme Euzenat, Manfred Hauswirth, Josiane Xavier Parreira, Jim Hendler, Guus Schreiber, Abraham Bern-stein, and Eva Blomqvist, Eds., *The Semantic Web—ISWC—11th International Semantic Web Conference, Boston, MA, November 11–15, Proceedings, Part II*, volume 7650 of *Lecture Notes in Computer Science*, pages 131–147. Springer, 2012. DOI: 10.1007/978-3-642-35173-0_9 111

Jens Lehmann, Robert Isele, Max Jakob, Anja Jentzsch, Dimitris Kontokostas, Pablo N. Mendes, Sebastian Hellmann, Mohamed Morsey, Patrick van Kleef, Sören Auer, and Chris-tian Bizer. DBpedia—A large-scale, multilingual knowledge base extracted from Wikipedia. *Semantic Web Journal*, 6(2):167–195, 2015. DOI: 10.3233/sw-140134 3, 111, 114, 133, 137, 145, 146, 158

Oliver Lehmberg, Dominique Ritze, Robert Meusel, and Christian Bizer. A large public corpus of web tables containing time and context metadata. In Bourdeau et al. [2016], pages 75–76. DOI: 10.1145/2872518.2889386 111

Yuangui Lei, Victoria Uren, and Enrico Motta. A framework for evaluating semantic metadata. In Derek Sleeman and Ken Barker, Eds., *Proc. of the 4th International Conference on Knowledge Capture*, pages 135–142. ACM Press, October 2007. DOI: 10.1145/1298406.1298431 120

Douglas B. Lenat. CYC: A large-scale investment in knowledge infrastructure. *Communications of the ACM*, 38(11):33–38, 1995. DOI: 10.1145/219717.219745 148

Mark Levene and Alexandra Poulovassilis. The hypernode model: A graph-theoretic approach to integrating data and computation. In Andreas Heuer, Ed., *Workshop on Foundations of Models and Languages for Data and Objects, Aigen, Austria, September 25–29*, volume 89-2 of *Informatik-Berichte des IfI*, pages 55–77. Technische Universität Clausthal, 1989. 12

Ninghui Li, Tiancheng Li, and Suresh Venkatasubramanian. t-closeness: Privacy beyond k-anonymity and l-diversity. In Rada Chirkova, Asuman Dogac, M. Tamer Özsu, and Timos K. Sellis, Eds., *Proc. of the 23rd International Conference on Data Engineering, ICDE, The Marmara Hotel, Istanbul, Turkey, April 15–20*, pages 106–115. IEEE Computer Society, 2007. DOI: 10.1109/icde.2007.367856 143

Girija Limaye, Sunita Sarawagi, and Soumen Chakrabarti. Annotating and searching web tables using entities, types and relationships. *Proc. of the VLDB Endowment*, 3(1):1338–1347, 2010. DOI: 10.14778/1920841.1921005 111

Yankai Lin, Zhiyuan Liu, Maosong Sun, Yang Liu, and Xuan Zhu. Learning entity and relation embeddings for knowledge graph completion. In Blai Bonet and Sven Koenig, Eds., *Proc. of the 29th AAAI Conference on Artificial Intelligence, January 25–30, Austin, TX*, pages 2181–2187. AAAI Press, 2015. 1, 78, 161

Zhiyuan Lin and Mahesh Tripunitara. Graph automorphism-based, semantics-preserving security for the resource description framework (RDF). In Gail-Joon Ahn, Alexander Pretschner, and Gabriel Ghinita, Eds., *Proc. of the 7th ACM on Conference on Data and Application Security and Privacy, CODASPY, Scottsdale, AZ, March 22–24*, pages 337–348. ACM Press, 2017. DOI: 10.1145/3029806.3029827 144

Xiao Ling and Daniel S. Weld. Fine-grained entity recognition. In Jörg Hoffmann and Bart Selman, Eds., *Proc. of the 26th AAAI Conference on Artificial Intelligence, July 22–26, Toronto, Ontario, Canada*, pages 94–100. AAAI Press, 2012. http://www.aaai.org/ocs/index.php/AAAI/AAAI12/paper/view/5152 107

Kun Liu and Evimaria Terzi. Towards identity anonymization on graphs. In Jason Tsong-Li Wang, Ed., *Proc. of the ACM SIGMOD International Conference on Management of Data, SIGMOD, Vancouver, BC, Canada, June 10–12*, pages 93–106. ACM Press, 2008. DOI: 10.1145/1376616.1376629 144

Yike Liu, Tara Safavi, Abhilash Dighe, and Danai Koutra. Graph summarization methods and applications: A survey. *ACM Computing Surveys*, 51(3):62:1–62:34, 2018. DOI: 10.1145/3186727 32

John W. Lloyd. *Foundations of Logic Programming*. Springer, 2012. DOI: 10.1007/978-3-642-83189-8 57

Colin Lockard, Xin Luna Dong, Prashant Shiralkar, and Arash Einolghozati. CERES: Distantly supervised relation extraction from the semi-structured web. *Proc. of the VLDB Endowment*, 11(10):1084–1096, 2018. DOI: 10.14778/3231751.3231758 109

Dave Longley and Manu Sporny. RDF dataset normalization, a standard RDF dataset normalization algorithm. *W3C Community Group Draft Report*, February 27, 2019. http://json-ld.github.io/normalization/spec/ 39

Yucheng Low, Joseph Gonzalez, Aapo Kyrola, Danny Bickson, Carlos Guestrin, and Joseph M. Hellerstein. Distributed GraphLab: A framework for machine learning in the cloud. *Proc. of the VLDB Endowment*, 5(8):716–727, 2012. DOI: 10.14778/2212351.2212354 70

Chun Lu, Philippe Laublet, and Milan Stankovic. Travel attractions recommendation with knowledge graphs. In Blomqvist et al. [2016a], pages 416–431. DOI: 10.1007/978-3-319-49004-5_27 3, 149

Chunliang Lu, Lidong Bing, Wai Lam, Ki Chan, and Yuan Gu. Web entity detection for semi-structured text data records with unlabeled data. *International Journal of Computational Linguistics and Applications*, 4(2):135–150, 2013. 109

Thomas Lukasiewicz, Maria Vanina Martinez, and Gerardo I. Simari. Complexity of inconsistency-tolerant query answering in datalog+/-. In Thomas Eiter, Birte Glimm, Yevgeny Kazakov, and Markus Krötzsch, Eds., *Informal Proceedings of the 26th International Workshop on Description Logics, ULM, Germany, July 23–26*, volume 1014 of *CEUR Workshop Proceedings*, pages 791–803. Sun SITE Central Europe (CEUR), 2013. http://ceur-ws.org/Vol-1014/paper_6.pdf DOI: 10.1007/978-3-642-41030-7_35 131

Gang Luo, Xiaojiang Huang, Chin-Yew Lin, and Zaiqing Nie. Joint entity recognition and disambiguation. In Lluís Màrquez, Chris Callison-Burch, Jian Su, Daniele Pighin, and Yuval Marton, Eds., *Proc. of the Conference on Empirical Methods in Natural Language Processing, EMNLP, Lisbon, Portugal, September 17–21*, pages 879–888. The Association for Computational Linguistics, 2015. https://www.aclweb.org/anthology/volumes/D15-1/ DOI: 10.18653/v1/d15-1104 109

Ricardo José Machado and Armando Freitas da Rocha. The combinatorial neural network: A connectionist model for knowledge based systems. In Bernadette Bouchon-Meunier, Ronald R. Yager, and Lotfi A. Zadeh, Eds., *Uncertainty in Knowledge Bases, 3rd International Conference on Information Processing and Management of Uncertainty in Knowledge-Based Systems, IPMU, Paris, France, July 2–6, Proceedings*, volume 521 of *Lecture Notes in Computer Science*, pages 578–587. Springer, 1990. DOI: 10.1007/bfb0028145 159, 160, 161

Jayant Madhavan, David Ko, Lucja Kot, Vignesh Ganapathy, Alex Rasmussen, and Alon Y. Halevy. Google's deep web crawl. *Proc. of the VLDB Endowment*, 1(2):1241–1252, 2008. DOI: 10.14778/1454159.1454163 111

Farzaneh Mahdisoltani, Joanna Biega, and Fabian M. Suchanek. YAGO3: A knowledge base from multilingual Wikipedias. In CIDR. http://cidrdb.org/cidr2015/Papers/CIDR15_Paper1.pdf 133, 146

Pierre Maillot and Carlos Bobed. Measuring structural similarity between RDF graphs. In Haddad et al. [2018], pages 1960-1967. DOI: 10.1145/3167132 69

Grzegorz Malewicz, Matthew H. Austern, Aart J. C. Bik, James C. Dehnert, Ilan Horn, Naty Leiser, and Grzegorz Czajkowski. Pregel: A system for large-scale graph processing. In Ahmed K. Elmagarmid and Divyakant Agrawal, Eds., *Proc. of the ACM SIGMOD International Conference on Management of Data, SIGMOD, Indianapolis, IN, June 6–10*, pages 135–146. ACM Press, 2010. DOI: 10.1145/1807167.1807184 1, 70, 71, 73

Stanislav Malyshev, Markus Krötzsch, Larry González, Julius Gonsior, and Adrian Bielefeldt. Getting the most out of Wikidata: Semantic technology usage in Wikipedia's knowledge graph. In Denny Vrandecic, Kalina Bontcheva, Mari Carmen Suárez-Figueroa, Valentina Presutti, Irene Celino, Marta Sabou, Lucie-Aimée Kaffee, and Elena Simperl, Eds., *The Semantic Web—ISWC—17th International Semantic Web Conference, Monterey, CA, October 8–12, Proceedings, Part II*, volume 11137 of *Lecture Notes in Computer Science*, pages 376–394. Springer, 2018. DOI: 10.1007/978-3-030-00668-6_23 139, 148

Ezio Marchi and Osvaldo Miguel. On the structure of the teaching-learning interactive process. *International Journal of Game Theory*, 3:83–99, 1974. DOI: 10.1007/bf01766394 158, 161

Jose L. Martínez-Rodríguez, Ivan López-Arévalo, and Ana B. Rios-Alvarado. OpenIE-based approach for knowledge graph construction from text. *Expert Systems With Applications*, 113:339–355, 2018. DOI: 10.1016/j.eswa.2018.07.017 109, 116

Jose L. Martínez-Rodríguez, Aidan Hogan, and Ivan Lopez-Arevalo. Information extraction meets the semantic web: A survey. *Semantic Web Journal*, 11(2):255–335, 2020. DOI: 10.3233/sw-180333 39, 106, 109, 120, 121

Cynthia Matuszek, John Cabral, Michael J. Witbrock, and John De Oliveira. An introduction to the syntax and content of Cyc. In *Formalizing and Compiling Background Knowledge and its Applications to Knowledge Representation and Question Answering, Papers from the AAAI Spring Symposium, Technical Report SS-06-05, Stanford, CA, March 27–29*, pages 44–49. AAAI Press, 2006. http://www.aaai.org/Library/Symposia/Spring/ss06-05.php 148

Mausam. Open information extraction systems and downstream applications. In Subbarao Kambhampati, Ed., *Proc. of the 25th International Joint Conference on Artificial Intelligence, IJCAI, New York, July 9–15*, pages 4074–4077. IJCAI/AAAI, 2016. 108

Mausam, Michael Schmitz, Stephen Soderland, Robert Bart, and Oren Etzioni. Open language learning for information extraction. In Tsujii et al. [2012], pages 523–534. 108

Diana Maynard, Kalina Bontcheva, and Isabelle Augenstein. *Natural Language Processing for the Semantic Web*. Morgan & Claypool, 2016. DOI: 10.2200/s00741ed1v01y201611wbe015 106, 109

John McCarthy. *Formalizing Commonsense*. Greenwood Publishing Group, 1990. 47

John McCarthy. Notes on formalizing context. In Ruzena Bajcsy, Ed., *Proc. of the 13th International Joint Conference on Artificial Intelligence. Chambéry, France, August 28–September 3*, pages 555–562. Morgan Kaufmann, 1993. 40

Sheila A. McIlraith and Kilian Q. Weinberger, Eds. *Proc. of the 32nd AAAI Conference on Artificial Intelligence, (AAAI), the 30th Innovative Applications of Artificial Intelligence (IAAI), and the 8th AAAI Symposium on Educational Advances in Artificial Intelligence (EAAI), New Orleans, LA, February 2–7*. AAAI Press, 2018. 179, 187

Edgar Meij. Understanding news using the Bloomberg knowledge graph. *Invited Talk at the Big Data Innovators Gathering (TheWebConf)*, 2019. Slides at https://speakerdeck.com/emeij/understanding-news-using-the-bloomberg-knowledge-graph 3, 149, 151

Pablo N. Mendes, Max Jakob, and Christian Bizer. DBpedia: A multilingual cross-domain knowledge base. In Nicoletta Calzolari, Khalid Choukri, Thierry Declerck, Mehmet Ugur Dogan, Bente Maegaard, Joseph Mariani, Jan Odijk, and Stelios Piperidis, Eds., *Proc. of the 8th International Conference on Language Resources and Evaluation, LREC, Istanbul, Turkey, May 23–25*, pages 1813–1817. European Language Resources Association (ELRA), 2012a. 146

Pablo N. Mendes, Hannes Mühleisen, and Christian Bizer. Sieve: Linked data quality assessment and fusion. In Divesh Srivastava and Ismail Ari, Eds., *Proc. of the Joint EDBT/ICDT Workshops, Berlin, Germany, March 30*, pages 116–123. Journal of the ACM, 2012b. DOI: 10.1145/2320765.2320803 123

Nandana Mihindukulasooriya, Mohammad Rifat Ahmmad Rashid, Giuseppe Rizzo, Raúl García-Castro, Óscar Corcho, and Marco Torchiano. RDF shape induction using knowledge base profiling. In Haddad et al. [2018], pages 1952–1959. DOI: 10.1145/3167132 155

Peter Mika, Tania Tudorache, Abraham Bernstein, Christopher A. Welty, Craig A. Knoblock, Denny Vrandecic, Paul T. Groth, Natasha Fridman Noy, Krzysztof Janowicz, and Carole A. Goble, Eds. *The Semantic Web—ISWC—13th International Semantic Web Conference, Riva del Garda, Italy, October 19–23. Proceedings, Part I*, volume 8796 of *Lecture Notes in Computer Science*. Springer, 2014. 215, 216

Tomas Mikolov, Kai Chen, Greg Corrado, and Jeffrey Dean. Efficient estimation of word representations in vector space. In Bengio and LeCun [2013]. http://arxiv.org/abs/1301.3781 88, 90

George A. Miller and Christiane Fellbaum. WordNet then and now. *Language Resources and Evaluation (LRE)*, 41(2):209–214, 2007. DOI: 10.1007/s10579-007-9044-6 106

Justin J. Miller. Graph database applications and concepts with Neo4j. In *Proc. of the Southern Association for Information Systems Conference, Atlanta, GA, March 23–24*, pages 141–147. AIS eLibrary, 2013. https://aisel.aisnet.org/sais2013/24 9, 11, 13, 38, 139

Marvin Minsky. A framework for representing knowledge. *MIT-AI Memo 306*, Santa Monica, 1974. 60, 157

Mike Mintz, Steven Bills, Rion Snow, and Daniel Jurafsky. Distant supervision for relation extraction without labeled data. In Keh-Yih Su, Jian Su, and Janyce Wiebe, Eds., *ACL, Proceedings of the 47th Annual Meeting of the Association for Computational Linguistics and the 4th International Joint Conference on Natural Language Processing of the AFNLP, August 2–7, Singapore*, pages 1003–1011. The Association for Computational Linguistics, 2009. DOI: 10.3115/1690219.1690287 108

Tom M. Mitchell, William W. Cohen, Estevam R. Hruschka Jr., Partha P. Talukdar, Bo Yang, Justin Betteridge, Andrew Carlson, Bhavana Dalvi Mishra, Matt Gardner, Bryan Kisiel, Jayant Krishnamurthy, Ni Lao, Kathryn Mazaitis, Thahir Mohamed, Ndapandula Nakashole, Emmanouil A. Platanios, Alan Ritter, Mehdi Samadi, Burr Settles, Richard C. Wang, Derry Wijaya, Abhinav Gupta, Xinlei Chen, Abulhair Saparov, Malcolm Greaves, and Joel Welling. Never-ending learning. *Communications of the ACM*, 61(5):103–115, 2018. DOI: 10.1145/3191513 108, 148

Federico Monti, Davide Boscaini, Jonathan Masci, Emanuele Rodolà, Jan Svoboda, and Michael M. Bronstein. Geometric deep learning on graphs and manifolds using mixture model CNNs. In *IEEE Conference on Computer Vision and Pattern Recognition, CVPR, Honolulu, HI, July 21–26*, pages 5425–5434. IEEE Computer Society, 2017. DOI: 10.1109/CVPR.2017.576 95

Elena Montiel-Ponsoda, Víctor Rodríguez-Doncel, and Jorge Gracia. Building the legal knowledge graph for smart compliance services in multilingual Europe. In Víctor Rodríguez-Doncel, Pompeu Casanovas, and Jorge González-Conejero, Eds., *Proc. of the 1st Workshop on Technologies for Regulatory Compliance Co-Located with the 30th International Conference on Legal Knowledge and Information Systems (JURIX), Luxembourg, December 13*, volume 2049 of *CEUR Workshop Proceedings*, pages 15–17. Sun SITE Central Europe (CEUR), 2017. http://ceur-ws.org/Vol-2049/02paper.pdf 149

Benjamin Moreau, Patricia Serrano-Alvarado, Matthieu Perrin, and Emmanuel Desmontils. Modelling the compatibility of licenses. In Hitzler et al. [2019], pages 255–269. DOI: 10.1007/978-3-030-21348-0_17 141

José Moreno-Vega and Aidan Hogan. GraFa: Scalable faceted browsing for RDF graphs. In Vrandečić et al. [2018], pages 301–317. DOI: 10.1007/978-3-030-00671-6_18 22

Andrea Moro and Roberto Navigli. Integrating syntactic and semantic analysis into the open information extraction paradigm. In Francesca Rossi, Ed., *IJCAI, Proceedings of the 23rd International Joint Conference on Artificial Intelligence, Beijing, China, August 3–9*, pages 2148–2154. IJCAI/AAAI, 2013. 109

Andrea Moro, Alessandro Raganato, and Roberto Navigli. Entity linking meets word sense disambiguation: A unified approach. *Transactions of the Association for Computational Linguistics*, 2:231–244, 2014. DOI: 10.1162/tacl_a_00179 107, 109

Boris Motik, Rob Shearer, and Ian Horrocks. Hypertableau reasoning for description logics. *Journal of Artificial Intelligence Research*, 36:165–228, 2009. DOI: 10.1613/jair.2811 62

Boris Motik, Bernardo Cuenca Grau, Ian Horrocks, Zhe Wu, Achille Fokoue, and Carsten Lutz. OWL 2 web ontology language profiles (2nd ed.). *W3C Recommendation, World Wide Web Consortium*, December 11, 2012. http://www.w3.org/TR/2012/REC-owl2-profiles-20121211/ 58, 59, 62

Varish Mulwad, Tim Finin, and Anupam Joshi. Semantic message passing for generating linked data from tables. In Alani et al. [2013a], pages 363–378. DOI: 10.1007/978-3-642-41335-3_23 111

Chris Mungall, Alan Ruttenberg, Ian Horrocks, and David Osumi-Sutherland. OBO flat file format 1.4 syntax and semantics. Editor's Draft, May 2012. http://owlcollab.github.io/oboformat/doc/obo-syntax.html 1, 49, 51

Emir Mu noz, Aidan Hogan, and Alessandra Mileo. Using linked data to mine RDF from Wikipedia's tables. In Ben Carterette, Fernando Diaz, Carlos Castillo, and Donald Metzler, Eds., *7th ACM International Conference on Web Search and Data Mining, WSDM, New York, February 24–28*, pages 533–542. ACM Press, 2014. DOI: 10.1145/2556195.2556266 111

Sergio Mu noz, Jorge Pérez, and Claudio Gutiérrez. Simple and efficient minimal RDFS. *Journal of Web Semantics*, 7(3):220–234, 2009. DOI: 10.1016/j.websem.2009.07.003 57

David Nadeau and Satoshi Sekine. A survey of named entity recognition and classification. *Lingvisticae Investigationes*, 30(1):3–26, 2007. DOI: 10.1075/li.30.1.03nad 107

Ndapandula Nakashole, Tomasz Tylenda, and Gerhard Weikum. Fine-grained semantic typing of emerging entities. In *Proc. of the 51st Annual Meeting of the Association for Computational Linguistics, ACL, August 4–9, Sofia, Bulgaria, Volume 1: Long Papers*, pages 1488–1497. The Association for Computational Linguistics, 2013. https://www.aclweb.org/anthology/volumes/P13-1/ 107

Arvind Narayanan and Vitaly Shmatikov. De-anonymizing social networks. In *30th IEEE Symposium on Security and Privacy (S&P), May 17–20, Oakland, CA*, pages 173–187. IEEE Computer Society, 2009. DOI: 10.1109/sp.2009.22 144

Roberto Navigli. Word sense disambiguation: A survey. *ACM Computing Surveys*, 41(2):1–69, 2009. DOI: 10.1145/1459352.1459355 106

Roberto Navigli and Simone Paolo Ponzetto. BabelNet: The automatic construction, evaluation and application of a wide-coverage multilingual semantic network. *Artificial Intelligence*, 193:217–250, 2012. DOI: 10.1016/j.artint.2012.07.001 106, 114, 148, 158, 160

Markus Nentwig, Michael Hartung, Axel-Cyrille Ngonga Ngomo, and Erhard Rahm. A survey of current link discovery frameworks. *Semantic Web Journal*, 8(3):419–436, 2017. DOI: 10.3233/sw-150210 127, 137

Sebastian Neumaier and Axel Polleres. Enabling spatio-temporal search in open data. *Journal of Web Semantics*, 55:21–36, 2019. DOI: 10.1016/j.websem.2018.12.007 114

Sebastian Neumaier, Jürgen Umbrich, Josiane Xavier Parreira, and Axel Polleres. Multi-level semantic labelling of numerical values. In Groth et al. [2016], pages 428–445. DOI: 10.1007/978-3-319-46523-4_26 111

David Newman. Knowledge graphs and AI: The future of financial data. In *Knowledge Graph Conference*, 2019. (Invited talk). 3, 151

Axel-Cyrille Ngonga Ngomo. Link discovery with guaranteed reduction ratio in affine spaces with Minkowski measures. In Cudré-Mauroux et al. [2012], pages 378–393. DOI: 10.1007/978-3-642-35176-1_24 129

Axel-Cyrille Ngonga Ngomo. ORCHID—reduction-ratio-optimal computation of geo-spatial distances for link discovery. In Alani et al. [2013a], pages 395–410. DOI: 10.1007/978-3-642-41335-3_25 129

Axel-Cyrille Ngonga Ngomo and Sören Auer. LIMES—A time-efficient approach for large-scale link discovery on the Web of data. In Walsh [2011], pages 2312–2317. 114, 137

Axel-Cyrille Ngonga Ngomo, Lorenz Bühmann, Christina Unger, Jens Lehmann, and Daniel Gerber. Sorry, I don't speak SPARQL: Translating SPARQL queries into natural language. In Schwabe et al. [2013], pages 977–988. DOI: 10.1145/2488388.2488473 129

Dat Ba Nguyen, Martin Theobald, and Gerhard Weikum. J-NERD: Joint named entity recognition and disambiguation with rich linguistic features. *Transactions of the Association for Computational Linguistics*, 4:215–229, 2016. DOI: 10.1162/tacl_a_00094 109

Vinh Nguyen, Olivier Bodenreider, and Amit Sheth. Don't like RDF reification?: Making statements about statements using singleton property. In Chung et al. [2014], pages 759–770. DOI: 10.1145/2566486.2567973 41

Maximilian Nickel and Volker Tresp. Tensor factorization for multi-relational learning. In Hendrik Blockeel, Kristian Kersting, Siegfried Nijssen, and Filip Zelezný, Eds., *Machine Learning and Knowledge Discovery in Databases—European Conference, ECML PKDD, Prague, Czech*

Republic, September 23–27, Proceedings, Part III, volume 8190 of *Lecture Notes in Computer Science*, pages 617–621. Springer, 2013. DOI: 10.1007/978-3-642-40994-3_40 6, 81

Maximilian Nickel, Kevin Murphy, Volker Tresp, and Evgeniy Gabrilovich. A review of relational machine learning for knowledge graphs. *Proc. of the IEEE*, 104(1):11–33, 2016a. DOI: 10.1109/jproc.2015.2483592 162

Maximilian Nickel, Lorenzo Rosasco, and Tomaso A. Poggio. Holographic embeddings of knowledge graphs. In Schuurmans and Wellman [2016], pages 1955–1961. 81, 87

Natalya F. Noy and Deborah L. McGuinness. Ontology development 101: A guide to creating your first ontology. *Technical Report*, Stanford Knowledge Systems Laboratory, 2001. https://protege.stanford.edu/publications/ontology_development/ontology101.pdf 115

Natasha F. Noy, Yuqing Gao, Anshu Jain, Anant Narayanan, Alan Patterson, and Jamie Taylor. Industry-scale knowledge graphs: Lessons and challenges. *ACM Queue*, 17(2):20, 2019. DOI: 10.1145/3329781.3332266 1, 3, 133, 149, 150, 151, 161, 163, 164

Sri Nurdiati and Cornelis Hoede. 25 years of development of knowledge graph theory: The results and the challenge. *Memorandum 1876*, University of Twente, September 2012. https://core.ac.uk/download/pdf/11468596.pdf 159

Ekpe Okorafor and Atish Ray. The path from data to knowledge. Accenture Applied Intelligence Blog, June 2019. https://www.accenture.com/us-en/insights/digital/data-to-knowledge 3, 151

Lawrence Page, Sergey Brin, Rajeev Motwani, and Terry Winograd. The PageRank citation ranking: Bringing order to the Web. *Technical Report 1999-66*, Stanford InfoLab, November 1999. http://ilpubs.stanford.edu:8090/422/ 70

Jeff Z. Pan, Guido Vetere, José Manuél Gómez-Pérez, and Honghan Wu, Eds. *Exploiting linked data and knowledge graphs in large organisations*. Springer, 2017. DOI: 10.1007/978-3-319-45654-6 1

Oleksandra Panasiuk, Simon Steyskal, Giray Havur, Anna Fensel, and Sabrina Kirrane. Modeling and reasoning over data licenses. In Aldo Gangemi, Anna Lisa Gentile, Andrea Giovanni Nuzzolese, Sebastian Rudolph, Maria Maleshkova, Heiko Paulheim, Jeff Z. Pan, and Mehwish Alam, Eds., *The Semantic Web: ESWC Satellite Events—ESWC Satellite Events, Heraklion, Crete, Greece, June 3–7, Revised Selected Papers*, volume 11155 of *Lecture Notes in Computer Science*, pages 218–222. Springer, 2018. DOI: 10.1007/978-3-319-98192-5_41 141

Harshvardhan J. Pandit, Axel Polleres, Bert Bos, Rob Brennan, Bud Bruegger, Fajar J. Ekaputra, Javier D. Fernández, Ramisa Gachpaz Hamed, Elmar Kiesling, Mark Lizar, Eva Schlehahn, Simon Steyskal, and Rigo Wenning. Data privacy vocabulary v0.1. *Draft Community Group Report, World Wide Web Consortium*, November 28, 2019. https://www.w3.org/ns/dpv 142

Vicky Papavasileiou, Giorgos Flouris, Irini Fundulaki, Dimitris Kotzinos, and Vassilis Christophides. High-level change detection in RDF(S) KBs. *ACM Transactions on Database Systems*, 38(1):1:1–1:42, 2013. DOI: 10.1145/2445583.2445584 138

Namyong Park, Andrey Kan, Xin Luna Dong, Tong Zhao, and Christos Faloutsos. Estimating node importance in knowledge graphs using graph neural networks. In Ankur Teredesai, Vipin Kumar, Ying Li, Rómer Rosales, Evimaria Terzi, and George Karypis, Eds., *Proc. of the 25th ACM SIGKDD International Conference on Knowledge Discovery and Data Mining, KDD, Anchorage, AK, August 4–8*, pages 596–606. ACM Press, 2019. DOI: 10.1145/3292500.3330855 91

Namyong Park, Andrey Kan, Xin Luna Dong, Tong Zhao, and Christos Faloutsos. Multi-Import: Inferring node importance in a knowledge graph from multiple input signals. In Rajesh Gupta, Yan Liu, Jiliang Tang, and B. Aditya Prakash, Eds., *KDD: The 26th ACM SIGKDD Conference on Knowledge Discovery and Data Mining, Virtual Event, CA, August 23–27*, pages 503–512. ACM Press, 2020. DOI: 10.1145/3394486.3403093 91

Jeff Pasternack and Dan Roth. Knowing what to believe (when you already know something). In Chu-Ren Huang and Dan Jurafsky, Eds., *COLING, 23rd International Conference on Computational Linguistics, Proceedings of the Conference, August 23–27, Beijing, China*, pages 877–885. Tsinghua University Press, 2010. https://www.aclweb.org/anthology/volumes/C10-1/ 130

Jeff Pasternack and Dan Roth. Making better informed trust decisions with generalized fact-finding. In Walsh [2011], pages 2324–2329. 130

Heiko Paulheim. Knowledge graph refinement: A survey of approaches and evaluation methods. *Semantic Web Journal*, 8(3):489–508, 2017. DOI: 10.3233/SW-160218 1, 76, 127, 128, 131, 162

Heiko Paulheim. How much is a triple? Estimating the cost of knowledge graph creation. In van Erp et al. [2018]. http://ceur-ws.org/Vol-2180/ISWC_2018_Outrageous_Ideas_paper_10.pdf 105

Heiko Paulheim and Christian Bizer. Type inference on noisy RDF data. In Alani et al. [2013b], pages 510–525. DOI: 10.1007/978-3-642-41335-3_32 128

Chaveevan Pechsiri and Rapepun Piriyakul. Explanation knowledge graph construction through causality extraction from texts. *Journal of Computer Science and Technology*, 25(5):1055–1070, 2010. DOI: 10.1007/s11390-010-9387-0 160

Charles S. Peirce. How to make our ideas clear. *Popular Science Monthly*, 12:286–302, 1878. 157

Tassilo Pellegrini, Giray Havur, Simon Steyskal, Oleksandra Panasiuk, Anna Fensel, Victor Mireles, Thomas Thurner, Axel Polleres, Sabrina Kirrane, and Andrea Schönhofer. DAL-ICC: A license management framework for digital assets. In *Proc. of the Internationales Rechtsinformatik Symposion (IRIS)*, 2019. 141

Thomas Pellissier Tanon, Denny Vrandečić, Sebastian Schaffert, Thomas Steiner, and Lydia Pintscher. From freebase to Wikidata: The great migration. In Jacqueline Bourdeau, Jim Hendler, Roger Nkambou, Ian Horrocks, and Ben Y. Zhao, Eds., *Proc. of the 25th International Conference on World Wide Web, WWW, Montreal, Canada, April 11–15*, pages 1419–1428. ACM Press, 2016. DOI: 10.1145/2872427.2874809 105, 114, 147, 148

Thomas Pellissier Tanon, Daria Stepanova, Simon Razniewski, Paramita Mirza, and Gerhard Weikum. Completeness-aware rule learning from knowledge graphs. In d'Amato et al. [2017], pages 507–525. DOI: 10.1007/978-3-319-68288-4_30 100, 104

Jeffrey Pennington, Richard Socher, and Christopher Manning. Glove: Global vectors for word representation. In Alessandro Moschitti, Bo Pang, and Walter Daelemans, Eds., *Proc. of the Conference on Empirical Methods in Natural Language Processing, EMNLP, October 25–29, Doha, Qatar, a meeting of SIGDAT, a Special Interest Group of the ACL*, pages 1532–1543. The Association for Computational Linguistics, 2014. https://www.aclweb.org/anthology/volumes/D14-1/ DOI: 10.3115/v1/d14-1162 88, 90

Silvio Peroni. A simplified agile methodology for ontology development. In Mauro Dragoni, María Poveda-Villalón, and Ernesto Jiménez-Ruiz, Eds., *OWL: Experiences and Directions—Reasoner Evaluation—13th International Workshop, OWLED, and 5th International Workshop, ORE, Bologna, Italy, November 20, Revised Selected Papers*, volume 10161 of *Lecture Notes in Computer Science*, pages 55–69. Springer, 2016. DOI: 10.1007/978-3-319-54627-8_5 115

Silvio Peroni, David M. Shotton, and Fabio Vitali. One year of the OpenCitations corpus—releasing RDF-based scholarly citation data into the public domain. In Claudia d'Amato, Miriam Fernández, Valentina A. M. Tamma, Freddy Lécué, Philippe Cudré-Mauroux, Juan F. Sequeda, Christoph Lange, and Jeff Heflin, Eds., *The Semantic Web—ISWC—16th International Semantic Web Conference, Vienna, Austria, October 21–25, Proceedings, Part II*, volume 10588 of *Lecture Notes in Computer Science*, pages 184–192. Springer, 2017. 148

David Peterson, Shudi Gao, Ashok Malhotra, C. M. Sperberg-McQueen, Henry S. Thompson, and Paul V. Biron. W3C XML schema definition language (XSD) 1.1 Part 2: Datatypes. *W3C Recommendation, World Wide Web Consortium*, April 5, 2012. https://www.w3.org/TR/2012/REC-xmlschema11-2-20120405/ 38

Giulio Petrucci, Chiara Ghidini, and Marco Rospocher. Ontology learning in the deep. In Blomqvist et al. [2016a], pages 480–495. DOI: 10.1007/978-3-319-49004-5_31 117

Minh-Duc Pham, Linnea Passing, Orri Erling, and Peter A. Boncz. Deriving an emergent relational schema from RDF data. In Gangemi et al. [2015], pages 864–874. DOI: 10.1145/2736277.2741121 32, 34

H. Sofia Pinto, C. Tempich, and Steffen Staab. Ontology engineering and evolution in a distributed world using DILIGENT. In Staab and Studer [2009], pages 153–176. DOI: 10.1007/978-3-540-92673-3 115

Alessandro Piscopo and Elena Simperl. Who models the world?: Collaborative ontology creation and user roles in Wikidata. *Proc. of the ACM on Human-Computer Interaction*, 2(CSCW):141:1–141:18, 2018. DOI: 10.1145/3274410 148

Alessandro Piscopo, Lucie-Aimée Kaffee, Chris Phethean, and Elena Simperl. Provenance information in a collaborative knowledge graph: An evaluation of Wikidata external references. In d'Amato et al. [2017], pages 542–558. DOI: 10.1007/978-3-319-68288-4_32 147

R. J. Pittman, Amit Srivastava, Sanjika Hewavitharana, Ajinkya Kale, and Saab Mansour. Cracking the code on conversational commerce. eBay Blog, April 2017. https://www.ebayinc.com/stories/news/cracking-the-code-on-conversational-commerce/ 1, 3, 149, 150

Aleksander Pivk, Philipp Cimiano, York Sure, Matjaz Gams, Vladislav Rajkovic, and Rudi Studer. Transforming arbitrary tables into logical form with TARTAR. *Data and Knowledge Engineering*, 60(3):567–595, 2007. DOI: 10.1016/j.datak.2006.04.002 111

Roel Popping. Knowledge graphs and network text analysis. *Social Science Information*, 42(91):91–106, 2003. DOI: 10.1177/0539018403042001798 159

Valentina Presutti, Enrico Daga, Aldo Gangemi, and Eva Blomqvist. eXtreme design with content ontology design patterns. In Eva Blomqvist, Kurt Sandkuhl, François Scharffe, and Vojtech Svátek, Eds., *Proc. of the Workshop on Ontology Patterns (WOP), collocated with the 8th International Semantic Web Conference (ISWC), Washington DC, October 25*, volume 516 of *CEUR Workshop Proceedings*. Sun SITE Central Europe (CEUR), 2009. http://ceur-ws.org/Vol-516/pap21.pdf 115

Valentina Presutti, Claudia d'Amato, Fabien Gandon, Mathieu d'Aquin, Stephen Staab, and Anna Tordia, Eds. *The Semantic Web: Trends and Challenges—11th International Conference, ESWC, Anissaras, Crete, Greece, May 25–29, 2014. Proceedings*, volume 8465 of *Lecture Notes in Computer Science*. Springer, 2014. 173, 181

Eric Prud'hommeaux and Gavin Carothers. RDF 1.1 turtle—terse RDF triple language. *W3C Recommendation, World Wide Web Consortium*, February 25, 2014. https://www.w3.org/TR/2014/REC-turtle-20140225/ 138

Eric Prud'hommeaux, Jose Emilio Labra Gayo, and Harold Solbrig. Shape expressions: An RDF validation and transformation language. In Sack et al. [2014], pages 32–40. DOI: 10.1145/2660517.2660523 27, 29

Jay Pujara, Hui Miao, Lise Getoor, and William W. Cohen. Knowledge graph identification. In Alani et al. [2013a], pages 542–557. DOI: 10.1007/978-3-642-41335-3_34 1

Guilin Qi, Huajun Chen, Kang Liu, Haofen Wang, Qiu Ji, and Tianxing Wu. *Knowledge Graph*. Springer, 2020. (to appear). 1

Ross Quillian. A notation for representing conceptual information: An application to semantics and mechanical English paraphrasing. SP-1395, system development corporation. *Technical Report SP-1395*, Systems Development Corp., Santa Monica, CA, 1963. 60, 157

Stephan Rabanser, Oleksandr Shchur, and Stephan Günnemann. Introduction to tensor decompositions and their applications in machine learning. *CoRR*, 2017. http://arxiv.org/abs/1711.10781 79, 80

Roy Rada. Gradualness eases refinement of medical knowledge. *Medical Informatics*, 11(1):59–73, 1986. DOI: 10.3109/14639238608994975 159, 160, 161

Filip Radulovic, Raúl García-Castro, and Asunción Gómez-Pérez. Towards the anonymisation of RDF data. In Haiping Xu, Ed., *The 27th International Conference on Software Engineering and Knowledge Engineering, SEKE, Wyndham Pittsburgh University Center, Pittsburgh, PA, July 6–8*, pages 646–651. KSI Research Inc. and Knowledge Systems Institute Graduate School, 2015. DOI: 10.18293/seke2015-167 143

Luc De Raedt, Ed. *Logical and Relational Learning: From ILP to MRDM (Cognitive Technologies)*. Springer-Verlag, 2008. 98

Yves Raimond, Christopher Sutton, and Mark B. Sandler. Interlinking music-related data on the Web. *IEEE MultiMedia*, 16(2):52–63, 2009. DOI: 10.1109/mmul.2009.29 149

Yves Raimond, Tristan Ferne, Michael Smethurst, and Gareth Adams. The BBC world service archive prototype. *Journal of Web Semantics*, 27–28:2–9, 2014. DOI: 10.1016/j.websem.2014.07.005 3, 148, 149

Alain T. Rappaport and Albert M. Gouyet. Dynamic, interactive display system for a knowledge base. U.S. Patent US4752889A, June 21, 1988. 159, 160, 161

Lev-Arie Ratinov and Dan Roth. Design challenges and misconceptions in named entity recognition. In Suzanne Stevenson and Xavier Carreras, Eds., *Proc. of the 13th Conference on Computational Natural Language Learning, CoNLL, Boulder, CO, June 4–5*, pages 147–155. The Association for Computational Linguistics, 2009. DOI: 10.3115/1596374.1596399 107

Pavan Reddivari, Tim Finin, and Anupam Joshi. Policy-based access control for an RDF store. In Lalana Kagal, Tim Finin, and James Hendler, Eds., *Policy Management for the Web, a Workshop Held at the 14th International World Wide Web Conference May 10, Chiba Japan*, pages 78–81, 2005. https://ebiquity.umbc.edu/_file_directory_/papers/159.pdf 141

Raymond Reiter. A theory of diagnosis from first principles. *Artificial Intelligence*, 32(1):57–95, 1987. DOI: 10.1016/0004-3702(87)90062-2 131

Xiang Ren, Ahmed El-Kishky, Chi Wang, Fangbo Tao, Clare R. Voss, and Jiawei Han. ClusType: Effective entity recognition and typing by relation phrase-based clustering. In Longbing Cao, Chengqi Zhang, Thorsten Joachims, Geoffrey I. Webb, Dragos D. Margineantu, and Graham Williams, Eds., *Proc. of the 21th ACM SIGKDD International Conference on Knowledge Discovery and Data Mining, Sydney, NSW, Australia, August 10–13*, pages 995–1004. ACM Press, 2015. DOI: 10.1145/2783258.2783362 107

Xiang Ren, Zeqiu Wu, Wenqi He, Meng Qu, Clare R. Voss, Heng Ji, Tarek F. Abdelzaher, and Jiawei Han. CoType: Joint extraction of typed entities and relations with knowledge bases. In Rick Barrett, Rick Cummings, Eugene Agichtein, and Evgeniy Gabrilovich, Eds., *Proc. of the 26th International Conference on World Wide Web, WWW, Perth, Australia, April 3–7*, pages 1015–1024. ACM Press, 2017. DOI: 10.1145/3038912.3052708 109

Juan L. Reutter, Adrián Soto, and Domagoj Vrgoc. Recursion in SPARQL. In Marcelo Arenas, Óscar Corcho, Elena Paslaru Bontas Simperl, Markus Strohmaier, Mathieu d'Aquin, Kavitha Srinivas, Paul T. Groth, Michel Dumontier, Jeff Heflin, Krishnaprasad Thirunarayan, and Stephen Staab, Eds., *The Semantic Web—ISWC—14th International Semantic Web Conference, Bethlehem, PA, October 11–15, Proceedings, Part I*, volume 9366 of *Lecture Notes in Computer Science*, pages 19–35. Springer, 2015. DOI: 10.1007/978-3-319-25007-6_2 76, 140

Sebastian Riedel, Limin Yao, and Andrew McCallum. Modeling relations and their mentions without labeled text. In José L. Balcázar, Francesco Bonchi, Aristides Gionis, and Michèle Sebag, Eds., *Machine Learning and Knowledge Discovery in Databases, European Conference, ECML PKDD, Barcelona, Spain, September 20–24, Proceedings, Part III*, volume 6323 of *Lecture Notes in Computer Science*, pages 148–163. Springer, 2010. DOI: 10.1007/978-3-642-15939-8_10 108

Petar Ristoski and Heiko Paulheim. RDF2Vec: RDF graph embeddings for data mining. In Groth et al. [2016], pages 498–514. DOI: 10.1007/978-3-319-46523-4_30 88

Richard H. Ritchens. General program for mechanical translation between any two languages via an algebraic interlingua. *Mechanical Translation*, 3(2):37, November 1956. 157

Giuseppe Rizzo, Claudia d'Amato, Nicola Fanizzi, and Floriana Esposito. Terminological cluster trees for disjointness axiom discovery. In Blomqvist et al. [2017], pages 184–201. DOI: 10.1007/978-3-319-58068-5_12 101

Giuseppe Rizzo, Nicola Fanizzi, and Claudia d'Amato. Class expression induction as concept space exploration: From DL-foil to DL-focl. *Future Gener. Comput. Syst.*, 108:256–272, 2020. DOI: 10.1016/j.future.2020.02.071 101, 104

Giuseppe Rizzo, Claudia d'Amato, and Nicola Fanizzi. An unsupervised approach to disjointness learning based on terminological cluster trees. *Semantic Web*, 12(3):423–447, 2021. DOI: 10.3233/SW-200391 101

Tim Rocktäschel and Sebastian Riedel. End-to-end differentiable proving. In Guyon et al. [2017], pages 3788–3800. http://papers.nips.cc/paper/6969-end-to-end-differentiable-proving 100

Marko A. Rodriguez. The Gremlin graph traversal machine and language. In James Cheney and Thomas Neumann, Eds., *Proc. of the 15th Symposium on Database Programming Languages, Pittsburgh, PA, October 25–30*, pages 1–10. ACM Press, 2015. DOI: 10.1145/2815072.2815073 13, 76

Stephen Roller, Douwe Kiela, and Maximilian Nickel. Hearst patterns revisited: Automatic hypernym detection from large text corpora. In Iryna Gurevych and Yusuke Miyao, Eds., *Proc. of the 56th Annual Meeting of the Association for Computational Linguistics, ACL, Melbourne, Australia, July 15–20, Volume 2: Short Papers*, pages 358–363. The Association for Computational Linguistics, 2018. https://www.aclweb.org/anthology/volumes/P18-2/ DOI: 10.18653/v1/p18-2057 108

Marco Rospocher, Marieke van Erp, Piek Vossen, Antske Fokkens, Itziar Aldabe, German Rigau, Aitor Soroa, Thomas Ploeger, and Tessel Bogaard. Building event-centric knowledge graphs from news. *Journal of Web Semantics*, 37–38:132–151, 2016. DOI: 10.1016/j.websem.2015.12.004 106

Jacobo Rouces, Gerard de Melo, and Katja Hose. Framebase: Representing *n*-ary relations using semantic frames. In Fabien Gandon, Marta Sabou, Harald Sack, Claudia d'Amato, Philippe Cudré-Mauroux, and Antoine Zimmermann, Eds., *The Semantic Web. Latest Advances and New Domains—12th European Semantic Web Conference, ESWC, Portoroz, Slovenia, May 31–June 4. Proceedings*, volume 9088 of *Lecture Notes in Computer Science*, pages 505–521. Springer, 2015. DOI: 10.1007/978-3-319-18818-8_31 109

Sebastian Rudolph, Markus Krötzsch, and Pascal Hitzler. Description logic reasoning with decision diagrams: Compiling SHIQ to disjunctive datalog. In Amit P. Sheth, Steffen Staab, Mike Dean, Massimo Paolucci, Diana Maynard, Timothy W. Finin, and Krishnaprasad Thirunarayan, Eds., *The Semantic Web—ISWC, 7th International Semantic Web Conference, ISWC, Karlsruhe, Germany, October 26–30. Proceedings*, volume 5318 of *Lecture Notes in Computer Science*, pages 435–450. Springer, 2008. 58

Anisa Rula, Matteo Palmonari, Andreas Harth, Steffen Stadtmüller, and Andrea Maurino. On the diversity and availability of temporal information in linked open data. In Cudré-Mauroux et al. [2012], pages 492–507. DOI: 10.1007/978-3-642-35176-1_31 121

Anisa Rula, Luca Panziera, Matteo Palmonari, and Andrea Maurino. Capturing the currency of DBpedia descriptions and get insight into their validity. In Olaf Hartig, Aidan Hogan, and Juan F. Sequeda, Eds., *Proc. of the 5th International Workshop on Consuming Linked Data, COLD co-located with the 13th International Semantic Web Conference (ISWC), Riva del Garda, Italy, October 20*, volume 1264 of *CEUR Workshop Proceedings*. Sun SITE Central Europe (CEUR), November 2014. http://ceur-ws.org/Vol-1264/cold2014_RulaPPM.pdf 121

Anisa Rula, Matteo Palmonari, Simone Rubinacci, Axel-Cyrille Ngonga Ngomo, Jens Lehmann, Andrea Maurino, and Diego Esteves. TISCO: Temporal scoping of facts. *Journal of Web Semantics*, 54:72–86, 2019. DOI: 10.1016/j.websem.2018.09.002 121

Owen Sacco and Alexandre Passant. A privacy preference ontology (PPO) for linked data. In Christian Bizer, Tom Heath, Tim Berners-Lee, and Michael Hausenblas, Eds., *WWW Workshop on Linked Data on the Web, Hyderabad, India, March 29*, volume 813 of *CEUR Workshop Proceedings*. Sun SITE Central Europe (CEUR), 2011. http://ceur-ws.org/Vol-813/ldow2011-paper01.pdf 141

Harald Sack, Agata Filipowska, Jens Lehmann, and Sebastian Hellmann, Eds. *Proc. of the 10th International Conference on Semantic Systems, SEMANTICS, Leipzig, Germany, September 4–5*. ACM Press, 2014. 211, 219

Ali Sadeghian, Mohammadreza Armandpour, Patrick Ding, and Patrick Wang. DRUM: End-to-end differentiable rule mining on knowledge graphs. In Wallach et al. [2019], pages 15321–15331. http://papers.nips.cc/paper/9669-drum-end-to-end-differentiable-rule-mining-on-knowledge-graphs 100, 104

Tomás Sáez and Aidan Hogan. Automatically generating Wikipedia info-boxes from Wikidata. In Pierre-Antoine Champin, Fabien L. Gandon, Mounia Lalmas, and Panagiotis G. Ipeirotis, Eds., *Companion of the The Web Conference on the Web Conference, WWW, Lyon, France, April 23–27*, pages 1823–1830. ACM Press, 2018. DOI: 10.1145/3184558.3191647 148

Tara Sainath, Alexander Rush, Sergey Levine, Karen Livescu, and Shakir Mohamed, Eds. *7th International Conference on Learning Representations, ICLR, New Orleans, LA, May 6–9*. OpenReview.net, 2019. https://openreview.net/group?id=ICLR.cc/2019/conference 220, 226

Muhammad Saleem, Muhammad Intizar Ali, Aidan Hogan, Qaiser Mehmood, and Axel-Cyrille Ngonga Ngomo. LSQ: The linked SPARQL queries dataset. In Marcelo Arenas, Óscar Corcho, Elena Paslaru Bontas Simperl, Markus Strohmaier, Mathieu d'Aquin, Kavitha

Srinivas, Paul T. Groth, Michel Dumontier, Jeff Heflin, Krishnaprasad Thirunarayan, and Stephen Staab, Eds., *The Semantic Web—ISWC—14th International Semantic Web Conference, Bethlehem, PA, October 11–15, Proceedings, Part II*, volume 9367 of *Lecture Notes in Computer Science*, pages 261–269. Springer, 2015. DOI: 10.1007/978-3-319-25010-6_15 139

Mehdi Samadi, Partha Talukdar, Manuela Veloso, and Manuel Blum. ClaimEval: Integrated and flexible framework for claim evaluation using credibility of sources. In Schuurmans and Wellman [2016], pages 222–228. http://dl.acm.org/citation.cfm?id=3015812.3015845 129, 130

Pierangela Samarati and Latanya Sweeney. Protecting privacy when disclosing information: k-anonymity and its enforcement through generalization and suppression. *Technical Report SRI-CSL-98-04*, Computer Science Laboratory, SRI International, 1998. http://www.csl.sri.com/papers/sritr-98-04/ 143

Georgios M. Santipantakis, Apostolos Glenis, Christos Doulkeridis, Akrivi Vlachou, and George A. Vouros. stLD: towards a spatio-temporal link discovery framework. In Sven Groppe and Le Gruenwald, Eds., *Proc. of the International Workshop on Semantic Big Data, SBD@SIGMOD, Amsterdam, The Netherlands, July 5*, pages 4:1–4:6. ACM Press, 2019. DOI: 10.1145/3323878.3325805 129

Eugene Santos Jr. and Eugene S. Santos. A framework for building knowledge-bases under uncertainty. *Journal of Experimental and Theoretical Artificial Intelligence*, 11(2):265–286, 1999. DOI: 10.1080/095281399146571 159, 160

Franco Scarselli, Marco Gori, Ah Chung Tsoi, Markus Hagenbuchner, and Gabriele Monfardini. The graph neural network model. *IEEE Transactions on Neural Networks*, 20(1):61–80, 2009. DOI: 10.1109/tnn.2008.2005605 91, 92, 93, 94

Max Schmachtenberg, Christian Bizer, and Heiko Paulheim. Adoption of the linked data best practices in different topical domains. In Mika et al. [2014], pages 245–260. DOI: 10.1007/978-3-319-11964-9_16 148

Manfred Schmidt-Schauß and Gert Smolka. Attributive concept descriptions with complements. *Artificial Intelligence*, 48(1):1–26, 1991. DOI: 10.1016/0004-3702(91)90078-X 63, 158

Edward W. Schneider. Course modularization applied: The interface system and its implications for sequence control and data analysis. In *Association for the Development of Instructional Systems (ADIS), Chicago, IL, April 1972*, 1973. DOI: 10.1037/e436252004-001 1, 158, 161

Michael Schneider and Geoff Sutcliffe. Reasoning in the OWL 2 full ontology language using first-order automated theorem proving. In Nikolaj Bjørner and Viorica Sofronie-

Stokkermans, Eds., *Automated Deduction—CADE-23—23rd International Conference on Automated Deduction, Wroclaw, Poland, July 31–August 5. Proceedings*, volume 6803 of *Lecture Notes in Computer Science*, pages 461–475. Springer, 2011. DOI: 10.1007/978-3-642-22438-6_35 55, 57

Christoph Schuetz, Loris Bozzato, Bernd Neumayr, Michael Schrefl, and Luciano Serafini. Knowledge graph OLAP: A multidimensional model and query operations for contextualized knowledge graphs. *Semantic Web Journal*, 2020. (Under open review). DOI: 10.3233/sw-200419 44, 45, 155

Dale Schuurmans and Michael P. Wellman, Eds. *Proc. of the 30th AAAI Conference on Artificial Intelligence, February 12–17, Phoenix, AZ*. AAAI Press, 2016. 207, 215

Daniel Schwabe, Virgílio A. F. Almeida, Hartmut Glaser, Ricardo Baeza-Yates, and Sue B. Moon, Eds. *22nd International World Wide Web Conference, WWW, Rio de Janeiro, Brazil, May 13–17*. ACM Press, 2013. 184, 206

Philipp Seifer, Johannes Härtel, Martin Leinberger, Ralf Lämmel, and Steffen Staab. Empirical study on the usage of graph query languages in open source Java projects. In Oscar Nierstrasz, Jeff Gray, and Bruno C. d. S. Oliveira, Eds., *Proc. of the 12th ACM SIGPLAN International Conference on Software Language Engineering, SLE, Athens, Greece, October 20–22*, pages 152–166. ACM Press, 2019. DOI: 10.1145/3357766.3359541 13

Juan F. Sequeda, Marcelo Arenas, and Daniel P. Miranker. On directly mapping relational databases to RDF and OWL. In Alain Mille, Fabien L. Gandon, Jacques Misselis, Michael Rabinovich, and Steffen Staab, Eds., *Proc. of the 21st World Wide Web Conference, WWW, Lyon, France, April 16–20*, pages 649–658. ACM Press, 2012. DOI: 10.1145/2187836.2187924 113

Juan F. Sequeda, Marcelo Arenas, and Daniel P. Miranker. OBDA: Query rewriting or materialization? In practice, both! In Mika et al. [2014], pages 535–551. DOI: 10.1007/978-3-319-11964-9_34 114

Juan F. Sequeda, Willard J. Briggs, Daniel P. Miranker, and Wayne P. Heideman. A Pay-as-you-go methodology to design and build enterprise knowledge graphs from relational databases. In Ghidini et al. [2019b], pages 526–545. DOI: 10.1007/978-3-030-30796-7_32 105

Stephan Seufert, Patrick Ernst, Srikanta J. Bedathur, Sarath Kumar Kondreddi, Klaus Berberich, and Gerhard Weikum. Instant espresso: Interactive analysis of relationships in knowledge graphs. In Bourdeau et al. [2016], pages 251–254. DOI: 10.1145/2872518.2890528 162

Nigel Shadbolt and Kieron O'Hara. Linked data in government. *IEEE Internet Computing*, 17(4):72–77, 2013. DOI: 10.1109/mic.2013.72 3, 133, 148, 149

Mohamed Ahmed Sherif and Axel-Cyrille Ngonga Ngomo. Semantic quran. *Semantic Web Journal*, 6(4):339–345, 2015. DOI: 10.3233/sw-140137 149

Mohamed Ahmed Sherif and Axel-Cyrille Ngonga Ngomo. A systematic survey of point set distance measures for link discovery. *Semantic Web Journal*, 9(5):589–604, 2018. DOI: 10.3233/SW-170285 129

Baoxu Shi and Tim Weninger. Discriminative predicate path mining for fact checking in knowledge graphs. *Knowledge-Based Systems*, 104:123–133, 2016. DOI: 10.1016/j.knosys.2016.04.015 129, 130

Cogan Shimizu, Quinn Hirt, and Pascal Hitzler. MODL: A modular ontology design library. *CoRR*, 2019. http://arxiv.org/abs/1904.05405 116

Solomon Eyal Shimony, Carmel Domshlak, and Eugene Santos Jr. Cost-sharing in Bayesian knowledge bases. In Dan Geiger and Prakash P. Shenoy, Eds., *UAI: Proceedings of the 13th Conference on Uncertainty in Artificial Intelligence, Brown University, Providence, Rhode Island, August 1–3*, pages 421–428. Morgan Kaufmann, 1997. 159, 160, 161

Prashant Shiralkar, Alessandro Flammini, Filippo Menczer, and Giovanni Luca Ciampaglia. Finding streams in knowledge graphs to support fact checking. In Vijay Raghavan, Srinivas Aluru, George Karypis, Lucio Miele, and Xindong Wu, Eds., *IEEE International Conference on Data Mining, ICDM, New Orleans, LA, November 18–21*, pages 859–864. IEEE Computer Society, 2017. DOI: 10.1109/icdm.2017.105 129, 130

Saurabh Shrivastava. Bring rich knowledge of people, places, things and local businesses to your apps. Bing Blogs, July 2017. https://blogs.bing.com/search-quality-insights/2017-07/bring-rich-knowledge-of-people-places-things-and-local-businesses-to-your-apps 1, 3, 149, 150

Rôney Reis C. Silva, Bruno C. Leal, Felipe T. Brito, Vânia M. P. Vidal, and Javam C. Machado. A differentially private approach for querying RDF data of social networks. In Bipin C. Desai, Jun Hong, and Richard McClatchey, Eds., *Proc. of the 21st International Database Engineering and Applications Symposium, IDEAS, Bristol, UK, July 12–14*, pages 74–81. ACM Press, 2017. DOI: 10.1145/3105831.3105838 144

Amit Singhal. Introducing the knowledge graph: Things, not strings. Google Blog, May 2012. https://www.blog.google/products/search/introducing-knowledge-graph-things-not/ 1, 3, 147, 149, 157, 161

Martin G. Skjæveland, Daniel P. Lupp, Leif Harald Karlsen, and Henrik Forssell. Practical ontology pattern instantiation, discovery, and maintenance with reasonable ontology templates. In Vrandečić et al. [2018], pages 477–494. DOI: 10.1007/978-3-030-00671-6_28 116

Jennifer Sleeman and Tim Finin.   Type prediction for efficient coreference resolution in heterogeneous semantic graphs.   In *IEEE 7th International Conference on Semantic Computing, Irvine, CA, September 16–18*, pages 78–85. IEEE Computer Society, 2013. DOI: 10.1109/icsc.2013.22 128

Alisa Smirnova and Philippe Cudré-Mauroux. Relation extraction using distant supervision: A survey. *ACM Computing Surveys*, 51(5):106:1–106:35, 2019. DOI: 10.1145/3241741 108

Richard Socher, Danqi Chen, Christopher D. Manning, and Andrew Ng.   Reasoning with neural tensor networks for knowledge base completion.   In Burges et al. [2013], pages 926–934.   http://papers.nips.cc/book/advances-in-neural-information-processing-systems-26-2013 82, 129

Arnaud Soulet, Arnaud Giacometti, Béatrice Markhoff, and Fabian M. Suchanek. Representativeness of knowledge bases with the generalized Benford's law. In Vrandečić et al. [2018], pages 374–390. DOI: 10.1007/978-3-030-00671-6_22 122

John Sowa.   Semantics of conceptual graphs.   In Norman K. Sondheimer, Ed., *17th Annual Meeting of the Association for Computational Linguistics, June 29–July 1, University of California at San Diego, La Jolla, CA*, pages 39–44. The Association for Computational Linguistics, 1979. https://www.aclweb.org/anthology/P79-1010/ DOI: 10.3115/982163.982175 157, 160

John Sowa. Semantic networks. In Stuart C. Shapiro, Ed., *Encyclopedia of Cognitive Science*. John Wiley & Sons, 1987. Revised version available at http://www.jfsowa.com/pubs/semnet.htm DOI: 10.1002/0470018860.s00065 157

Blerina Spahiu, Riccardo Porrini, Matteo Palmonari, Anisa Rula, and Andrea Maurino. AB-STAT: Ontology-driven linked data summaries with pattern minimalization. In Harald Sack, Giuseppe Rizzo, Nadine Steinmetz, Dunja Mladenic, Sören Auer, and Christoph Lange, Eds., *The Semantic Web—ESWC Satellite Events, Heraklion, Crete, Greece, May 29–June 2, Revised Selected Papers*, volume 9989 of *Lecture Notes in Computer Science*, pages 381–395. Springer, 2016. DOI: 10.1007/978-3-319-47602-5_51 32

Alessandro Sperduti and Antonina Starita.   Supervised neural networks for the classification of structures.   *IEEE Transactions on Neural Networks*, 8(3):714–735, 1997. DOI: 10.1109/72.572108 91

Manu Sporny, Gregg Kellogg, Markus Lanthaler, Dave Longley, and Niklas Lindström. JSON-LD 1.0, A JSON-based serialization for linked data. *W3C Recommendation, World Wide Web Consortium*, January 16, 2014. 114, 137

Rajan Srikanth and Matthias Jarke.   The design of knowledge-based systems for managing ill-structured software projects. *Decision Support Systems*, 5(4):425–447, 1989. DOI: 10.1016/0167-9236(89)90020-1 159, 160

Steffen Staab and Rudi Studer, Eds. *Handbook on Ontologies*. International Handbooks on Information Systems. Springer, 2009. DOI: 10.1007/978-3-540-92673-3 187, 210

Claus Stadler, Jens Lehmann, Konrad Höffner, and Sören Auer. LinkedGeoData: A core for a web of spatial open data. *Semantic Web Journal*, 3(4):333–354, 2012. DOI: 10.3233/sw-2011-0052 3, 114, 148

Simon Steyskal and Axel Polleres. Defining expressive access policies for linked data using the ODRL ontology 2.0. In Sack et al. [2014], pages 20–23. DOI: 10.1145/2660517.2660530 141

Patrick Stickler. CBD—Concise bounded description. *W3C Member Submission*, June 3, 2005. https://www.w3.org/Submission/2005/SUBM-CBD-20050603/ 138

Radu Stoica, George H. L. Fletcher, and Juan F. Sequeda. On directly mapping relational databases to property graphs. In Hogan and Milo [2019]. http://ceur-ws.org/Vol-2369/short06.pdf DOI: 10.1145/2187836.2187924 113

Frans N. Stokman and Pieter H. de Vries. Structuring knowledge in a graph. In Gerrit C. van der Veer and Gijsbertus Mulder, Eds., *Human-Computer Interaction*, chapter 11, pages 186–206. Springer, 1988. DOI: 10.1007/978-3-642-73402-1_12 159, 160, 161

Umberto Straccia. A minimal deductive system for general fuzzy RDF. In Axel Polleres and Terrance Swift, Eds., *Web Reasoning and Rule Systems, 3rd International Conference, RR, Chantilly, VA, October 25–26, Proceedings*, volume 5837 of *Lecture Notes in Computer Science*, pages 166–181. Springer, 2009. DOI: 10.1007/978-3-642-05082-4_12 42

Philip Stutz, Daniel Strebel, and Abraham Bernstein. Signal/Collect12. *Semantic Web Journal*, 7(2):139–166, 2016. DOI: 10.3233/sw-150176 1, 70

Jian Su, Xavier Carreras, and Kevin Duh, Eds. *Proc. of the Conference on Empirical Methods in Natural Language Processing, EMNLP, Austin, TX, November 1–4*. The Association for Computational Linguistics, 2016. 179, 187

Mari Carmen Suárez-Figueroa, Gong Cheng, Anna Lisa Gentile, Christophe Guéret, C. Maria Keet, and Abraham Bernstein, Eds. *Proc. of the ISWC Satellite Tracks (Posters and Demonstrations, Industry, and Outrageous Ideas) co-located with 18th International Semantic Web Conference (ISWC), Auckland, New Zealand, October 26–30*, volume 2456 of *CEUR Workshop Proceedings*. Sun SITE Central Europe (CEUR), 2019. http://ceur-ws.org/Vol-2456 171, 190

Fabian M. Suchanek, Gjergji Kasneci, and Gerhard Weikum. YAGO: A core of semantic knowledge unifying WordNet and Wikipedia. In Carey L. Williamson, Mary Ellen Zurko, Peter F. Patel-Schneider, and Prashant J. Shenoy, Eds., *Proc. of the 16th International Conference on World Wide Web, WWW, Banff, Alberta, Canada, May 8–12*, pages 697–706. ACM Press, 2007. 145, 146, 158

Fabian M. Suchanek, Gjergji Kasneci, and Gerhard Weikum. YAGO: A large ontology from Wikipedia and WordNet. *Journal of Web Semantics*, 6(3):203–217, 2008. DOI: 10.1016/j.websem.2008.06.001 111, 146

Fabian M. Suchanek, Jonathan Lajus, Armand Boschin, and Gerhard Weikum. Knowledge representation and rule mining in entity-centric knowledge bases. In Markus Krötzsch and Daria Stepanova, Eds., *Reasoning Web. Explainable Artificial Intelligence—15th International Summer School, Bolzano, Italy, September 20–24, Tutorial Lectures*, volume 11810 of *Lecture Notes in Computer Science*, pages 110–152. Springer, 2019. DOI: 10.1007/978-3-030-31423-1_4 98, 99

Yizhou Sun and Jiawei Han. Mining heterogeneous information networks: Principles and methodologies. *Synthesis Lectures on Data Mining and Knowledge Discovery*. Morgan & Claypool Publishers, 2012. DOI: 10.2200/S00433ED1V01Y201207DMK005 8

Yizhou Sun, Jiawei Han, Xifeng Yan, Philip S. Yu, and Tianyi Wu. Pathsim: Meta path-based top-k similarity search in heterogeneous information networks. *Proc. of the VLDB Endowment*, 4(11):992–1003, 2011. DOI: 10.14778/3402707.3402736 8, 130, 160

Zhiqing Sun, Zhi-Hong Deng, Jian-Yun Nie, and Jian Tang. RotatE: Knowledge graph embedding by relational rotation in complex space. In Sainath et al. [2019]. https://openreview.net/group?id=ICLR.cc/2019/conference 79, 86

Mihai Surdeanu, Julie Tibshirani, Ramesh Nallapati, and Christopher D. Manning. Multi-instance multi-label learning for relation extraction. In Tsujii et al. [2012], pages 455–465. 108

Zafar Habeeb Syed, Michael Röder, and Axel-Cyrille Ngonga Ngomo. FactCheck: Validating RDF triples using textual evidence. In Cuzzocrea et al. [2018], pages 1599–1602. DOI: 10.1145/3269206.3269308 129, 130

Zafar Habeeb Syed, Michael Röder, and Axel-Cyrille Ngonga Ngomo. Unsupervised discovery of corroborative paths for fact validation. In Ghidini et al. [2019a], pages 630–646. DOI: 10.1007/978-3-030-30793-6_36 129, 130

James Joseph Sylvester. Chemistry and algebra. *Nature*, 17:284, 1878. DOI: 10.1038/017284a0 157

Jeremy Tandy, Ivan Herman, and Gregg Kellogg. Generating RDF from tabular data on the Web. *W3C Recommendation, World Wide Web Consortium*, December 17, 2015. https://www.w3.org/TR/2015/REC-csv2rdf-20151217/ 113

Jeni Tennison and Gregg Kellogg. Metadata vocabulary for tabular data. *W3C Recommendation, World Wide Web Consortium*, December 17, 2015. https://www.w3.org/TR/2015/REC-tabular-metadata-20151217/ 113

The R. Foundation. The R. project for statistical computing, 1992. https://www.r-project.org 76

The UniProt Consortium. UniProt: A hub for protein information. *Nucleic Acids Research*, 43(D1):D204–D212, 2014. 133, 135

Bryan B. Thompson, Mike Personick, and Martyn Cutcher. The bigdata® RDF graph database. In Andreas Harth, Katja Hose, and Ralf Schenkel, Eds., *Linked Data Management*, pages 193–237. CRC Press, 2014. 139

Katherine Thornton, Harold Solbrig, Gregory S. Stupp, José Emilio Labra Gayo, Daniel Mietchen, Eric Prud'hommeaux, and Andra Waagmeester. Using shape expressions (ShEx) to share RDF data models and to guide curation with rigorous validation. In Hitzler et al. [2019], pages 606–620. DOI: 10.1007/978-3-030-21348-0_39 29, 123, 158

Felice Tobin. Thomson Reuters launches first of its kind knowledge graph feed allowing financial services customers to accelerate their AI and digital strategies. Thomspon Reuters Press Release, October 2017. https://www.thomsonreuters.com/en/press-releases/2017/october/thomson-reuters-launches-first-of-its-kind-knowledge-graph-feed.html 3, 149, 151

Dominik Tomaszuk, Renzo Angles, Lukasz Szeremeta, Karol Litman, and Diego Cisterna. Serialization for property graphs. In Stanislaw Kozielski, Dariusz Mrozek, Pawel Kasprowski, Bozena Malysiak-Mrozek, and Daniel Kostrzewa, Eds., *Beyond Databases, Architectures and Structures. Paving the Road to Smart Data Processing and Analysis—15th International Conference, BDAS, Ustroń, Poland, May 28–31, Proceedings*, volume 1018 of *Communications in Computer and Information Science*, pages 57–69. Springer, 2019. DOI: 10.1007/978-3-030-19093-4_5 138

Gerald Töpper, Magnus Knuth, and Harald Sack. DBpedia ontology enrichment for inconsistency detection. In Valentina Presutti and Helena Sofia Pinto, Eds., *I-SEMANTICS—8th International Conference on Semantic Systems, I-SEMANTICS, Graz, Austria, September 5–7*, pages 33–40. ACM Press, 2012. DOI: 10.1145/2362499.2362505 101, 131

Jeffrey Travers and Stanley Milgram. An experimental study of the small world problem. *Sociometry*, 32(4):425–443, 1969. DOI: 10.2307/2786545 157

Théo Trouillon, Johannes Welbl, Sebastian Riedel, Éric Gaussier, and Guillaume Bouchard. Complex embeddings for simple link prediction. In Maria-Florina Balcan and Kilian Q. Weinberger, Eds., *Proc. of the 33nd International Conference on Machine Learning, ICML, New York, June 19–24*, volume 48 of *JMLR Workshop and Conference Proceedings*, pages 2071–2080. JMLR.org, 2016. http://proceedings.mlr.press/v48/ 81, 84, 86

Jun'ichi Tsujii, James Henderson, and Marius Pasca, Eds. *Proc. of the Joint Conference on Empirical Methods in Natural Language Processing and Computational Natural Language Learning,*

EMNLP-CoNLL, July 12–14, Jeju Island, Korea. The Association for Computational Linguistics, 2012. 202, 220

Ledyard R. Tucker. The extension of factor analysis to three-dimensional matrices. In *Contributions to Mathematical Psychology*, pages 110–127. Holt, Rinehart and Winston, 1964. 81

Giovanni Tummarello, Christian Morbidoni, Reto Bachmann-Gmür, and Orri Erling. RDF-Sync: Efficient remote synchronization of RDF models. In Aberer et al. [2007], pages 537–551. DOI: 10.1007/978-3-540-76298-0_39 138

Octavian Udrea, Diego Reforgiato Recupero, and V. S. Subrahmanian. Annotated RDF. *ACM Transactions on Computational Logics*, 11(2):10:1–10:41, 2010. DOI: 10.1145/1656242.1656245 42

Jacopo Urbani, Spyros Kotoulas, Jason Maassen, Frank van Harmelen, and Henri E. Bal. WebPIE: A web-scale parallel inference engine using MapReduce. *Journal of Web Semantics*, 10:59–75, 2012. DOI: 10.1016/j.websem.2011.05.004 58

Marieke van Erp, Medha Atre, Vanessa López, Kavitha Srinivas, and Carolina Fortuna, Eds. *Proc. of the ISWC Posters and Demonstrations, Industry and Blue Sky Ideas Tracks Co-Located with 17th International Semantic Web Conference (ISWC), Monterey, October 8–12*, volume 2180 of *CEUR Workshop Proceedings*. Sun SITE Central Europe (CEUR), 2018. http://ceur-ws.org/Vol-2180 195, 208

Hernán Vargas, Carlos Buil Aranda, Aidan Hogan, and Claudia López. RDF explorer: A visual SPARQL query builder. In Ghidini et al. [2019a], pages 647–663. DOI: 10.1007/978-3-030-30793-6_37 22

Shikhar Vashishth, Prince Jain, and Partha Talukdar. CESI: Canonicalizing open knowledge bases using embeddings and side information. In Champin et al. [2018], pages 1317–1327. DOI: 10.1145/3178876.3186030 76

Paola Velardi, Stefano Faralli, and Roberto Navigli. OntoLearn reloaded: A graph-based algorithm for taxonomy induction. *Computational Linguistics*, 39(3):665–707, 2013. DOI: 10.1162/coli_a_00146 116

Petar Velickovic, Guillem Cucurull, Arantxa Casanova, Adriana Romero, Pietro Liò, and Yoshua Bengio. Graph attention networks. In *6th International Conference on Learning Representations, ICLR, Vancouver, BC, Canada, April 30–May 3, Conference Track Proceedings*. OpenReview.net, 2018. https://openreview.net/forum?id=rJXMpikCZ 95

Ruben Verborgh, Miel Vander Sande, Pieter Colpaert, Sam Coppens, Erik Mannens, and Rik Van de Walle. Web-scale querying through linked data fragments. In Christian Bizer, Tom Heath, Sören Auer, and Tim Berners-Lee, Eds., *Proc. of the Workshop on Linked Data on the*

Web, Co-Located with the 23rd International World Wide Web Conference (WWW), Seoul, Korea, April 8, volume 1184 of *CEUR Workshop Proceedings*. Sun SITE Central Europe (CEUR), 2014. http://ceur-ws.org/Vol-1184/ldow2014_paper_04.pdf 137, 140

Ruben Verborgh, Miel Vander Sande, Olaf Hartig, Joachim Van Herwegen, Laurens De Vocht, Ben De Meester, Gerald Haesendonck, and Pieter Colpaert. Triple pattern fragments: A low-cost knowledge graph interface for the Web. *Journal of Web Semantics*, 37–38:184–206, 2016. DOI: 10.1016/j.websem.2016.03.003 139

Serena Villata and Fabien Gandon. Licenses compatibility and composition in the Web of data. In Juan F. Sequeda, Andreas Harth, and Olaf Hartig, Eds., *Proc. of the 3rd International Workshop on Consuming Linked Data, COLD, Boston, MA, November 12*, volume 905 of *CEUR Workshop Proceedings*. Sun SITE Central Europe (CEUR), 2012. http://ceur-ws.org/Vol-905/VillataAndGandon_COLD2012.pdf 141

Serena Villata, Nicolas Delaforge, Fabien Gandon, and Amelie Gyrard. An access control model for linked data. In Robert Meersman, Tharam S. Dillon, and Pilar Herrero, Eds., *On the Move to Meaningful Internet Systems: OTM Workshops—Confederated International Workshops and Posters: EI2N+NSF ICE, ICSP+INBAST, ISDE, ORM, OTMA, SWWS+MONET+SeDeS, and VADER, Hersonissos, Crete, Greece, October 17–21. Proceedings*, volume 7046 of *Lecture Notes in Computer Science*, pages 454–463. Springer, 2011. DOI: 10.1007/978-3-642-25126-9_57 141

Johanna Völker, Daniel Fleischhacker, and Heiner Stuckenschmidt. Automatic acquisition of class disjointness. *Journal of Web Semantics*, 35(P2):124–139, 2015. DOI: 10.1016/j.websem.2015.07.001 101, 116

Julius Volz, Christian Bizer, Martin Gaedke, and Georgi Kobilarov. Discovering and maintaining links on the Web of data. In Bernstein et al. [2009], pages 650–665. DOI: 10.1007/978-3-642-04930-9_41 114, 137

Denny Vrandečić and Markus Krötzsch. Wikidata: A free collaborative knowledgebase. *Communications of the ACM*, 57(10):78–85, 2014. DOI: 10.1145/2629489 3, 36, 105, 114, 133, 137, 145, 147, 158

Denny Vrandečić, Kalina Bontcheva, Mari Carmen Suárez-Figueroa, Valentina Presutti, Irene Celino, Marta Sabou, Lucie-Aimée Kaffee, and Elena Simperl, Eds. *The Semantic Web—ISWC—17th International Semantic Web Conference, Monterey, CA, October 8–12, Proceedings, Part I*, volume 11136 of *Lecture Notes in Computer Science*. Springer, 2018. 176, 179, 191, 204, 217, 218, 224

Andreas Wagner, Duc Thanh Tran, Günter Ladwig, Andreas Harth, and Rudi Studer. Top-*k* linked data query processing. In Elena Simperl, Philipp Cimiano, Axel Polleres, Óscar Corcho, and Valentina Presutti, Eds., *The Semantic Web: Research and Applications—9th Extended*

Semantic Web Conference, ESWC, Heraklion, Crete, Greece, May 27–31. Proceedings, volume 7295 of *Lecture Notes in Computer Science*, pages 56–71. Springer, 2012. DOI: 10.1007/978-3-642-30284-8_11 75

Claudia Wagner, Eduardo Graells-Garrido, David García, and Filippo Menczer. Women through the glass ceiling: Gender asymmetries in Wikipedia. *EPJ Data Science*, 5(1):5, 2016. DOI: 10.1140/epjds/s13688-016-0066-4 122

Hanna M. Wallach, Hugo Larochelle, Alina Beygelzimer, Florence d'Alché-Buc, Emily B. Fox, and Roman Garnett, Eds. *Advances in Neural Information Processing Systems 32: Annual Conference on Neural Information Processing Systems, NeurIPS, December 8–14, Vancouver, BC, Canada*, 2019. http://papers.nips.cc/book/advances-in-neural-information-processing-systems-32-2019 168, 214

Toby Walsh, Ed. *IJCAI, Proceedings of the 22nd International Joint Conference on Artificial Intelligence, Barcelona, Catalonia, Spain, July 16–22*. IJCAI/AAAI, August 2011. 182, 206, 208

Meng Wang, Ruijie Wang, Jun Liu, Yihe Chen, Lei Zhang, and Guilin Qi. Towards empty answers in SPARQL: Approximating querying with RDF embedding. In Vrandečić et al. [2018], pages 513–529. DOI: 10.1007/978-3-030-00671-6_30 76, 155

Quan Wang, Bin Wang, and Li Guo. Knowledge base completion using embeddings and rules. In Qiang Yang and Michael J. Wooldridge, Eds., *Proc. of the 24th International Joint Conference on Artificial Intelligence, IJCAI, Buenos Aires, Argentina, July 25–31*, pages 1859–1866. IJCAI/AAAI, 2015. 90

Quan Wang, Zhendong Mao, Bin Wang, and Li Guo. Knowledge graph embedding: A survey of approaches and applications. *IEEE Transactions on Knowledge and Data Engineering*, 29(12):2724–2743, December 2017. DOI: 10.1109/TKDE.2017.2754499 1, 2, 77, 79, 82, 162, 163

Xiao Wang, Houye Ji, Chuan Shi, Bai Wang, Yanfang Ye, Peng Cui, and Philip S. Yu. Heterogeneous graph attention network. In Ling Liu, Ryen W. White, Amin Mantrach, Fabrizio Silvestri, Julian J. McAuley, Ricardo Baeza-Yates, and Leila Zia, Eds., *The World Wide Web Conference, WWW, San Francisco, CA, May 13–17*, pages 2022–2032. ACM Press, 2019. DOI: 10.1145/3308558.3313562 8

Zhen Wang, Jianwen Zhang, Jianlin Feng, and Zheng Chen. Knowledge graph embedding by translating on hyperplanes. In Carla E. Brodley and Peter Stone, Eds., *Proc. of the 28th AAAI Conference on Artificial Intelligence, July 27–31, Québec City, Québec, Canada*, pages 1112–1119. AAAI Press, 2014. DOI: 10.1016/j.knosys.2020.106564 1, 78, 161

Gerhard Weikum and Martin Theobald. From information to knowledge: Harvesting entities and relationships from web sources. In Jan Paredaens and Dirk Van Gucht, Eds.,

Proc. of the 29th ACM SIGMOD-SIGACT-SIGART Symposium on Principles of Database Systems, PODS, June 6–11, Indianapolis, IN, pages 65–76. ACM Press, 2010. DOI: 10.1145/1807085.1807097 106

Robert West, Evgeniy Gabrilovich, Kevin Murphy, Shaohua Sun, Rahul Gupta, and Dekang Lin. Knowledge base completion via search-based question answering. In Chung et al. [2014], pages 515–526. DOI: 10.1145/2566486.2568032 127

Mark D. Wilkinson, Michel Dumontier, IJsbrand Jan Aalbersberg, Gabrielle Appleton, Myles Axton, Arie Baak, Niklas Blomberg, Jan-Willem Boiten, Luiz Bonino da Silva Santos, Philip E. Bourne, Jildau Bouwman, Anthony J. Brookes, Tim Clark, Mercè Crosas, Ingrid Dillo, Olivier Dumon, Scott Edmunds, Chris T. Evelo, Richard Finkers, Alejandra Gonzalez-Beltran, Alasdair J. G. Gray, Paul Groth, Carole Goble, Jeffrey S. Grethe, Jaap Heringa, Peter A. C 't Hoen, Rob Hooft, Tobias Kuhn, Ruben Kok, Joost Kok, Scott J. Lusher, Maryann E. Martone, Albert Mons, Abel L. Packer, Bengt Persson, Philippe Rocca-Serra, Marco Roos, Rene van Schaik, Susanna-Assunta Sansone, Erik Schultes, Thierry Sengstag, Ted Slater, George Strawn, Morris A. Swertz, Mark Thompson, Johan van der Lei, Erik van Mulligen, Jan Velterop, Andra Waagmeester, Peter Wittenburg, Katherine Wolstencroft, Jun Zhao, and Barend Mons. The FAIR guiding principles for scientific data management and stewardship. *Scientific Data*, 3, 2016. DOI: 10.1038/sdata.2016.18 133, 135

William A. Woods. What's in a link: Foundations for semantic networks. In Daniel G. Bobrow and Allan Collins, Eds., *Representation and Understanding*, Studies in Cognitive Science, pages 35–82. Elsevier, 1975. DOI: 10.21236/ada022584 157, 160

Gong-Qing Wu, Ying He, and Xuegang Hu. Entity linking: An issue to extract corresponding entity with knowledge base. *IEEE Access*, 6:6220–6231, 2018. DOI: 10.1109/access.2017.2787787 107, 108

Zonghan Wu, Shirui Pan, Fengwen Chen, Guodong Long, Chengqi Zhang, and Philip S. Yu. A comprehensive survey on graph neural networks. *CoRR*, 2019. http://arxiv.org/abs/1901.00596 DOI: 10.1109/tnnls.2020.2978386 2, 91, 95, 96

Marcin Wylot, Manfred Hauswirth, Philippe Cudré-Mauroux, and Sherif Sakr. RDF data storage and query processing schemes: A survey. *ACM Computing Surveys*, 51(4):84:1–84:36, 2018. DOI: 10.1145/3177850 13

Guohui Xiao, Diego Calvanese, Roman Kontchakov, Domenico Lembo, Antonella Poggi, Riccardo Rosati, and Michael Zakharyaschev. Ontology-based data access: A survey. In Lang [2018], pages 5511–5519. DOI: 10.24963/ijcai.2018/777 114

Reynold S. Xin, Joseph E. Gonzalez, Michael J. Franklin, and Ion Stoica. GraphX: A resilient distributed graph system on spark. In Peter A. Boncz and Thomas Neumann, Eds.,

1st International Workshop on Graph Data Management Experiences and Systems, GRADES, Co-Loated with SIGMOD/PODS, New York, June 24, page 2. CWI/ACM, 2013a. DOI: 10.1145/2484425.2484427 1, 70, 76

Reynold S. Xin, Josh Rosen, Matei Zaharia, Michael J. Franklin, Scott Shenker, and Ion Stoica. Shark: SQL and rich analytics at scale. In Kenneth A. Ross, Divesh Srivastava, and Dimitris Papadias, Eds., *Proc. of the ACM SIGMOD International Conference on Management of Data, SIGMOD, New York, June 22–27*, pages 13–24. ACM Press, 2013b. DOI: 10.1145/2463676.2465288 70

Keyulu Xu, Weihua Hu, Jure Leskovec, and Stefanie Jegelka. How powerful are graph neural networks? In Sainath et al. [2019]. https://openreview.net/forum?id=ryGs6iA5Km 71, 96

Wei Xu, Raphael Hoffmann, Le Zhao, and Ralph Grishman. Filling knowledge base gaps for distant supervision of relation extraction. In *Proc. of the 51st Annual Meeting of the Association for Computational Linguistics, ACL, August 4–9, Sofia, Bulgaria, Volume 2: Short Papers*, pages 665–670. The Association for Computational Linguistics, 2013. https://www.aclweb.org/anthology/volumes/P13-2/ 108

Bishan Yang, Wen-tau Yih, Xiaodong He, Jianfeng Gao, and Li Deng. Embedding entities and relations for learning and inference in knowledge bases. In Yoshua Bengio and Yann LeCun, Eds., *3rd International Conference on Learning Representations, ICLR, San Diego, CA, May 7–9, Conference Track Proceedings*, 2015. http://arxiv.org/abs/1412.6575 80, 84

Fan Yang, Zhilin Yang, and William W. Cohen. Differentiable learning of logical rules for knowledge base reasoning. In Guyon et al. [2017], pages 2319–2328. http://papers.nips.cc/paper/6826-differentiable-learning-of-logical-rules-for-knowledge-base-reasoning 100, 104

Luwei Yang, Zhibo Xiao, Wen Jiang, Yi Wei, Yi Hu, and Hao Wang. Dynamic heterogeneous graph embedding using hierarchical attentions. In Joemon M. Jose, Emine Yilmaz, Jo ao Magalh aes, Pablo Castells, Nicola Ferro, Mário J. Silva, and Flávio Martins, Eds., *Advances in Information Retrieval—42nd European Conference on IR Research, ECIR, Lisbon, Portugal, April 14–17, Proceedings, Part II*, volume 12036 of *Lecture Notes in Computer Science*, pages 425–432. Springer, 2020. DOI: 10.1007/978-3-030-45442-5_53 8

Taha Yasseri, Robert Sumi, András Rung, András Kornai, and János Kertész. Dynamics of conflicts in Wikipedia. *PLOS One*, 7(6), June 2012. DOI: 10.1371/journal.pone.0038869 105

Xiaoxin Yin, Jiawei Han, and Philip S. Yu. Truth discovery with multiple conflicting information providers on the Web. *IEEE Transactions on Knowledge and Data Engineering*, 20(6):796–808, 2008. DOI: 10.1109/tkde.2007.190745 129

Dani Yogatama, Daniel Gillick, and Nevena Lazic. Embedding methods for fine grained entity type classification. In *Proc. of the 53rd Annual Meeting of the Association for Computational Linguistics and the 7th International Joint Conference on NaturalLanguage Processing of the Asian Federation of Natural Language Processing, ACL, July 26–31, Beijing, China, Volume 1: Short Papers*, pages 291–296. The Association for Computational Linguistics, 2015. https://www.aclweb.org/anthology/volumes/P15-2/ DOI: 10.3115/v1/p15-2048 107

Amrapali Zaveri, Anisa Rula, Andrea Maurino, Ricardo Pietrobon, Jens Lehmann, and Sören Auer. Quality assessment for linked data: A survey. *Semantic Web Journal*, 7(1):63–93, 2016. DOI: 10.3233/sw-150175 119, 124, 125

Fuzheng Zhang, Nicholas Jing Yuan, Defu Lian, Xing Xie, and Wei-Ying Ma. Collaborative knowledge base embedding for recommender systems. In Balaji Krishnapuram, Mohak Shah, Alexander J. Smola, Charu C. Aggarwal, Dou Shen, and Rajeev Rastogi, Eds., *Proc. of the 22nd ACM SIGKDD International Conference on Knowledge Discovery and Data Mining, San Francisco, CA, August 13–17*, pages 353–362. ACM Press, 2016. DOI: 10.1145/2939672.2939673 76

Lei Zhang. Knowledge graph theory and structural parsing. Ph.D. thesis, University of Twente, 2002. 159

Weizhen Zhang, Han Cao, Fei Hao, Lu Yang, Muhib Ahmad, and Yifei Li. The Chinese knowledge graph on domain-tourism. In *Advanced Multimedia and Ubiquitous Engineering, MUE/FutureTech*, volume 590 of *Lecture Notes in Electrical Engineering*, pages 20–27. Springer, 2019. DOI: 10.1007/978-981-32-9244-4_3 3, 149

Mingbo Zhao, Tommy WS Chow, Zhao Zhang, and Bing Li. Automatic image annotation via compact graph based semi-supervised learning. *Knowledge-Based Systems*, 76:148–165, 2015. DOI: 10.1016/j.knosys.2014.12.014 130

Suncong Zheng, Feng Wang, Hongyun Bao, Yuexing Hao, Peng Zhou, and Bo Xu. Joint extraction of entities and relations based on a novel tagging scheme. In Regina Barzilay and Min-Yen Ka, Eds., *Proc. of the 55th Annual Meeting of the Association for Computational Linguistics, ACL, Vancouver, Canada, July 30–August 4, Volume 1: Long Papers*, pages 1227–1236. The Association for Computational Linguistics, 2017. https://www.aclweb.org/anthology/volumes/P1&-1/ DOI: 10.18653/v1/p17-1113 109

Weiguo Zheng, Jeffrey Xu Yu, Lei Zou, and Hong Cheng. Question answering over knowledge graphs: Question understanding via template decomposition. *Proc. of the VLDB Endowment*, 11(11):1373–1386, 2018. DOI: 10.14778/3236187.3236192 23

Bin Zhou and Jian Pei. Preserving privacy in social networks against neighborhood attacks. In Alonso et al. [2008], pages 506–515. DOI: 10.1109/icde.2008.4497459 144

Bin Zhou and Jian Pei. The k-anonymity and l-diversity approaches for privacy preservation in social networks against neighborhood attacks. *Knowledge and Information Systems*, 28(1):47–77, 2011. DOI: 10.1007/s10115-010-0311-2 143

Guodong Zhou, Jian Su, Jie Zhang, and Min Zhang. Exploring various knowledge in relation extraction. In Knight et al. [2005], pages 427–434. DOI: 10.3115/1219840.1219893 108

Antoine Zimmermann, Nuno Lopes, Axel Polleres, and Umberto Straccia. A general framework for representing, reasoning and querying with annotated semantic web data. *Journal of Web Semantics*, 12:72–95, 2012. DOI: 10.1016/j.websem.2011.08.006 11, 42, 43, 155

Lei Zou, Lei Chen, and M. Tamer Özsu. K-automorphism: A general framework for privacy preserving network publication. *Proc. of the VLDB Endowment*, 2(1):946–957, 2009. DOI: 10.14778/1687627.1687734 144

Authors' Biographies

AIDAN HOGAN

Aidan Hogan is an Associate Professor at the Department of Computer Science, Universidad de Chile, where he also holds the position of Associate Researcher in the Millennium Institute for Foundational Research on Data (IMFD). He received a B.Eng. and Ph.D. from the National University of Ireland, Galway, in 2006 and 2011, respectively. His primary research interests center on the Semantic Web and Knowledge Graphs. He is the author of over 100 research publications on these topics, including 2 other books: *Reasoning Techniques for the Web of Data* and *The Web of Data*.

EVA BLOMQVIST

Eva Blomqvist is an Associate Professor at the Department of Computer and Information Science, Linköping University. She received a Ph.D. from Linköping University, Sweden, in 2009, in the area of Ontology Learning for the Semantic Web. After a postdoc at ISTC-CNR in Rome, Italy, she has been a member of the Semantic Web group at Linköping University since 2011. Her primary research interests include the Semantic Web and Knowledge Graphs, more specifically the development and use of ontologies as schemas for Knowledge Graphs. She is the author of over 50 research publications in the area, and has served as scientific program chair of several of the top conferences in the field.

MICHAEL COCHEZ

Michael Cochez is an Assistant Professor in the Knowledge Representation and Reasoning Group at the Computer Science department of the Vrije Universiteit, Amsterdam. He received his B.Sc. from the University of Antwerp, Belgium and his M.Sc. and Ph.D. degrees from the University of Jyväskylä, Finland. His research interests are in the intersection of Machine Learning and Knowledge Graphs.

CLAUDIA D'AMATO

Claudia d'Amato is an Associate Professor at the Department of Computer Science, University of Bari, Italy and a member of the Knowledge Acquisition and Machine Learning Lab. She also holds a habilitation as Full Professor for the scientific sectors: INF/01 and ING-INF/05. She received her Master's Degree and Ph.D. from the University of Bari, Italy, in 2003 and 2007, respectively. Over the years, she has also spent several invited-researcher stays in different international universities and research institutes. Her primary research interests center on Machine Learning for the Semantic Web and Knowledge Graphs. She is the author of over 100 research publications on these topics.

GERARD DE MELO

Gerard de Melo is a Full Professor at the Hasso Plattner Institute for Digital Engineering and at the University of Potsdam, where he holds the Chair for Artificial Intelligence and Intelligent Systems and heads the corresponding research group. Previously, he was a faculty member at Rutgers University in New Jersey and at Tsinghua University in Beijing, and a Post-Doctoral Research Scholar at ICSI/UC Berkeley. He has published over 150 papers on Natural Language Processing, Knowledge Graphs, and AI, and received a number of best paper awards.

CLAUDIO GUTIERREZ

Claudio Gutierrez is Full Professor at the Department of Computer Science, Universidad de Chile. He is also a Senior Researcher in the Millennium Institute for Foundational Research on Data (IMFD). His main research interests are the computational foundations of data and knowledge. He has worked and published extensively in the areas of the Semantic Web and Databases, fields in which he received test of time awards (ISWC and PODS). He also devotes time to research in the field of the History of Science and Technology.

SABRINA KIRRANE

Sabrina Kirrane is an Assistant Professor at the Vienna University of Economics and Business Institute for Information Systems and New Media, where she is also a member of the Research Institute for Cryptoeconomics and the Sustainable Computing Lab. Her research interests include Security, Privacy, and Policy aspects of the Next Generation Internet (NGI), Distributed and Decentralized Systems, Big Data, and Data Science, with a particular focus on policy representation and reasoning (e.g., access constraints, usage policies, regulatory obligations, societal norms, business processes), and the development of transparency and trust techniques for the Web.

JOSE EMILIO LABRA GAYO

Jose Emilio Labra Gayo is an Associate Professor at the University of Oviedo, Spain. He founded the WESO (Web Semantics Oviedo) research group in 2004, whose main goal is to apply semantic technologies to solve practical problems. He was a member of the W3C Data Shapes working group and is a member of the W3C Community Groups: Shape Expressions and SHACL. He is coauthor of the *Validating RDF Data* book and maintains the ShEx and SHACL library SHaclEX as well as the online tools RDFShape and Wikishape. Previously, he was coordinator of the Master in Web Engineering and Dean of the School of Computer Science Engineering at the University of Oviedo (2004–2012).

ROBERTO NAVIGLI

Roberto Navigli is a Full Professor of Computer Science at the Sapienza University of Rome, where he leads the Sapienza NLP Group. His research is focused on multilingual Natural Language Understanding, a field in which he received two grants of the European Research Council. In 2015, he received the META prize for groundbreaking work in overcoming language barriers with the BabelNet lexical-semantic knowledge graph, a project also highlighted in *The Guardian* and *Time* magazine, and winner of the *Artificial Intelligence Journal* prominent paper award 2017. He is the co-founder of Babelscape, a successful company which enables Natural Language Understanding in dozens of languages.

SEBASTIAN NEUMAIER

Sebastian Neumaier is a researcher in the Data Intelligence group at the St. Poelten University of Applied Sciences, Austria. He received an M.Sc. and Ph.D. from the Vienna University of Technology, in 2015 and 2019, respectively. His Ph.D. thesis is centered around methods to facilitate the integration and semantic enrichment of Open Data sources using Knowledge Graph technologies. His current research focuses on different aspects of semantic data management.

AXEL-CYRILLE NGONGA NGOMO

Axel-Cyrille Ngonga Ngomo is a Full Professor for Data Science at Paderborn University. He obtained his M.Sc., Ph.D., and habilitation from the University of Leipzig, where he also led the Agile Knowledge Engineering and Semantic Web Group. His research focuses on the automation of the lifecycle of knowledge graphs. Thus, his works include the development of approaches for the extraction, integration, fusion, storage, analysis, and exploitation of knowledge graphs.

AXEL POLLERES

Axel Polleres heads the Institute for Data, Process, and Knowledge Management of Vienna University of Economics and Business (WU Wien), which he joined in September 2013 as a Full Professor in the area of "Data and Knowledge Engineering". He is also a faculty member of the Complexity Science Hub Vienna and was a visiting professor at Stanford University in 2018. He obtained his Ph.D. and habilitation from Vienna University of Technology. His research focuses on ontologies, query languages, logic programming, configuration technologies, Artificial Intelligence, Semantic Web, Linked Open Data, Knowledge Graphs, and their applications for Knowledge Management. Moreover, he actively contributed to international standardization efforts within the World Wide Web Consortium (W3C) where he co-chaired the W3C SPARQL working group.

SABBIR M. RASHID

Sabbir M. Rashid is a Ph.D. candidate at Rensselaer Polytechnic Institute (RPI) working with Deborah L. McGuinness on research related to data annotation and harmonization, ontology engineering, knowledge representation, and various forms of reasoning. Prior to RPI, Sabbir completed a double major at Worcester Polytechnic Institute, where he received B.Sc. degrees in both Physics and Electrical & Computer Engineering. Much of his graduate studies at RPI have involved research related to data annotation and transformation using Semantic Data Dictionaries. His current work includes the application of deductive and abductive inference techniques over Linked Health Data, such as in the context of chronic diseases like diabetes.

ANISA RULA

Anisa Rula has been an Assistant Professor in Computer Science at the Department of Information Engineering, University of Brescia since January 2021 and a researcher at the University of Bonn in the SDA group since January 2017. She obtained her doctoral degree in Computer Science from the University of Milano-Bicocca in 2014. Her research interests are in the intersection of semantic knowledge technologies and data quality with a particular focus on data integration. She is researching new solutions to data integration with respect to the quality of data modeling and efficient solutions for large-scale data sources. Recently, she has been working on data understanding for large and complex datasets, on knowledge extraction, and on semantic data enrichment and refinement.

LUKAS SCHMELZEISEN

Lukas Schmelzeisen is a Ph.D. candidate working with Steffen Staab in the Analytic Computing group at the University of Stuttgart, Germany. He holds a B.Sc. in Computer Science, which he received in 2015 at University of Koblenz–Landau. His main research interests are continuous representations of both natural language corpora and knowledge graphs. In particular, his current focus is on how such representations can be updated over time.

JUAN SEQUEDA

Juan Sequeda is the Principal Scientist at data.world. He joined through the acquisition of Capsenta, a company he founded as a spin-off from his research. His academic and industry work has been on designing and building Knowledge Graph for enterprise data integration where he has researched and developed technologies for semantic and graph data virtualization, ontology and graph data modeling and schema mapping, and data integration methodologies. Juan holds a Ph.D. in Computer Science from the University of Texas at Austin. He is the recipient of the NSF Graduate Research Fellowship, received 2nd Place in the 2013 Semantic Web Challenge for his work on ConstituteProject.org, Best Student Research Paper at International Semantic Web Conference 2014, and the 2015 Best Transfer and Innovation Project awarded by the Institute for Applied Informatics. Juan bridges academia and industry through standardization committees, being a co-chair of the Property Graph Schema Working Group, and past member of the Graph Query Languages task force of the Linked Data Benchmark Council (LDBC), as well as a past invited expert member and standards editor at the World Wide Web Consortium (W3C).

STEFFEN STAAB

Steffen Staab holds a Cyber Valley endowed chair for Analytic Computing at the University of Stuttgart, Germany, and a chair for Web and Computer Science at the University of Southampton, UK. Steffen is a fellow of the European Association for Artificial Intelligence. His research interests range from knowledge graphs and machine learning to the semantics of human–computer interaction. He is co-director of the Interchange Forum for Reflecting on Intelligent Systems (IRIS) at the University of Stuttgart.

ANTOINE ZIMMERMANN

Antoine Zimmermann is an Associate Professor at Mines Saint-Étienne in France. He received M.Sc. and Ph.D. degrees from the University of Grenoble, France in 2004 and 2008, respectively. He spent two years at the Digital Enterprise Research Institute in Galway, Ireland, from 2009 to 2010, then one year at INSA Lyon, France, before getting a position at Mines Saint-Étienne, where he has been a permanent researcher since 2012. In 2021, he received his habilitation from Université Jean Monnet, Saint-Étienne. His research interests are related to the Semantic Web, more specifically on knowledge representation, knowledge engineering, reasoning, data management, and context on the Web.

Printed in the United States
by Baker & Taylor Publisher Services